The Sherpas of the Himalayas

About the Authors

Manis Kumar Raha, M.Sc., Ph.D.(b. 1937) during his service period (1962-1995) served Cultural Research Institute, Government of West Bengal (1962-1970) and Anthropological Survey of India, Government of India (1970-1995) in different capacities. He retired as Joint Director from Anthropological Survey of India. In 1981 he completed a course on Management Development Programme for Educational Administrator from Indian Institute of Management, Joka, Kolkata. For last fifty years or so he has undertaken many anthropological research projects among different tribes, castes and religious groups inhabiting Jammu & Kashmir, Himachal Pradesh, Uttaranchal, Andaman and Nicobar Islands, West Bengal, and Sikkim. In 1996 he was elected as the Sectional President, Anthropology and Archaeology Section of 83rd Indian Science Congress. He was paper setter, moderator, and examiner and Ph.D. Examiner of different Universities. He was also members of Ph.D. Committee and P.G. Board of Studies of Vidyasagar University. As Visiting Fellow he was in Rajib Gandhi University (Arunachal Pradesh) and Dibrugarh University. He was also in the Editorial Board of different scientific journals. He has published 34 books, over 200 articles and over 100 book reviews.

Palash Chandra Coomar, M.Sc. Ph.D. (b. 1956) is at present working as Joint Director, Directorate of Census Operations, Government of India. Before joining Census Operation in 1996 he served Anthropological Survey of India from 1984 to 1996. During his service period he has undertaken research work among both tribal and non-tribal communities living in West Bengal, Sikkim, Bihar and Andaman and Nicobar Islands. He is also paper setter and examiner of post-graduate classes and also Ph.D. examiner of different universities. He has published twelve books, more than fifty articles and book reviews.

Sri Sudip Bhui, M.Sc. (Anth), M.Sc. (Bot), M.Phil (b. 1977) is at present Assistant Professor, Department of Anthropology and Tribal Studies, Sidho-Kanho-Birsha University. Earlier he was an academic staff of Mahishadal Girls' College and Haldia Government College. Before that as research assistant he undertook research work in different research projects at Netaji Institute for Asian Studies. He is at present undertaking research work on indigenous health care system. He is also the author of some books and articles.

The Sherpas of the Himalayas

Their Life, Culture and Society

Manis Kumar Raha
Palash Chandra Coomar
Sudip Bhui

CONCEPT PUBLISHING COMPANY PVT. LTD.
NEW DELHI-110059

ISBN-13: 978-93-5125-194-1

First Published 2016

Published and Printed by

Concept Publishing Company Pvt. Ltd.
Regd. Office:
A/15-16, Commercial Block, Mohan Garden,
New Delhi-110059 (INDIA)
Phones : 25351460, 25351794, *Fax* : 091-11-25357109
E-mail : publishing@conceptpub.com
Website: www.conceptpub.com

Editorial Office: H-13, Bali Nagar, New Delhi-110 015, India.

Cataloging in Publication Data—DK Courtesy: D.K. Agencies (P) Ltd. <docinfo@dkagencies.com>
Raha, Manis Kumar, author.
The Sherpas of the Himalayas : their life, culture and society / Manis Kumar Raha, Palash Chandra Coomar, Sudip Bhui.
pages cm
Study conducted in Darjeeling District of West Bengal and Sikkim, India.
Includes bibliographical references and index.
ISBN 9789351251941

1. Sherpa (Nepalese people)—India—Darjeeling (District)—Social life and customs. 2. Sherpa (Nepalese people)—India—Sikkim—Social life and customs. 3. Darjeeling (India : District)—Social life and customs. 4. Sikkim (India)—Social life and customs. I. Coomar, Palash Chandra, 1956- author. II. Bhui, Sudip, author. III. Title.

DS432.S54R34 2016 DDC 305.800954 23

Dedicated
to
Mr. Sarajit Kumar Chatterjee
Our friend and well-wisher

PREFACE

The people of the Himalayas differ considerably from the people of the plains of India both ethnically and culturally. They are distinct in their social, economic, political and religious characters. Again the people of the Eastern Himalayas are significantly different from those of the Western and Central Himalayas. The former have many distinct cultural features, quite different from those of the later. The first author, who has the credit of having long research experience in the Western and Central Himalayas, was keen to undertake research work in some communities living in the Eastern Himalayas, and so the present research project cropped up. The first and the second authors selected the Sherpas of Kalimpong Sub-Division of Darjeeling District in West Bengal and South District of Sikkim for this purpose. The main reason for selecting the Sherpas is that they are one of the most important tribes of the Eastern Himalayas though they are included in the broader groups of the Bhutia. Another important reason for selecting the Sherpas of Darjeeling and Sikkim is that very little ethnographic information are available on the Sherpas of these two areas. Almost no research work in true sense, has so far been published on the Sherpas of Darjeeling. The Sherpas of Sikkim is also no doubt, quite less known. But on the other hand, the Sherpas of Nepal have been studied in great details by many distinguished scholars and academicians. So detailed ethnographic and other information are easily available on the Sherpas of Nepal whereas in case of the Sherpas of Darjeeling and Sikkim the same is almost blank.

We divided the whole job of the research project from selection of the villages in the two areas to the writing the manuscripts and make it publication ready into four parts: (1) Selection of the villages in Darjeeling and Sikkim and undertaking field work, (2) Preparation of the questionnaires and schedules for field work, preparation for Tables for tabulation work, library consultation, (3) Tabulation of the quantitative data, and (4) writing of the report and make it publication worthy. Like our other research project on the Karens of Andamans and Nicobar Islands, we distributed the four parts of the research work among the three authors of this book. The first part was taken up mainly by the second author (Palash Chandra Coomar) and partly by the first author (Manis Kumar Raha). The second part of the project was done mainly by the first author and partly by the third author. The third part was undertaken mainly by the third author (Sri Sudip Bhui) and partly by the first author. The fourth part was totally done by the first author.

The present book is a detailed study of the Sherpas of Darjeeling and Sikkim, and most probably, as far as we know, the only detailed study on the Sherpas of these two areas, Darjeeling and Sikkim. We have also added different aspects of the culture of the Sherpas of Nepal written by different authors in order to present before our learned readers an almost complete picture of the Sherpas of the Himalayas.

We firmly believe that our readers will be satisfied with the present book as they will be able to know the Sherpas of Darjeeling and Sikkim who were hitherto very little known, and will also be able to compare the life and activities of the Sherpas of the three areas, Darjeeling, Sikkim and Nepal. We also believe that those scholars and academicians who are interested of the tribal shudies, particularly of the Himalayas and Northeast India, will consider it an important contribution.

Authors

ACKNOWLEDGEMENTS

When an anthropologist takes up a research project to study some community may be a caste, a tribe or a religious group or a village, he or she depends on the help and cooperation of different persons. For field work he or she depends on the district and local government officials, Panchayat Pradhan and members, teachers and others and also the inhabitants of the village or the members of the ethnic group selected for study. For consulting different literature he or she has to study books, reports, journals etc. in different libraries. So, he or she depends on the help and co-operation of the authority of these libraries. Without active co-operation and help of all of them, the anthropologist cannot successfully complete his or her research project.

The same are true for us. For fieldwork, for consultation of books, reports, journals etc. we had to depend on the active support, help and cooperation of many people. We depended on a good number of people of Kalimpong town of Darjeeling District and Gangtok, and South District of Sikkim. They spontaneously came forward to extend their help and co-operation to us. We express our deep sense of gratitude to all of them. We are also thankful to the authority of National Library, library of Anthropological Survey of India and also library of the Asiatic Society for allowing us to consult different books, journals, reports etc. But we are extremely grateful to all our Sherpa informants of all the four villages, two from Kalimpong Sub-Division, Darjeeling District and two from South District, Sikkim, for their tireless help and co-operation to us. They have supplied us very valuable information about the life and activities of the Sherpas. Their active support, help and co-operation, have enabled us to successfully complete our research project on the Sherpa of Darjeeling and Sikkim.

We are also thankful to Sri Mantu Ram Das of Baruipur who tirelessly helped us by typing the whole manuscripts and also by sending the publication ready manuscripts to the publisher through e-mail.

Finally, we are also greatly indebted to the authority of Concept Publishing Company (P) Ltd., New Delhi, for publishing this book on the Sherpas.

Authors

CONTENTS

LIST OF COLOURED PHOTOGRAPHS

LIST OF TABLES

1
INTRODUCTION

The self exists within the lotus of heart,
    And is the master of one's life and body.
With mind illumined by the purity and meditation,
    The wise know Him as the blissful, the immortal.

Mundaka Upanishad
Book-3, Chapter-1, Hymn 5

If you want others to be happy, practise compassion.
    If you want to be happy, practise compassion

H.H. The Dalai Lama

The Great Himalayas the King of Mountains, situated in the north-western, north-eastern and eastern borders of India, have both ethical and physical, sacred and secular existence. Many religious and mythological literature have described the Himalayas as the abode of many gods and goddesses. The Mount Kailash is considered as the home of Lord Shiva, one of the Trinities of the Hindus. Goddess Parvati is the daughter of the Himalayas and so on. The Hindu mythologies have vividly described the divine feature of this great mountain. The *Skanda Purana* has beautifully described feelings of the Hindus about the Himalayas:

> He who thinks on Himachal, though he should not behold him, as greater than he who performs all worships in Kashi. In hundred ages of the gods I could not tell thee of the glories of Himachal. As the dew is dried up by the morning sun, so are the sins of mankind by the sight of Himachal.

Pandit Jawaharlal Nehru, the great leader and the first Prime Minister of India, has also echoed the sentiment of every Indian about the Himalayas:

> Himalayas are not only near to us, but also very dear, for they have always been a part of our history and tradition, our thinking and poetry, our worship and devotion.... They are not only physically present in India, dominating the vast Indian plain, but for every Indian, they convey a deeper message.

But apart from the divine features and sacredness, this great mountain also has its very physical existence.

From the conversation between King Milinda and the sage Nagasena, we get a beautiful description of the physical features of the Himalayas. When King Milinda wanted to know about the Himalayas, the sage Nagasena described this mountain in the following way:

> The Himalayas, the king of the mountains, five and three thousand leagues in existent at the circumference, with its ranges of eight and forty thousand peaks, the source of five hundred rivers, the dwelling place of multitudes of mighty creatures, the producer of manifold perfumes, enriched with hundreds of magical drugs, is seen to rise afloat, like a cloud, the centre [of the earth].

Thus we see the "Through all the known ages of man, the Himalayas have evoked wonder, praise and veneration...." (Lall 1981: XII). Besides the sacred and divine sides of the Himalayas and the physical existence, there is another side of the Himalayas, that is the people these great mountain ranges have given shelter to.

The Himalayas are great to every human being living far and near. The mighty tract of the Great Himalayas "with its varying ecological conditions, has not only acted as the centre for meditation for the sages, saints and other holy men but also has given shelter to a large number of ethnic groups with diverse cultural identity and social formations" (Raha 1987:XIX). These ethnic groups have different material culture, different economy, different social organization, different systems of social control and different magico-religious beliefs, practices and world view. For centuries they are occupying different parts of the Himalayas and settled there. For centuries many parts of the Himalayas were quite inaccessible to the outsiders. And this helped the inhabitants there to keep their life style and tradition more or less undisturbed.

> "They could master the difficulties created by the inhospitable environment of the rugged, unkempt mountainous terrains of

> the Himalayas they dwell, and could adapt themselves accordingly for their mere survival. The culture built by these sturdy denizens of the Himalayas in such an environment is somewhat different from that prevalent in the plains areas" (*ibid*).

In the Himalayas while some of the ethnic groups "live in almost arid high altitude regions which remain show clad for at least five months a year, some live in the foothill areas amidst thick vegetation with heavy monsoon rain. While some people live on the beautiful valleys, some live on the rugged, inhospitable steep slopes of the mountain" (Raha 1992: XVIII).

Though the Indian plain land faced several invasions particularly in the India's north-east and north-west relgions, but because of the semi-inaccessible and ruggedness of the terrain and inhospitable environment, the invaders mostly kept themselves away from the Himalayan region (Raha 1995: XVII-XVIII). As a result the people there led somewhat peaceful life and remained satisfied with their own culture and traditions.

The three tracts of the Himalayas, Western, Central and Eastern Himalayas, are considered for centuries, as the suitable places of settlements for a very large number of people who belong to different ethnic groups. They live in different altitudes and also in different eco-zones. Many of these ethnic groups are living in the Himalayas for centuries, but there are people who have migrated to this mountain tract not many decades ago. We get some detailed information about some of these ancient and modern communities, but unfortunately we have very little or no information about many of them also. While this is true for the Western and Central Himalayas, this is also true for the Eastern Himalayas.

The Eastern Himalayas which include some north-eastern States of India and also sovereign countries like Bhutan, Nepal etc. are also the habitat of many well known as well as little known communities. For many reasons the anthropologists felt the importance of the ethnographic study, particularly of those who are little known or about whom no information is available. Strategically and also for the purpose of proper planning for the development, knowledge about people and the area they inhabit, is essential. This is must for the planners and also for those who will execute the development programmes. Only the detailed ethnographic study of the little known or unknown communities, can supply such information.

This is one of the reasons why we selected the Sherpas of Darjeeling and Sikkim for the purpose of our study. We selected the Sherpas of these two areas because people have very little knowledge about them to share with. So far save except a few scrapy and very brief accounts, no detailed anthropological and/or ethnographic study has so far been done on this tribe of the above areas till date. Furthermore, the Sherpas of Darjeeling are even less known than their brethren living in Sikkim. And in comparison to the Sherpas of Nepal, these people from Darjeeling and Sikkim are very much little known. The detailed study on the Sherpas of Nepal by Fürer-Haimendorf (1964, 1984), Ortner (1979), Robert A. Paul (1982), R.R. Kumar (1989), S.T. *Lama* (1971) and others, give us enough knowledge about them living in Nepal. So, one gets enough of information about the Sherpas of Nepal. Moreover, the Sherpas, particularly of Nepal, are quite well known for many many decades to the mountaineers who wanted to conquer the known and unknown mighty peaks of the Great Himalayas and also to the adventurers who love to go to the very rugged, unkempt terrains of the Himalayas which are seldom visited by the people who live far from the Himalayas. The Sherpas of Nepal acted and are still acting as the guides and porters to these mountaineers and adventurers for many many decades. Without their help it was almost impossible for the mountaineers and adventurers to move in the Himalayas. Because one of the main professions of the Sherpas of Nepal is to work as porters and guides, so, they are quite popular. But the case of the Sherpas of Darjeeling and Sikkim is somewhat different. Though some of them acted and still act as the guides and porters to the mountaineers and adventurers, but because most of the Himalayan expeditions particularly to the Mount Everest and many other important peaks of the Himalayas, took place and are still taking place from Nepal, so the Sherpas there are very popular to all of them, and through them all over the world.

Therefore, realizing that no much of information about the Sherpas of Darjeeling and Sikkim are available, so we planned to study the Sherpas of these two areas anthropologically with the hope that our study of the Sherpas of Darjeeling and Sikkim and the studies of the Sherpas of Nepal will help the readers to get a complete picture of the life and activities of the Sherpas of the Himalayas as a whole. Our study is mostly ethnographic. We have made some comparison between the Sherpas of these two areas, and at the same time, we have also referred to the relevant portion from the published materials on the Sherpas of Nepal in our text. This will help our readers to trace out the similarities and differences in the cultural pattern of not only the Sherpas of the two areas we have studied, but at the same time, between the Sherpas of those two areas and the Sherpas of Nepal. Thus, our readers will easily get enough idea about the total cultural pattern of the Sherpas as a whole, that means the Sherpas of the three worlds, Darjeeling, Sikkim and Nepal.

For the purpose of our study we have selected four villages, two from Kalimpong Sub-Division, Darjeeling District of West Bengal (Sherpaguri and Sherpapur) and two from South District of Sikkim (Sherpagaon and Sherpahat). For obvious reason we have used the pseudonym for all the four selected villages. All these villages are multi-ethnic villages and the Sherpas are one of the ethnic groups. A good number of the Sherpa families live in all these villages.

As regards chapterization, we have divided the book into ten chapters apart from Preface and Acknowledgements. Introduction is as usual, included in the first chapter. In the second chapter we have discussed something about the two areas of our study, that is, Darjeeling and Sikkim. The third chapter includes the origin, migration and distribution of the Sherpas. In Chapter Four we have discussed about the population of the Sherpas, mainly from our household census and Census of 2001. Land and livelihood are two very important aspects of any human groups with agro-based economy, particularly of those who have a rural base. These two are also probably the most important asset to those who are agriculturists. In Chapter Five of this book we have included the land and economy of the Sherpas. Like many other human societies the Sherpa society is likewise divided into some social divisions. This we have discussed in Chapter Six. Family is the basic and most important social unit of each and every society. The Sherpas also live in families which are in a similar way, very important to them. In Chapter Seven of this book we have discussed about the families of the Sherpas. Similarly, marriage is equally important, equally to both individuals and also to the society. While marriage is very important turning point of life to every individual, it is also very important to the family and the society in which the individual belongs. So, our Chapter Eight deals with the marriage system of the Sherpas. In our book the last but one chapter (Chapter Nine) has covered the crises of life. Here we have discussed about the pregnancy, childbirth, name-giving ceremony, marriage and death ceremonies etc. All these are very important events in the life of all human being, and similarly in the life of the Sherpas also. While the Sherpas welcome a new child when it is born, with great enthusiasm and joy, they mourn for a person whose life is snatched away by the death. Between these two, birth and death, gain and loss, stands marriage balancing the two. So, all these phases of life are equally important to the Sherpas. In the last chapter we have discussed about the religious beliefs and practices of the Sherpas as in the life of the Sherpas religion is the most important aspect. Religion is also very vital to all members of the Sherpa society in all the three areas, Darjeeling, Sikkim and Nepal.

Another important thing we like to highlight here. We have dedicated this book to our very good friend and well-wisher, Mr. Sarajit Kumar Chatterjee I.P.S. Mr. Chatterjee is engaged since long in an in-depth study of many important social and political issues some of which are harming the basic fabric of integration of our country, India. He has published a good number of highly emotive books, and most of these books cover both historical and constitutional facts and documents. From all these books the readers will get enough food for thought as all these books are on the current problems which India is facing today.

2
IN THE WORLD THEY LIVE

A. Darjeeling District

Geographical Situation

The district of Darjeeling (or Darjiling) is situated in the northern-most part of West Bengal. This district is mostly mountainous but part of it is in the plains or Tarai region. This district lies between 26°31′ and 27°13′ north latitude and between 87°50′ and 88°53′ east longitude. It has an area of 3,149.00 Sq. Kms of which 3,073.77 Sq. Kms go to the rural area. The urban areas cover only 75.23 Sq. Kms according to 2001 Census. This district has 318,737 households of which 219, 401 are found in the rural areas and 99,336 in the urban sectors. Darjeeling district is bounded on the north by Sikkim, in the south by State of Bangladesh and West Dinajpur district of West Bengal, in the west by State of Nepal and on the east by State of Bhutan and Jalpaiguri district of West Bengal.

Darjeeling Hill area is unique from the environmental and ecological points of view.

> The Darjeeling Hill area has a fragile terrestrial system, which is much too often disturbed by various environmental catastrophes. Landslide hazard is most important and recurring catastrophy. The region lies within the lesser and Sub-Himalayan belt of the Eastern Himalayas .... (Desai 2003a:8)

Darjeeling district has two distinct natural tracts-firstly the hilly tract and secondly the Terai area. The latter area, which is just beneath the hilly tract and valleys of the lower Himalayas, "is a low-lying belt of country traversed by numerous rivers and streams rushing down from the hills and by the upland ridges which mark their courses" (O'Malley

1985:2). Again from Terai "the mountains tower abruptly from the plains, which are here only about 300 feet above sea level, in lofty spurs reaching to 6000 and 10,000 feet, and culminate a series of long ridges and valleys" (*ibid*). In the past mountains were completely covered with forest, and this was what was seen by a traveller in 1830. On the higher levels of the mountains one can see pine forests and masses of rhododendron with flowers of various colours.

Mountains

In this part of the Himalayas the ranges may be divided into three distinct zones. These zones are: (I) the great ranges of the snowy peaks, which form the main axis of the chain (II); the Lower or Outer Himalayas, forming the broad belt of mountains of inferior altitude south of the snows, and (III) comparatively low hills forming Sub-Himalayan zone, either as ridges or spurs contiguous with outer hills or separated from them by the flat-bottomed valleys known as Duars' (O'Malley 1985:2). In fact the snowy ranges lie beyond the limits of the district of Darjeeling in the north. Here there is a long range of mountains stretching from East to West, and this range forms the backbone of the Darjeeling Himalayas. The important snowy ranges near Darjeeling is the Kanchanjunga, Dongkya, Singalila, Gipmochi, Tanglu and the Senchal.

River System

The district of Darjeeling is washed by the network of rivers like the Mechi, Balasan, Mahanadi, Teesta and the Jaldhaka. The first three rivers drain the valleys on the south-eastern side of the Sangalila ridge. The rest of the districts are washed by the Teesta and the Jaldhaka. The Teesta which forms the boundary between Sikkim and Darjeeling, enters this district from Sikkim. Here in this district this river receives the river, Rangit. The main tributaries of the Teesta are the Rangpo, Rilli, Rangit, Reyang and the Sivok. The affluents of the river, Rangit are the Rangnu, the Little Rangit, and the Ramman. The Ramman is again joined by the rivers, the Rathu and the Siri. The Mahanadi, Mahananda or Mahaldi is another important river of the district of Darjeeling. The river Balasan are receiving water from the Rinchingtong, Rangbang, Rakti and the Rohini. The Jaldhaka makes the eastern boundary of Darjeeling and separates the district from Bhutan and Western Duars. The principal tributaries of this river are the Paralangchhu, Rangchhu, and the Machhu.

Forest

In Darjeeling district there are three forest divisions, namely Darjeeling, Kalimpong and Kurseong. The forest areas of Darjeeling may be divided into five zones. These zones are situated in different altitudes. The Tropical Moist Deciduous forest type is found between 300 to 1000 meters, the Tropical Evergreen Lower Montane between 1000 to 2000 meters, the Tropical Evergreen Upper Montane between 2000 to 3000 meters and the Sub-Alpine is spread over above 3500 meters. But with the spread of tea gardens and settlements in Darjeeling district, the forests faced catastrophic deforestation operation. In 1830 Captain Herbert, the then Deputy Surveyor-General found the whole hills were "completely clothed with forest from the very top to bottom", and General Lloyd also found the hills "clothed from top of the hills to the very bottom of the valleys with a dense forest" (O'Malley 1985: 98). In 1901 the forest areas were 51.54 per cent of the total geographical areas, the same came down to 34.12 per cent. In 1951 just after India achieved independence the forest cover was 46.01 per cent but according to West Bengal State Forest Report, 2000 the District of Darjeeling has only 38.23 per cent of the total geographical area under forest. Parallely 1901 the arable land was 19.76 per cent the same was increased to 36.67 per cent in 1951 and in 1991 it became 56.40 per cent. The most deforested areas are found in (I) Tea Garden areas (II) Forest area along the principal thoroughfares including NH-55 and (III) Forest area at the fringe of the urban centres/settlements. Massive deforestation has been recorded in Kurseong, Sukna, Bugdogra, Pankhabari, Kalimpong, Chel, Jaldhaka and some other areas (Desai 2003a: 59-61).

Climate

"Climate plays a significant role in the landform development, especially in case of the slope stability" (Desai 2003a:53). The temperature of Darjeeling district is markedly variable. The temperature starts rising from April-May when summer sets in. Winter months start from October, and the whole area becomes very chilly in the months from December to middle of March. "During winter the weather remains generally dry and in summer the situation alters, when precipitation occurs from humid air masses from the Bay of Bengal" (*ibid*). In Darjeeling district the mean maximum temperature is 12°C (53°F). The mean maximum temperature in Kalimpong is 26.7°C (80°F) and the mean minimum temperature there is 7.8°C (46°F) (Das & Bhuimali 2011: 29). In Darjeeling district July is the month when highest rainfall (792.2 mm on an average) is received. Then it continues to reduce and finally becomes lowest in December (6.3 mm on an average). In Kalimpong also the same feature of the rainfall is noticed. The month of July experiences the highest rainfall (612.9 mm on an average), and December receives the lowest rainfall (6.06 mm on average). Normally, the higher amount of rainfall falls in the months from May to September in both Darjeeling and Kalimpong.

Origin of the Name

The name Darjeeling has probably a Tibetan origin. The word 'Darjeeling' means the place where Indra's (the Hindu God) thunderbolt or scepter rested (*Dorje* – the majestic thunderbolt, *Ling*-place, hence 'the place of thunderbolt') (Das & Bhuimali 2011:24). According to Waddel (1891) 'Darjeeling means cave of the mystic thunderbolt on the Observatory Hill from which cave Dorje-ling or Darjeeling derives its name" (*ibid*). The Earl of Ronoldsay is of the view that Darjeeling district had derived its name from the name of a *Lama* (Dorjerinzing) "who founded monastery on the Observatory Hill" (*ibid*). Sen thinks that this district got its name from the word 'Durjaya-Linga' meaning "Siva of invincible prowess, who rules the Himalayas" (Sen 1989 cf Das & Bhuimali 2011:24).

History

At the beginning of the 19th Century, this tract of the country, at present within West Bengal, was a part of the dominion of the Raja of Sikkim. In 1706 the Bhutanese occupied the area what is at present the Kalimpong Sub-Division. The King of Sikkim also faced the aggression of the Gorkhas of Nepal, but fought an unsuccessful battle against the Gurkhas of Nepal (O'Malley 1985:19). In 1780 the Gorkha invaded Sikkim and continued their battle against the Raja of Sikkim for the next 30 years. Afterwards, they conquered a major part of Sikkim as far east as the Teesta and annexed the Terai. The East India Company during this period "was engaged in unavailing remonstrances against the Nepalese and war was finally broke out in 1814" (*ibid*). The Nepalese were driven away from the occupied part, the Raja of Sikkim was reinstated. Under a treaty Titaliya of 1817 with the East India Company, the Raja of Sikkim got his sovereignty back and started ruling the whole tract between the rivers, Mechi and Teesta (about 4000 sq. miles). But the East India Company assumed the paramount power in Sikkim, though it guaranteed the sovereignty of the king over his kingdom. With this action of the East India Company, Sikkim including the present district of Darjeeling remained as the buffer state between Nepal and Bhutan (*ibid*).

During late twenty's of the nineteenth century disputes arose at Sikkim and Nepal boarder, between the two countries, Sikkim and Nepal; and in order to settle this dispute, Captain Lloyd along with Mr. J.W. Grant, the Commercial Resident at Malda, moved through this area. On June 1829 Captain Lloyd wrote in a report that they visited a place which was "the old Goorka station called Dorjeling" and "was immediately struck with its being well adopted for the purpose of a sanitarium." He narrated the strategic importance of this place and also the importance for the trade purpose. He impressed upon the then "Governor-General, Lord William Bentinck, the numerous advantages promised by the establishment of a sanitarium at Darjeeling and strongly advocated its occupation for military purposes as the key of a pass into the Nepal territory" (*ibid*: 20). Lord William Bentinck gave due importance to this report of General Lloyd, and on 1st February, 1835 a Deed of Grant was executed by the Raja of Sikkim, and Darjeeling was handed over to the East India Company in exchange of an allowance of Rs. 3000/- given to the Raja of Sikkim. This allowance was raised to Rs. 6000/- in 1846. In this way Darjeeling came under the control of the British. Thereafter slowly and gradually Darjeeling was developed into a famous hill station. Captain Herbert reported that in 1830s about 1200 able-bodied Lepcha who settled in some areas of the then Darjeeling were compelled to leave Darjeeling for Nepal because of the oppression of the King of Sikkim. The King also prohibited people of Sikkim from going to Darjeeling. In 1839 Dr. Campbell became the first Superintendent of Darjeeling.

Again the Kalimpong area of Darjeeling was under the control of the Bhutan Government since 1706 when the Bhotias wrested this area from Sikkim. During 1780 the Gorkhas invaded this part and ultimately conquered this area by defeating the Bhotias. (Chatterjee & Mondal 1911:146). In 1864 the British army during Anglo-Bhutan War defeated the Bhutanese army who were forced to sign a treaty known as the Treaty of Sinchula later in 1865. Under this treaty Bhutan had to handover the territory east of the Teesta River to the British East India Company. In 1866 Kalimpong was added to Darjeeling and so it became a part of the district of Darjeeling (*ibid*).

During the colonial period, Darjeeling got different administrative arrangements "just to have a sole control over the flourishing resources of the Hills" during different period of time. These administrative status were 'Non-regulated Area', 'Scheduled District', 'Backward Tract' and 'Partially Excluded Area' (Sarkar 2011: 140).

> Thus, from the very beginning Darjeeling Hills had experienced, 'a specialized administration'. In case of Darjeeling activation of this colonial play had been maintained as a double edge sword. The specialized administration resulted into the isolation of Darjeeling from Bengal mainstream, which did help the British control not only the physical space of the hill station but the hill resources as well (*ibid*).

Administrative Division

Darjeeling is one of the districts of West Bengal and is situated on the northern most part of this state. It is divided into four Sub-divisions, namely, Darjeeling Sadar, Kurseong, Kalimpong and Siliguri. These sub-divisions are further divided into twelve Community Development Blocks. These C.D. Blocks are Darjeeling Pulbazar, Rangli Rangliot, Kalimpong-I, Kalimpong-II, Gorubathan, Jore Bunglow Sukiapokhri, Mirik, Kurseong, Matigara, Naxalbari, Phansidewa and Kharibari. In addition there are nine urban units, namely, Pattabong Tea Estate, Darjeeling, Kalimpong, Mirik, Kurseong, Cart Road, Uttar Bagdogra, Bairatisal, and Siliguri according to 2001 Census. Census 1991 has returned a total of 710 villages in this district of which 620 are inhabited and 90 uninhabited. The district has a total of 238,669 occupied residential houses, 243, 872 households according to 1991 Census.

Ethnic Composition

Before 1830 Darjeeling district was inhabited by a good number of the Lepcha, but during 1830 because of the oppression of the Raja of Sikkim they were forced to flee to Nepal and to take refuge there (O'Malley 1985:22). The Gurkha people of Nepal were also present in some parts of Darjeeling during this period. Later on with the development of this district a large number of people belonging to different castes, tribes and religious groups, flocked in Darjeeling. Particularly, with the development of the tea estates, a large number of the labour force was required, and many of these labourers were brought from different areas of Nepal, Bhutan, Bengal and Bihar (now Jharkhand). In addition a large number of people from different parts of India and Nepal came to Darjeeling for service, business etc. At present different Nepali castes like the Khambus or Jimdar, Murmis, Limbus, Chettri, Mangar, Gurung, Newar, Yakha, Kanil, Damai, Sarki, and others are found in Darjeeling. In addition one also finds the Bengali, Marwari, Sikh or Punjabi, Bihari and others inhabiting in different areas of Darjeeling District. According to 1951 Census the population of different Nepali caste groups as follows were living there (Chatterjee & Mondal 2011:153):

> Khambus (63,745), Murmis (49,890), Limbu (19,838), Chetri or Khas (30,463), Bahun or Brahmin (11,317), Magar (19,413), Gurung (17,864), Newar (48,827), Garlhi (998), and Bhujel (5,745).

According to 1941 Census the Yakhas had 824 population. According to 1991 census the Kami had population of 30, 713, Dami 8,482, and Sarki 6,611.

The District of Darjeeling has a total of 204, 167 Scheduled Tribe population forming 4.63 per cent of the total Scheduled Tribe population of West Bengal and of 12.69 per cent of the total population of Darjeeling District.

Among the numerically important Scheduled Tribes who live in this district are the Bhutias (45,014), Lepcha (31,210), Munda (17,189), Oraon (66,978), Santal (14,709), Nagesia (3,589), Mech (2,159), Chik Baraik (2,699) and the Lodha (2001). The other Scheduled Tribes have less than 2000 population each.

In Darjeeling District the Scheduled Castes have a total of 258,881 population forming 1.40 per cent of the total Scheduled Caste population of West Bengal and 16.09 per cent of the total population of Darjeeling District. Among these Scheduled Castes, the numerically important are the Rajbansi (1,29,904) Namasudra (41,555), Kami (31,195), Damai (10,082), Sarki (5,454), Lohar (4,562), Hari (4,478), Chamar (3,275), Dom (2,350), Mallah (2,396) and the Dosadh (2,120). While the Dhoba, Bhuimali, Nunia and the Jelia Kaibarta have population between 1,000 and 2,000, the rest of the Scheduled Castes have less than 1000.

Population

During early twenty's of the nineteenth century Darjeeling was practically unpopulated. Even when in 1835 the East India Company took over the possession of this tract of land mass, it was a "worthless uninhabited mountain" (O'Malley 1985:21). But in early thirty's of the nineteenth century that this hilly tract was inhabited by the Lepcha, was proved from the writings of O'Malley. He writes

> "About 10 years previously 1200 able bodied Lepchas, forming, according to Captain Herbert, two-thirds of the population of Sikkim, had been forced by the oppression of the Raja to fly from Darjeeling and its neighbourhood, and to take refuge in Nepal" (*ibid*: 22)

Even in 1852 Dr. Campbell, a member of the Indian Medical Service, found "Darjeeling an inaccessible tract of forest with a very scanty population...." (*ibid*). Dr. Campbell's inspection report states that the population of Darjeeling which was about 100 in 1839, rose to about 10,000 in 1849 "chiefly by immigration from neighbouring States of Nepal, Sikkim and Bhutan in all of which slavery was prevalent" (*ibid*). The British authority considered it to be of foremost important job to populate this hilly tract. For this reason all possible facilities were granted to the settlers. They were given forest land for cultivation and settlements. With the development of tea and Cinchona industries, attention of many people was drawn toward Darjeeling and gradually people started pouring in this hilly station. In 1869 Darjeeling had 22,000 inhabitants (Banerjee *et. al.* 1980). During the first census of 1871-72 population rose to 94,712 persons and the Census of 1881 reported the population of Darjeeling as 155,179. 1891 Census returned 223,314 souls in Darjeeling, and in 1901 we get 249,117 people in this hilly region. In this way Darjeeling got speedily populated. This speedy growth of population was definitely linked with the fast

Table 2.1: Population of Darjeeling District with Density of population per sq. km in different Census year

Year	*Total Geographical Area in sq. km*	*Total population*	*Density of Population per sq. km*
1901	3015	249117	83
1921	3015	282748	94
1941	3087	376369	122
1961	3108	624640	201
1981	3149	1024269	325
2001	3149	1609172	511

Source: Das & Bhuimali 2011: 40.

development of the Darjeeling district. In Darjeeling district the population has steadily grown. The growth of population has also helped in increasing the density of population. The table below (Table 2.1) gives us a clear picture of the same for different Census years. While in 1901 the population of Darjeeling district was 2,49,117 and the density of population per sq. km. was 83 (the rural geographical area being 3015 sq. km.), in 2001 the population was increased to 16,09,127 with the density of population being 511. In 2001 the total geographical area was 3149 sq. km.

During first census of 1872 the total population Darjeeling was a little below one lakh and that of Kalimpong Sub-Division, only 6,446 (Table 2.2). But after nine years, in 1881 the population of Darjeeling crossed one lakh and became 115,179. In Kalimpong the same also became almost double (12,683). Since 1872 one can notice a steady growth of population in both Darjeeling District and Kalimpong Sub-Division. In 2001 the population of Darjeeling was 16,09,172 and that of Kalimpong 2,22,220 (Table 2.2). The population variation of both Darjeeling and Kalimpong (Table 2.3) also highlights the steady growth of population. These growths of population are due to both natural growth as also influx of population from outside. Apart from the natural growth, tea industry is primarily responsible for inviting a very large number of people from outside Darjeeling both as labourers and also for other business. Of course, there were other reasons also for such population growth. Table 2.3 shows the quantum of growth of population in Darjeeling District and Kalimpong Sub-Division.

Table 2.2: Population of Darjeeling 1872-2001

Year	*Darjeeling District*	*Kalimpong Sub-Division*
1872	94412	6446
1881	155179	12683
1891	223314	26631
1901	249117	41511
1911	265550	49520
1921	282748	60093
1931	319635	68203
1941	376369	79042
1951	445260	93441
1961	624640	120526
1971	781777	134538
1981	1024269	158726
1991	1299919	190266
2001	1609172	225220

Source: Das and Bhuimali 2011: 38-39.

When we look at the sex-ratio (number of female per 1000 males) in different decades, we see from Table 2.4 that in 1901 the sex-ratio of the population of Darjeeling was quite low. In rural areas the same is also true. But in urban centres it was significantly low. This type of low sex-ratio continued till 1991. In 2001 it became only 937 females per 1000 males in total population and 956 females per 1000 males in rural population. The urban population still has quite a low sex-ratio (2001 it is 899 females per 1000 males only).

Table 2.3: Population Variation of Darjeeling District, 1872-2001

Year	*Darjeeling District*	*Kalimpong Sub-Division*
1872-81	+60467	+6237
1881-91	+68135	+13948
1891-1901	+25803	+14880
1901-11	+16433	+8009
1911-21	+17198	+10573
1921-31	+36887	+8110
1931-41	+56734	+10839
1941-51	+68891	+14399
1951-61	+75023	+27085
1961-71	+157137	+14012
1971-81	+242492	+24188
1981-91	+275650	+31540
1991-2001	+309253	+34954

Source: Das & Bhuimali 2011: 42.

Table 2.4: Sex-Ratio (Females per 1000 Males), 1901-2001

	2001	*1991*	*1981*	*1971*	*1961*	*1951*	*1951*	*1941*	*1931*	*1921*	*1911*	*1901*
Total	937	914	888	882	864	867	863	883	879	896	869	873
Rural	956	934	911	910	909	907	905	912	905	911	892	892
Urban	899	868	830	793	731	717	721	736	728	777	666	690

Source: Das & Bhuimali 2011: 49.

Now, we shall move to the present day population of Darjeeling. We shall give emphasis on the general population, Scheduled Tribe population and the Bhutias population. As we have already said we do not get the population figures of the Sherpa separately as the Sherpa have been merged with the Bhutias and enumerated along with the Bhotia. So, we give here 2001 census figures of the Bhutias. But before that we shall cite the population of Darjeeling District according to 2011 Census. According to 2011 Census the total population of Darjeeling is 18,46,823 who live in an area of 3,149 sq. km. Out of this total population 9,37,259 (50.75%) are males and 9,09,564 (49.25%) are females. The decennial growth rate (2001-2011) is 14.47 per cent. 2011 Census also returns the sex-ratio of 970 females per 1000 males.

According to 2001 census Darjeeling District has a population of 1,609,172 of which 51.62 per cent are males and the rest 48.38 per cent are females. In rural areas 1,088,740 persons live, and of this population a little over half are males and a little less than half are females. Same is the numerical position of males and the females living in the urban sector of this district (Table 2.5).

Table 2.5: Distribution of Total Population, Scheduled Tribe Population and Bhutias Population in Rural and Urban Areas of Darjeeling District, 2001

Total	*Sex*	*Total*		*Rural*		*Urban*	
		No	*%*	*No*	*%*	*No*	*%*
Population	P	1,609,172	100.00	1088,740	100.00	520,432	100.00
	M	830,664	51.62	556,633	51.13	274,011	52.65
	F	778,528	48.38	532,107	48.87	246,421	47.35
Scheduled Tribe population	P	204,167	100.00	178,878	100.00	25,289	100.00
	M	102,287	50.10	89,740	50.17	12,547	49.62
	F	101,880	49.90	89,138	49.83	12,742	50.38
Bhutia population	P	45,014	100.00	27,855	100.00	17,159	100.00
	M	22,440	49.85	13,812	49.59	8628	50.28
	F	22,574	50.15	14,043	50.41	8531	49.72

Source: Census of India, 2001.

This district has also a population of 204,167 Scheduled Tribes in its fold. The strength of the Scheduled Tribe males is slightly over half, and the same of the Scheduled Tribe females, a little less then half. The condition of the Scheduled Tribe population living in the rural areas is almost similar. In the rural areas while the males are slightly higher in number than the females, in the urban centres we find totally opposite picture. Here the Scheduled Tribe females are a little more in number than their males counterpart.

Now, we come down to the sex-wise numerical position of the Bhutias population in Darjeeling (Table 2.5). In case of the total Bhutias population and the Bhutias population living in the urban centres, the number of males is slightly more than that of the females. Contrarily, in the rural areas their male members are a little less in number than their female counterpart.

In Darjeeling district, according to 2001 Census, a total of 1,609,172 people live. Out of this population majority (67.66%) live in the rural areas. Still a significant number of population (32.34%) reside in the urban centres. Almost similar distribution pattern can be seen in case of the rural and urban dwelling male and female population (Table 2.5).

But in case of the Scheduled Tribe population overwhelming majority (87.61%) actually live in the rural areas. Quite a small number of this population (12.39%) preferred to live in the urban centres. In case of the Scheduled Tribe male and female population the same type of distribution is seen. 87.73 per cent Scheduled Tribe males and 87.49 per cent Scheduled Tribe females live in the rural areas. The remaining 12.27 per cent males and 12.51 per cent females are found to have taken shelter in the urban centres.

The rural-urban distribution of the Bhutias population show a little different picture. Though majority of the Bhutias population (61.88%) live in the rural areas, still a significant number (38.12%) reside in the urban centres. The distribution of the male and female Bhutias in the rural and urban areas is almost same (Table 2.6).

Table 2.6: Distribution of Population, Scheduled Tribe Population and Bhutias Population in Rural and Urban Areas of Darjeeling District, 2001

Total	Sex	Total		Rural		Urban	
		No	%	No	%	No	%
Population	P	1,609,172	100.00	1088,740	67.66	520,432	32.34
	M	830,664	100.00	556,633	67.01	274,011	32.99
	F	778,528	100.00	532,107	68.35	246,421	31.65
Scheduled Tribe population	P	204,167	100.00	178,878	87.61	25,289	12.39
	M	102,287	100.00	89,740	87.73	12,547	12.27
	F	101,880	100.00	89,138	87.49	12,742	12.51
Bhutia population	P	45,014	100.00	27,855	61.88	17,159	38.12
	M	22,440	100.00	13,812	61.55	8628	38.45
	F	22,574	100.00	14,043	62.21	8531	37.79

Source: Census of India, 2001.

Now, let us examine the numerical position of the Bhutias population in the total population of the district of Darjeeling and also in the total Scheduled Tribe population in this district.

In the total population and also in the rural population the strength of the Bhutias population is less than 3.0 per cent. But in the urban centres they are 3.30 per cent of the total urban population. In case of the Bhutias males, their strength in the total male population and also in the rural male population is less than 3.00 per cent but in the urban centres they occupy 3.15 per cent. Almost same is the numerical position of the Bhutias females in the total female population and total rural female population. In the total female population they are 2.90 per cent and in the rural female population their strength is 2.64 per cent. But in the urban centes they have a little higher strength (3.46%) (Table 2.7).

Table 2.7: Numerical Position of the Bhutias Population of Darjeeling in the Total Population and Total Scheduled Tribe Population of Darjeeling District, 2001

(in per cent)

Bhutia population	*Population*			*Scheduled Tribe Population*		
	Total (%)	*Rural (%)*	*Urban (%)*	*Total (%)*	*Rural (%)*	*Urban (%)*
Person	2.80	2.56	3.30	22.05	15.57	67.85
Male	2.70	2.48	3.15	21.94	15.39	68.77
Female	2.90	2.64	3.46	22.16	15.75	66.95

Source: Census of India, 2001.

But among the Scheduled Tribe population the position of the Bhutias population is somewhat better (Table 2.7). In the total population the numerical strength of the Bhutias persons, males and females lies between 21.94 per cent and 22.16 per cent. In the rural Scheduled Tribe population they have somewhat higher strength. Their sex-wise numerical strength ranges between 15.39 per cent and 15.75 per cent. But in the urban centres their number is very high among the total Scheduled Tribe population. They cover more than half of the total Scheduled Tribe population inhabiting urban centres, and their strength goes as follows: persons 67.85 per cent, males 68.77 per cent and females 66.95 per cent. It can thus clearly be stated that the Bhutias are numerically the most important Scheduled Tribe in Darjeeling district.

B. Sikkim

Geographical Situation

Sikkim, the 22nd State of the Indian Union, is situated in the eastern Himalayas. It is a totally mountainous and undulating country, and is located between 28°07′48″ and 27°04′46″ north latitudes and 88°00′58″ and 88°55′25″ east longitude. It covers on area of 7,300 sq. km. (Bhatt and Bhargava 2005:25). The State has derived its name from the Limboo word, *Su-Khim* meaning happy palace or home. According to Debnath the word *Su-Khim* means "a place of peace and happiness (2009:4)". It is bounded in the north by the vast stretches of the Tibetan plateau, on the west, Nepal, on the east, Bhutan and Chambi valley of Tibet (China) and on the south, Darjeeling district (Subba 2008:75).

> Sikkim is a land of rich and varied scenic beauty, magnificent mountains, eternal snows, dark forests, green fertile valleys, raging torrents and calm placid lakes....Sikkim contains within its border a variety of non-tropical and geographic environments from the low snow-free outer hills to the high peaks with permanent snow and glaciers (*ibid*: 26).

This State extends 114 km. (approx) from south to north and 64 km. east to west. The altitude ranges from 250 to 8,598m (Subba 2008:75).

Sikkim is totally a mountainous area with no flat land. This State "forms the part of the Inner Himalayan range of mountains which projects southward" (Desai 1988:2-3). It is separated from Nepal, Tibet and Bhutan by the mountainous walls ranging from 3600 meters to 9100 meters above mean sea level. But there is no such wall that separates this state from West Bengal. In Sikkim the hilly regions may be divided into four ecological zones namely, lower hills, middle hills, high hills and very high hills (Bhasin 1997: 157). The lower hills have temperate climate. The part of the lower hills is sub-tropical in nature. The middle hills are having temperate climate. But the high hills are either sub-alpine or alpine in nature. On the other hand, the very high hills are totally alpine (*ibid*).

Mountains

Sikkim is situated in the inner mountain ranges of the Great Himalayas. It is totally rugged, mountainous and its elevation ranges from 300 meters to 8540 meters. "But the habitable areas are only up to the altitude of 2100 meters, constituting only 20 per cent of the total area of the state" (*ibid*:26). Sikkim has a number of mountains which are situated mostly in the north-west direction. These snow covered mountains include Kanchenjunga (8,598 m), Kumbha Karna (7,711 m), Pendem (6,706 m), Narsingh (5,825 m), Kabru Dome (6,545 m) etc. 'The State of Sikkim is geographically a basin". In the north of this State lies the Great Himalayan Range, in the east the Chola Ranges and in the West, the Singalila Range. The foot hills surround the south (Debnath 2009: 5). The mountains have varied elevations ranging from 300 to 8540 meters. "But the habitable areas are only up to the altitude of 2100 meters' covering only 20 per cent of the total areas of the State" (Bhatt & Bhargava 2005: 26).

Rivers

The Teesta, the largest river in Sikkim, divides the State into two parts. It has a number of tributaries, like the Zemu, Lachung, Rangyong, Dikchu, Rongli, Rongpo, and the Rangit. A large number of human settlements are found to be present on the banks of this great river, Teesta. According to White Sikkim is drained by the Teesta and its tributaries which are the Rangeet, the Rungnu-chhu, the Lachen and the Lachung rivers (1971:3).

Forests

In this mountainous State the forests cover 2,646 sq. km. or 36 per cent of total area of the State. According to Bhatt and Bhargava (2005:27-28) these forests may be divided into the following types:

1. Sub-tropical deciduous monsoon forest.
2. Sub-tropical evergreen hill forest.
3. Lower temperate broadleaf forest.
4. Rhododendron forest.
5. Extensive moist alpine scrub.
6. Lower hill forest.
7. Sal forest.
8. Dry mixed forests.
9. Wet mixed Forests.

Rai has mentioned about two different classifications of the forests of Sikkim (1994: 256). These two are:

1. (a) Tropical 1000′ to 3000′
   (b) Lower Temperate 3000′ to 5000′
   (c) Upper Temperate 5000′ to 7000′
   (d) Sub-Alpine 7000′ to 11000′
   (e) Alpine 11000′ – tree-line
   (This system is usually expressed in feet amsl)
2. (a) Sub-tropical Sal forest
   (b) Sub-Tropical Terminalia forest
   (c) Warm temperate mixed forest
   (d) Temperate Magnolia-Betula forest
   (e) Temperate Oak-Chestnut forest
   (f) Cool temperate mixed forest
   (g) Sub-Alpine Fir forest.

According to Debnath forests in Sikkim can be grouped into two categories:

1. The 'deciduous' forests in the lower attitude which have greatly been cleared, and
2. Above this the coniferous forests with either persistent or deciduous leaves (2009:7).

On the basis of the vegetation the whole State has been divided into three zones, namely, (I) Tropical zone (up to 1700 metres), (II) Temperate zone (1700 to 4300 metres) and (III) Alpine zone (above 4300 metres to the perpetual snowline of 5000 metres) (Shresta 1993:13).

Climate

The climate of this State of Sikkim has some peculiarities because of its peculiar location in the Himalayas. "As such the temperature conditions vary from sub-tropical in southern lower parts to cold deserts in the snowy north. It is the most humid region in the whole range of the Himalayas, because of its proximity to the Bay of Bengal and direct exposure to Southwest monsoon" (Subba 2008:76-77). In this State "the climate varies from tropical heat in the valleys to Alpine cold in the higher altitudes. The tropical climate prevails in the deep valleys with elevation up to 5000 ft. The temperate zone comprises areas having elevations between 5000 ft. and 13,000 ft." (Bhatt & Bhargava 2005:25). The perpetual snow-clad areas start from 16,000 ft. and beyond. *The Imperial Gazetteer of*

India referring to Sir J.D. Hooker, the famous Botanist who made extensive study of Sikkim, divided Sikkim into three similar zones, namely, Tropical (upto 5000 ft.), Temperate (5000 ft. to 13,000 ft.) and Alpine (beyond 13,000 ft.) with perpetual snow line at 16,000 ft. (1908: Vol. 22:366). In this state the rainfall varies from 841 mm to 4500 mm. The mean annual humidity stands around 82 per cent. The maximum and minimum temperature which depends on season and elevations, varies from 31.1°C to 4.2°C (Subba *ibid*: 77). "Most of the rainfall is received during the months of May to October. Through the Teesta valley the south-west monsoon penetrates to quite far north thereby extending the humid belt right up to the lower reaches of the snow-capped mountains" (Desai 1988:7). However, the rainy season is followed by long spells of sunshine and bright weather. Thereafter come the biting cold days. "Because of the copious rainfall many areas in the State of Sikkim face hardship. The landslide not only cause traffic bottle-necks but sometimes cause loss to human and animal life too" (Chib 1977:33). Sikkim also faces different natural calamities like heavy snow fall, heavy rain, drought, flood and storm in different seasons of the year. Similarly, heavy rain and heavy snowfall also cause land-slides. All these are responsible for heavy damage of land, crops, property and other resources and also responsible for the death of human and animal lives.

History

Sikkim has a long history though very little is known about its early history. This State has travelled a long way for 333 years from antiquity to monarchy (1642-1975). In 1975 it achieved statehood in Independent India and still continuing with that status (Subba 2008:73). The history of this state prior to the beginning of monarchy i.e. 1642 is somewhat obscure. From the chronology given by Subba (2008: XIX-XXXI) we come to know that the Lepcha chieftains ruled this area known as Mayel Lyang, i.e. Sikkim from sometimes in 7th Century and continued till 1642. The last Lepcha chieftain (*Panu*), Thekong Mun Solong Panu survived from 1595 to 1642 AD when the first Chogyal of Namgyal Dynastry, Phuntsog Namgyal was consecrated in 1642.

Besides the Lepcha some other communities were also present in Sikkim. These communities were the Limboos or Tsongs, the Mangars or Magars or Mong-pas, and the Bhutias or Lhorees or Lhopos or Lhopas who also had their chiefs and they also occupied certain territories.

From 1642 Sikkim was ruled by several Chogyals. The First Chogyal Phuntso Namgyal reigned from 1642 to 1670 and the Second Chogyal, Tensung Namgyal reigned from 1670 to 1700. Sikkim was under the control of third Chogyal, Chogdor Namgyal, from 1700 to 1716 and the Fourth Chogyal Gyurmed Namgyal was on the throne from 1717 to 1733. The Fifth Chogyal, Gyurmed Namgyal was consecrated in 1733 and continued upto 1780. The next Chogyal, Tenzing Namgyal enthroned in 1780 and reigned upto 1793. In 1793 the Seventh Chogyal Tsungphud Namgyal came into power and continued to rule upto 1864. In 1815 the Teaty of Sugouli was signed by the British and the Nepal. In 1816 the seventh Chogyal, Tsugphud Namgyal signed the Treaty of Titalia with the British authority of India. From 1817 Sikkim became a Protectorate of the British Government. The Eight Chogyal, Sridkyong Namgyal, became the Chogyal of Sikkim in 1863 and continued to rule Sikkim till 1874. After his death, Thutub Namgyal who became Ninth Chogyal in 1874, continued upto 1914. The reign of the Tenth Chogyal, Sidkyong Tulku started from 1914, but he was a Chogyal only for less than a year. After his untimely death Sir Tashi Namgyal became the eleventh Chogyal. He continued upto 1963. In 1949 a *Satyagraha* was launched in Sikkim. In the same year a democratic Government was formed and Tashi Tshering became its first Chief Minister. In 1950 Sikkim became a Protectorate of India and continued with that status till 1974. Sikkim got Palden Thondup Namgyal as its Twelfth Chogyal in 1963 who remained as the Chogyal till 1975 when Sikkim became 22nd State of Independent India and Sikkim lost its identity as the Himalayan Kingdom (Subba 2008: XIX-XXXi).

Origin of the Name

The State, Sikkim derived its name from the word *Sukhim* which means a place of peace and happiness (Kakodkar 1955:7; Debnath 2009:4). Sikkim is called *Denjong* in Tibetan and Bhotia languages. The word, *Denjong* has been originated from *Bay Yul Demo Jong* meaning "the hidden valley of rice". When the Bhotias started entering Sikkim at the beginning of the 14th Century they found the Lepchas who were already there, cultivating paddy in the Teesta and other valleys of Sikkim (*ibid*). In 1642 when "Phuntsho Namgyal was consecrated as the Chogyal of Sikkim, the autonomous Lepcha and Tsong (Limboo) Chieftains accepted the supremacy of Namgyal Dynasty and signed a Tripartite Treaty of *Lho-Mon-Tsong-Sum* by which they integrated their land resources with the migrant Bhotias. The country thus formed was called as '*Mayel*' and later on *Renjong* by the Lepcha, *Yioksom* (fort or a fortified place) by the Limboos and *Deyjong* by the Bhutias which was later on named *Song Khim* (New Home or Palace) by the Limbooni Queen Thungwamukma of Tensung Namgyal, second Maharaja of Namgyal Dynasty and then corrupted to *Sukhim* and again to *Sikhim*" (Subba 2008:1; Risley, 1984: 1-38; Chemjong 1967: 1967: 162-164, Namgyal & Dolma 1908: 27).

Administrative Settings

Sikkim which was once a princely state, was controlled by the king for many years. It has come a long way from antiquity to Monarchy for 333 years (1642-1975) and it became the 22nd state of India on April 26, 1975. But before it became a state of India, Sikkim became a Protectorate of India after the signing of the Indo-Sikkim Treaty 1950 (Chib 1977:15). Earlier during British rule "Sikkim was associated to India as a hereditary monarchy subject to the 'British Paramountcy'. In May 1974 the then Sikkim Assembly passed the Government of Sikkim Act 1974 for providing a responsible Government and furthering its relations with India" (Chakravarthi 1994: 110-111). Sikkim was given an 'Associate State' status within the framework of the Constitution of India. Later on by the Constitution (36th Amendment) Act, 1975 of India Sikkim finally became 22nd state of the Indian Union with effect from 26th April, 1975 (*ibid*: 111) by a franchise (97% vote of positive accent) (Bhatt & Bhargava 2005:62). In the past when Sikkim was a princely state, it was ruled by a hereditary king. He was assisted by large landowners, the *Kajis,* in the administration of the State. The *Kajis* were hereditary ministers. During the British rule, the Maharaja was also assisted by the British Political Officers along with the hereditary *Kajis* (Bhasin 1997: 154).

Sikkim, the 22nd State of India has been divided into four districts, namely North District, East District, South District and West District. Again each district is further sub-divided into two sub-Divisions. The North District has Chungthang and Mangan Sub-Divisions. East District has Gangtok and Pakyong Sub-Divisions. South District has Namchi and Ravong Sub-Divisions and West District has Gyalshing and Soreng Sub-Divisions. Here in this district there are 9 Tehsils, 20 C.D. Blocks, 9 towns, 698 inhabited villages and 87 uninhabited villages (Bhatt & Bhargava 2005:32). The East District has an area of 954 sq. km., North District 4,226 sq. km., South District 750 sq. km and West District 1166 sq. km. (*ibid*: 64).

The South District wherefrom we selected two locations inhabited by the Sherpas for our study, has two sub-divisions, namely, Namchi and

Ravong, while Namchi Sub-Division has two towns, ninety one revenue blocks, and six forest blocks, the other sub-division, Ravong, does not have any town, but has forty four revenue blocks, and four forest blocks, according to 1991 Census. The head quarters of South district is Namchi.

Ethnic Composition

The present day Sikkim is inhabited by a large number of ethnic and religious groups. But in the remote past during the prehistoric era this state was inhabited by three tribes namely the Naong, Chang, and the Mon. The Lepcha entered Sikkim a little latter and afterwards absolved these three tribes completely (Bhatt and Bhargava 2005: 17). During early 17th century came the Tibetans. Thereafter came other groups.

According to Bhatt and Bhargava the Lepcha are the earliest settlers of Sikkim. They are also known as the *RongKup*, meaning the children of Rong. Similarly, the Bhutias are the descendants of the early settlers of Sikkim. They came from Tibet and Bhutan escorted by the ancestors of the first Chogyal, Phuntsok Namgyal. In Sikkim the Nepalese is a broad term that includes different ethnic groups like the Majars, Murmis, Tamangs, Gurungs, Rais, Limbus, Damis, Kamis, Bahuns and the Chhetris (2005: 34-35). Out of them the Limbus and the Magars are also living Sikkim from very early times.

But at present the three main groups of Sikkim are the Nepali, the Bhutias and the Lepcha. The Nepali are mostly the Hindu except a few who are Buddhists. The Bhutias and the Lepcha practice Buddhism. In Sikkim there are some Scheduled Castes like the Dami, Kami, Majhi, Sarki and some generic castes who are treated as the Scheduled Castes.

In this state the Bhutias and the Lepcha are two main Scheduled Tribes. But the Bhutias include different ethnic groups also, and they are the Chumbipa, Dopthapa, Dukpa, Kagatey, Sherpa, Tibetan, Tromopa and the Yolmo. In recent years two more tribes have been included in the list of the Scheduled Tribes. They are the Limboo and the Tamang, according to the *Annual Report of 2006-2007* of the Ministry of Tribal Affairs, Government of India (p. 135). As these two tribes have not been shown separately in the Census of India, Sikkim, 2001, they may have most probably, been included in the generic tribes of Sikkim in Census 2001.

In addition there are some state-wise Other Backward Classes (OBC). They include the Bhujel, Gurung, Limboo, Rai, Manger, Sunwar and the

Tamang. Besides, the Sannyasi, Thami and the Jogi are also treated as the Other Backward Classes. Among them the Limbo include the Tsong, Subba and the Yakthungba, and the Sunuwar cover the Koincha and the Mukhia. In Sikkim the Nepalis include a number of caste groups, and they are the Limta, Gurung, Magar Rai, Tamang, Brahmin, Thakur and the Chhetris. In addition there are Pradhan (Newar), and the Gurkha. Over and above many people from different parts of India have also gone to Sikkim in connection with business, service, or some other purposes and ultimately settled there (Bhatt and Bhargava 2005: 47-57).

Population

Sikkim returns a total population of 6,10,577 in 2011 with 323,070 (52.93%) males and 287,507 (47.07%) females. The decadal growth of population of this state in 2001-2011 is 12.9 per cent and the sex-ratio is 890 females per 1000 females (Table 2.8). The density of population is 86 person per sq. km. But in 1891, that means 120 years ago this mountainous State had a population of 30,458 (Table 2.8). In South District of Sikkim the total population according to 2011 census, is 1,46,850 with male 76,670 (52.21%) and female 70,180 (47.79%).

This population of Sikkim of 1891 was increased to 59,014 in 1901. The same became 87,920 in 1911 and then increased to 81,721 in 1921, to 109,908 in 1931, to 121,520 in 1941, to 137,725 in 1951, and ultimately reached 607, 688 in 2011. The number of females is less than male population as indicated by all the census years. The above table also shows that though the population is increasing in different decades, still the growth rate fluctuates. The maximum growth is noticed in 1901 when the population of Sikkim was increased from the 1891 population by 93.7 per cent. The next higher decadal growth of population in 1981 from the year 1971 (50.77%) followed by the year 1911 (49.0%). There was a negative growth only in the year 1921 (–7.1%). It is not clear why the population of Sikkim went down to 41,492 from 1911 to 1921 (45,059) population.

As regards sex-ratio the Sikkim population always returns low sex-ratio. From the sex-ratio of 916 females per 1000 males in 1901, it came down as low as 889 (provisional) in 2011. The highest sex-ratio was in 1921 when it was 970 females per 1000 males followed by 1931 (967 females per 1000 males) and 1911 (890 females per 1000 males). Since 1921 the sex-ratio of the population of Sikkim started lowering down till it reached 1971 when the sex-ratio became lowest (863 females per 1000 males). Thereafter, it got improved slightly till it reached 2011.

Table 2.8: Growth of Population of Sikkim During the period 1891 to 2011

Year	Person	Male	Female	Percentage Variation	Sex-Ratio
1891	30,458	—	—	—	—
1901	59,014	30,795	28,219	93.7	916
1911	87,920	45,059	42,861	49.0	951
1921	81,721	41,492	40,229	–7.1	970
1931	109,808	55,825	53,983	34.4	967
1941	121,520	63,289	58,231	10.7	920
1951	137,725	72,210	65,515	13.3	907
1961	162,189	85,193	76,996	17.8	904
1971	209,843	112,662	97,181	29.38	863
1981	316,385	172,440	143,945	50.77	875
1991	406,457	216,427	190,030	28.47	878
2001	540,851	288,484	252,367	33.06	875
2011	607,688*	321,661*	286,027*	12.36*	889*

Source: Census of India.
*Provisional figures.

The State of Sikkim has a total population of 540,851 according to 2001 Census (Table 2.9). Out of this population 53.34 per cent are male and the remaining 46.66 per cent are females. In both rural and urban areas of Sikkim more than half are males and less than half (46.82% and 45.36% respectively) are females.

Here in this State the population of the Scheduled Tribes number 111,405. Out of this total like the general population, a little over half are males and a little less than half are females. In the rural areas the number of males among the Scheduled Tribes is 52.27 per cent while that of the females is 48.73 per cent. But reverse is the case with the sex-wise distribution of the Scheduled Tribe population in the urban areas of Sikkim. Here the strength of the males is a little less (49.02%) than that of the females (50.98%).

We now come down to the Bhutias population (Table 2.9). We have discussed here about the Bhutias population because the Sherpa which we have studied and on whom we are writing this book, are included in the broad category of the Bhutias, along with some other groups. We have already stated this elsewhere. In Sikkim there are a total of 70,308 Bhutias of which 50.88 per cent are males and 49.12 per cent females. In case of the Bhutias inhabiting rural area the number of the male Bhutias is a little higher (51.10%) than that of the female (48.90%). But the case is different in case of the Bhutias living in urban areas. Here the number of the female Bhutias (50.98%) is a little more than that of the male Bhutias (50.98%).

Table 2.9: Sex-wise Distribution of Total Population, Scheduled Tribe Population and Bhutias Population of Sikkim, 2001

Population	Sex	Total		Rural		Urban	
		No.	%	No.	%	No.	%
Total	P	540,851	100.00	480,981	100.00	59,870	100.00
	M	288,485	53.34	255,774	53.18	32,710	54.64
	F	252,367	46.66	225,207	46.82	27,160	45.36
Scheduled Tribe Population	P	111,405	100.00	101,909	100.00	9,496	100.00
	M	56,940	51.11	52,249	51.27	4,691	49.40
	F	54,465	48.89	49,660	48.73	4,805	50.60
Bhutia Population	P	70,308	100.00	62,662	100.00	7,646	100.00
	M	35,770	50.88	32,022	51.10	3,748	49.02
	F	34,538	49.12	30,640	48.90	3,898	50.98

Source: Census of India, 2001.

Now, let us examine the distribution of the population of Sikkim in the rural and urban areas according to 2001 Census. Out of a total population of Sikkim overwhelming majority (88.93%) actually live in the rural areas. Only a very small number (11.07%) of them have preferred urban centres to live. This is equally true for the male and female population.

In case of the Scheduled Tribe population over 90 per cent live in the rural areas, and only 8.52 per cent stay in the urban areas. The distribution is also equally similar in case of the male ana female Scheduled Tribe population. A little over 90 per cent of the total Scheduled Tribe population of both sexes (91.76% and 91.18% respectively) dwell in the rural areas. It means that a very small number of the Scheduled Tribe population (less than 10.00%) have preferred urban centres as suitable for their dwelling.

The same is the condition with the Bhutias population of Sikkim. About 90 per cent of the total Bhutias population, total Bhutias males and total Bhutias females reside in the rural sector. So, the remaining small number of them have actually accepted urban centres as their place of residence.

Table 2.10: Distribution of Total Population, Scheduled Tribe Population and Bhutias Population in Rural and Urban Areas of Sikkim, 2001

Population	*Sex*	*Total*		*Rural*		*Urban*	
		No.	*%*	*No.*	*%*	*No.*	*%*
Total	P	540,851	100.00	480,981	88.93	59,870	11.07
	M	288,484	100.00	255,774	88.66	32,710	11.34
	F	252,367	100.00	225,207	89.24	27,160	10.76
Scheduled Tribe Population	P	111,405	100.00	101,909	91.48	9,496	8.52
	M	56,940	100.00	52,249	91.76	4,691	8.24
	F	54,465	100.00	49,660	91.18	4,805	8.82
Bhutia Population	P	70,308	100.00	62,662	89.12	7,646	10.88
	M	35,770	100.00	32,022	89.52	3,748	10.48
	F	34,538	100.00	30,640	88.71	3,898	11.29

Source: Census of India, 2001.

It is further seen that out of the total population of Sikkim (540, 851) according to 2001 Census, the total Scheduled Tribe population covers only 20.60 per cent. The total Scheduled Tribe males form only 19.94 per cent and the total Scheduled Tribe females 21.58 per cent, out of the total male and female population respectively. In the rural areas the total Scheduled Tribe population form 21.19 per cent of the total population of rural Sikkim. Similarly, total Scheduled Tribe males of the rural areas are only 20.43 per cent of the total rural male population. The total Scheduled Tribe females residing in the rural areas, covers only 22.05 per cent of the total female population of the rural Sikkim. In the urban areas of Sikkim the total of 9,496 Scheduled Tribe live and they form 15.86 per cent of the total population inhabiting the urban areas. As regards the urban centre dwelling Scheduled Tribe males, they rest on 14.34 per cent of the total male population living in the urban centres. Similarly, the total Scheduled Tribe females settled in the urban centres, constitute of 17.59 per cent of the total population of Sikkim living the urban centres.

In South District according to 2001 Census, the Scheduled Tribe population was 20,483 forming 15.57 per cent of the total population of this district. In the urban centres of this district the strength of the Scheduled Tribes is 7.10 per cent and in the rural areas the same is 15.84 per cent. Again out of this total Scheduled Tribe population of this district 10,322 (50.39%) are males and 10,161 (49.61%) females with sex-ratic being 984 females per 1000 males.

We shall now see the strength and distribution of the Bhutias population among the total population of the district. There are a total of 70,308 Bhutias in Sikkim according to 2001 Census. This Bhutias population form 13.00 per cent of the total population of the district. Again 35,770 Bhutias males of this district come to 12.40 per cent of the total male population of the district. Similarly, 34,538 Bhutias females rest 13.69 per cent of the total female population of the district.

In rural Sikkim a total of 62,662 Bhutias live, and they form 13.03 per cent of the total population inhabiting rural areas of Sikkim. Again the total Bhutias males in rural areas are 32,022, and they cover 12.52 per cent of the total male population of the rural areas of the State. In case of the Bhutias female population, there are 30,640 of them in the rural areas of Sikkim forming 13.61 per cent of the total females of the rural areas of Sikkim. As we move to the urban centres, we find 7,646 Bhutias live in these urban centres. They constitute 12.77 per cent of the total urban population of the State. The Bhutias males in the urban centres of Sikkim are 3,748, and they form 11.46 per cent of the total urban males of the State. There are 3,898 Bhutias females live in the urban centres here. Their strength is 14.35 per cent of the total female population of the state.

Now, we shall discuss about the numerical position of the Bhutias, Lepcha and other generic tribe population among the Scheduled Tribe population of the State of Sikkim. In this state there are 70,308 Bhutias who form 63.11 per cent of the total Scheduled Tribe population of the State. The total male Bhutias (35,770) have a share of only 62.82 per cent of the total Scheduled Tribe males of this state. In the same way the Bhutias females form 63.41 per cent of the total Scheduled Tribe females of Sikkim. When we look at the rural-based Bhutias population we see that the Bhutias here form 61.49 per cent of the total Scheduled Tribe population inhabiting the rural Sikkim. The rural-based Bhutias males have registered 61.29 per cent of the total Scheduled Tribe males living in rural areas. In the same way, the rural Bhutias females remain satisfied with 61.70 per cent of the total Scheduled Tribe females residing rural area. But the picture is different in urban centres. Here there are only 7,646 Bhutias who form 80.54 per cent of the total Scheduled Tribe population inhabiting urban centres. The urban dwelling Bhutias males have got a share of 79.90 per cent of total Scheduled Tribe males and the urban dwelling Bhutias females have accepted 81.12 per cent share of the total female Bhutias living in the urban centres (Table 2.11).

So, we see that in Sikkim the Scheduled Tribe population have never exceeded over 22 per cent of the total population of Sikkim and the Bhutias population have also not reached 14 per cent of the total population throughout Sikkim. On the other hand, the Bhutias population form overwhelming majority (always over 60%) of the total Scheduled Tribe population of this state and ranges between 61.00 per cent and 82.00 per cent. So, it may clearly be said that the Bhutias stand as the major Scheduled Tribe numerically.

Table 2.11: Numerical Position of the Bhutias Population of Sikkim in the Total Population and Total Scheduled Tribe Population of Sikkim, 2001

(in per cent)

Bhutia population	*Population*			*Scheduled Tribe Population*		
	Total	*Rural*	*Urban*	*Total*	*Rural*	*Urban*
Person	13.00	13.03	12.77	63.11	61.49	80.52
Male	12.40	12.52	11.46	62.88	61.29	61.29
Female	13.69	13.61	14.35	63.41	61.70	61.70

Source: Census of India, 2001.

Table 2.11 gives us a good idea about the numerical position of the Bhutias of Sikkim in the total population and total Scheduled Tribe population of this State. It is seen from this table that in the total population of Sikkim, the total Bhutias population has a share of only 13.00 per cent according to 2001 Census. The total Bhutias males and females have almost identical share in the total male and female population of this State, only that the Bhutias females have a little higher strength (13.69%) than the Bhutias males (12.40%). In the rural areas of Sikkim the numerical position of the Bhutias population is almost identical position with the total Bhutias population. Here also the total rural Bhutias population have a strength of only 13.03 per cent of the total population of the rural areas of Sikkim. The Bhutias males and females inhabiting in the rural areas of Sikkim cover only 12.52 per cent and 13.61 per cent of the total rural male and female populations. The urban centres also give the same picture only that females are of a little higher strength (14.35%) than the males.

After having a brief discussion on the population of the State of Sikkim, we shall now discuss about the population of the South district of Sikkim wherefrom we selected two locations inhabited by the Sherpas for our study. In this South district 131,506 people live of which 15.58

per cent are Scheduled Tribe population and 4.76 per cent Scheduled Caste population. Again out of the total male population 15.13 per cent are Scheduled Tribe males and 4.61 per cent Scheduled Caste males. Similarly, out of a total female population (63,279) 16.06 per cent are Scheduled Tribe females and 4.92 per cent Scheduled Caste females.

Table 2.12: Sex-wise Distribution of Population in the South District of Sikkim, 2001

Population	Person		Male		Female	
	No	%	No	%	No	%
Population	131,506	100.00	68,227	51.88	63,279	48.12
Scheduled Tribe	20,483	100.00	10,322	50.39	10,161	49.61
Scheduled Caste	6,262	100.00	3,148	50.27	3,114	48.73

Source: Bhatt & Bhargava 2005: 31, 49, 53.

Again out of the total population in South district 51.88 per cent are males and a little less than half are females. Similarly, among the Scheduled Tribe of this district a little over half are males and a little less than half are females. In the same way the male population of the Scheduled Castes form 50.27 per cent of the total Scheduled Caste population and Scheduled Castes females, a little less than half.

3

THEIR ORIGIN, MIGRATION AND DISTRIBUTION

Origin and Identity

The Sherpa are included in the broad category of the Bhutias in both West Bengal and Sikkim. As the Bhutias are the Scheduled Tribe in West Bengal as well as in Sikkim, so the Sherpas are also treated as the Scheduled Tribe in both West Bengal and Sikkim. In Nepal the Sherpas are recognized as one of the *Janjati* (Scheduled Tribe) since, Panchayat system was introduced in Nepal in 1959-60 (Kunwar 1989:122).

The Dukpa, Kagatay, Tibetan and the Yolmo are included in the broad category of the Bhutias. But in Sikkim apart from the Dukpa, Kagatey, Sherpa and the Tibetan, a few more communities like the Chumbipa, Dopthapa and the Tromopa are also included in the category of the Bhutias as reported in the *Annual Report, 2006-2007 of the Ministry of Tribal Affairs, Government of India*. It has not been mentioned why these groups are included in the broad category of the Bhutias in both West Bengal and Sikkim.

It is also not clear whether they are the sub-tribes of the Bhutias or whether they have some relation with the Bhutias. On the other hand, T.B. Subba is of the opinion that though the Sherpas are constitutionally under the Bhutias group, but the Sherpas "consider themselves to be Nepali" (1989:8). According to him the Nepalese of Darjeeling are constituted of the groups like the Bahun, Thakuri, Chhetri, Newar, Rai, Limbu, Yakha, Sunuwar, Tamang, Magar, Gurung, Jog, Bhujel, Thami, Yelmu, Sherpa, Sunar, Kami, Sarki and the Damai (*ibid*). Whatever may be their status in the Bhutias society, the Sherpas are an ethnic Tibetan group (Ortner 1978: 263). Bagchi is also of the view that the Sherpa is a "hardy hill race of Tibetan stock with marked Mongolia feature" (1991:169). Subba also thinks that "the Sherpas are of Tibetan origin" (2008:279).

The Sherpa got their name 'Sherpa' from the word '*shar-pa*' meaning "people from the east". Fürer-Haimendorf also has the same view. According to him.

> The name Sherpa is derived from the Tibetan word *shar-pa* which means 'easterner', but it is not clear in what manner this term came to be associated with this particular group. From the Tibetan point of view Sherpas are southerners rather than easterners, and even with a purely Nepalese setting the term has not real justification for other Bhotia groups dwell to the east as well as to the west of the Sherpa country. Yet, the term has gained wide currency and must be accepted as the name of an ethnic group with a pronounced sense of separateness from other Bhotia groups (1964: 1-2).

In his other book (*The Sherpa Transformed*, 1984), Fürer-Haimendorf again repeated the same thing as mention above. But he has also added that "there is a tradition that before their migration to their present habitat they had been settled in Eastern Tibet" (1984: 1-2). Possibly this could be the reason why the Sherpas are called the *Shar-pa* meaning *easterner.* Shrestha, Singh and Pradhan also think that ' "Sherpa" in Tibetan language means "easterners" ' (1975:13). Subba T.B. feels that the word 'Sherpa' is supposed to be the corrupt form of the word "Sharva" which means people "living in the east" (1989:46). The All India Survey of *People of India* by Anthropological Survey of India, reveals that the word "Sherpa" is derived from the word "Sharva", meaning 'east', and "pa" meaning 'resident/people" (Gangopadhyay 1993:154; Mitra 2008:1183). Bista has also found the same word '*Sharva* meaning 'living in the east' responsible for the term, 'Sherpa' (1976:160). Bagchi thinks that "Their origin from eastern Tibet is presumably indicated by the philology of the term Sherpa which, in Tibetan language, denotes a man (*pa*) of the east (*Sher*)" (1991:169).

Bankoti has also tuned with the others by saying that "The word 'sherpa' is derived from the word 'sharya' meaning 'east' and 'pa' meaning 'resident/people' (2004:1452). According to Subba," The name "Sherpa" means "Eastern people in the Tibetan language" (2008:279).

Oppitz after consulting historical documents, reported that the Kham region of eastern Tibet was the home land of the Sherpas which is about 1300 miles from their present habitat Solu-Khumbu areas of Nepal (1974:122).

There is a strong belief among the scholars, academicians and others who have studied the Sherpas that they came to Nepal from their homeland in eastern Tibet, and then to Sikkim-Darjeeling and elsewhere from eastern Nepal. That is why they got the name the Sherpa which is derived from the word 'Sharva' meaning 'easterners'. Hermanns as early as the middle of the last century, reported that—

> the Sherpa are believed to have come from the eastern part of Tibet, and they are considered to have a originally lived in the frontier district in Tsing-Lai-Sechwan provinces of China (1954:23).

The Sherpas involved in the profession of mountaineering for much over a century. The earliest reference to the Sherpas in the Annals of Mountaineering was cited in 1907 when "Dr. A.M. Kedlas recruited a few Sherpas from Darjeeling to accompany him to the Sikkim Himalayas as high altitude porters" (Kohli and Verghese 1962:61). Thus, it is clear that the Sherpa immigrants of Darjeeling were the first to use the word "Sherpa" (Subba 2008:281). The people of Solu and Khumbu borrowed the term "Sherpa" from the Sherpas of Darjeeling. The latter while going for mountaineering and trekking expeditions to the Nepal Himalayas as high attitude porters, they came in contact with the people of Solu and Khumbu, and from the Sherpas of Darjeeling they borrowed the term, 'Sherpa' and used the same as surname.

> "But the land mark of using the term 'Sherpa' by the people of Solu-Khumbu should be 1950s. Previously they were known as 'Sherpa' (easterners) or 'Nubripa' (westerner), Bhot or Lama. Finally, this term 'Sherpa' was given separate, independent and full ethnic identity. Even though they use two terms while giving their identity with insiders and outsiders, which is used here by auto-name, i.e. "Serwa' and exo-name, i.e. 'Sherpa'. One would say *nga Serwa hin*, meaning "I am Serwa". But for the outsiders, he would prefer to say "I am Sherpa" (Subba 2008:281).

Ortner is of the view that the Sherpas after their migration from Tibet and settled in the new areas in Nepal, they came to have an ethnic identity separate from the Tibetans, and to develop a dialect not mutually intelligible with the Tibetan spoken just over the border (just over the border meaning a seven day trek over a 1900-foot pass) (1978:10).

Bista, in connection with the identity of the Sherpas, thinks that before these people became highly publicized by mountaineering expeditions, the Sherpas of Khumbu (Nepal) area identified themselves to the non-Sherpa people by the term, '*Shar Khombo*' meaning inhabitants of Shar-Khumbu area. Bista further states that "Despite their close affinity with the Tibetan language, culture and religion, the Sherpas feel as much Nepali as any other people. In line with this they dislike being associated with the term '*bhote*'" (1976:160).

According to Nawang (1995) the word 'Sherpa' is made by combining two words—*shyar* (meaning East) and *Pa* (meaning people). That means the word 'Sherpa' means "People of the East". The ancestral home of the Sherpas is on the northern side of Solu Khumbu district along the Dudh Koshi River and its tributary at Solu Khola. The Solu Khumbu Sherpas are among the best known Himalayan people. So, the Solu Khumbu region is also popularly known as 'Sherpa land' or 'Shyar Khumbu'.

It is not clear why and when these people were given the name 'Sherpa'. Some Sherpas think that originally they were not addressed by the term 'Sherpa' though they were sure of the term by which they were addressed in the past before they were given this term 'Sherpa'. Another group of them is of the view that the word, 'Sherpa' actually means "*man from rising sun area*". That is why other groups of that area are not called the Sherpas. Further, according to some other Sherpas those people who live in the western part of Nepal are called the 'Nubripa' while those inhabit in the Eastern Nepal are known as the Sherpas, though both the Nubripas and the Sherpas belong to the same type of culture group.

According to the reincarnated *Lama* of Tengboche monastery, Palzin Thimi, the first man who came to Khumbu, came from Kham-Salmo-Gang (east of Tibet), and was believed to be incarnated from the god Wosal. When he went back to Tibet, the people these areas wanted to know wherefrom he came. "From the east part of Kham", he replied. So, this way the name 'Sherpa' (easterner) came into being. But some Sherpas of Solu (Nepal) think that the name 'Sherpa' is of recent origin (*Source*: internet).

Allen is of opinion that "the great majority of the Sherpas descent from people who, migrated south over the Himalayan Passes".

There was a problem of identity of the Sherpas. According Oppitz after the migration of the Sherpas from Eastern Tibet via Dingri, Central Tibet and settling down in the Solu Khumbu region, some other groups of people also came to Solu Khumbu region and settled there. "Because of their general cultural similarity they were easily integrated into the tribal community" (1977:234). Besides these people another set of people who included members from some Nepalese groups like the Tamang, Gurung, Chetri and the Newar, also came and settled in this region, entered into marital or casual unions with the Sherpa girls'.

> The offspring of these alliances, now mainly living in Pharak, were also assimilated into Sherpa culture despite the fact that they had from distinctly different cultural background. They started to wear Sherpa dress and ornaments, took Sherpa names, were converted to Buddhist religion and adopted Sherpa language. The ultimate feature of their assimilation, however, was the transformation of their original tribal names into substitutive clan names (*ibid*: 235).

But this is not the end of the infiltration of other groups into the Sherpa society. The so-called Khamba who were the last batch of immigrants to Khumbu region, also integrated into the Sherpa society. But even they were integrated in the Sherpa society still the original Sherpas have not accepted them at par with them so far as social status is concerned, because, "*khamba* is relatively empty category in local terminology."

> "For all people who had within the last four generations, moved into Khumbu from the north, were lebelled in this way. Some of them were just northern neighbours, whereas a number of them had their place of origin as far away as the west Nepalese areas of Mustangbhot and Manangbhat. Lacking the most important status symbol in the eyes of the Sherpa i.e. an acknowledged clan name these Khamba were looked upon as socially inferior (Oppitz 1977: 235).

The term, *Sherpa* is also used to refer particularly to those males who are employed as guides for mountaineering expeditions and adventures in the Himalayas to conquer the mighty snow clad peaks of the Himalayas, particularly, the Great Mount Everest. They are highly respected as the elite mountaineers and have expert knowledge about the very difficult undulated, unkempt and dangerous terrains of the Himalayas. To all explorers, mountaineers and adventurers of the Himalayas the Sherpas are the assets. The Sherpas serve all these people as guides and portars and particularly, the guide for those explorers and mountaineers who venture for the mighty peaks of the Himalayas crossing high altitudes, and braving extreme environment, hazards, avalanches, death traps, land and snow slides etc. The Sherpas carry heavy equipments, foods, tents, dresses etc. extremely essential for the expeditions. But now a days the term 'Sherpa' is loosely used to refer to almost any porters nd guides employed fo mountaineering expeditions. This definitely hurt the sentiments of the original Sherpas, who insist on making the distinction between themselves and the ordinary portars who are not the original Sherpas. This has to some extent, identity crisis among the original Sherpas.

Migration

In connection with the migration of the Sherpas, Ortner is of the view that

> It has been well established that the Sherpas migrated into their present location in Nepal from the Khams region of eastern Tibet about 450 years ago. It is not clear why they left; harassment by marauding Mongal tribes, or religious persecution by the reformed Tibetan Buddhist sect have been suggested, although it seems equally plausible that there was some local upheaval in the feudal social structure. In any event, they made their way, a journey of some 1,250 miles, to north-eastern Nepal, where they settled in the then uninhabited region in the general environs of Mount Everest (1979:10).

Ortner has further stated that "A second influx of immigrants apparently came into the Sherpa area from the immediately adjacent part of Tibet about 150 years ago, and became incorporated as Sherpas" (*ibid*). Before the Chinese occupation of the Tibet, the Sherpas used to go on frequent trade across the border and played the role of the middlemen in Nepal for trade between Tibet and India (Ortner: *ibid*). Bagchi, on the other hand, has reported that "the Sherpas migrated from Tibet to Nepal in 13th or 14th century and "gradually spread to the adjoining Pharak and Solu in" Nepal (1951: 169).

Paul is of the view that the ancestors of the Sherpas most probably migrated in 17th Century A.D. (1982). Fürer-Haimendorf is of view that "all Sherpa share the tradition of having migrated from Tibet, but the document relating to the migration of the Sherpas in the Khumbu and Solu regions are lacking." He further states:

> "This lack of legendary, as well as historical, accounts of their ancestors' arrival in their present habitat is all the more surprising as many Sherpas are literate and well acquainted with myths and traditions regarding establishment of Buddhism in Tibet and fates of such historical figures as the 'lotus-born' saint, Padmasambhaba, known to Tibetans and Sherpas as Guru Rimpoche ('Precious Master'). There is no agreement even about the route of migration from Tibet to Khumbu and Solu" (1964: 18).

Fürer-Haimendorf further states that the Sherpas in general, believe that their ancestors from their homeland in eastern Tibet moved towards southern directions along the Rongshar Chu which is west of the Rolwaling Himal where from they turned east, reached Solu area and settled there. But on reaching Solu area they involved in a hard task of ousting the earlier Kiranti population. After some times they further moved towards north and then reached Khumbu (1964: 18).

But it is believed that the ancestors of some of the Sherpas of Khumbu came to Khumbu straight from Tibet across Nangpa La, the present main trade-route between Khumbu and Tingri region.

> Thus, it is said that the forefathers of the Mende clan came from the vicinity of Karte in Tibet and that after crossing the Nangpa La, they first lived in a cave above a place called Mende between the present villages of Thami and Khumjung (*ibid*).

It is also believed that the ancestors of all the clans of the Sherpas came to this area almost at the same time (*ibid*).

The Sherpas of Solu-Khumbu area and also of all the districts of Sikkim are not the original inhabitants of this area (Oppitz 1974: 122; Kunwar 1989:118). Subba referring to Sherpas (1982) mentioned that the ancestors of the Sherpas came to Khumbu directly from Tibet crossing Nangpa La (19,050 ft) the main trade route between Khumbu and Dingri region of Tibet (2008: 280).

Hermanns also believe that these people are believed to have come from original habitat in the frontier district in Tsing-Lai-Sechwen provinces of China (1954: 23) wherefrom they migrated to different parts of the eastern Himalayas particularly to Nepal. From Nepal some of them migrated to Sikkim and settled there. Again some of them finally migrated to Darjeeling and settled there. According to Bankati

> "The Sherpa penetration of the Himalayan region on the south of the Sagarmatha occurred approximately 600 years ago, when they commenced the migration through the Nangpa La" (2004: 1482).

From their original homeland they migrated to the "land south of their homeland and thus initially settled in the Khumbu area and from there they re-migrated to other outlying areas" (*ibid:* 1482: 1483). According to Mitra these people were living in places like Solu, Khumbu, Parak and other areas which were in Tibet upto A.D. 1792 (2008: 1183).

Oppitz in connection with the Sherpa migration, tells that their first migration started in 1530 AD and continued till 1850 AD because of the "politico-religious and internal religious conflict" (1974: 122 cf Subba 2008: 279). But according to *Lama* the Sherpas were compelled to migrate as they were harassed by the Mongals (1971: 150-160 cf Subba 2008: 279). The same is the view of Downs (1980: 3). The *Mola* (a speech-making tradition which is orally narrated sometimes like a story on the occasion of wedding in Bigu) as cited by Subba, tells that "the original home land of the Sherpas was in Kham. People from other country came to attack over there and then the inhabitants of Kham ran away .... Some of them settled in Khumbu. Even from Khumbu some people got down to Solu and settled in Gomba dzyung (present Junbesi). Later on population increased and some people reached Chortung La (the ridge of Jiri) from where they look to north-western side. There they saw some empty land like a granary in six which was present Bigu. Very few of them settled in that village" (Subba 2008: 280).

The said *Mola* further states that the villages like Khartal, Labtang, Khasa, and Lamobagar were already settled by the Sherpas. The Sherpas migrated from their original homeland. They had to migrate because of the political conflict, as mentioned in the said *Mola*. The Sherpas first settled at Khumbu and then at Solu. Thereafter, they moved to north-western and also to north-eastern direction though the date of their migration could not be ascertained (Kunwar 1989: 120). An oral tradition that tells us that "the Sherpas immigrated into Kalimpong about two centuries ago, most of them directly from Solu-Khumbu and some *via* Sikkim for the purpose of better fortune" (Gupta 1980: 95).

Allen referring to strict historicity of the documents translated by Oppitz (1968), states that the founders of the Sherpas "are supposed to have arrived in what is now Napal more or less simultaneously around 1530" (1978: 12). According to Chatterjee the Sherpas who are clearly ethnic Tibetan, moved towards South (1951 cf. Doherty 1978: 435).

As regards migration of the Sherpas, Gautom reports that the Sherpas started migrating from Tibet about 600 years ago through Nangpala Pass. Narrating a legend of the Sherpas, Gautam states that the Mongol king Tsokpo Ddzangubrae who belonged to the Gelukpa sect, attempted to preach the people about the principles and ethics of this sect of Buddhism. He also converted the people into this sect forcefully. The followers of the Nyingmapa sect (the Sherpas for example) were totally against to get converted to Gelukpa, and in order to get rid of the wrath of the king, they fled towards south of their homeland and finally took refuge at Khumbu region of Nepal. Many of them again migrated from Khumbu to some other areas within and outside Nepal. Zangbu is also of the openion that the first person to come to Khumbu, came from Kham to Khumbu *via* Rolwaling and Tashi Lapcha Pass about 600 years ago (1995). According to some Chinese account, some Sherpas believe that they were descendants of the Tibetan from the Kham region of Sichuan Province. According to a legend, their ancestors settled down at Kham region after they completed their pilgrimage to different Buddhist monasteries and temples of India and Nepal (*Source*: internet). Another *internet* source reveals that the Sherpas migrated from eastern Tibet to Nepal within last 300 to 400 years.

In connection with the migration of the Sherpas of Solu-Khumbu region of Eastern Nepal, Oppitz is of the opinion that though at present Solu-Khumbu region are the main settlements of the Sherpas, but it was not so always. Even these areas were not inhabited by others before the coming of the Sherpas.

> It was not until the middle of the sixteenth century that the first ancestors of the Sherpas immigrated into this region. These ancestors had come a long way. According to written accounts and oral information their original homeland was a region in the Eastern Tibetan Province of Kham named Salmo Gang, that is a region approximately 1300 miles away from their present home (Oppitz 1977: 233).

It is guessed that the Sherpas migrated from their original habitat at Salmo Gang in Kham Province in Eastern Tibet to Solu-Khumbu region of Eastern Nepal because of the "politico-religious tension between the Kham people and their powerful neighbours in the north, the Mongals" (*ibid*). Oppitz further states that this migration of the Sherpas from Kham areas took place in two successive phases. In the first phase they moved from their habitat in Kham Province to Tinkye region in Central Tibet, and then from Tinkye region they migrated to their present habitat in Nepal, that is, Solu-Khumbu region. In the midway they halted in Central Tibet. But another politico-religious thrust compelled them to leave this newly acquired home for the second time.

> In the years 1531-33, Mirza Muhammed Haidar Dughlat, the General of the religious Muslim zealot, Sultan Sa'id Khan from Kashgar, invaded Tibet with army from the west, and although he did not quite achieve his aim – the destruction of the city temple Lhasa—the army generated a lot of fear and turmoil in those parts through which the martial campaign led. Supposing that this foreign invation was directly related to the Sherpas' escape across the Himalayan range into Nepal, as the indications suggest, we can date their arrival in Solu-Khumbu very precisely. It must have been round 1533 (*ibid*).

So, Oppitz thinks that the Sherpas finally started migrating from Tibet around 1533 because of the invasion on Tibet by the army of Sultan Sa'id Khan of Kashgar.

In this way the ancestors of the Sherpas after crossing the Nangpa La Pass, entered the valleys situated in the south of Mt. Everest and established their first settlements there. And this, according to Oppitz, began the "history of the colonization of Solu-Khumbu". These immigrant Sherpas were divided into four clans and each clan consisted of only a few families. These four clans were Minyagpa, Thimi, Serwa and Chappa. They immediately moved to Solu. Later on majority of the Sherpas came and settled in this region (*ibid*: 234).

After their occupation of Solu region, the next batch came and settled at Khumbu region. They were earlier settled in and around Dingri, the adjacent area north of the main Himalayan range. "They started to move into Nepal from about the middle of the 18th Century. Because of their general cultural similarity they were easily integrated into the tribal community" (*ibid*).

The whole tribe of the Sherpa immigrants of Solu-Khumbu regions did not come to this area at a time. Rather they came in small batches and in different period of time. Considering this Oppitz has hypothised that the people who are now known as the Sherpas, an important hill tribe of Eastern Nepal, are

> the result of the numerical expansion of a very small population that followed mechanically its own rate of growth (doubling rate for population: 49 years) within the confines of a single area (Solu-Khumbu) and a demarcated period of time (ca 450 years) (*ibid*:237).

During their stay in Solu-Khumbu region the Sherpas faced waves of people belonging to different other ethnic groups who came and settled in this region.

Finally, some other groups from western Nepal infiltrated into the Solu-Khumbu area and settled there retaining their own traditional culture. This movement started in 19th Century and till continuing. They all are now settled in Solu area (*ibid*:235).

Distribution

The Sherpas are found to live in different parts of Nepal, particularly in eastern Nepal. They are also found in all the four districts of Sikkim. In West Bengal they are mostly found to settle in Darjeeling district. Here their main concentration is in Kalimpong sub-division. Some of them are also found to get settled in Darjeeling and Kurseong Sub-Divisions. They are also reported to be settled in Arunachal Pradesh. But nothing is known to us about their population, life and activities in Arunachal Pradesh. Some of them may have settled in Bhutan. But we do not have any authentic source of information about their settlement in Bhutan. Some of them have also settled in some parts of Europe and America. In Darjeeling district they live in the altitudes ranging from 4000 ft. to 9000 ft.

In Sikkim they are found in all the four districts, but their number is more in western district. "Okhray, Tikpur, Rumbuk Ripdi, Bhareng, Sapray-Nagi, Bhurikhop, Soreng, Singling, Dentam (in West District), Damthong, Jawbari (in South District), Rongli, Phadamchen, Penlong and Pakyong (East District) are the areas where a good number of the Sherpas are found to stay" (Gangopadhyay 1993:155; Bankati 2004:1489). Subba has found higher concentration of the Sherpas in the areas like Ribdi, Bharang, Okharey, Upper Thambong, Higher elevation areas of Tashiding constituency, Begha, Upper Bermiok, Siribadam, Singling, and Buriokhop of West District, Ralang, Nayabasti, Wok, Domthang of South District, Regu, Pathing and Khamdong of East District and Kabi Tingda area of North District of Sikkim (2008: 281).

In Nepal they are found to live in Namcha Bazar, Khumjung, Kunde, Phortse, Pangboche, Milingbo and Changmitang, Thamo, Thami, and Thamote villages beside Khumbu and Solu (Fürer-Haimandorf 1964:5). According to Bankoti the Sherpa are found to inhabit "in the regions of Oolangchung, Gola, Laelep, Papung and Yamfuddin in the eastern district of Taplejung and then to west of these people occupy 11 out of 50 VDCs in the Solu and Khumbu region". They are also found to get settled in the Kathmandu Valley and other eastern areas (2004:1483). Bista is of the openion that in Nepal the Sherpas "live in the northern districts of Sangarmatha Zone along the Dudh Kosi River and its tributary valley and in the Helmu hill districts, although their original homeland is traditionally the district of Solu-Khumbu" (1976:160). According to another source the Sherpas are found to inhabit all along the eastern hill districts of Nepal like Taplejung, Panchthar, Ilam, Bhojpur, Sankhuwasabha, Ramechhap, Dolakha, Sindhupalchowk, Udaypur, and Okhaldhunga. They are also found in Kathmandu valley and Namche Bazar area (*Source*: *internet*).

The Sherpas, apart from West Bengal, Sikkim, Nepal and Bhutan, are also found to Arunachal Pradesh. Outside India some of them are living in some of the European countries and also in U.S.A. In New York a good number of them are found to inhabit. A few of them also live in Korea.

4

THEIR NUMERICAL POSITION

It is difficult to say how many Sherpas are there in India particularly in West Bengal, Sikkim and Arunachal Pradesh. We get the census figures of the Sherpa of Darjeeling District in 1901 and from 1931 to 1951. In 1901 their population in Darjeeling was 3,450, in 1931 they were 5,295 in number, in 1941, 6,929 and in 1951, they were 8998. Their numerical strength is not available for the census year 1911 and 1921. As they were included in the broad group, *Bhutias*, so no separate census figure for the Sherpa of Darjeeling or of West Bengal is available. But in 1981 their population in West Bengal was 14,195 as mentioned by Mitra (2008:1183). In case of Sikkim no census figure is available. Subba has traced out 25,808 Sherpas in Sikkim from the voters' list of 2004 forming 4.31 per cent of the total population of Sikkim (2008:281). Subba after referring to Gordon (1979:85), has also reported 7,173 Sherpas in India according to 1961 Census (2008:281).

According to an information available from internet there are 80,000 Sherpas live in both sides of the Himalayan range. More than 45,000 of the 80,000 Sherpa population live primarily in Darjeeling District of West Bengal and some are in Sikkim and Arunachal Pradesh. Fürer-Haimendorf cited a figure of 7,929 Sherpas in 1947 in Darjeeling district (1964:3-4). But in 1984 Fürer-Haimendorf has not mentioned anything about the population of the Sherpas in Nepal or in his studied areas.

According to 1971 Census the population of the Bhote Sherpas was 79,218 (Subba 2008:281). Oppitz could trace over 14,000 Sherpas in Solu-Khumbu area in 1965 (1968:109). Ortner has faced difficulty in finding out exact population figures of the Sherpas, but she could get about 7,000 Sherpas in Darjeeling area. This figure she got from a British report of 1965. Ortner also guessed about 3,000 to 4,000 Sherpas in Kathmandu. So, she has counted about 24,000 to 25,000 Sherpas live in Nepal and Darjeeling (1979:12).

In Nepal an *internet* source has mentioned that in 1990 the Bhote Sherpa population was 28,600, in 1995 it was 32,600, in 2000, 36,900 and on 08.07.2010 the Sherpa population was 45,000. Another internet source has traced 30,000 Sherpas in Nepal, especially in Solu-Khum District and in and around Namcha Bazar. The third internet source has reported that 1,54,622 Sherpas in Nepal according to 2001 Census forming 0.68 per cent of the total population of Nepal (2,31,51,423 according to 2001 census). This Sherpa population includes 92.83 per cent Buddhists, 6.26 per cent were Hindus, 0.63 per cent were Christians and 0.20 per cent embraced *Bon* religion of Tibet.

Bankoti has also reported that in Nepal there were 1,10,358 Sherpas according to 1991 Census.

Gupta, in order to study the comparative demographic profile of the Sherpas living in high altitude and lower altitude areas, selected 1 Upper Khumbu village of Eastern Nepal, which is situated in the altitude between 10,000 and 14,000 ft. above mean sea level. The villages selected by Gupta in lower altitude areas, are Upper Eachhay, Sherpagaon, Algarah, Lava, Pashiting and Munsong Cinchona Plantation. These villages are situated in the altitudes between 3000 and 6000 ft. above mean sea level (1980: 96-100).

At Upper Khumbu village Gupta got a total of 539 Sherpas of which 272 (50.46%) are males and 267 (49.54%) females. Again out of the total of 539 Sherpas of this village 233 (43.23%) belonged to the age-group 0-14, 246 (45.64%) belonged to the age-group 15 to 49 and 60 (11.13%) belonged to the age-group 50+. Again in the age-group 0-14 out of a total Sherpa population of 233, 110 (47.21%) were males and 123 (52.79%) females. In the age-group 15 to 49 total males were 130 (52.85%) and females 116 (47.15%) out of a total of 246 Sherpas and in the age-group 50+ out of a total of 60 Sherpas, the total males were 32 (53.33%) and total females 28 (46.67%).

The combined Sherpa population of all the villages of Kalimpong sub-Division of Darjeeling studied by Gupta, was 1446. Out of this total Sherpa population as found by Gupta from his studied villages of Kalimpong 766 (52.97%) were males and 680 (47.03%) females. Again out of this total of 1446 Sherpas 573 (39.63%) belonged to the age-group, 0-14, 717 (49.58%) belonged to the age-group, 15 to 49 and the rest 156 (10.79%) belonged to the age-group, 50+.

Again out of a total of 573 Sherpas belonging to the age-group 0-14 of the villages of Kalimpong, 306 (53.40%) were males and 267 (46.60%) females. In case of the age-group 15-49, out of a total of 717 Sherpas,

378 (52.72%) were males and 339 (47.38%) females. Again out of a total of 156 Sherpas belonging to the age-group 50+, 72 (52.56%) were males and 74 (47.44%) females (Gupta 1980: 96-100).

Besides Darjeeling, Sikkim and Nepal, there are 3000 to 4000 Sherpas live in Bhutan, about 1,000 in China and about 2,500 in New York (*Source: internet*).

So, we get from different sources available to us, different figures of the Sherpas of Darjeeling, Sikkim and Nepal. Therefore, it is difficult to ascertain the exact number of the Sherpas in the countries they live, that is, India, Nepal, Bhutan, China including Tibet, Korea, U.S.A. and any other places.

Sherpa Population of our Studied Villages

So, far we have counted the Sherpa population in different places like West Bengal, Darjeeling, Sikkim, Nepal, Tibet, China and New York as mentioned by different sources. Now, we shall turn our attention towards the villages of Darjeeling and Sikkim we have studied, and check the population of the Sherpa inhabiting these villages.

Now, when we examine the sex-wise distribution of the Sherpa population of the two villages of Sikkim and also two villages of Darjeeling, we find that out of the combined total Sherpa population of these four villages (1260), the combined male population (643) is slightly higher (51.03%) than the combined Sherpa female population (48.97% of Table 4.1). In the two Sikkim villages also the combined Sherpa male population (363 or 52.46%) is higher than the combined Sherpa female population (329 or 47.54%). On the other hand, in two Darjeeling villages, the combined Sherpa female population is slightly higher (50.70%) than the combined Sherpa male population (49.30%) (Table 4.1).

Now, we like to examine the distribution of the Sherpa population of these four villages of two areas, Sikkim and Darjeeling (Table 4.1). On examination we find the quantum of population belongs to each of three categories ("upto 14", "15 to 59" and "60+"). In the age-group "upto 14" the combined population of the four studied villages is 447 of which the total combined female population (51.01%) is slightly higher than the combined male population (48.99%) of these two villages (Table 4.1).

When we turn out attention towards the distribution of the Sherpa population of the studied villages of Sikkim and Darjeeling of these categories separately, we get some peculiar data. While the combined population of the studied villages of Sikkim shows very low numerical dominance of the male Sherpas over the female Sherpas, the studied villages of Darjeeling district on the other hand, reveal the opposite trend. Here the Sherpa female population is higher in number than the male Sherpa population (Table 4.1). In the age –group 15-59, the combined population of the four villages of the two areas, Sikkim and Darjeeling, the combined population of the studied villages of Sikkim and the combined population of the studied villages of Darjeeling show a common trend. Everywhere in this age-group the male Sherpas population is higher in number than the female Sherpa population though in the combined population of the four villages the numerical difference between male and female Sherpas is not much (52.05% and 47.95% respectively). In the villages of Darjeeling this difference is very low (50.44% and 49.56% respectively). But the gap between the two sexes in the Sikkim villages, is little wider (53.45% and 46.55% respectively). In the last age-group category, i.e. 60+ the combined Sherpa population of all four villages of Sikkim and Darjeeling reveals that the male population of this category is higher in number than the female population (53.09% over 46.91%). The same trend is seen in the two villages of Sikkim and also two villages of Darjeeling when taken separately. But it is also true that the male power at Sikkim villages is higher than that of the Darjeeling villages (54.17% over 51.52%). It is also seen that in general the Sherpa males are numerally stronger than the female Sherpas.

We shall now shift our discussion from sex-wise distribution of the Sherpa population to the sex-ratio in three different age-groups mentioned above. Among the combined total population of the four villages the sex-ratio is 960 females per 1000 males. But in the combined population of two villages of Sikkim the sex-ratio is 906 females per 1000 males whereas among the combined population of the two villages of Darjeeling is 1029 females per 1000 males. When we turn our attention to the age-groupwise distribution of the Sherpa population of all the four studied villages and also combined Sherpa population of two villages of Darjeeling district is quite high, 1041 and 1132 per village. The sex-ratio of two villages of Sikkim is only 977 females per 1000 males.

But in the age-group 15-59 the sex-ratio of the Sherpa population is somewhat low. While the combined Sherpa population of all the four villages and same of two villages of Sikkim have sex-ratio of 921 and 871 females per 1000 males respectively, the combined Sherpa population of two villages of Darjeeling has a sex-ratio of 983 females per 1000 males. The trend of sex-ratio of the age-group 60+ is almost similar to that of the age-group 15-59. Here in the total combined study areas and study areas of Sikkim the sex-ratio is less than 900 (884 and 846 females per 1000 males respectively). Only in the study areas of Darjeeling the same is 941 females per 1000 males.

Table 4.1: Distribution of the Combined Sherpa Population of the Studied Villages of Sikkim and Darjeeling in Three Age-group Categories

Sl. No.	Age Group	Settings	Person		Male		Female		Sex-Ratio
			No.	%	No.	%	No.	%	
1.	4-14	Total study area	447	1000.00	219	48.99	228	51.01	1041
		Two villages of Sikkim	253	100.00	128	50.59	125	49.41	977
		Two villages of Darjeeling	194	100.00	91	46.91	103	53.09	1132
2.	15-59	Total study area	732	100.00	381	52.05	351	47.95	921
		Two villages of Sikkim	391	100.00	209	53.45	182	46.55	871
		Two villages of Darjeeling	341	100.00	172	50.44	169	49.56	983
3.	60+	Total study area	81	100.00	43	53.09	38	46.91	884
		Two villages of Sikkim	48	100.00	26	54.17	22	45.83	846
		Two villages of Darjeeling	33	100.00	17	51.52	16	48.48	941
4.	Total	Total study area	1260	100.00	643	51.03	617	48.97	960
		Two villages of Sikkim	692	100.00	363	52.46	329	47.54	906
		Two villages of Darjeeling	568	100.00	280	49.30	288	50.70	1029

Source: Field Study by the authors.

It is thus seen that while in Darjeeling villages the Sherpas have satisfactory sex-ratio, the female population is either higher or close to the male populations, in the studied villages of Sikkim the same quite low.

Distribution of the Sherpa Population of the Studied Villages of Sikkim and Darjeeling in Three Age-group Categories

We have already said that we have selected two villages (Sherpaguri and Sherpapur) from Darjeeling and two villages (Sherpagaon and Sherpahat) from South district of Sikkim. After tabulating the sex and age-groupwise Sherpa population of these four villages, we have grouped them into three broad categories. The first such category is "upto 14" years of age which we have termed as the population of children. The second category is the adolescent and adult category in which we have included all Sherpa population of 15-59 years of age. We have termed the last category as the category of old people, and so, we have included all Sherpa population of 60 and above years of age. Now, the Sherpa population of the first and the last categories are expected dependents who remain economically dependent on the Sherpa population of the second category, i.e. adolescent and adult group, who are the expected workers and earners. Here through this Table 4.2 we have tried to show the sex-wise population strength of each category of the studied villages of both Darjeeling and Sikkim.

Now, from Table 4.2 we see that in total there is a combined total of 1260 Sherpas of these four villages belonging to all age-groups. Out of this population 54.92 per cent live in the two villages of Sikkim and the remaining 45.08 inhabit in two villages of Darjeeling. While we compare the Sherpa population of Sikkim and Darjeeling belonging to the three age-group categories, we see that in all the categories the combined Sherpa population of two Sikkim villages is more than that of the two Darjeeling villages. Particularly the Sherpa population of the 60+ category of the Sikkim villages is significantly higher than that of the Darjeeling villages (Table 4.2).

When we come down to the combined Sherpa male population of two villages of Sikkim and two villages of Darjeeling, we see that the

Table 4.2: Distribution of the Sherpa Population of the Studied Villages of Sikkim and Darjeeling in Three Age-groups

Age group	*Population under study area belongs to*	*Person*		*Male*		*Female*	
		No.	*%*	*No.*	*%*	*No.*	*%*
Upto 14	Total	447	100.00	219	100.00	228	100.00
	Two villages of Sikkim	253	56.60	128	58.45	125	54.82
	Two villages of Darjeeling	194	43.40	91	41.55	103	45.18
15-59	Total	732	100.00	381	100.00	351	100.00
	Two villages of Sikkim	391	53.42	209	54.86	182	51.85
	Two villages of Darjeeling	341	46.58	172	45.14	169	48.15
60+	Total	81	100.00	43	100.00	38	100.00
	Two villages of Sikkim	48	59.26	26	60.47	22	57.89
	Two villages of Darjeeling	33	40.74	17	39.53	16	42.11
Total	Total	1260	100.00	643	100.00	617	100.00
	Two villages of Sikkim	692	54.92	363	56.45	329	53.32
	Two villages of Darjeeling	568	45.08	280	43.55	288	46.68

Source: Field study by the authors.

Sherpa male population of two Sikkim villages is significantly higher (56.45%) than that of the two Darjeeling villages (43.55%). The same is true for all the Sherpa male population of the villages of Sikkim and Darjeeling of all the three categories. Though the Sherpa male population of Sikkim villages of all the categories are much higher than that of Darjeeling villages, but the male population of the two categories, "upto 14" and "60+" of Sikkim villages are significantly higher (58.45% and 60.47% respectively).The Sherpa female population of the two villages of Sikkim and two villages of Darjeeling has followed the same trend (Table 4.2). Here also the total Sherpa female population of Sikkim Villages for all the three categories is higher than that of the Darjeeling villages.

The above trend is due to the higher number of the Sherpa population in the two Sikkim villages.

Distribution of the Sherpa Population of the Studied Villages of Sikkim and Darjeeling in Three Age-group Categories

We have already said that we have selected two villages from Kalimpong, Darjeeling (Sherpaguri and Sherpapur) and two villages (Sherpagaon and Sherpahat) from South District of Sikkim. After tabulating the sex and age-groupwise Sherpa population of these four villages, we have grouped them into three broad age-group categories. The first such category is 'upto 14' years of age in which we have included the population of children. The second category is the adolescent and adult category in which we have included all Sherpa population from 15 to 59 years of age. We have termed the last category as the category of old people, and so we have included all Sherpa population of 60 and above years of age. Now, the Sherpa population of the first and the last categories are expected dependents who are expected to remain economically dependent on the Sherpa population of the second category, i.e. adolescent and adult group, who are the expected workers and as well as earners. Here through this Table 4.3 we have tried to show the sex-wise population strength of each category of the Sherpa population of the studied villages of both Darjeeling and Sikkim.

Now, from Table 4.3 we see that there are a combined total of 1260 Sherpas of these four villages belonging to all age-groups. Out of this population 54.92 per cent live in the two villages of Sikkim and the remaining 45.08 per cent inhabit two villages of Darjeeling. While we compare the Sherpa population of Sikkim belonging to all the three age-group categories with those of Darjeeling, we see that in all the categories the combined Sherpa population of two Sikkim villages is more than that of the two Darjeeling villages. Particularly the Sherpa population of the 60+ category of the Sikkim villages is significantly higher than that of the Darjeeling villages (Table 4.3).

When we come down to the combined Sherpa male population of two villages of Sikkim and two villages of Darjeeling, we see that the Sherpa male population of two Sikkim villages is significantly higher (56.45%) than that of the two Darjeeling villages (43.55%). The same is true for all the Sherpa male population of the villages of Sikkim and Darjeeling of all the three categories. Though the Sherpa male population of Sikkim villages of all the categories is much higher than that of the Darjeeling villages, but the male population of the two categories, 'upto 14' and '60+' of Sikkim villages, is significantly higher (58.45% and 60.47% respectively).

Table 4.3: Distribution of the Sherpa Population of the Studied Villages of Sikkim and Darjeeling in Three Age-group Categories

Sl. No.	*Age-group*	*Population of the study areas*	*Person*		*Male*		*Female*	
			No.	*%*	*No.*	*%*	*No.*	*%*
1.	Upto 14	Total	447	100.00	219	100.00	228	100.00
		Two villages of Sikkim	253	56.60	128	58.45	125	54.82
		Two villages of Darjeeling	194	43.40	91	41.55	103	45.18
2.	15-59	Total	732	100.00	381	100.00	351	100.00
		Two villages of Sikkim	391	53.42	209	54.86	182	51.85
		Two villages of Darjeeling	341	46.58	172	45.14	169	48.15
3.	60+	Total	81	100.00	43	100.00	38	100.00
		Two villages of Sikkim	48	59.26	26	60.47	22	57.89
		Two villages of Darjeeling	33	40.74	17	39.53	16	42.11
4.	Total	Total	1260	100.00	643	100.00	617	100.00
		Two villages of Sikkim	692	54.92	363	36.45	329	53.32
		Two villages of Darjeeling	568	45.08	280	43.55	288	46.68

Source: Field study by the authors.

The Sherpa female population of the two villages of Sikkim and two villages of Darjeeling have followed the same trend (Table 4.3). Here also the total Sherpa female population, and the same of all the three categories of Sikkim villages are higher than that of the Darjeeling villages.

The above trend is due to the higher number of the Sherpa population in the two Sikkim villages.

Distribution of the Combined Sherpa Population of the Studied Villages of Sikkim and Darjeeling in Three Age-group Categories

When we examine the sex-wise distribution of the Sherpa population of the two villages of Sikkim and also two villages of Darjeeling, we find that out of the combined total Sherpa population of these four villages (1,260) the combined male population (643) is slightly higher (51.03%) than the combined Sherpa female population (Table 4.4). In the two Sikkim villages also the combined Sherpa male population (363 o4 52.46%) is higher than the combined Sherpa female population (329 or 47.54%). But in the two Darjeeling villages, the combined Sherpa female population is slightly higher (50.70%) than the combined Sherpa male population (49.30%).

Table 4.4: Distribution of the Combined Sherpa Population of the Studied Villages of Darjeeling and Sikkim in Three Age-groups

Age groups	*Population under study area belongs to*	*Person*		*Male*		*Female*	
		No.	*%*	*No.*	*%*	*No.*	*%*
Upto 14	Total	447	35.48	219	34.06	228	36.95
	Two villages of Sikkim	253	36.56	128	35.26	125	37.99
	Two villages of Darjeeling	194	34.15	91	32.50	103	35.76
15-59	Total	732	58.10	381	59.25	351	56.89
	Two villages of Sikkim	391	56.50	209	57.58	182	55.32
	Two villages of Darjeeling	341	60.04	172	61.43	169	58.68
60+	Total	81	6.43	43	6.69	38	6.16
	Two villages of Sikkim	48	6.94	26	7.16	22	6.69
	Two villages of Darjeeling	33	5.81	17	6.07	16	5.56
Total	Total	1260	100.01	643	100.00	617	100.00
	Two villages of Sikkim	692	100.00	363	100.00	329	100.00
	Two villages of Darjeeling	568	100.00	280	99.98	288	100.00

Source: Field study by the authors.

Now, we like to examine the distribution of the Sherpa population of these four villages of two areas, Sikkim and Darjeeling (Table 4.4). On examination we find the quantum of population belongs to each of these three categories ('upto 14', '15 to 59' and '60+'). In the age-group 'upto 14' the combined population of the four studied villages is 447 of which the total combined female population (51.01%) is slightly higher than the combined male population (48.99%) of these four villages.

When we turn our attention towards the distribution of the Sherpa population of the studied villages of Sikkim and Darjeeling of this category separately, we get some peculiar data. While the combined population of the studied villages of Sikkim show a very low numerical dominance of the male Sherpas over the female Sherpas, the studied villages of Darjeeling district on the other hand, reveal the opposite trend. Here the Sherpa female population are significantly higher in number than the male Sherpa population (Table 4.4).

In the age-group 15-59, the combined population of the four villages of the two areas, Sikkim and Darjeeling, the combined population of the studied villages of Sikkim and the combined studied villages of Darjeeling show a common trend. Everywhere in this age-group the male Sherpa population are higher in number than the female Sherpa population though in the combined population of the four villages the numerical difference between male and female Sherpas is not much (52.05% and 47.95% respectively). In the villages of Darjeeling this difference is even lower (50.44% and 49.56% respectively). But the gap between the two sexes in the Sikkim villages a little wider (53.45% and 46.55% respectively).

In the last age-group category, i.e. '60+' the combined Sherpa population of all four villages of Sikkim and Darjeeling reveal that the male population of this category is higher in number than the female population (53.09% over 46.91%). The same trend is seen in the two villages of Sikkim and also two villages of Darjeeling when taken separately. But it is also true that the male power at Sikkim villages is higher than that of the Darjeeling villages (54.17% over 51.52% respectively).

It is thus seen that in general the Sherpa males are numerically stronger than the female Sherpas.

We shall now shift our discussion from sex-wise distribution of the Sherpa population to the sex-ratio in three different age-groups mentioned above. Among the combined total population of the four villages the sex-ratio is 960 females per 1000 males. But in the combined population of two villages of Sikkim the sex-ratio is 906 whereas among the combined population of the two villages of Darjeeling the same is 1029 females per 1000 males.

When we turn our attention tot the age-group-wise Sherpa population, we see that in the age-group, 'upto 14', the sex-ratio of both combined Sherpa population of all the four studied villages and also combined Sherpa population of two villages of Darjeeling district is quite high, 1041 and 1132 female per 1000 males respectively. But the same for the combined Sherpa population of two villages of Sikkim is only 977 females per 1000 males.

But in the age-group '15-59' the sex-ratio of the Sherpa population is somewhat low. While the combined Sherpa population of all the four villages and same of the two villages of Sikkim have sex-ratio of 921 and 871 females per 1000 males respectively, the combined Sherpa population of two villages of Darjeeling has a sex-ratio of 983 females per 1000 males.

The trend of sex-ratio of the age-group '60+' is almost similar to that of the age-group '15-59'. Here in the total study areas and study areas of Sikkim the sex-ratio is less than 900 (884 and 846 females per 1000 males respectively). Only in the study-areas of Darjeeling the same is 941 females per 1000 (Table 4.5).

Table 4.5: Distribution of the Combined Sherpa Population of the Studied Villages of Sikkim and Darjeeling in Three Age-group Categories

Sl. No.	*Age-group*	*Settings*	*Person*		*Male*		*Female*		*Sex-ratio*
			No.	*%*	*No.*	*%*	*No.*	*%*	
1.	Upto 14	Total study area	447	100.00	219	48.99	228	51.01	1041
		Two villages of Sikkim	253	100.00	128	50.59	125	49.41	977
		Two villages of Darjeeling	194	100.00	91	46.91	103	53.09	1132
2.	15-19	Total study area	732	100.00	381	52.05	351	47.95	921
		Two villages of Sikkim	391	100.00	209	53.45	182	46.55	871
		Two villages of Darjeeling	341	100.00	172	50.44	169	49.56	983
3.	60+	Total study area	81	100.00	43	53.09	38	46.91	884
		Two villages of Sikkim	48	100.00	26	54.17	22	45.83	846
		Two villages of Darjeeling	33	100.00	17	51.52	16	48.48	941
4.	Total	Total study area	1260	100.00	643	51.03	617	48.97	960
		Two villages of Sikkim	692	100.00	363	52.46	329	47.54	906
		Two villages of Darjeeling	568	100.00	280	49.30	288	50.70	1029

Source: Field study by the authors.

Sex-wise Distribution of the Sherpa Population

A. Two Villages of Darjeeling District

In the Kalimpong Sub-Division of Darjeeling District, West Bengal we have studied the Sherpas living in two villages, Sherpaguri and Sherpapur. In these two villages a total of 115 families live of which majority (62.61%) live in Sherpapur village and the remaining 37.39 per cent inhabit at Sherpaguri village. In these two villages a total of 568 Sherpas live of which 49.30 per cent are males and 50.70 per cent females. When we come down to the village level, we see that at among the Sherpas of Sherpaguri village majority (50.23%) are females whereas the males are a little less than half (49.77%). At Sherpapur village the same is the situation. Here also the female Sherpas are a little more in number (51.00%) than the Sherpa males (49.00%). This means that in these two villages the females have numerically slightly overshadowed the males (Tables 4.6 and 4.7).

When we further analyse our Sherpa population data of these two villages, we see that out of the total population of these two villages (568), majority (61.80%) live at Sherpapur village while only 38.20 per cent inhabit at the other village. The same is the condition with sex-wise distribution of the Sherpas these two villages. The female Sherpas are majority in these two villages (61.43% and 62.15% respectively) whereas males are much less in number (Table 4.6).

Table 4.6: Sex-wise Distribution of the Sherpa Population in Two Villages of Kalimpong, Darjeeling

Sl. No.	*Villages*	*Families*		*Person*		*Male*		*Female*	
		No.	*%*	*No.*	*%*	*No.*	*%*	*No.*	*%*
1.	Total	115	100.00	568	100.00	280	100.00	288	100.00
2.	Sherpaguri	43	37.39	217	38.20	108	38.57	109	37.85
3.	Sherpapur	72	62.61	351	61.80	172	61.43	179	62.15

Source: Field study by the authors.

Table 4.7: Sex-wise Distribution of the Sherpa Population in Two Villages of Kalimpong, Darjeeling

Sl. No.	*Villages*	*Families*		*Person*		*Male*		*Female*	
		No.	*%*	*No.*	*%*	*No.*	*%*	*No.*	*%*
1.	Total	115	100.00	568	100.00	280	49.30	288	50.70
2.	Sherpaguri	43	37.39	217	100.00	108	49.77	109	50.23
3.	Sherpapur	72	62.61	351	100.00	172	49.00	179	51.00

Source: Field study by the authors.

Sex-wise Distribution of the Sherpa Population in Three Age-Groups

A. Two Villages of Darjeeling District

When we divide the Sherpa population into three major age-group categories, representing children (upto 14 years of age), adolescents and adults (15 to 59 years of age) and old people (60+ years and above), we get some interesting and important results. From the combined total Sherpa population of the two villages, Sherpaguri and Sherpapur of Kalimpong Sub-division, Darjeeling district, we get a total of Sherpa population of 568. Out of this total Sherpa population majority (60.03%) belong to the age-group, 15 to 59. The next higher number of the Sherpas belongs to the age-group, 'upto 14' (34.15%). The old-age people here have the lowest population strength.

The same trend is noticed in the two villages separately. At Sherpaguri village out of a total of 217 Sherpas, majority (62.67%) as usual, is found in the age-group, 15 to 59 followed by the age-group, 'upto 14' in which 29.95 per cent Sherpas belong. At Sherpapur village similarly majority (58.40%) out of the total 351 Sherpas of this village, come under the age-group, 15 to 59. In this village also the next higher number of the Sherpas (36.75%) is found in the age-group, 'upto 14'. The age group, 60+ as usual has the lowest numerical strength (Table 4.8).

Table 4.8: Sex-wise Distribution of the Sherpa Population in Two Villages of Darjeeling in Three Age-groups

Age Group	Villages	Person		Male		Female	
		No.	%	No.	%	No.	%
Upto 14	Total	194	34.15	91	32.50	103	35.76
	Sherpaguri	65	29.95	33	30.56	32	29.36
	Sherpapur	129	36.75	58	33.72	71	39.66
15-59	Total	341	60.03	172	61.43	169	58.68
	Sherpaguri	136	62.67	67	62.04	69	63.30
	Sherpapur	205	58.40	105	61.05	100	55.87
60+	Total	33	5.81	17	6.07	16	5.56
	Sherpaguri	16	7.37	8	7.41	8	7.34
	Sherpapur	17	4.84	9	5.23	8	4.47
Total	Total	568	99.99	280	100.00	288	100.00
	Sherpaguri	217	99.99	108	100.01	109	100.00
	Sherpapur	351	99.99	172	99.97	179	100.00

Source: Field study by the authors.

When we come down to the combined Sherpa male population of these two villages, we get that out of a total of 172, the majority (61.43%) belong to the age-group, 15 to 59. The age-group, 'upto 14' has secured the next higher strength. The age- group 60+ remains satisfied with the lowest number of the Sherpa population (Table 4.8).

In case of the combined female Sherpa population, as usual the highest female population (58.68%) is found in the age-group 15 to 59. The age-group 'upto 14' has the next higher strength. The old-age people bear the lowest population. The same is the picture with the two villages, Sherpaguri and Sherpapur if seen separately. In both villages the age-group, 15 to 59 has kept the highest number of the Sherpa females. The age-group 'upto 15' has the next higher number of the Sherpa females. The age-group 60+ has the minimum number of the Sherpa females.

In another Table (Table 4.9) also we have discussed about the sex-wise distribution of the Sherpa population of two villages of Kalimpong Sub-Division, Darjeeling District with sex-ratio. When we see the combined Sherpa population of the two villages and also of the villages separately, we see that the female Sherpa population everywhere is higher than that of the male Sherpa population. In fact a little over half the population is of the female Sherpas, and therefore, the male Sherpas are a little less than 50.00 per cent. But the same type of the distribution is not found in three different age-groups. In the age-group, 'upto 14' the combined Sherpa population of the two villages and of Sherpapur village, the females are more in number than the males. They are little over half of the total Sherpa population (59.09% and 55.04% respectively). But Sherpaguri has male Sherpa population a little higher (50.77%) than the female Sherpas. In case of the age-group, 15 to 59, the opposite is the picture. In this age-group the combined Sherpa population and the Sherpa population of Sherpapur have the male Sherpa population a little over 50.00 per cent than the female Sherpa population. But at Sherpaguri village the female Sherpa population has slightly overshadowed the Sherpa male population. The same is the picture in the age-group 60+. Here like the age-group, 15 to 59, the combined Sherpa population and the Sherpa population of Sherpapur have a little over 50.00 per cent of the total population as the Sherpa males. That means, the Sherpa males here are a little over half. But at Sherpaguri the Sherpa males and females have equal strength (Table 4.9).

When we examine the sex-ratio of the Sherpa population, we get that in the age-group 'upto 14' the combined total Sherpa population of the two villages of Darjeeling District, and in the village, Sherpapur the sex-ratio is high but in the other village, i.e. Sherpaguri the same is only

970 females per 1000 males. In the age-group, 15 to 59, reverse is the case. Here in this age-group the combined total Sherpa population and total Sherpas of Sherpapur have low sex-ratio but at Sherpaguri the same is high (1030 females per 1000 males). In the age-group 60+ the combined total Sherpa population of Sherpapur village has low sex-ratio (941 and 889 females per 1000 males). But at Sherpaguri the sex-wise distribution of population being equal,

Table 4. 9: Sex-wise Distribution of the Sherpa Population of Two Villages of Darjeeling in Three Age-groups with Sex-ratio

Age Group	Villages	Person		Male		Female		Sex-Ratio
		No	%	No	%	No	%	
Upto 14	Total	194	100.00	91	46.91	103	53.09	1132
	Sherpaguri	65	100.00	33	50.77	32	49.23	970
	Sherpapur	129	100.00	58	44.96	71	55.04	1224
15-59	Total	341	100.00	172	50.44	169	49.56	983
	Sherpaguri	136	100.00	67	49.26	69	50.74	1030
	Sherpapur	205	100.00	105	51.22	100	48.78	952
60+	Total	33	100.00	17	51.52	16	48.48	941
	Sherpaguri	16	100.00	8	50.00	8	50.00	1000
	Sherpapur	17	100.00	9	52.94	8	47.06	889
Total	Total	568	100.00	280	49.30	288	50.70	1029
	Sherpaguri	217	100.00	108	49.77	109	50.23	1009
	Sherpapur	351	100.00	172	49.00	179	51.00	10

Source: Field study by the authors.

the sex-ratio is also balanced. In all age-groups the combined total Sherpa population of two villages and also separate Sherpa population of the two villages, Sherpaguri and Sherpapur the sex-ratio is higher (1029, 1009 and 1041 respectively).

Sex-wise and Age-group-wise Distribution of the Sherpa Population

A. Two Villages of Darjeeling District

Now, let us examine the strength of the combined Sherpa male and female population belonging to different age-groups of the two villages of Darjeeling districts. From Table 4.10 we find that in the age-groups 5-9, 15-19, 25-29, 35-39, 45-49, 55-59 and 70+ the male population is higher in number than the female population. In other age-groups (upto 4, 10-14, 20-24, 30-34, 50-54, 60-64 and 65-69) the number of the Sherpa males of these two villages is less than that of the Sherpa females. The age-group 40-44 is the only age-group which has equal number of male as well as female members. The reverse is the case with the females. The age-groups, upto 5, 10-14, 20-24, 30-34, 50-54, 60-64 and 65-69 have the Sherpa females who have numerically overshadowed the Sherpa males. But in the remaining age-groups they are lesser in number than their male counterparts (Table 4.10).

When we look into the sex-ratio of different age-groups (Table 4.11) we see that the sex-ratio is highest in age-group upto 4 (1933) followed by the age-group 60-64 (1667) and 65-69 (1500). But we find lowest sex-ratio in the age-group 55-59 (556) followed by the age-groups 70+(667) and 5-9 (676). The sex-ratio is 1000 females per 1000 males in the age-group of 40-44 as the number of males and females in this age-group is equal (each 19).

Table 4.10: Age-Group-wise Distribution of Sherpa Population of Two Villages of Darjeeling, West Bengal

Sl. No.	*Age Groups*	*Person*		*Male*		*Female*	
		No.	*%*	*No.*	*%*	*No.*	*%*
1.	Upto 4	44	7.75	15	5.36	29	10.07
2.	5-9	62	10.92	37	13.21	25	8.68
3.	10-14	88	15.49	39	13.93	49	17.01
4.	15-19	73	12.85	39	13.93	34	11.81
5.	20-24	44	7.75	19	6.79	25	8.68
6.	25-29	50	8.80	26	9.29	24	8.33
7.	30-34	42	7.39	18	6.43	24	8.33
8.	35-39	36	6.34	20	7.14	16	5.56
9.	40-44	38	6.69	19	6.79	19	6.60
10.	45-49	30	5.28	16	5.71	14	4.86
11.	50-54	14	2.46	6	2.14	8	2.78
12.	55-59	14	2.46	9	3.21	5	1.74
13.	60-64	8	1.41	3	1.07	5	1.74
14.	65-69	5	0.88	2	0.71	3	1.04
15.	70+	20	3.52	12	4.29	8	2.78
	Total	568	99.99	280	100.00	288	100.01

Source: Field study by the authors.

While studying the population structure of the Sherpas of the two villages of Kalimpong Sub-Division, Darjeeling District, we have examined the Sherpa population of these two villages belonging to different age-groups. Out of the total Sherpa population of these two villages we see that maximum number of the Sherpas (15.49%) belong to the age-group 10 to 14. Next in order come age-group 15-19 (12.85%) followed by the age-group 5 to 9 (10.92%). The rest of the age-groups have all below 10.00 per cent, the lowest being age-group 65 to 69 (0.88%).

In case of the male Sherpas of these two villages, we find that age-groups 10 to 14 and 15 to 19 have accommodated highest number of male Sherpas as each of these two age-groups having 13.93 per cent of the total male Sherpas of these two villages. Next comes age-group 5 to 9 which has 13.21 per cent Sherpa males in its credit. Each of the remaining age-groups has less than 10.00 per cent Sherpa males. Age group 65-69 has the lowest strength (0.71%).

The maximum number of the female Sherpas of these two villages belong to the age-group 10 to 14 (17.01%). Next comes age-group 15 to 19 which has taken in its fold 11.81 per cent of the Sherpa females of these two villages. The age-group 5 to 9 follows the previous age-group (15 to 19) as it has taken a share of 10.07 per cent of the total Sherpa females of these two villages of Kalimpong. The age-group 65-69 has secured only 1.04 per cent of the combined total Sherpa female population of these two villages.

Table 4.11: Age-Group-wise Distribution of Sherpa Population of Two Villages of Darjeeling, West Bengal

Sl. No.	Age Groups	Person		Male		Female		Sex Ratio
		No.	%	No.	%	No.	%	
1.	Upto 4	44	100.00	15	34.09	29	65.91	1933
2.	5-9	62	100.00	37	59.68	25	40.32	676
3.	10-14	88	100.00	39	44.32	49	55.68	1256
4.	15-19	73	100.00	39	53.42	34	46.58	872
5.	20-24	44	100.00	19	43.18	25	56.82	1316
6.	25-29	50	100.00	26	52.00	24	48.00	923
7.	30-34	42	100.00	18	42.86	24	57.14	1333
8.	35-39	36	100.00	20	55.56	16	44.44	800
9.	40-44	38	100.00	19	50.00	19	50.0	1000
10.	45-49	30	100.00	16	53.33	14	46.67	875
11.	50-54	14	100.00	6	42.86	8	57.14	1333
12.	55-59	14	100.00	9	64.29	5	35.71	556
13.	60-64	8	100.00	3	37.50	5	62.50	1667
14.	65-69	5	100.00	2	40.00	3	60.00	1500
15.	70+	20	100.00	12	60.00	8	40.00	667
	Total	568	100.00	280	49.30	288	50.70	1029

Source: Field study by the authors.

As we come down to the individual village level, we see that at Sherpaguri village of Kalimpong, Darjeeling, there are a total of 217 Sherpas live in this village. Out of these 217 Sherpas the highest number (17.51%) is found in the age-group 10-14. The next higher strength (16.13%) is noticed in the age-group 15-19. The age-group 5-9 which secures the third position numerically, has only 7.83 per cent Sherpas out of a total of 217. Age-group 60-64 has held the lowest number (0.92%) of the total Sherpa population followed by age-group 65-69 (1.38%) (Table 4.12).

Among the male Sherpas of this village Sherpaguri, the age-group 15-19 covers the highest number of the Sherpas (17.59%) out of a total of 108 male Sherpas. The next higher strength (16.67%) is found to be present in the age-group of 10-14. The age-group 5-9 has also held a good number of the Sherpas (11.11%). The rest of the age-groups has less than 10.00 per cent each. While age-group 65-69 has kept the lowest number of the Sherpas (1.85%), age-group 60-64 does not have a single Sherpa male in its credit.

Regarding the distribution of the female Sherpas of the village, Sherpaguri of Kalimpong Sub-Division, Darjeeling District, we see that the highest number of the Sherpas is found in the age-group of 10-14 (18.35%). The next higher number of the Sherpa females (14.68%) comes under the age-group 15-19. The rest of the age-groups have less than 10.00 per cent each. The age-group 65-69 has the lowest number of the Sherpa females (0.92%).

Table 4.12: Age-Group-wise Distribution of Sherpa Population of Sherpaguri Village of Darjeeling, West Bengal

Sl. No.	*Age Groups*	*Person*		*Male*		*Female*	
		No.	*%*	*No.*	*%*	*No.*	*%*
1.	Upto 4	10	4.61	3	2.78	7	6.42
2.	5-9	17	7.83	12	11.11	5	4.59
3	10-14	38	17.51	18	16.67	20	18.35
4.	15-19	35	16.13	19	17.59	16	14.68
5.	20-24	14	6.45	6	5.56	8	7.34
6.	25-29	16	7.37	8	7.41	8	7.34
7.	30-34	11	5.07	5	4.63	6	5.50
8.	35-39	10	4.61	5	4.63	5	4.59
9.	40-44	15	6.91	6	5.56	9	8.26
10.	45-49	14	6.45	8	7.41	6	5.50
11.	50-54	12	5.53	4	3.70	8	7.34
12.	55-59	9	4.15	6	5.56	3	2.75
13.	60-64	2	0.92			2	1.83
14.	65-69	3	1.38	2	1.85	1	0.92
15.	70+	11	5.07	6	5.56	5	4.59
	Total	217	99.99	108	100.02	109	100.00

Source: Field study by the authors.

On further examination of the age-group-wise distribution of the Sherpas of the village Sherpaguri of Kalimpong, Darjeeling District, we see that out of a total of 217 Sherpas of this village the number of males is slightly lower than that of the Sherpa females, 49.77 per cent against 50.23 per cent. But in the age-groups 5-9, 15-19, 45-49, 55-59, 65-69 and 70+ the number of male Sherpas is higher than that of the female Sherpas. In the rest of the age-groups, i.e. 10-14, 20-24, 30-34, 40-44, and 50-54 the number of the Sherpa females is more than that of the Sherpa males. In the age-groups 25-29 and 35-39 the number of the male and the female Sherpas is the same. On the other hand, the age-group 60-64 does not have any Sherpa male, but in this age-group there are only two Sherpa females (Table 4.12).

As we look into the sex-ratio in different age-groups of the Sherpas of the village Sherpaguri, we find that the highest sex-ratio is in the age-group 'upto 4' which is 2333. This means that in this age-group there are 2333 female Sherpas per 1000 male Sherpas. The next higher sex-ratio (2000) is found in the age-group 45-49 followed by the age-groups 30-34 (1200), 10-14 (1111) and 70+ (1009). Age-groups 25-29 and 35-39 have balanced sex-ratio. That means in these two age-groups there are 1000 female Sherpas per 1000 male Sherpas. The lowest sex-ratio is found in the age-group 20-24 where for 1000 Sherpa males there are only 333 Sherpa females (Table 4.13).

Now, we shall come to the village Sherpapur of Kalimpong Sub-division in the district of Darjeeling, West Bengal. In this village a total of 351 Sherpas live. Out of these 351 Sherpas, the highest number (14.25%) are found in the age-group 10-14. The next higher number is present in the age-group 5-9 (12.82%) followed by the age-group 15-19 (10.83%). Each of the other age-groups has less than 10.00 per cent. the lowest number of the Sherpas (0.57%) is found in the age-groups 50-54 and 65-69 (Table 4.13).

In this village there are 172 Sherpa males, and of these males highest number is found in the age-group 5-9 (14.53%). The age-group 10-14 has the next higher strength. This age-group (10-14) is followed by the age-groups 15-19 (11.63%) and 25-29 (10.47%). The rest of the age-groups have each with less than 10.00 per cent of the Sherpa males. The lowest number of the Sherpa males of this village is in the age-groups 50-54 with of the total Sherpa males of this village, Sherpapur. There is no Sherpa males present in the age group 65-69.

The village Sherpapur has a total of 179 Sherpa females, and out of these Sherpa females the highest number of the Sherpa females is present

Table 4.13: Age-Group-wise Distribution of Sherpa Population of Sherpaguri Village of Darjeeling, West Bengal

Sl. No.	*Age Groups*	*Person*		*Male*		*Female*		*Sex Ratio*
		No.	*%*	*No.*	*%*	*No.*	*%*	
1.	Upto 4	10	100.00	3	30.00	7	70.00	2333
2.	5-9	17	100.00	12	70.59	5	29.41	417
3.	10-14	38	100.00	18	47.37	20	52.63	1111
4.	15-19	35	100.00	19	54.29	16	45.71	742
5.	20-24	14	100.00	6	42.86	8	57.14	333
6.	25-29	16	100.00	8	50.00	8	50.00	1000
7.	30-34	11	100.00	5	45.45	6	54.55	1200
8.	35-39	10	100.00	5	50.00	5	50.00	1000
9.	40-44	15	100.00	6	40.00	9	60.00	750
10.	45-49	14	100.00	8	57.14	6	42.86	2000
11.	50-54	12	100.00	4	33.33	8	66.67	500
12.	55-59	9	100.00	6	66.67	3	33.33	—
13.	60-64	2	100.00	—	—	2	100.00	500
14.	65-69	3	100.00	2	66.67	1	33.33	833
15.	70+	11	100.00	6	54.55	5	45.45	1009
	Total	217	100.00	108	49.77	109	50.23	—

Source: Field study by the authors.

in the age-group 10-14 (16.20%). The next higher number of the Sherpa females is found in the age-group 'upto 4' (12.29%) followed by the age-group 5-9 (11.17%). The age-group 15-19 also has a good number of the Sherpa females (10.06%). Each of the remaining age-groups has less that 10.00 per cent of the Sherpa females of this village. The lowest number of the Sherpa females is present in the age-groups 55-59 and 65-69 each with 1.12 per cent of the Sherpa females. The age-group 50-54 does not have a single Sherpa woman.

Now, we come down to the other aspects of the age-group-wise distribution of the Sherpa females of the village, Sherpapur (Table 4.14). In this village out of a total of 351 Sherpas a little over half (51.00%) are females and a little less than half (49.00%) are males. While we count the age-groupwise distribution of the Sherpas of this village, we see that in the age-groups 5-9, 15-19, 25-29, 35-39, 40-44, 55-59 and 70+ the number of the Sherpas males is higher than that of the Sherpa females. In case of the age-group 50-54 all are males as there was no female Sherpas in this age-group. But in the age-groups 'upto 4', 10-14, 20-24 and 30-34 the female Sherpas have outnumbered their male counterpart. In the age-groups 45-49 and 60-64 the number of the male and female Sherpas is equal (Table 4.14).

Table 4.14: Age-Group-wise Distribution of Sherpa Population of Sherpapur Village of Darjeeling, West Bengal

Sl. No.	Age Groups	Person		Male		Female	
		No.	%	No.	%	No.	%
1.	Upto 4	34	9.69	12	6.98	22	12.29
2.	5-9	45	12.82	25	14.53	20	11.17
3.	10-14	50	14.25	21	12.21	29	16.20
4.	15-19	38	10.83	20	11.63	18	10.06
5.	20-24	30	8.55	13	7.56	17	9.50
6.	25-29	34	9.69	18	10.47	16	8.94
7.	30-34	31	8.83	13	7.56	18	10.06
8.	35-39	26	7.41	15	8.72	11	6.15
9.	40-44	23	6.55	13	7.56	10	5.59
10.	45-49	16	4.56	8	4.65	8	4.47
11.	50-54	2	0.57	2	1.16		
12.	55-59	5	1.42	3	1.74	2	1.12
13.	60-64	6	1.71	3	1.74	3	1.68
14.	65-69	2	0.57			2	1.12
15.	70+	9	2.56	6	3.49	3	1.68
	Total	351	100.01	172	100.00	179	100.03

Source: Field study by the authors.

As we calculate the sex-ratio of the Sherpa males and females of different age-groups, we find that the highest sex-ratio belong to the age-group 'upto 4' (1833 females per 1000 males). The next higher sex-ratio is found in the age-group 30-34 followed by the age-group 10-14 and 20-24 (1385, 1381 and 1301 females per 1000 males respectively). In the age-groups 45-49 and 60-64 the sex-ratio is the same. But in the rest of the age-groups (except age-group 50-54 in which there is no member) the sex-ratio varies from 500 (age-group 70+) to 900 (age-group 15-19). In the age-group 65-69 there is no male. The sex-ratio of the total Sherpa population of this village is 1041 females per 1000 males (Table 4.15).

Sex-wise Distribution of the Sherpa Population in Three Age-Groups

A. The Two Villages of Kalimpong, Darjeeling District

We see that the majority of the Sherpas of two villages of Kalimpong, Darjeeling belong to the age-group, 15 to 59 (60.04%). The same is the case with the male (61.43%) and female (58.68%) Sherpas. Next in order come those who belong to the age-group 'upto 14'. In this category the strength of the Sherpas is 34.15 per cent and that of the male and female Sherpas are 32.50 per cent and 35.76 per cent respectively. The strength

Table 4.15: Age-Group-wise Distribution of Sherpa Population of Sherpapur Village of Darjeeling, West Bengal

Sl. No.	Age Groups	Person		Male		Female		Sex Ratio
		No.	%	No.	%	No.	%	
1.	Upto 4	34	100.00	12	35.29	22	64.71	1833
2.	5-9	45	100.00	25	55.56	20	44.44	800
3.	10-14	50	100.00	21	42.00	29	58.00	1381
4.	15-19	38	100.00	20	52.63	18	47.37	900
5.	20-24	30	100.00	13	43.33	17	56.67	1308
6.	25-29	34	100.00	18	52.94	16	47.06	889
7.	30-34	31	100.00	13	41.94	18	58.06	1385
8.	35-39	26	100.00	15	57.69	11	42.31	733
9.	40-44	23	100.00	13	56.52	10	43.48	769
10.	45-49	16	100.00	8	50.00	8	50.00	1000
11.	50-54	2	100.00	2	100.00	—	—	—
12.	55-59	5	100.00	3	60.00	2	40.00	667
13.	60-64	6	100.00	3	50.00	3	50.00	1000
14.	65-69	2	100.00	—	—	2	100.00	—
15.	70+	9	100.00	6	66.67	3	33.33	500
	Total	351	100.00	172	49.00	179	51.00	1041

Source: Field study by the authors.

of the elderly Sherpas who belong to 60 and above, is quite low (Table 4.16).

Table 4.16: Distribution of the Combined Sherpa Population of the Two Villages of Kalimpong, in Three Age-groups

Sl. No.	Age Group	Person		Male		Female	
		No.	%	No.	%	No.	%
1.	Upto 14	194	34.15	91	32.50	103	35.76
2.	15-59	341	60.04	172	61.43	169	58.68
3.	60+	33	5.81	17	6.07	16	5.56
	Total	568	100.00	280	100.00	288	100.00

Source: Field study by the authors.

Again from Table 4.17 we get the sex-wise numerical distribution of the Sherpa population of three different age-groups ('upto 14', 15-59 and 60 and above) of the combined population of two Sherpa villages of Kalimpong Sub-Division of Darjeeling District. From this table we get that out of the total Sherpa population of these two villages the number of females (50.70%) is a little more than that of the males (49.30%). The same (that is higher strength of the female Sherpas over the male Sherpas) is found in the age-group category of 'upto 14' (53.09% and 46.91% respectively). But in other two age groups, i.e., 15-59 and 60+ the numerical position of the male Sherpas is slightly higher than that of the female Sherpas (Table 4.17).

As we find out the sex-ratio from Table 4.17 we see that in case of the total Sherpa population of these two villages and also in case of the age-group 'upto 14' female sex-ratio is higher (1029 and 1132 females respectively per 1000 males). But in case of the other two age-groups (15 to 59 and 60+) males have outnumbered the females in case of the sex-ratio (983 and 941 females respectively per 1000 males).

Now, we like to come to see the status of the individual villages. At Sherpaguri village of Kalimpong, Darjeeling a little over half (50.23%) of the total Sherpa population is females and the remaining a little less than half (49.77%) is males. In case of the age-groups 'upto 14' the male Sherpas are marginally higher in number than the female Sherpas, but reverse is the case of the age-group 15-59. In this case the female Sherpas are slightly more than the male Sherpas.

Table 4.17: Distribution of Sherpa Population of Two Villages of Darjeeling in Three Age Groups

Sl. No.	Age Groups	Person		Male		Female		Sex Ratio
		No.	%	No.	%	No.	%	
1.	Upto 14	194	100.00	91	46.91	103	53.09	1132
2.	15-59	341	100.00	172	50.44	169	49.44	983
3.	60+	33	100.00	17	51.52	16	48.48	941
	Total	568	100.00	280	49.30	288	50.70	1029

Source: Field study by the authors.

On the other hand, the senior Sherpa males and females (60+) are equal in number. So far as the sex-ratio is concerned while in case of the age-group 'upto 14', there are 970 female Sherpas per 1000 male Sherpas' in two other age-groups and also in case of the total Sherpa population of this village, the female Sherpas are 1030 in case of 15-59 age-group, 1000 in case of 60+ age-group and 1009 per 1000 male Sherpas in case of the total Sherpa population (Table 4.18).

In another table (Table 4.19) on the Sherpa population of Sherpaguri village we find that out of 217 Sherpas of this village majority belong to the age-group 15-59 (62.67%). The next higher number of the Sherpas of this village come under the age-group 'upto 14' (29.95%) and the lowest number rests in the age-group 60+(7.37%). The same trend is noticed in case of the Sherpa males and the females of this village. In both these cases majority belong to the age-group 15-59 (62.04% and 63.30% respectively) and the lowest number of the Sherpas are in the age-group 60+(7.41% and 7.34% respectively).

Table 4.18: Distribution of Sherpa Population of Sherpaguri Village of Darjeeling in Three Age Groups

Sl. No.	Age Groups	Person		Male		Female		Sex Ratio
		No.	%	No.	%	No.	%	
1.	Upto 14	65	100.00	33	50.77	32	49.23	970
2.	15-59	136	100.00	67	49.26	69	50.74	1030
3.	60+	16	100.00	8	50.00	8	50.00	1000
	Total	217	100.00·	108	49.77	109	50.23	1009

Source: Field study by the authors.

Table 4.19: Distribution of Sherpa Population of Sherpaguri Village of Darjeeling in Three Age Groups

Sl. No.	Age Groups	Person		Male		Female	
		No.	%	No.	%	No.	%
1.	Upto 14	65	29.95	33	30.55	32	29.36
2.	15-59	136	62.67	67	62.04	69	63.30
3.	60+	16	7.37	8	7.41	8	7.34
	Total	217	99.99	108	100.00	109	100.00

Source: Field study by the authors.

At Sherpapur village of Kalimpong, Darjeeling, we get somewhat different picture. Here, in this village out of total Sherpa population, the male Sherpas are a little less in number (49.00%) than the female Sherpas who are a little more than half (51.00%). The same is the condition in case with the age-group 'upto 14'. But in two other age-groups the number of the male Sherpas is a little more than that of the female Sherpas (Table 4.20).

Now, as we examine the sex-ratio we find that in case of the total Sherpa population of this village (Sherpaguri) there are 1041 Sherpa females per 1000 Sherpa males. In case of the age-group 'upto 14' the females are significantly higher in number than the males (1224 female Sherpas per 1000 male Sherpas). In case of other two age-groups the number of females are 952 (in case of the age-group 15-59) and 889 (in case of age-group 60+) per 1000 Sherpa males.

When we look into Table 4.21 we find that out of a total of 351 Sherpas of this village Sherpapur, majority (58.41%) of the Sherpas belong to the age-group 15-59. The next higher strength is present in the age-group 'upto 14' (36.75%). The lowest number of the Sherpas of Sherpapur comes under the age-groups. 60+ (4.84%). The same trend is noticed in case of both male and female Sherpas of this village.

Table 4.20: Distribution of the Sherpa Population of Sherpapur Village of Darjeeling in Three Age-Groups

Sl. No.	Age Groups	Person		Male		Female		Sex Ratio
		No.	%	No.	%	No.	%	
1.	Upto 14	129	100.00	58	44.26	71	55.04	1224
2.	15-59	205	100.00	105	51.22	100	48.78	952
3.	60+	17	100.00	9	52.94	8	47.06	889

Source: Field study by the authors.

In both cases the majority of the Sherpas belong to the age-group 15-59 (61.05% and 55.87% respectively). The lowest number of the Sherpa males and females of this village of Sherpapur come under the age-group 60+ (5.23% and 4.47% respectively). When we come to examine the distribution of the Sherpas of these two villages, we find that at Sherpaguri more number of the Sherpas (person, male and female) are found in the age-groups, 15-59 and 60+ than that of Sherpapur, but in the latter village more Sherpas (person, male and female) are found in the age-group 'upto 14'.

Table 4.21: Distribution of the Sherpa Population of Sherpapur Village of Darjeeling in Three Age-Groups

Sl. No.	Age Groups	Person		Male		Female	
		No.	%	No.	%	No.	%
1.	Upto 14	129	36.75	58	33.72	71	39.66
2.	15-59	205	58.41	105	61.05	100	55.87
3.	60+	17	4.84	9	5.23	8	4.47
	Total	351	100.00	172	100.00	179	100.00

Source: Field study by the authors.

B. Two Villages of Sikkim

In Sikkim as already said, we have studied two Sherpa villages, Sherpagaon and Sherpahat. These two villages when combined together, have 124 Sherpa families (Table 4.22). Out of these Sherpa families 64 (51.61%) are at Sherpagaon and a little less, 60 (48.39%) are at Sherpahat. The combined Sherpa population of these two villages is 692 of whom 340 (49.13%) live at Sherpagaon but the majority (352 or 50.87%) at Sherpahat. The combined Sherpa males of these two villages are 363. Out of them the Sherpas (192 or 52.89%) of Sherpagaon are more than that of Sherpahat (171 or 47.11%). On the other hand, the picture is totally opposite in case of the Sherpa females. Out of a total of 329 Sherpa females of the two villages, Sherpagaon has a share of 148 or 44.98 per cent which is much less than that of Sherpahat where the number of females is 181 or 55.02 per cent. Apparently it may seem to be peculiar. While one village has significantly more Sherpa males and the other village has significantly more Sherpa females. But this is a reality (Table 4.22).

Table 4.22: Sex-wise Distribution of the Sherpa Population of Two Villages of Sikkim

Sl. No.	*Villages*	*Families*		*Person*		*Male*		*Female*	
		No.	*%*	*No.*	*%*	*No.*	*%*	*No.*	*%*
1.	Total	124	100.00	692	100.00	363	100.00	329	100.00
2.	Sherpagaon	64	51.61	340	49.13	192	52.89	148	44.98
3.	Sherpahat	60	48.39	352	50.87	171	47.11	181	55.02

Source: Field study by the authors.

In our two studied villages in Sikkim, that is Sherpagaon and Sherpahat, there are a total of 129 Sherpa families of which 64 (51.61%) are located at Sherpagaon and 60 (48.39%) in Sherpahat (Table 4.22). In 129 Sherpa families of two villages 692 Sherpas live. Out of these 692 Sherpa individuals 363 (52.46%) are males and 329 (47.54%) females.

Table 4.23: Sex-wise Distribution of the Sherpa Population in Two Villages of Sikkim

Sl. No.	*Villages*	*Families*		*Person*		*Male*		*Female*	
		No.	*%*	*No.*	*%*	*No.*	*%*	*No.*	*%*
1.	Total	124	100.00	692	100.00	363	52.46	329	47.54
2.	Sherpagaon	64	51.61	340	100.00	192	56.47	148	43.53
3.	Sherpahat	60	48.39	352	100.00	171	48.58	181	51.42

Source: Field study by the authors.

When we come down to the village level, we see that at Sherpagaon 340 Sherpas live in 64 families. Out of these 340 Sherpas, 192 (56.47%) are males, but only 148 (43.53%) are females. On the other hand, at Sherpahat 352 Sherpas live in 60 families of this village. Out of these 352 Sherpas 171 (48.58%) are males and 181 (51.42%) females. This means that Sherpahat gives totally opposite picture from that present at Sherpagaon. At Sherpahat village number of the Sherpa females overshadows the number of the Sherpa females (Table 4.23).

Sex and Age-group-wise Distribution of the Sherpa Population

A. Two Villages of South District, Sikkim

On analyzing the age-group and sex-wise population data of the Sherpas of the two villages, Sherpagaon and Sherpahat (Table 4.24) we again find some peculiarities. We have already got the combined total Sherpa population of these two villages as 692 including 363 males and 329 females. Now, when we divide this total Sherpa population of these two villages in different age-groups, the highest number of the combined Sherpa population belongs to the age-group, 5 to 9 (12.86%) followed by the age-group 10 to 14 (12.43%), age-group 15 to 19 (11.71%) and age-group upto 4 (11.27%). The next three age-group that is, 20 to 24, 25-29 and 30-34 have the next higher strengths (9.54%, 8.96% and 8.53% respectively). The rest of the age-groups have a strength of below 5.00 per cent except age-group 35-39 which has a strength of 5.20 per cent. The lowest strength (1.88%) goes to each of the age-groups, 60-64 and 65-69 (Table 4.24).

When we come down to the age-group and sex-wise distribution of the combined Sherpa male population (Table 4.24), we find almost the same picture as we find in case of the combined total. Here, in case of the total male Sherpas the age-group 5-9 has the largest number of persons (13.50%). Next in order come the age-groups (15-19 (12.12%), 10-14 (11.57%) and 'upto 4' (10.19%). The age-groups 20-24 (9.37%), 30-34 (9.09%) and 25.29 (8.26%) also have significant strength. The rest of the age-groups except 35-39 (6.06%) have strength below 5.0 per cent. The age-group 60-64 has the lowest strength (1.65%).

In case of the combined age-group and sex-wise female Sherpa population of these two villages, the trend is similar to that of the total and male population. Here also the age-group 10-14 has the numerically highest population (13.37%). The age-groups upto 4 has the next higher strength of 12.46 per cent followed by the age-group 5-9 (12.16%) and age-group 15-59 (11.25%). The age-groups 20-24 and 25-29 both have significant strength as both are having a strength of 9.73 per cent each. The rest of the age-groups except 30-34 (7.90%) and 45-49 (5.17%) have the strength below 5.00 per cent. The age-group 65-69 has the lowest strength (1.22%).

Table 2.24: Sex and Age-group-wise Distribution of the Combined Sherpa Population of Two Villages in Sikkim

Sl. No.	*Age-group*	*Population*		*Male*		*Female*	
		No.	*%*	*No.*	*%*	*No.*	*%*
1.	Upto 4	78	11.27	37	10.19	41	12.46
2.	5-9	89	12.86	49	13.50	40	12.16
3.	10-14	86	12.43	42	11.57	44	13.37
4.	15-19	81	11.71	44	12.12	37	11.25
5.	20-24	66	9.54	34	9.37	32	9.73
6.	25-29	62	8.96	30	8.26	32	9.73
7.	30-34	59	8.53	33	9.09	26	7.90
8.	35-39	36	5.20	22	6.06	14	4.26
9.	40-44	19	2.75	9	2.48	10	3.04
10.	45-49	31	4.48	14	3.86	17	5.17
11.	50-54	14	2.02	9	2.48	5	1.52
12.	55-59	23	3.32	14	3.86	9	2.74
13.	60-64	13	1.88	6	1.65	7	2.13
14.	65-69	13	1.88	9	2.48	4	1.22
15.	70+	22	3.18	11	3.03	11	3.34
	Total	692	100.01	363	100.00	329	100.02

Source: Field study by the authors.

It is thus seen the higher combined population strength among the Sherpas of Sherpagaon and Sherpahat villages of Sikkim is found in the lower age-groups. That means among the children and adolescent groups the numerical strength is higher. Next comes the age-groups of the adults who also have significant strength. Normally, the strength of the population recedes from the age-group 35-39. The lowest strength lies in the age-groups 60-64 and 65-69.

Further analysis of the age-group and sex-wise distribution of the Sherpa population of the two villages, Sherpagaon and Sherpahat of Sikkim, gives us some other peculiarities of the Sherpa population (Table 4.25). The sex-wise distribution of the Sherpa population of different age-groups shows marked variation of the numerical strength of the members of both sexes, and therefore marked variation in the sex-ratio is also seen. While in some of the age-groups the males supercede the females by numerical strength, in some other age-groups, the reverse picture is seen. In the age-groups, 5-9, 15-19, 30-34, 35-39, 50-54, 55-59, and 65-69 the number of males is more than that of the females. On the other hand, in the other age-groups (upto 4,10-14, 20-24, 25-29, 40-44, 45-49 and 60-64, the females have overshowed the males numerically. Here it may be mentioned that in the total Sherpa population of these two villages, the number of males is slightly higher than that of the females. Table 4.25 also shows that the highest strength of the Sherpa males is in the age-group of 65-69 (69.13%), followed by the age-group, 50-59 where the Sherpa males form 64.29 per cent. The strength of the Sherpa males is also very high in the age-groups of 35-39 (61.11%) and 55-59 (60.87%). Age-groups of 30-34 (55.93%) and 5-9 (55.06%) also have significant strength of male population. On the other hand, age-group 45-49 has the lowest number of the Sherpa population (46.15%), followed by the age-groups 60-64 (46.15%), 40-44 (47.37%) and 'upto 4' (47.44%).

Now, as we look at the age-group-wise distribution of the female Sherpas of these two studied villages of Sikkim taken jointly, we find that the highest number of the Sherpa females (54.84%) is found in the age-group of 45-49. The next higher strength of the female Sherpas is in the age-group of 60-64 (53.85%). Thereafter come age groups, 40-44 (52.63%) and 'upto 4, (52.56). The age-group-wise lowest strength of the combined Sherpa females of the two villages is found in the age-group, 65-69, in which the strength of the Sherpa females is only 30.77%. Next in order come age-groups, 50-54 (35.71%), 35-39 (38.89%) and 55-59 (39.13%).

Now, let us move to count the age-group-wise distribution of the sex-ratio (Table 4.25). The highest sex-ratio is found in the age-group of 45-49 where there are 1214 females per 1000 males. The age-groups, 60-64, 40-44, and 'upto 4' also have quite high sex-ratio (1167, 1111 and 1108 females respectively per 1000 males). The age-groups, 25-29 and 10-14 also have significantly high sex-ratio. The age-group 70+ where the number of male and female Sherpa being equal, has an equal sex-ratio. But the lowest sex-ratio is found in the age-group of 65-69 where there are 444 females per 1000 males. The age-groups, 50-54, 35-39, 55-59 and 30-34, also have very low sex-ratio (556, 363, 643 and 788 females respectively per 1000 males). The sex-ratio is also low in the age-groups of 5-9 and 15-19.

It is thus seen that the age-group-wise distribution of the combined Sherpa population of the two villages in Sikkim does not show any uniform

Table 4.25: Sex and Age-Group-wise Distribution of the Combined Sherpa Population of Two Villages of Sikkim with Sex-Ratio

Sl. No.	Age-group	Population		Male		Female		Sex Ratio
		No.	%	No.	%	No.	%	
1.	Upto 4	78	100.00	37	47.44	41	52.56	1108
2.	5-9	89	100.00	49	55.06	40	44.94	816
3.	10-14	86	100.00	42	48.83	44	51.17	1048
4.	15-19	81	100.00	44	54.32	37	45.68	841
5.	20-24	66	100.00	34	51.52	32	48.48	941
6.	25-29	62	100.00	30	48.39	32	51.61	1067
7.	30-34	59	100.00	33	55.93	26	44.07	788
8.	35-39	36	100.00	22	61.11	14	38.89	636
9.	40-44	19	100.00	9	47.37	10	52.63	1111
10.	45-49	31	100.00	14	45.16	17	54 84	1214
11.	50-54	14	100.00	9	64.29	5	35.71	556
12.	55-59	23	100.00	14	60.87	9	39.13	643
13.	60-64	13	100.00	6	46.15	7	53.85	1167
14.	65-69	13	100.00	9	69.23	4	30.77	444
15.	70+	22	100.00	11	50.00	11	50.00	1000
	Total	692	100.00	363	52.46	329	47.54	906

Source: Field study by the authors.

pattern. The sex-ratio in a similar way does not reflect any uniformity also.

Sex and Age-group-wise Distribution of the Sherpa Population of Sherpagaon village of Sikkim

After analyzing the combined Sherpa population of the two studied villages in Sikkim Sherpagaon and Sherpahat, we shall now come down to examine the pattern of the age-group and sex-wise distribution of the Sherpa population in the individual villages of Sikkim. We shall first take up Sherpagaon.

At Sherpagaon, as already said, there are 340 Sherpa individuals with 192 males and 148 females. In this village the largest number of the Sherpas belongs to the age-groups of 10-14 and 15-19 each having 11.76 per cent of the total Sherpa population. Next in order comes the age-group of 5-9 which has covered 11.47 per cent of the total Sherpa population followed by age-group, 20-24 (10.59%). Age-groups 'Upto 4', 25-29 and 30-34, also have significant strength. The lowest strength is shared by age-groups, 60-64 and 65-64 each of which has covered 1.47 per cent of the total Sherpa population (Table 4.26).

In case of the male Sherpa population of Sherpagaon the age-group-wise distribution shows somewhat different trend. The age-group, 5-9 has the highest strength (13.54%) while the second place has been secured by the age-group, 15-19 with 12.50 per cent male population in its fold. Next in order comes age-group, 10-14 with 10.42 per cent strength followed by the age-groups, 20-24 and 30-34 each with 9.90 per cent strength. Age-groups, 25-29 (9.38%) and 'upto-4' (8.33%) also have significant coverage of the male Sherpa population (Table 4.26).

Finally, we come down to the female population of the Sherpas of Sherpagaon (Table 4.26). Among the Sherpa females of these villages, the age-group, 10-14 has captured the highest number of the females (13.51%). Next in order come age-groups, 'upto-4' and 20-24 each has kept 11.49 per cent of the Sherpa females of Sherpagaon village in its fold. The age-group, 15-19 has held 10.81 per cent of the female population. At the same time, the age-groups, 5-9 and 25-29 have significant strength. Again the lowest number of population is found in the age-group, 65-69 (2.03%). The age-groups, 60-64 and 70+ also have very few members, each with 2.70 per cent.

Table 4.26: Sex and Age-Group-wise Distribution of the Sherpa Population of Sherpagaon Village of Sikkim

Sl. No.	*Age-group*	*Population*		*Male*		*Female*	
		No.	*%*	*No.*	*%*	*No.*	*%*
1.	Upto 4	33	9.71	16	8.33	17	11.49
2.	5-9	39	11.47	26	13.54	13	8.78
3.	10-14	40	11.76	20	10.42	20	13.51
4.	15-19	40	11.76	24	12.50	16	10.81
5.	20-24	36	10.59	19	9.90	17	11.49
6.	25-29	30	8.82	18	9.38	12	8.11
7.	30-34	29	8.53	19	9.90	10	6.76
8.	35-39	21	6.18	11	5.73	10	6.76
9.	40-44	12	3.53	6	3.13	6	4.05
10.	45-49	16	4.71	8	4.17	8	5.41
11.	50-54	7	2.06	4	2.08	3	2.03
12.	55-59	15	4.41	10	5.21	5	3.38
13.	60-64	5	1.47	1	0.52	4	2.70
14.	65-69	5	1.47	2	1.04	3	2.03
15.	70+	12	3.53	8	4.17	4	2.70
	Total	340	100.00	192	100.02	148	100.01

Source: Field study by the authors.

It thus appears from the age-group-wise distribution of the Sherpa population of Sherpagaon from Table 4.26 that the lower age-groups have higher number of people (total, male and female) while the higher age groups have significantly lower number of members. Particularly, the number of old age people (both male and female) is markedly low.

Sex and Age Group-wise Distribution of the Sherpa Population of Sherpagaon with Sex-Ratio

In Table 4.27 we have further analyzed the age-group and sex-wise distribution and the sex-ratio of the Sherpa population at Sherpagaon village. It appears from Table 4.27 that in most of the age-groups of this village there is numerical dominance of the males over the females. Only in the age-groups, 'upto 4', 60-64, and 65-69, the females have outnumbered the males. In the age-groups 40-44, and 45-49 the numerical strength of both the sexes is equal. Among the Sherpas of this village in the age-groups, 5-9, 55-59 and 70+ the males have the highest strength, each with 66.67 per cent, and in each of these age-groups the females have covered only 33.33 per cent of the total members of that particular age-group.

The next higher member of males is found in the age-group, 30-34 where the numerical strength of the males is 65.52 per cent followed by the age-groups, 15-19 and 25-29, each with 60.00 per cent male members. But among the male Sherpas of Sherpagaon village in Sikkim the lowest number of the male population is found in the age-group, 60-64 in which the number of male members is only 20.00 per cent. The next lowest number of the male members is in the age-group of 65-69 with 40.00 per cent male members belong to its fold (Table 4.27).

Among the female Sherpas of Sherpagaon village the dominance of the fair sex is found only in the age-groups, 'upto-4' and 65-69. These age-groups have 51.52 per cent, and 60.00 per cent of the female population of the respective age-group. But the highest number of female members is in the age-group of 60-64 where 80.00 per cent members are females. The next higher number of females is found in the age-groups, 65-69. But the lowest number of the females is found to belong in the age-groups, 5-9, 30-34, 55-59 and 70+. Each of these age-groups has only 33.33 per cent of the total members of the respective age-group as females (Table 4.27).

It is therefore seen that in most of the age-groups the females occupy a secondary position and have accepted the numerical dominance of the male members.

Table 4.27: Sex and Age-Group-wise Distribution of the Sherpa Population of the Sherpagaon Village with Sex-Ratio

Sl. No.	Age-group	Population		Male		Female		Sex Ratio
		No.	%	No.	%	No.	%	
1.	Upto 4	33	100.00	16	48.48	17	51.52	1063
2.	5-9	39	100.00	26	66.67	13	33.33	500
3.	10-14	40	100.00	20	50.00	20	50.00	1000
4.	15-19	40	100.00	24	60.00	16	40.00	667
5.	20-24	36	100.00	19	52.78	17	47.22	895
6.	25-29	30	100.00	18	60.00	12	40.00	667
7.	30-34	29	100.00	19	65.52	10	33.48	526
8.	35-39	21	100.00	11	52.38	10	47.62	909
9.	40-44	12	100.00	6	50.00	6	50.00	1000
10.	45-49	16	100.00	8	50.00	8	50.00	1000
11.	50-54	7	100.00	4	57.14	3	42.86	750
12.	55-59	15	100.00	10	66.67	5	33.33	500
13.	60-64	5	100.00	1	20.00	4	80.00	4000
14.	65-69	5	100.00	2	40.00	3	60.00	1500
15.	70+	12	100.00	8	66.67	4	33.33	500

Source: Field study by the authors.

While in two age-groups they have been able to retain dominant position, in three other age-groups they have equal strength with the male members.

We shall now come down to the sex-ratio of the age-group-wise population of the Sherpas of Sherpagaon. The sex-ratio of the Sherpas of Sherpagaon in general is as low as 771. This means that here in this village there are 771 Sherpa females per 1000 males. In the Sherpa population of this village in Sikkim only three age-groups have higher sex-ratio. These three age-groups are 60-64, 65-69 and 'upto 4' which have sex-ratio of 4000, 1500 and 1063 respectively. This means age-group, 60-64 has as large number as 4000 females per 1000 males which is undoubtedly very high. The age-group 65-69 has 1500 females per 1000 males and age-group, 'upto 4' has 1063 females per 1000 males. In the age-groups 10-14, 40-44, and 45-49 the male and the female Sherpas are equal in number. That means in these age-groups there are 1000 females per 1000 males. The age-group, 35-39 has 909 females per 1000 females. But in the rest of the age-groups the number of females per 1000 males is less than 900. The lowest number of females (only 500) per 1000 males is found in the age-groups, 5-9, 55-59 and 70+.

Sex and Age-group-wise Distribution of the Sherpa Population at Sherpahat

At Sherpahat as we look into the age-group and sex-wise distribution of the Sherpa population, we see that like Sherpagaon, the higher number of the Sherpa population is found in the lower age-groups and the lower number of these people belong to the higher age groups (Table 2.28). The highest concentration of the Sherpas is found in the age-group of 5-9 where 14.20 per cent of the total Sherpa population of this village is found. The next higher concentration is found to belong in the age-group, 10-14 (13.07%) followed by the age-group, 'upto-4'. 12.78% Sherpas belong to this age-group ('Upto-4'). The age-group, 15-19 also has a significant number of the Sherpas of this village (11.65%). On the contrary, the lowest concentration of the Sherpas of this village is present in the age-groups, 40-44 and 50-54 each with 1.99 per cent of the total Sherpas of this village. The age-groups, 55-59, 60-64 and 65-69 also have very low concentration each with 2.27 per cent of the Sherpa population of this village. The age-group, 70+ also does not have a high concentration. Here also like other higher age-groups, very small number of the Sherpas (2.84%) belong.

The Sherpa males of this village, Sherpahat have in a similar way, variable age-groupwise distribution. Their age-group-wise distribution shows that the higher concentration of the male Sherpas of this village is located in the lower age-groups and the lower number of the Sherpa males are held in the higher age-groups. The highest concentration of the Sherpa males is in the age-group, 5-9. Here the strength is 13.45 per cent. The next higher concentration is found in the age-group, 10-14 (12.87%) followed by the age-groups, 'upto 4' (12.28%) and 15-19 (11.70%). On the other hand, the lowest concentration of the Sherpa males at Sherpahat is found in the age-groups, 40-44 and 70+ each with 1.75 per cent of the total Sherpa males. The next lowest number of the Sherpa males of this village is in the age-group 55-59 having 2.34 per cent of the Sherpa male concentration. This age-group is followed by the age-groups, 50-54 and 60-64 each with 2.92 per cent of the Sherpa males of Sherpahat in their possession. Therefore, the strength of the Sherpa males of different age-groups at Sherpahat varies from 1.75 per cent to 13.45 per cent (Table 4.28).

When we examine the age-group-wise distribution of the Sherpa females of the village Sherpahat, we find that the age-group-wise distribution of the Sherpa females of this village varies from 1.10 per

Table 4.28: Sex and Age-Group-wise Distribution of the Sherpa Population at Sherpahat, Sikkim

Sl. No.	*Age-group*	*Person*		*Male*		*Female*	
		No.	*%*	*No.*	*%*	*No.*	*%*
1.	Upto 4	45	12.78	21	12.28	24	13.26
2.	5-9	50	14.20	23	13.45	27	14.92
3.	10-14	46	13.07	22	12.87	24	13.26
4.	15-19	41	11.65	20	11.70	21	11.60
5.	20-24	30	8.52	15	8.77	15	8.29
6.	25-29	32	9.09	12	7.02	20	11.05
7.	30-34	30	8.52	14	8.19	16	8.84
8.	35-39	15	4.26	11	6.43	4	2.21
9.	40-44	7	1.99	3	1.75	4	2.21
10.	45-49	15	4.26	6	3.51	9	4.97
11.	50-54	7	1.99	5	2.92	2	1.10
12.	55-59	8	2.27	4	2.34	4	2.21
13.	60-64	8	2.27	5	2.92	3	1.66
14.	65-69	8	2.27	7	4.09	1	0.55
15.	70+	10	2.84	3	1.75	7	3.87
	Total	352	99.98	171	99.99	181	100.0

Source: Field study by the authors.

cent to 14.92 per cent (Table 2.28). The highest concentration is found in the age-group, 5-9. In this age-group 14.92 per cent Sherpa females of this village belong. The next higher concentration is found in the age-group 'upto 4' and 10-14 each having 13.26 per cent of the Sherpa females in its fold. Both age-group 15-19 and age-group 25-29 also have significant concentration of the Sherpa females of Sherpahat. The age-group, 15-19 has 11.60 per cent and the age-group, 25-29 has 11.05 per cent of the Sherpa females. But the lowest frequency of the Sherpa females at Sherpahat is found to be present in the age-group 65-69 where only 0.55 per cent of the Sherpa females of Sherpahat is present. The next lower strength of the Sherpa females of this village is found in the age-group 50-54. In this age-group only 1.10 per cent of the Sherpa females are found. The age-group, 60-64 also holds only 1.66 per cent of the Sherpa females. Similarly, age groups 35-39, 55-59 keep only a very small number of the Sherpa females (2.21% each).

It is thus found that among the Sherpa females as among their male counterparts in the village Sherpahat in Sikkim, the lower age-groups have higher number of females than the higher age-groups which have retained smaller number of the females.

Now, we shall further look at the age-group-wise distribution of the Sherpas of Sherpahat and their sex-ratio through Table 2.29. This table shows that in a few age-groups the males have outnumbered the females while in most of the other age-groups the females have overshadowed the Sherpa males numerically. In the age-groups, 35-39, 50-54, 60-64 and 65-69 the Sherpa males are higher in number than the Sherpa females. The highest strength of the Sherpa males is in the age-group of 65-69 where the overwhelming majority of the male Sherpas (87.50%) is found. The next higher strength of the Sherpa males is in the age-group, 35-39. This age-group holds 73.33 per cent of the total Sherpa population of this age-group. The age-group 50-54 also holds very large number of the Sherpa males (71.43%). The lowest number of the Sherpa males is found to remain in the age-group, 70+ which keeps only 30.00 per cent of the total Sherpa population of this age-group as the male. The next lower strength of the Sherpa males is found in the age-group 25-29 (37.50%). In the age-groups, 20-24 and 55-59 the male and female Sherpas are in equal number, each sharing half of the population of these age-groups. But in the remaining age-groups the Sherpa females have out-numbered the males. The largest number of the Sherpa females is found in the age-group 70+ which has held 70.00 per cent of the total Sherpa population of this age-group. The next higher number of the Sherpa females is found in the age-group, 25-29 per cent (62.50%) followed by the age-group, 45-49 (60.00%). The lowest number of the Sherpa females is observed in the age-group, 65-69 which holds only 12.50 per cent of the female population. The next lowest number of the Sherpa females of Sherpahat village is located in the age-group, 35-39 where 26.67 per cent of the total population are females. The age-group, 50-54 also has a very small number of the Sherpa females (28.57%).

As we examine the sex-ratio of the Sherpas of Sherpahat in different age-groups, we find that in many age-groups the number of females per 1000 males is much higher. The highest sex-ratio, 2333 females per 1000 males is found in the age-group 70+. The next higher sex-ratio is found in the age-group, 25-29 where there are 1667 females per 1000 males. The age-groups 40-44, 5-9, 'upto 4' and 30-34 also have quite high sex-ratio, while 40-44 has 1333 females per 1000 males, age-group, 5-9 has 1174 females per 1000 males. The other two age-groups have 1143 females per 1000 males each. The lowest sex-ratio is found in the age-group 65-69 which has only 143 females per 1000 males. The age-groups,

35-39, 50-54 and 60-64 also have very low sex-ratio. These age-groups have 364, 400 and 600 females respectively per 1000 males. But sex-ratio is equal in the age-groups 20-24 and 55-59. Each of these two age-groups have held equal number of the members of both sexes. Thus, we get a very variable sex-ratio in different age-groups of the Sherpas of Sherpahat village (Table 4.29).

Table 4.29: Sex and Age-Group-wise Distribution of the Sherpa Population at Sherpahat Village, Sikkim with Sex-Ratio

Sl. No.	*Age-group*	*Population*		*Male*		*Female*		*Sex Ratio*
		No.	*%*	*No.*	*%*	*No.*	*%*	
1.	Upto 4	45	100.00	21	46.67	24	53.33	1143
2.	5-9	50	100.00	23	46.00	27	54.00	1174
3.	10-14	46	100.00	22	47.83	24	52.17	1091
4.	15-19	41	100.00	20	48.78	21	51.22	1050
5.	20-24	30	100.00	15	50.00	15	50.00	1000
6.	25-29	32	100.00	12	37.50	20	62.50	1667
7.	30-34	30	100.00	14	46.67	16	53.33	1143
8.	35-39	15	100.00	11	73.33	4	26.67	364
9.	40-44	7	100.00	3	42.86	4	57.14	1333
10.	45-49	15	100.00	6	40.00	9	60.00	1500
11.	50-54	7	100.00	5	71.43	2	28.57	400
12.	55-59	8	100.00	4	50.00	4	50.00	1000
13.	60-64	8	100.00	5	62.50	3	37.50	600
14.	65-69	8	100.00	7	87.50	1	12.50	143
15.	70+	10	100.00	3	30.00	7	70.00	2333
	Total	352	100.00	171	48.58	181	51.42	1050

Source: Field study by the authors.

B. Two Villages of Sikkim

When we divide the whole Sherpa population into three major age-group categories representing children (up to 14 years of age), adolescents and adults (15 to 59 years of age) and old people (60 years and above), we get some interesting and important figures. Among the combined Sherpa population of the above mentioned two villages (Table 4.30) we find that there are 253 individuals who belong to the age-group, 'up to 14'. They form 36.56 per cent of the total population. But the combined Sherpa population of these two villages belonging to the age-group 15 to 59, that is adolescent and adult population, comes to 391 and secures the highest strength (56.50%). That means more than half of the total Sherpa population of these two villages are either adolescents or adults. But the number of the elderly Sherpas of these two villages is only 48 (6.94%). It clearly shows that the strength of the elderly persons in the combined Sherpa population of these two villages is the lowest and the some of the adolescent and adult population is the highest. The children lie in between (Table 4.30).

When we treat the two Sherpa villages of Sikkim separately, we see that the picture of the Sherpa minors, adolescents and adults and old people is almost same. At Sherpagaon village out of the total of 340 Sherpas the strength of the children (112 or 32.94%) is a little less than the same of the combined children population of these two villages and also less than the same of the Sherpahat village. But the strength of the adolescent and adult Sherpa population at Sherpagaon is the highest (60.59%), much higher than the combined adolescent and adult Sherpa population of the two villages and also the same of the Sherpahat village. Again here in this village, population of the elderly Sherpas is the lowest (22 or 6.47%).

Table 4.30: Sex-wise Distribution of the Sherpa Population of Three Age-Groups of Two Villages of Sikkim

Sl. No.	*Age group*	*Villages*	*Population*		*Male*		*Female*	
			No.	*%*	*No.*	*%*	*No.*	*%*
1.	Up to 14	Total	253	36.56	128	35.26	125	37.99
		Sherpagaon	112	32.94	62	32.30	50	33.78
		Sherpahat	141	40.06	66	38.60	75	41.44
2.	15 – 59	Total	391	56.50	209	57.58	182	55.32
		Sherpagaon	206	60.59	119	61.98	87	58.78
		Sherpahat	185	52.56	90	52.63	95	52.49
3.	60+	Total	48	6.94	26	7.16	22	6.69
		Sherpagaon	22	6.47	11	5.73	11	7.43
		Sherpahat	26	7.39	15	8.77	11	6.08
	Total	Total	692	100.00	363	100	329	100.00
		Sherpagaon	340	100.00	192	100.01	148	99.99
		Sherpahat	352	100.01	171	100.00	181	10.01

Source: Field study by the authors.

Next we come down to the other village, i.e. Sherpahat. Here, though the strength of the adolescent and adult population is the highest (52.56%), it is much lower than the combined adolescent and adult Sherpa population of these two villages and even lower than the same of the other village, Sherpagaon. But the population strength of the minors ('up to 14') is quite high (141 or 40.06%) much higher than that of the combined Sherpa population of the two villages and also significantly higher than that of Sherpagaon. Even at Sherpahat the strength of the elderly Sherpas (7.39%) is higher than that of the combined Sherpa population of the two villages and also higher than that of the Sherpa population of Sherpagaon. Therefore, it may be said that at Sherpahat though the adult population is the highest in strength but the population of the minors is also significantly high. The number of the elderly Sherpas of this village is quite low (Table 4.30).

Now, let us come down to the male members of the Sherpa society in the studied villages, that is, Sherpagaon and Sherpahat, in Sikkim. The combined male Sherpa population of these two villages is 363. Among these population the largest strength (209 or 57.58%) goes to adolescent and adult population. Next to this population comes population of the male children who stands at 128 or 35.26 per cent. The combined male population of the elderly persons (60 and above years of age) is as usual, very low, only 26 or 7.16 per cent. It is therefore clear that out of the combined total male Sherpa population of the two villages the share of the adolescent and the adult male population is more than half. Next in order come the population of the male minor who have secured more than one third of the combined population.

Now, we like to count the female Sherpa population in order to get the population figures of female minor, adolescent and adult and the elderly Sherpas of these two villages (Sherpagaon and Sherpahat) of Sikkim. The combined total female population of these two villages is 329 of which the adolescent and adult population (182 or 55.32%) has the highest strength followed by the minor female population who stands at 125 or 37.99 per cent. The old female population (60+ age-group) is as usual very low (22 or 6.69%).

After analyzing the combined Sherpa population of the two villages of Sikkim, we now come down to the individual village level. At Sherpagaon the total Sherpa male population is 192. Out of this male population the adolescents and adult male population secures much above half of the male population (61.98%). The next comes the population of the children who covers about one third of the total population (32.30%). The strength of the elderly persons in the Sherpa society of this village is as low as 5.73 per cent.

At Sherpahat on the other hand, the adolescent and adult population (15-59) is a little over half of the total Sherpa population of this village (52.63%). Reversely, the strength of the children is quite significant (38.60%), much more than that at Sherpagaon. The elderly persons also have a strength (8.77%), much over that of Sherpagaon.

Next, we come down to the children, adolescent and adult and old age people among the Sherpas of these two villages. At Sherpagaon the much over half (58.78%) of the total Sherpa population are adolescents and the adults. The population of the female children comes next. Their strength is 33.38 per cent. As usual the elderly persons are only a few in number (7.43%). But at Sherpahat the female adolescent and the adult population have a strength of a little over half, 52.49 per cent, but the female children of the village closely follow their female adolescent and adult members with a population of 41.44 per cent. The strength of the old age female is as low as 6.08 per cent.

It is thus seen that among the Sherpas of the two villages of Sikkim studied by us, the adolescent and the adult population (total, male and female) is always more than half of the respective population. On the other hand, at Sherpahat number of Sherpa children (total, male and female) are significantly high. The old age population is always below one tenth of the respective total population.

Table 4.31: Sex-wise Distribution of Population of Three Different Age-Groups of the Sherpas of Two Villages of Sikkim

Sl. No.	*Age group*	*Villages*	*Population*		*Male*		*Female*		*Sex Ratio*
			No.	*%*	*No.*	*%*	*No.*	*%*	
1.	Up to 14	Total	253	100.00	128	50.59	125	49.41	977
		Sherpagaon	112	100.00	62	55.36	50	44.64	806
		Sherpahat	141	100.00	66	46.81	75	53.19	1136
2.	15-59	Total	391	100.00	209	53.45	182	46.55	871
		Sherpagaon	206	100.00	119	57.77	87	42.23	731
		Sherpahat	185	100.00	90	48.65	95	51.35	1056
3.	60+	Total	48	100.00	26	54.17	22	45.83	846
		Sherpagaon	22	100.00	11	50.00	11	50.00	1000
		Sherpahat	26	100.00	15	57.69	11	42.31	733
	Total	Total	692	100.00	363	52.46	329	47.54	906
		Sherpagaon	340	100.00	192	56.47	148	43.53	771
		Sherpahat	352	100.00	171	48.58	181	51.42	1058

Source: Field study by the authors.

When we further count on the children, adolescent and adult and elderly population, we further see that in the combined total Sherpa population of these two villages the difference between male and female child population is quite thin. While male population is 50.59 per cent the female population stands closely behind the male population with 49.41 per cent as its strength. In case of the adolescent and adult population (15-59 years of age) out of a total 391 persons of the two villages combined together, the male population has overshadowed the female population (53.45% against 46.55%). There are only 48 senior Sherpas in these two villages. Out of these 48 senior Sherpas, 54.17 per cent are males and 45.83 per cent females (Table 4.31).

Now, let us come down to the village level. At Sherpagaon out of a total of 112 Sherpa belonging to the age-group 'up to 14', majority (55.36%) are males. The female Sherpa population in this village is proportionately low covering 44.64 per cent. Same is the condition of the Sherpas of this village belonging to the age-group, 15-59. Here in this age-group 57.77 per cent are males and only 42.23 per cent females. Among the senior Sherpas of this village (60 years and above) the number of the male and the female is same.

At Sherpahat on the other hand, the female Sherpas (53.19%) numerically dominate over the male Sherpas (46.81%) in the age-group 'upto 14'. Same is the case with the sex-wise distribution of the Sherpa population of Sherpahat where there are 95 female Sherpas in the age-group of 15 to 59. Here also the female Sherpas have overshadowed the male Sherpas numerically (51.35% against 48.65%). But the deviation is noticed in case of the senior Sherpas (60+ age-group) of this village. In this age-group the male Sherpas have got domination by securing 59.69 per cent of the total population of the age-group, while the Sherpa females rest on a meager 42.31 per cent.

It is thus seen that while the combined Sherpa population of the two villages and also the Sherpa population of Sherpagaon show the numerical dominance, may be narrow, of the male population over the female ones, but at Sherpahat on the other hand, we find the reverse picture in case of the age-groups 'upto 14' and 15 to 59. In these two age-groups the Sherpa females dominate numerically over their male counterpart. But in case of the elderly population (60+), the population picture is like that of Sherpagaon or the combined Sherpa population of the two villages. The elderly males here are higher in number than the elderly females (Table 4.31).

Now, let us examine the sex-ratio of the Sherpas of the two villages. In case of the total combined Sherpa population of these two villages the number of females per 1000 males is 906. But at Sherpagaon this sex-ratio is very low, only 771 females per 1000 males. This means the number of female is much lower than that of the male. But at Sherpahat on the other hand, the sex-ratio is higher. Here there are 1058 females per 1000 males. That is the Sherpa females here have outnumbered the Sherpa males in this regard.

When we examine the sex-ratio among the children, adolescent and the adult and the old-age people of the combined population of the two villages, and also at Sherpagaon and Sherpahat, we see that the sex-ratio is quite variable. In the age-group of 'up to 14', in the combined population we get 977 females per 1000 males. But at Sherpagaon the sex-ratio in this age-group is only 806 females per 1000 males. Reversely in case of the Sherpas of Sherpahat there are 1136 females per 1000 males in this age group (up to 14).

In case of the adolescent and adult age-group (15 to 59) the combined population of the two villages has a sex-ratio of only 871. This means that in this population the number of female per 1000 males is quite low. But at Sherpagaon the sex-ratio in this age-group of the Sherpas is even lower, 731 only, that is, only 731 females per 1000 males. At Sherpahat on the other hand, the sex-ratio is quite high. In this age-group (15 to 59) among the Sherpa, the sex-ratio is 1056 females per 1000 males. This proves that at Sherpahat the females are numerically higher than the males among the Sherpas (Table 4.31).

The senior Sherpas who belong to the age-group, 60 and more, have the sex-ratio is 846 females per 1000 males in case of the combined Sherpa population of these two villages. But it is interesting to mention here that at Sherpagaon the ratio of male and the female is the same. On the other hand, reverse is the case with the elderly Sherpas (60 and more) of Sherpahat village where the sex-ratio is 733 females per 1000 males. That means here the number females is very low in comparison to that of the males.

It is thus seen that among the Sherpas of different age-groups the number of persons of different sexes, is highly variable. The uniformity has not been maintained always, and thereby the sex-ratio has also become very much variable.

5

THEIR LAND AND LIVELIHOOD

Land is very important in the life of all human beings particularly those who depend on land for their livelihood. Even those who are not cultivators, also depend on land for their shelter and other purposes. So, land is very precious and very sacred to all. To the Sherpas like all the human beings, land is very precious and sacred asset. In Sikkim and Darjeeling the Sherpas depend mostly on the land for their shelter and livelihood. Their major earning comes from the land.

Among the Sherpas of both Sikkim and Darjeeling the land tenure system as prevalent among them is somewhat different from that present among the people of other areas. In fact the Sherpas follow different land tenure system, and this is related to different types of land or land producing different types of crops. Many Sherpa land owners, instead of cultivation their own land by themselves or by agricultural labourers, are often found to lease out whole or part of their cultivable lands to the tenants for cultivation, and in these lands the tenants cultivate different types of crops. But for different types of land as said earlier or the lands where different types of crops are grown, the terms and conditions for leasing out the land are different. That means the system of land tenure and also its terms and conditions as followed by the Sherpa, are in reality, different. Below we have discussed the said systems as followed by the Sherpas of Sikkim and Darjeeling.

Adhiya

Under this system the Sherpa land owners let out part or whole of their land to one or more tenants depending on the size of the land possessed by the land owners. The land owners set-up certain terms and conditions which the tenants are to oblige. Under this system the tenants are to give 50 per cent of the yields which they harvest from the land owner's land to the land owners after the harvest. The land owners will not bear any expenditure incurred by the tenants for cultivating the land. The tenants have to bear the whole expenditure on cultivating the land. For cultivating the land they always spend a good amount of money for the procurement of seeds of the crops they will cultivate, manure, insecticides etc. Even they have to use their own agricultural implements and bullocks. They do not get any help from the land owners in this regard. In case if any tenant does not have some implements or the bullocks, they can take the same from the owner on rent or one time payment if the owner has any. If not they have to take these from other villagers on rent. In case the tenant requires labourers as helpers in cultivating the land, he has to bear the expenditure. He gets nothing from the land owners. The land owner only bears the amount which he pays as the revenue for his land to the government.

Among the Sherpa of *Adhiya* type of tenure system is applicable to such lands which are let out for cultivating crops like maize, millet and potato. If the land which some land owner lets out to some tenant, is less fertile and the yield is quite low, then the land owner comes to an agreement with the tenant for a 25 per cent share of the yield from the tenant. That means in such type of land, the tenant has to pay only 25 per cent share of the total yield of that land to the land owner as per agreement made by the land owner and the tenant on this land. Because the yield is low and the tenant has to bear the expenditure on seeds, manure, implement (if any), insecticide etc., so, he is compelled to make such an agreement with the land owner. The land owner being fully aware of the condition of the land which he is letting out, agrees to these terms as set up by the tenant. In such a case the tenant gets 75 per cent of the yield though he has to bear other things. During the initial year of harvest of large cardamom, generally during 3rd or 4th year, the Sherpas follow this type of share cropping system. They apply 25 per cent-75 per cent share of production during the initial year because during these initial years, the yield of the large cardamom usually becomes less. So, the tenant puts forward his condition i.e., 25 per cent-75 per cent share of the yield, and the land owner usually accepts it. Although the yield is less but not the expenditure for the cultivation. The expenditure remains the same. After the initial years when the production of cardamom increases the owner-tenant share of production becomes 50:50 (Coomar & Raha 2013:38-39).

Kud or Kudhiya

Kud or Kudhiya is also a system of land tenure found among the Sherpas. Under this system the Sherpa land owner makes a deal with the share cropper *(Kudhiya)* in which the latter has to pay certain amount of crops to the former. This amount depends on the type, location and fertility of the soil of the land. The share-cropper (*Kudhiya*) has the option to pay that amount of money which is equivalent to the the amount of crops to be paid by the share-cropper to the land owner. Before the agricultural season starts the land owner and the share-cropper sit together to settle the amount of crop or money to be paid by the latter to the former. Like the other land tenure system (*Adhiya*) in this system also the share cropper (*Kudhiya*) has to bear the total expenditure to be incurred for cultivating such land. The land owner in no way, bears any expenditure. He only pays the land revenue to the Government. The *Kudhiya* bears the expenditure for seed, manure, insecticide, wage of the labourer if employed etc. The share-cropper before bringing his share of the crop, has to pay the land-owner his share of the crops or equivalent amount of money as was fixed by the deal which was finalized by him and the land-owner (Coomar & Raha 2013:39).

The land owner and the share-cropper make fresh contract every year in case of all share cropping system.

Owner-Cultivator

Among the Sherpas those who have small area of land, more man-power in the family or do not remain engaged in some other job, that means those who have time and capability to cultivate their own land, usually cultivate their own land instead of giving the land on share basis to the share-croppers. In case they do not have sufficient man-power in this respective family or if the size of the land is larger in comparison to the man-power they have in their respective family, they hire agricultural labourers (*Khethala*) and employ them on daily wage basis. For employing such *Khethala* on daily basis the land owners give them wage in cash and also lunch for the days they are employed. Now, whether the land owners themselves with their family members cultivate the land or in case they employ daily wage labourers they have to bear all expenditure for cultivating the land. In case the land-owners do not have implements and bullocks they have to hire these from others. Again in case they do not have seeds of the crops, fertilizer and insecticide they have to purchase these.

In Darjeeling and Sikkim there are two types of land – the hilly or rocky land and the valley or plain land. The hilly lands are mostly rocky and undulating and situated on the hill slopes. The fertility of this type of land is quite low and the owner has to build ridges on all sides of the land with stones and mud to preserve rain or spring water for cultivation. The hilly lands are often subjected to land slides particularly during rainy season. Even in case proper ridges are not built on the slope side, then there is every possibility of erosion of surface soil.

On the other hand, the valley lands are somewhat plain, less rocky, more muddy and more fertile. The possibility of landslide and erosion of surface soil during rainy season are also less. Moreover, this type of and can preserve sufficient quantity of rain water. Again in the state of Sikkim, the entire area of land have been divided into three broad circles, namely, Circle-A, Circle-B and Circle-C. The Circle-A land includes all the plain or valley land. This type of land being quite fertile and less rocky, normally produce two crops a year. The Circle-B type of land covers partly plain and partly hilly land. Though double cropping is possible at least in some parts of this type of land, but normally this is avoided because of the lack of sufficient fertility. The third category, i.e. Circle-C is formed mostly of the hilly land. Most of this type of land are situated on the hilly slopes. This type of land is mostly rocky and least fertile. In this type of land normally double cropping is avoided because of the lack of sufficient fertility (*ibid*).

So, it is seen that two crops are produced in Circle-A type of land, but the same is avoided in the land belonging to other two circles. The quantity of the land belonging to all three circles differs in quality as also in the rate of fertility. With the variation of quality and fertility of the land of these three types of land, the crops produced also vary in rate of production and also in varieties of crops produced.

Again in Darjeeling and Sikkim the whole land has been classified on the basis of attitude. The land type varies with the variation of altitude. Those lands which are situated up to 2500 feet above mean sea level, are categorized as No. I. The Category No. II land are those lands which are situated between 2501 and 3500 feet above mean sea level. The third category, i.e. No. III category of lands are such lands which are situated between 3500 feet and 5000 feet above mean sea level and Category No. IV comprises land situated beyond 5000 feet above mean sea level. In case of the categorization of land on the basis of altitude, the fertility of land also varies according to the altitude where the land is situated. The lands under Category No. I are more fertile than other three categories. Again the fertility of Category No. II is comparatively better than that of the Categories No. III and IV. Category No. III is somewhat better than Category No. IV so far as fertility is concerned. The rate of fertility of these four categories of land categorized on the basis of their location in different altitudes, can be well depicted if we examine the rate of production of large cardamom in these categories of land. In Table 5.1 we give the production of large cardamom in Sikkim in different categories of land.

Table 5.1: Rate of Production of Large Cardamom in Different Categories of Land

Sl. No.	*Category of Land*	*Rate of production of large cardamom (approx.)*
1.	Lands of Category No. I	480 to 500 Kgs per hectare
2.	Lands of Category No. II	290 to 500 Kgs per hectare
3.	Lands of Category No. III	180 to 200 Kgs per hectare
4.	Lands of Category No. IV	70 to 80 Kgs per hectare

Source: Field study by the authors.

It is thus clearly seen that while the land under Category No. I produces highest yield, Category No. IV land the lowest. It is further seen that the production of large cardamom in Category No. I is much higher than that the same of Category No. II, and again the rate of production of the large cardamom in the lands of Category No. II is much higher that that of Category No. III. And the difference of rate of production of large cardamom between Category No. III and Category No. IV is also quite wide.

So, it is seen that the Sherpas prefer first category of land as its yield is highest at the first instance and their preference is least for the last Category because its yield is the lowest. To them Category No. I is the best land for cardamom cultivation and Category No. IV the worst land for the same purpose.

Apart from the above types of land classifications, the Sherpas further classify the land in the following way on the basis of availability of the irrigation facility and the composition of the soil. This fourfold classification goes as follows:

1. Wet Field

This type of land receives irrigational water from the springs and small canals. Normally, two crops a year are produced because of the availability of irrigational facility. Paddy is generally cultivated in this type of field because paddy cultivation requires good amount of water.

2. Dry Field

In the Sherpa country dry lands do not get irrigational facility. So for the irrigational purpose, the land owner totally depends on the rain water. Normally this type of land produces only one crop a year, and obviously the rate of production is much less in this type of land in comparison to that of the wet land. Usually maize, millet, potato etc. are cultivated in this type of land.

3. Cardamom Field

The third categories of land are those lands where large cardamoms are cultivated. No irrigational facility is available in this type of field. The Sherpas depend solely on the rain water. The large cardamom fields are classified into four categories. We have already discussed about these categories.

4. Banjo Field

The *Banjo* fields are those lands which are mostly rocky. Normally, edible food crops are not grown here. This type of land is mainly utilized for the growth of fuel wood, cattle fodder, bamboo groves etc.

In addition to all those types of land there are Government Khas lands totally owned the State Government. Normally, the forest lands are owned by the Forest Department of the State Government where forests are grown. Besides forest land the Government has also *Khas* lands for other purposes such as construction work etc. No *Khas* land belongs to the Sherpas. The Sherpas cannot purchase or otherwise receive this type of land for any reason. Only the Government can utilize this type of and for some particular purposes like implementing development schemes etc. Of course, the Sherpas get some facilities from the forest such as fodder for their domestic animal, fuel such as dry wood and leaves, wood for furniture and house building and so on. In the forest they have their sacred groves in some place in the forest, where they have their deities and spirits whom they worship at a regular interval. They also dispose the dead bodies in the forest.

In the district of Darjeeling the Sherpas also follow a local classification of land. Locally the lands, both cultivable and non-cultivable, have been classified into different types on the basis of its utilization. Each type is meant for a particular purpose. Following are the types:

Table 5.2: Local Classification of Land in Darjeeling

Sl. No.	*Local Term of the Categories*	*English Term*	*Nature of Utilization*
1.	Sukha Khet	Dry field	Cultivation of maize, millet, ginger, potato, wheat and vegetables.
2.	Pani Khet	Wet field	Cultivation of paddy.
3.	Old Fallow	Grazing ground	Grazing of domestic animals.
4.	New Fellow	Grazing ground	Grazing of domestic animals.
5.	Ghareri	Homestead land	For construction of houses.
6.	Sirubari	Land for cultivation thatching grass	Fodder, plantation, broomstick, bamboo etc. plantation.
7.	Bansbari	Bamboo grove	For bamboo.
8.	Pahiro	Landslide area	Barren land.
9.	Jungle	Forest land	Different big trees.
10.	Jhori	Bushy land	Fuel wood, broomstick etc.
11.	Jhora	Stream	For boulders, stones, sand, etc., and irrigation water.
12.	Khola	River	For boulders, stones, sand, etc., and irrigation water.
13.	Goath	Cowshed	For building cowshed.
14.	Maidan	Playground	For sports and outdoor games.
15.	Sadak	Metalled road	For communication and transport.
16.	Bato	Narrow hilly path	For communication.
17.	Pokhari	Pond	For fishes and other aquatic animals, and also for domestic use of water.
18.	Alchibari	Cardamom field	For cultivation of cardamom.
19.	Suntola Bagan	Orange Orchard	For Orange cultivation.
20.	Cha Bagan	Tea garden	For cultivation of tea plants.

Source: Field study by the authors.

In both Sikkim and Darjeeling the market value of different types of land varies. The rate depends on the economic value, fertility or importance of the land. Obviously, the land that produces better crops or gives higher production, has higher market value. Here, particularly in Sikkim the cardamom land has the highest economic value. The reason is that cardamom is the main cash crop of the people of Sikkim. On the other hand, very little crops are grown in the *Banjo* land and therefore the people get very little value from this type of field. So, to the Sherpas the *Banjo* land has very little economic value. Therefore, the market value of this type of land is quite low. We give below the approximate rates of different types of land, though no doubt, the rates always vary. The rates in Table 5.3 are collected by us from local source and those in Table 5.4 are Government rates:

Table 5.3: Market Value of Different Types of Land

Kind of land	*Circle-A*	*Circle-B*	*Circle-C*
Cardamom field	75,000/-	70,000/-	62,500/-

Source: Field study by the authors.

Table 5.4: Market Value of Different Types of Land

Kind of Lands	*Class of Lands*	*Different Circle of Lands*		
		Circle–A	*Circle–B*	*Circle–C*
Paddy Field	I	Rs. 69,160/- per hectare	Rs. 64,220/- per hectare	Rs. 59,280/- per hectare
		Rs. 28,000/- per hectare	Rs. 26,000/- per hectare	Rs. 24,000/- per hectare
	II	Rs. 63,232/- per hectare	Rs. 59,280/- per hectare	Rs. 54,340/- per hectare
		Rs. 25,600/- per hectare	Rs. 24,000/- per hectare	Rs. 22,000/- per hectare
	III	Rs. 54,340/- per hectare	Rs. 51,870/- per hectare	Rs. 49,400/- per hectare
		Rs. 22,000/- per hectare	Rs. 21,000/- per hectare	Rs. 20,000/- per hectare
Wet Land Dry Field	I	Rs. 48,906/- per hectare	Rs. 44,460/- per hectare	Rs. 39,520/- per hectare
		Rs. 19,800/- per hectare	Rs. 18,000/- per hectare	Rs. 16,000/- per hectare
	II	Rs. 44,460/- per hectare	Rs. 39,520/- per hectare	Rs. 37,050/- per hectare
		Rs. 18,000/- per hectare	Rs. 16,000/- per hectare	Rs. 15,000/- per hectare
	III	Rs. 39,520/- per hectare	Rs. 37,050/- per hectare	Rs. 29,640/- per hectare
		Rs. 16,800/- per hectare	Rs. 15,000/- per hectare	Rs. 12,000/- per hectare
Banjo Field (No Class)		Rs. 34,580/- per hectare	Rs. 32,110/- per hectare	Rs. 29,640/- per hectare
		Rs. 14,000/- per hectare	Rs. 13,000/- per hectare	Rs. 12,000/- per hectare
Cardamom Field (No Circle Class)	I	Rs. 74,100/- per hectare	—	—
		Rs. 30,000/- per hectare	—	—
	II	Rs. 69,160/- per hectare	—	—
		Rs. 28,000/- per hectare	—	—
	III	Rs. 61,750/- per hectare	—	—
		Rs. 25,000/- per hectare	—	—
	IV	Rs. 51,870/- per hectare	—	—
		Rs. 21,000/- per Acre	—	—

Source: Land Revenue Department Government of Sikkim *vide* Notification No.22/LR(S) dated 20/11/90. See also Coomar & Raha 2013: 41-42.

This rate is applicable to Government purchase. But in case of a person or a private body, i.e. Monastery Committee the rate depends on the negotiation between the seller and the buyer. The rates varies according to the location of the land, whether the land is situated near the road side, or near the market place, the lands which have good communication facility etc. generally have the higher rate than other lands (*Source*: Land Revenue Department Government of Sikkim *vide* Notification No. 22/ LR(S) dated 20/11/90).

The rates of different types of land also vary for different other reasons. The presence of trees or presence of bolders also brings changes in the rates. The land which has big trees surely fetches higher price as big trees have their own economic value. On the other hand, if the land is having big boulders which often disturbs in smooth agricultural operations, obviously it has a lower price as the presence of boulder in the cultivable land reduces the price of the land. The boulders eat up some portion of land and also disturb in smooth agricultural operators. So, the rate of yield per unit of land is also reduced, and, therefore, price of the land is also lower.

The rate of the land also varies according to the altitude of the land. The higher the altitude, the lower the price of the land and the lower the altitude the higher the rate of land. It is the general rule. In the high altitude the snow fall damages the crops and the land cannot be cultivated throughout the year. So, the price of the lower altitude land where there is no snowfall, obviously the market value of the land is higher as this type of land can be cultivated through the year. Similarly, the area which is prone to the landslide, fetches lower price as the land cannot be utilized during and after the land slide for a considerable period. Thus, it is seen that for various factors the price of the land in both Darjeeling and Sikkim varies for varied reasons.

People of both Darjeeling and Sikkim acquire land, mainly by two ways, i.e. either through inheritance of the ancestral property or by self acquisition. Generally, the sons inherit the land of their father. If a person does not have son, in that case the daughter/daughters (if any) inherit her/their father's land. In certain cases father during his lifetime, may arrange to distribute part or whole of his landed property equally among his sons. But in other case this person keeps the land with him during his life time and does not part with his land. After his death his sons divide their father's landed property equally according to the arrangement. Thus, each son takes a part of the father's land. Now a days same offspring from the modernized and educated families apply for succession certificate to the Sub-Divisional Magistrate mentioning that they are the only legal successors of their father. After verification, authority issues succession certificate to the concerned family. On receipt of the succession certificate, all the legal owners hand over the deed of the land along with the succession certificate to the office of Sub-Divisional Magistrate for the transfer of ownership of land from their father's name to their names. Sometimes without proper registration and mutation of land in their names they go on cultivating their father's land. When an individual distributes his landed property during his life time among his offspring, he sometimes demarcates the portion of his land in the name of each of his sons and daughters, and then applies to the Sub-Divisional Magistrate/Sub-Registrar for necessary transfer of ownership of a particular plot of land in the name of a particular son or daughter. Apart from inheriting paternal land they sometimes purchase land from others. The price of the land is mutually settled by both the seller and the buyer depending on the location and the quality of the land. The owner of the land follows the normal procedure of applying to the Sub-Divisional Magistrate mentioning the land he/she wants to sell to the buyer. The office of the Sub-Divisional Magistrate then sends the case to the Gram Panchayat and V.L.O. for the proper verification. The Gram Panchayat and the V.L.O. verify whether the land has any litigation and whether the owner of the land is proper. The ownership of the land is verified by the owners of the land situated on the boundary of that particular land as it is essential to get the signature of the boundary land owners for selling a plot of land. If the verification reports of Gram Panchayat and V.L.O. are satisfactory then the Sub-Divisional Magistrate grants permission for the transfer of ownership of land. Both parties make a sale deed mentioning the sale value, area of land, boundary of land, etc. Signature of both parties is required in the sale deed. For preparing any sale deed, they pay stamp duty to the Government. The landless Sherpas can apply to the Government for the allotment of land. The Government after proper investigation and verification may allot a portion of the vested land to the landless after getting the recommendation of Gram Panchayat and finding the person concerned as actually landless.

Large cardamom is the main crop among the Sherpas of Sikkim as already said. But the Sherpas in general cultivate potato, maize, millet, and different other types of vegetables. For the cultivation of these crops they depend on either the high yielding or the local variety of seeds. To increase the fertility they use manure and to protect the crops from any type of diseases or infestation of the insects they also use pesticides.

Sometimes, the Sherpas for the cultivation, take cash loan under different schemes either from bank or from the Government. In case of Bank loan they pay interest as per prevailing rate fixed by the Bank, but if it is from the Government it is in certain case either interest free or with low interest. The loans/credits are available on different schemes. But for the re-plantation of large cardamom and for cultivation of large cardamom, they normally go for '*Agricultural Term Loan-Long term*'. When the scheme is sponsored by the Government, they get 50 per cent subsidy on the loan amount but they do not get any subsidy if the scheme is sponsored by the Bank. In both cases whether it is Government or the Bank they repay the loan amount along with interest if any, after three years but definitely within the six years from the date of taking the loan in accordance with terms and conditions.

The Sherpas are not in much in favour of employing any modern knowhow in the cultivation of different types of crops though in the recent years some of them are using these. Normally in cultivation they follow their age-old plough cultivation and use their traditional agricultural implements and know-how. Generally, they do not use the tractor, mechanized tilling machine or husking machine. Even in order to get bumper production only some of them use chemical fertilizer and improved seeds. Only those Sherpas, particularly those who are economically well off and well informed, use chemical fertilizer particularly at the time of potato cultivation. In cultivation of the different varieties of crops majority of them depend on the organic manure like cow-dung, ash of fuel wood, etc. If the crops are affected by any kind of diseases or insects they use pesticides to get rid of these. On enquiry the informants revealed that they were using pesticides for several years.

For ginger cultivation they avail themselves of the facility of *Agricultural Cash Credit (ACC)- Short Term Loan*. Like the *Agricultural Term Loan* if it is the Government ACC scheme then they get 50 per cent subsidy of the loan amount but in case of the Bank they do not get any subsidy for such scheme. In this scheme the rate of interest and the eligibility condition of the loan receiver are also the same like that of the *Agricultural Term Loan*. In case of ACC scheme a loan taker will have to repay the amount within one year from the date of the receipt of the loan amount.

Apart from these agricultural schemes, they also avail themselves of the loan facility for the cultivation of large cardamom, ginger, potato, starting of piggery and goatary, purchase of bullock for the purpose of cultivation and some such purposes under the *Integrated Rural*

Development Project (I.R.D.P). These schemes have been prepared either by the Rural Development Agency (R.D.A) or by the District Rural Development Agency. From the I.R.D.A. Scheme as sponsored by the Sikkim State Government; they get 30 per cent subsidy on the loan amount. But if it is the central scheme sponsored by the Central Government, then they get higher subsidy. In case of the Central Government sponsored schemes 50 per cent of the total subsidy, is borne by the State Government and the rest 50 per cent by the Central Government. Under this scheme the entire amount is financed by the State Bank of India. Again the National Agricultural and Rural Development Bank finances 60 per cent amount (except subsidy) of this scheme to the State Bank of India. No security is required for a loan up to Rs. 10,000/- under priority sector, i.e. agriculture, animal husbandry etc. An individual can get maximum three times loan under this scheme, if he/she does not have any outstanding loan or clears his/her previous loan amount before the loan is taken. If someone takes loan for the purpose of large cardamom cultivation, he/she must repay the loan after three years, but definitely within six years from the date of receipt of the loan. For the loan taken for the ginger cultivation one has to repay the loan amount within one year. If the loan taken for the establishment of piggery or goatary or for the purchase of bullock then the loan receiver has to repay the loan amount after one year, but definitely within three years from the date of receipt of the loan. With the help of the Gram Panchayat, the Rural Development Agency selects the persons eligible to get loan under this scheme.

After the selection of the candidates, the Rural Development Agency recommends the names of the selected person to the State Bank of India, and Bank finances those candidates. The loan receivers pay interest at the rate as fixed by the Bank from time to time.

After harvest the Sherpas often sell if they have any surplus agricultural and kitchen garden products. They normally sell those in the local market (weekly and regular). In some cases these markets are about 2 to 3 km. away from their village. For cash they take the pain of going to the market and with that cash, they purchase their daily necessities from these markets.

It is thus seen that the Sherpas of both Darjeeling and Sikkim depend basically on land for their livelihood as they are basically the agriculturists and horticulturists. They get supply of their much needed income from land. Therefore, their connection with their land is very deep-rooted. (Coomar & Raha 2013:47).

Land Holding of the Sherpa

Like all other agricultural societies of India, may even be of outside India, the Sherpas of Darjeeling and Sikkim also have land to cultivate as they are also agriculturists. No doubt all the Sherpa families of these two regions do not have land, but most of them have land. The area and types of land possessed, vary from family to family. In order to get some idea about the size and type of land they possess, we studied four villages inhabited by the Sherpas, two from Darjeeling and two from Sikkim. To the Sherpas of the two areas, land is their most valuable asset and most important source of their livelihood.

When we look at the type and size of holding of land by the Sherpas of Darjeeling and Sikkim, we see that in the four villages studied, there are 225 (94.14%) families out of a total of 239 Sherpa families, have land. The remaining 14 (5.86%) families do not have land. Now, these 225 Sherpa families having land, have 1198 members and hold a total of 572.18 acres of land; therefore, the average per family land holding is 2.54 acres. As in these 225 families 1198 Sherpa live, so, the average per head land holding is only 0.48 acre. Here in these four villages the average Type-I land holding per families is 2.23 acres and average per head land holding is 0.42 acre. On the other hand, the average per family land holding only of Type-II land is 2.50 acres and average per head holding is 0.51 acre among the Sherpas. When we examine the holding of Type-III land we find that the per family holding is 2.43 acres and the average per head holding of Type-III land is 0.43 acre. But the Sherpas have larger area of "Other Type" of land. Among these people of four villages studied the average per family possession of 'Other type' of land is 4.15 acres area and average per head possession of this type of land is 0.69 acre (Table 5.5).

When we co-relate between size of the family and holding of different types of land we see that there is significant variation in the holding of different types of land by different sizes of families. In the small size of family (1-3 members per family) the average land holding per family is 1.96 acres, but the same is 2.28 acres per family in the medium size (4-6 members), 3.29 acres in the large size (7-9 members) and 4.29 acres per family in the very large size (10+ members).

In case of the Type-I land the average per family possession of small sized families is 1.55 acres, the same is 1.81 acres in case of the medium sized families, 2.79 acres in case of the large sized families and 5.13 acres in case of the very large sized families.

Table 5.5: Average Land Holding Among the Sherpas of the Studied Villages

Family Size	Land Type I: No. of Family	Population	Total Land in Acres	Avg. Land Per Family	Avg. Land Per Head	II: No. of Family	Population	Total Land in Acres	Avg. Land Per Family	Avg. Land Per Head	III: No. of Family	Population	Total Land in Acres	Avg. Land Per Family	Avg. Land Per Head	IV: No. of Family	Population	Total Land in Acres	Avg. Land Per Family	Avg. Land Per Head	Total: No. of Family	Population	Total Land in Acres	Avg. Land Per Family	Avg. Land Per Head
1-3	21	48	32.55	1.55	0.68	20	51	40.19	2.01	0.79	8	17	25.00	3.13	1.47	4	10	6.03	1.51	0.60	53	126	103.78	1196	0.82
4-6	43	214	78.02	1.81	0.36	41	189	104.09	2.54	0.55	20	99	36.25	1.81	0.37	11	62	43.38	3.94	0.70	115	564	261.74	228	0.46
7-9	11	86	30.73	2.77	0.36	12	94	32.40	2.70	0.34	14	106	44.47	3.18	0.41	5	41	34.73	6.95	0.85	42	327	142.33	3.39	0.44
10+	9	105	46.14	5.13	0.45	3	39	14.00	4.67	0.36	2	23	1.25	0.63	0.05	1	14	2.94	0.21	0.21	15	181	64.33	4.29	0.36
Total	84	453	187.44	2.23	0.42	76	373	190.68	2.50	0.51	44	245	106.97	2.43	0.43	21	127	87.08	2.94	0.69	225	1198	572.18	2.54	0.48

Source: Field study by the authors.

But the holding of Type-II land is a bit larger. In case of the small size families the average per families holding of Type-II land is 2.01 acres, but the same average per family holding of medium size families is 2.54 acres. For the large size families the same is 2.70 acres and the very large family, 4.67 acres (Table 5.5).

In case of the Type-III land the average per family possession of land is 2.43 acres among the Sherpas and in the small size Sherpa families, this average is 3.13 acres but the same in the medium size families is only 1.81 acres. In the large size families it is 3.18 acres and for the very large families the same is very meager (0.63 acre)

The average per family possession of 'Other Type' land is comparatively higher. In case of the small families it is 1.51 acres and in case of medium families it is 3.94 acres. The large families hold 6.95 acres of land and the very large families 2.94 acres on an average per family.

We now move to the per head per family possession of different types of land by different sizes of families of these four Sherpa villages of two areas namely Darjeeling district, West Bengal, and South District, Sikkim.

Among the Sherpas of all the four villages the average per head land holding is 0.48 acres. Among these people average per head Type-I land is 0.42 acre. Type-II land is 0.51 acre, Type-III land 0.43 acre and the 'Other Type' land 0.69 acre. The per head holding of all the first three types of land is highest in small families (1-3 members) except per head holding on 'Other type' which is highest in large family (7-9 members). Again in the small families per head holding of Type-III land is much higher than other types. But in the medium size families per head 'Other Types' of land is higher than other types. In the large family per head land holding of 'Other type' land is much higher than any other types. In the very large family per head holding of Type-I is higher than any other type. Finally, when we look at the average per head total holding of different sizes of land we see small size families have the highest per head land (0.82 acre) followed by medium size families (0.46 acre). Then comes large size family (0.44 acre) followed by very large size families which have the lowest per head holding (0.36 acre). We shall now move to the combined holding of two villages of Darjeeling district.

In Darjeeling district when we look into two villages, Sherpaguri and Sherpapur, we find that out of 115 families, 104 (90.43%) families with 515 members have land and the remaining 11 families (9.57%) do not have land. Again out of these 104 land-owning families, the highest

Table 5.6: Average Land Holding Among the Sherpas of Two Villages of Darjeeling

	Land Type																								
	I					II					III					IV					TOTAL				
Family Size	No. of Family	Population	Total Land in Acres	Avg. Land Per Family	Avg. Land Per Head	No. of Family	Population	Total Land in Acres	Avg. Land Per Family	Avg. Land Per Head	No. of Family	Population	Total Land in Acres	Avg. Land Per Family	Avg. Land Per Head	No. of Family	Population	Total Land in Acres	Avg. Land Per Family	Avg. Land Per Head	No. of Family	Population	Total Land in Acres	Avg. Land Per Family	Avg. Land Per Head
1-3	18	41	27.08	1.50	0.66	2	6	1.00	0.50	0.17	5	12	11.70	2.21	0.92	2	6	0.50	0.25	0	27	65	39.65	1.49	0.61
4-6	34	170	63.58	1.87	0.37	—	—	—	—	—	20	78	17.01	1.06	0.22	5	26	32.50	6.50	1	55	274	113.09	2.06	0.41
7-9	9	70	26.50	2.94	0.38	1	7	4.50	4.50	0.64	16	70	28.46	3.16	0.41	1	7	1.50	1.50	0.21	20	154	60.96	3.05	0.40
10+	1	12	1.50	1.50	0.13	—	—	—	—	—	9	10	1.00	6.00	0.10	—	—	—	—	—	2	22	2.50	1.25	0.11
Total	62	293	118.66	1.91	0.40	3	13	5.50	1.83	0.42	31	170	57.54	1.86	0.34	8	39	34.50	4.31	0.88	104	515	216.20	2.08	0.42

Source: Field study by the authors.

number of families (62 or 59.62%) have Type-I land. Next come 31 (29.81%) families who have Type-III land. Families having Type-II and 'Other type' land are only a few in number (2.88% and 7.69% respectively).

These 104 Sherpa families have a total of 216.20 acres of land. Therefore, the average per family land holding is 2.08 acres. Out of the 104 families 62 families have Type-I land, and the average per family land holing is 1.91 acres. The average per family land holding is 1.83 acres. Only 3 families have such land. Again 31 families have Type-III land with an average per family holding is 1.86 acres. Only 8 Sherpa families have 'Other type' land, and they have an average per family holding of 1.31 acres. Now as we come down to the average per family holding of land by different sizes of families, we see that highest holding (2.94 acres) of Type-I land is by the large size families (7-9 members). Then come medium size families which have an average of 1.87 acres of land per family. Small and very large families have the same average per family land (Table 5.6).

In case of the Type-II land only small and large families have such land. There are only two small families which have land, and the average per family holding is 0.50 acre. Only one large family has 4.50 acres of Type-II land. In case of the Type-III land large families among the Sherpas have the highest average per family of such land (3.16 acres) followed by the small families (2.21 acres per family).

The highest average per family of 'Other type' of land (6.50 acres) is held by the medium size families. Again when we examine the total land, we see that large size families have the highest average per family land holding (3.05 acres) followed by the medium size families (2.06 acres).

Now, let us examine the per head land holding. When we look at the total combined land of the two villages of Darjeeling, we see that the highest average per head holding of total land is possessed by small families (0.61 acre) and the lowest average by very large size families (0.11 acre). While the average per head holding land is 0.42 acre, Type-I is 0.40 acre, Type-II 0.42 acre, Type-III 0.34 acre and 'Other type' 0.88 acre. Further we see from Table 5.6 that the highest average per head possession of Type-I land is by the small families (0.66 acre) and the lowest by the very large families (0.13 acre). In case of the Type-II land the highest possession of average per head land holding is held by large families (0.64 acre). The highest average per head holding of Type-III land is held by the small families (0.92 acre) and the highest average per head holding of 'Other type' land is by the medium families (1.25 acres).

It is thus seen that among the Sherpas of Darjeeling district, different sizes of the families hold the highest average of different types of land.

Now, as we come down to the individual villages we see that at Sherpaguri village of Darjeeling district out of a total of 43 Sherpa families 36 (83.72%) have land and 7 (16.28%) families do not have land. Again when the overwhelming majority of the families (80.56%) have Type III land, 6 or 16.67% families have Type I land. Only one family (2.78%) has Type-II and none has 'Other type' land. Again when we go to the other studied village of Darjeeling district that is, Sherpapur, we see that out of 72 Sherpa families 68 (94.44%) have land and the remaining 4 (5.56%) are landless. When we examine the distribution of families having different types of land, we get that the overwhelming majority of the families (82.35%) have Type-I land. The next larger number of families having different types of land, we get 8 (11.46%) families having 'Other Type' of land. But Type-II and Type-III land are held by two families (2.94% each).

When we look at the individual Sherpa village of Darjeeling district, we see that among the Sherpas of Sherpaguri village of Darjeeling there are 36 Sherpa families who hold 58.45 acres of land, that means, average per family holding comes to 1.46 acres (Table 5.7). When we examine different types of land we see that out of different types of land the average per family Type-III land is the highest which is 1.59 acres among the Sherpas of this village. Next comes Type-I land. The average per family of this type of land is 1.32 acres. Again out of the total land large families (7-9 members) have the highest per family holding (2.44 acres). Next comes small families whose average per family holding is 1.77 acres.

We are now coming drawn to the per family holding of different types of land by different size of family. The highest average per family holding of Type-I land is held by the medium size families (1.61 acres). But Type-II land is held only by the large size families (7-9 members) which have only 0.64 acre as the per family average. The small families have the highest average per family holding of Type-III land (2.21 acres). The large size families are quite close to the holding of small size families (2.18 acres). No family possesses 'Other type' of land in this village (Table 5.7).

When we examine per head holding of land by the Sherpas of Sherpaguri village of Darjeeling we see that per head holding of the total land is only 0.33 acre. Of the different types of land held by the Sherpas of this village, the per head holding of Type-II land is the highest (0.64 acre) among these people followed by Type-I land (0.44 acre). Again when we examine per head holding of total land by different sizes of the Sherpa families, we see that small size families hold highest average per head land (0.83 acre) and the very large families the lowest (0.10 acre). Again among different sizes of families, we see that small size families among the Sherpas have the highest possession of per head Type-I land (0.62 acre). Per head Type-II land is only possessed by the large families (0.64 acre). The highest average of per head Type-III land is held by small families (0.92 acre). In this village no Sherpa has got any 'Other type' of land (Table 5.7).

Now, we come down to the other village of Darjeeling district, i.e. Sherpapur studied by us (Table 5.8). In this village there are a total of 68 Sherpa families with 335 members. These 68 families possess a total of 157.75 acres of land. The average per family holding here comes to 2.32 acres. Out of different sizes of the Sherpa families of this village the large size families have the highest average per family holding (3.55 acres) followed by the medium size families (2.48 acres). When we look at different types of land, we see that the highest average per family land possessed by the Sherpas of this village is Type-III land (5.75 acres) and then 'Other Type' (4.31 acres).

Out of the different type of land possessed by different sizes of families, we get that the large families possess highest per family of Type-I land (2.94 acres). Type-II land is only possessed by the small families. The highest per family Type-III land is possessed by large families (11.00 acres) and medium size families possess the highest per family 'Other type' land (6.50 acres). Now, let us look into the average per head land holding in this village (Table 5.8). Here the average per head land holding of the total land is 0.47 acre. In case of different types of land the average per head holding of the 'Other type' land is the highest (0.88 acre) whereas average per head holding of Type-II land is the lowest (0.17 acre). In case of different sizes of families the very large families have the highest per head holding (1.25 acres) whereas the large families have the lowest average per head land (0.45 acre). In a village in Kalimpong Sub-Division of Darjeeling District, Raha has calculated the average per family land holding among the Sherpas to be 2.34 acres and average per head holding, 0.48 acre. In the small sized Sherpa families (1 to 3 members each), the average per family and average per capita land holding are 1.28 and 0.54 acre respectively. In medium sized families (4 to 5 members each) the same are 1.75 and 0.37 acre respectively. The large families (6 to 8 members) have per family and per capita holdings as 3.64 and 0.54 acre

Table 5.7: Average Land Holding Among the Sherpas of Sherpaguri Village, Darjeeling

Family Size	Land Type I					II					III					Other Type					Total				
	No. of Family	Population	Total Land in Acres	Avg. Land Per Family	Avg. Land Per Head	No. of Family	Population	Total Land in Acres	Avg. Land Per Family	Avg. Land Per Head	No. of Family	Population	Total Land in Acres	Avg. Land Per Family	Avg. Land Per Head	No. of Family	Population	Total Land in Acres	Avg. Land Per Family	Avg. Land Per Head	No. of Family	Population	Total Land in Acres	Avg. Land Per Family	Avg. Land Per Head
1-3	3	5	3.08	1.03	0.62	—	—	—	—	—	5	12	11.07	2.21	0.92	—	—	—	—	—	8	17	14.15	1.77	0.83
4-6	3	13	4.83	1.61	0.37	—	—	—	—	—	15	72	16.51	1.10	0.23	—	—	—	—	—	18	85	21.54	1.02	0.25
7-9	—	—	—	—	—	1	7	4.5	4.5	0.64	8	61	17.46	2.18	0.29	—	—	—	—	—	9	68	21.96	2.44	0.32
10+	—	—	—	—	—	—	—	—	—	—	1	10	1.00	1.00	0.10	—	—	—	—	—	1	10	1.00	1.00	0.10
Total	6	18	7.91	1.32	0.44	1	7	4.5	4.5	0.64	29	155	46.04	1.59	0.30	—	—	—	—	—	36	180	58.45	1.46	0.33

Source: Field study by the authors.

Table 5.8: Average Land Holding Among the Sherpas of Sherpapur Village, Darjeeling

	Land Type																								
	I					*II*					*III*					*Others*					*Total*				
Family Size	No. of Family	Population	Total Land in Acres	Avg. Land Per Family	Avg. Land Per Head	No. of Family	Population	Total Land in Acres	Avg. Land Per Family	Avg. Land Per Head	No. of Family	Population	Total Land in Acres	Avg. Land Per Family	Avg. Land Per Head	No. of Family	Population	Total Land in Acres	Avg. Land Per Family	Avg. Land Per Head	No. of Family	Population	Total Land in Acres	Avg. Land Per Family	Avg. Land Per Head
1-3	15	36	24.00	1.60	0.67	2	6	1.00	0.50	0.17	—	—	—	—	—	2	6.0	0.50	0.25	0.08	19	48	25.50	1.34	0.53
4-6	31	157	58.75	1.90	0.37	—	—	—	—	—	1	6	0.50	0.50	0.08	5	26.0	32.50	6.50	1.25	37	189	91.75	2.48	0.49
7-9	9	70	26.50	2.94	0.38	—	—	4.50	4.50	—	1	9	11.00	11.00	1.22	1	7.0	1.50	1.50	0.21	11	86	39.00	3.55	0.45
10+	1	12	1.50	1.50	0.13	—	—	—	—	—	—	—	—	—	—	—	—	—	—	—	1	12	1.50	1.50	1.25
Total	56	275	110.75	1.98	0.40	2	6	1.00	0.50	0.17	2	15	11.50	5.75	0.76	8	39.0	34.50	4.31	0.88	68	335	157.8	2.32	0.47

Source: Field study by the authors.

respectively. The same for very large families are 5.83 and 0.58 acre respectively (2011:81).

Now, we shall look at the land holding scenario of Sikkim. In the two studied villages of this State there are a total 124 Sherpa families of which 121 (97.58%) have land and the remaining only 3 (2.42%) do not have land. If we take up the land holding figures of the two villages of Sikkim we shall see that in the two villages studied the total number of families having land is 121 and the total number of members of these 121 families is 683. The total area of land possessed by these families is 355.98 acres, thereby the per family holding comes to 2.94 acres. Among these 121 families the per family distribution of different types of land is variable. Among these families only 22 families have Type-I land (total 68.78 acres) and the per family holding of Type-I land is 3.13 acres. Similarly 73 families have Type-II land, and per family holding is 2.54 acres. 13 families have Type-III land and per family holding is 3.80 acres and finally only 13 families have 'Other type' land and the per family holding comes to 1.44 acres (Table 5.9).

Again if we examine the distribution of total land in different sizes of families, we get that very large families have the highest per family of land (4.75 acres). The large size families have the next higher per family holding (3.70 acres). Small and medium size families have almost equal per family holding.

Now, we like to examine the land holding pattern of the two studied villages of Sikkim. The total number of the Sherpa families reside in these two villages are 124, and out of these 124 families 121 are with land (97.58%) and only 3 (2.42%) Sherpa family in these two villages are landless. Again the majority of these 121 families (60.33%) have Type-II land (Table 5.9).

The next larger number of families (18.18%) have Type-I land. Equal number of families (13 or 10.74%) have each Type-III and 'Other Type' of land (Table 5.9). When we come down to the individual studied villages of Sikkim we see that at Sherpagaon village of South District of Sikkim there are 60 Sherpa families and all these 60 Sherpa families (100.00%) have land. No Sherpa family is landless now. Out of these 60 Sherpa families overwhelming majority (83.33%) have Type-II land. Only 6.67 per cent families have Type-I land. Type-II and 'Other Type' of land are owned by 5.00 per cent families each (Table 5.10). In the other village (Sherpahat) of Sikkim 61 Sherpa families have land. Here only 3 Sherpa families are without land. In this village largest number of families (37.70%) have Type-II land whereas 29.51 per cent families have Type-I

Table 5.9: Average Land Holding Among the Sherpas of Two Villages of Sikkim

Family Size	Land Type: i — No. of Family	Population	Total Land in Acres	Avg. Land Per Family	Avg. Land Per Head	II — No. of Family	Population	Total Land in Acres	Avg. Land Per Family	Avg. Land Per Head	III — No. of Family	Population	Total Land in Acres	Avg. Land Per Family	Avg. Land Per Head	Others Type — No. of Family	Population	Total Land in Acres	Avg. Land Per Family	Avg. Land Per Head	Total — No. of Family	Population	Total Land in Acres	Avg. Land Per Family	Avg. Land Per Head
1-3	3	7	5.47	1.82	0.78	18	45	39.19	2.18	0.87	3	5	13.94	4.65	2.79	2	4	5.53	2.77	1.38	26	61	64.13	2.47	1.05
4-6	9	44	14.44	1.6	0.33	41	189	104.09	2.54	0.55	4	21	19.24	4.81	0.92	6	36	10.88	1.81	0.3	60	290	148.65	2.48	0.51
7-9	2	16	4.23	2.12	0.26	11	87	27.9	2.54	0.32	5	36	16.01	3.2	0.44	4	34	33.23	8.31	0.98	22	173	81.37	3.7	0.47
10+	8	93	44.64	5.58	0.49	3	39	14.0	4.67	0.36	1	13	0.25	0.25	0.02	1	14	2.94	2.94	0.21	13	159	61.83	4.75	0.39
Total	22	160	68.78	3.13	0.44	73	360	185.18	2.54	0.51	13	75	49.44	3.8	0.66	13	88	52.58	4.04	0.6	121	683	355.98	2.94	0.52

Source: Field study by the authors.

land. Like the former village (Sherpagaon) each of the Type-III and 'Other Type' land is owned by 16.39 per cent Sherpa families each of Sherpahat village (Table 5.11).

It is thus seen that in both Darjeeling district and South District of Sikkim there are some landless Sherpa families, though Darjeeling village has definitely higher number in this regard than that of the South District of Sikkim.

Now, we shall go for the combined holding of different types of land by different sizes of families of the two villages of Sikkim. When we take up Type-I land we see that very large families have the highest average per family holding of Type-I land (5.58 acres). Next comes large size families with 2.12 acres of per family holding. The medium size families have the lowest average per families holding of Type-I land. In case of the Type-II land the highest average per family holding (4.67 acres) is held also by the very large families. The medium and large families come next with equal average per family holding of 2.54 acres each. The highest average per family holding of Type-III land has been secured by the medium size families (4.81 acres) followed by small families (4.65 acres). The very large families have the lowest average per family holding of Type-III land, only 0.25 acre. In case of the 'Other Type' land the average size families have the highest average per family holding (8.31 acres). The next come very large families having an average per family holding of 'Other type' land of 2.94 acres. The medium families have the lowest average per family holding of this type of land (Table 5.09).

Now, we shall examine the average per head holding in the combined land holding of these two villages of South district of Sikkim (Table 5.09). The average per head holding of the total land here is only 0.52 acre. In case of different types of land the highest average per head holding of Type-III land is 0.66 acre. The Type-I land has the lowest average per head holding which comes to 0.44 acre. In case of the average per head holding of in different sizes of families, we see that small families have the highest average per head holding (1.05 acres) whereas very large families have the lowest average per head holding (0.39 acre). Now, as we examine the average per head holding of different types of land by different sizes of families we see that small families have the highest average per head holding of Type-III land (2.79 acres) and the lowest average of per head land holding is held by very large families (0.02 acre of Type-III land).

We shall now move to the individual studied villages of Sikkim and see the nature and extent of the land holding. At Sherpagaon village of

South District, Sikkim there are 61 Sherpa families where 331 members inhabit. These 61 Sherpa families hold a total of 156.53 acres of land. So, the average per family holding comes to 2.57 acres. As we examine the holding of different types of land, we get that among the Sherpas of this village per family holding of Type-I land is 0.81 acres, Type-II land is 2.55 acres. Type-III land is 3.81 acres and 'Other Type' land is 3.59 acres. Again we have further examined the holding of land by different sizes of families and we get that very large families (10+members) have the highest per families holding (3.88 acres). Next in order come large families (2.86 acres) followed by medium size families (2.38 acres). The small families have the lowest average per family holding (2.32 acres). When we took at the per family land holding of different sizes of families, we get among the Sherpas of Sherpagaon village of Sikkim that the very large families have the highest per family holding of Type-I land (1.50 acres). The next come small families, which have 1.00 per family. The highest average per family of Type-II land (4.67 acres) goes also to the very large families followed by large and medium families (2.49 and 2.47 acres respectively). On the other hand, the highest average per family Type-II land (4.94 acres) is held by small families. Next in order comes large families (3.65 acres). The large families among the Sherpas of Sherpagaon village hold highest average per family 'Other Type' land (5.00 acres).

Now, let us examine the per head land holding in this village (Sherpagaon). The average per head holding of the total land is only 0.47 acre. In this village the credit of holding highest per head area of land is of Type-III land (0.69 acre) whereas the holding of the average per head Type-I land is the lowest (0.14 acre). In case of the highest and lowest per head land held by different sizes of families, the small families have the highest average per head land (0.94 acre) and the very large families have the lowest per head holding of land (0.30 acre). When we examine the average per head land holding of different types of land held by different sizes of families, we get that all sizes of families have less than one acre as the average per head holding of different types of and except Type-III land held by small families. In this case the average per head holding of Type-III land by the small families is 2.47 acres (Table 5.10).

We shall now take up the next village of Sikkim, i.e. Sherpahat of South District and its land holding pattern (Table 5.11). In this village the average per family holding of the total land of the village is 3.32 acres as this village is inhabited by 352 Sherpas who live in 60 families and hold a total of 199.45 acres. Therefore, the average per family holding comes to 3.32 acres. In this village the average per family holding of

Table 5.10: Average Land Holding Among the Sherpas of the Sherpagaon Village of Sikkim

	Land Type																								
	I					II					III					IV					Total				
Family Size	No. of Family	Population	Total Land in Acres	Avg. Land Per Family	Avg. Land Per Head	No. of Family	Population	Total Land in Acres	Avg. Land Per Family	Avg. Land Per Head	No. of Family	Population	Total Land in Acres	Avg. Land Per Family	Avg. Land Per Head	No. of Family	Population	Total Land in Acres	Avg. Land Per Family	Avg. Land Per Head	No. of Family	Population	Total Land in Acres	Avg. Land Per Family	Avg. Land Per Head
1-3	1	3	1.00	1.00	0.33	11	27	24.19	2.20	0.90	1	2	4.94	4.94	2.47	—	—	—	—	—	13	32	30.13	2.32	0.94
4-6	2	9	0.75	0.38	0.08	26	120	64.19	2.47	0.53	1	6	3.06	3.06	0.50	2	12	5.76	2.88	0.48	31	147	73.70	2.38	0.50
7-9	—	—	—	—	—	10	79	24.90	2.49	0.32	2	14	3.65	3.65	0.52	1	8	5.00	5.00	0.63	13	101	37.20	2.86	0.37
10+	1	12	1.50	1.50	0.13	3	39	14.00	4.67	0.36	—	—	—	—	—	—	—	—	—	—	4	51	15.50	3.88	0.30
Total	4	24	3.25	0.81	0.14	50	265	127.28	2.55	0.48	4	22	15.24	3.81	0.69	3	20	10.76	3.59	0.54	61	331	156.53	2.57	0.47

Source: Field study by the authors.

Table 5.11: Average Land Holding Among the Sherpas of the Sherpahat Village of Sikkim

Family Size	*Land Type* I					II					III					IV					*Total*				
	No. of Family	Population	Total Land in Acres	Avg. Land Per Family	Avg. Land Per Head	No. of Family	Population	Total Land in Acres	Avg. Land Per Family	Avg. Land Per Head	No. of Family	Population	Total Land in Acres	Avg. Land Per Family	Avg. Land Per Head	No. of Family	Population	Total Land in Acres	Avg. Land Per Family	Avg. Land Per Head	No. of Family	Population	Total Land in Acres	Avg. Land Per Family	Avg. Land Per Head
1-3	1	2	4.00	4.47	2.24	7	18	15.00	2.14	0.83	2	3	9.00	4.50	3.00	2	4	5.53	2.77	1.98	13	29	34.00	2.62	1.17
4-6	7	35	13.69	1.96	0.56	15	69	39.90	2.66	0.58	3	15	16.24	5.41	1.08	4	24	5.12	1.28	0.21	29	143	74.95	2.58	0.52
7-9	2	16	4.23	2.12	0.26	1	8	3.00	3.00	0.38	3	22	8.71	2.90	0.40	3	26	28.23	9.41	1.09	9	72	44.17	4.91	0.61
10+	7	81	43.14	6.16	0.53	—	—	—	—	—	1	13	0.25	0.25	0.02	1	14	2.94	2.94	0.21	9	108	46.33	5.15	0.43
Total	18	136	65.53	3.64	0.48	23	95	57.9	2.52	0.61	9	53	34.20	3.80	0.65	10	68	41.82	4.18	0.62	60	352	199.45	3.32	0.57

Source: Field study by the authors.

different type of land is quite variable. Here in this village average per family holding of 'Other type' land is the highest (4.18 acres) among all the types of land. The next higher average per family holding goes to Type-III land (3.80 acres) followed by Type-I land (3.64 acres). The lowest average per family holding is of Type-II.

As we look into the average per family land held by different sizes of families we shall see that the very large family holds the highest average per family holding (5.15 acres). Next come large families which have 4.91 acres of per family holding. The medium size families have the lowest such land. In case of the average per family holding of different types of land by different sizes of families, we get that while medium size families have the highest average per family of "Other type" land (9.41 acres), the very large families have the highest per family of Type-I land. The highest average Type-II land goes to large families (3.00 acres) but the highest average of Type-III land is held by medium size families (5.41 acres) (Table 5.11).

Now, let us examine her head land holding by the Sherpas of this village (Sherpahat). The average per head holding of the total land among the Sherpas of Sherpahat is 0.57 acre. Of the different types of land the highest average per head land held by the Sherpas of this village, is of Type-III (0.65 acre) followed by 'Other type' land (0.62 acre). Among the different sizes of land the average per head holding is the highest among the small families (1.17 acres) and the lowest is among the very large families (0.43 acre). Again the highest average per head of holding of all type of land is held by small families. Other sizes of families have varied but smaller area of per head holding.

Workers: Main and Marginal: The Scheduled Tribes and the Bhutias

We have already mentioned elsewhere that the Sherpas have not been enumerated separately by the Census authority as they are included along with some other tribes, within the broad Scheduled Tribe category, the Bhotia/Bhutias in both West Bengal and Sikkim. As a result we do not get any separate census figures for the Sherpa. For this reason we have no option but to state the Census figures of the Bhotia/Bhutias, so that the readers get some faint idea the numerical strength of the Sherpas of the two areas as returned by the Census Authority.

In Table 5.12 we have tried to show the distribution of the workers, main workers and marginal workers of the Scheduled Tribe and the Bhotia/ Bhutias population of West Bengal. According to Census 2001, 48.77

per cent of the Scheduled Tribe population of West Bengal are workers, and at the same time, 53.76 per cent of the Scheduled Tribe male population and 48.69 per cent of the Scheduled Tribe female population are also workers. Again out these total workers of the Scheduled Tribes of West Bengal 65.70 per cent are the main workers and 34.30 per cent marginal workers. Similarly among the total Scheduled Tribe male workers of West Bengal 78.32 are the main workers and 21.68 per cent marginal workers. Among the female Scheduled Tribe workers 49.89 per cent are the main and the remaining 50.11 per cent are the marginal workers. That means the strength of the female Scheduled Tribe marginal workers is slightly higher than that of the main workers.

As we come among the Bhotia/Bhutias population of West Bengal 36.33 per cent of the total Bhotia/Bhutias population (60091) are workers, 45.79 per cent are male workers out of the total Bhutias male population (30055) and 26.86 per cent female workers out of the total Bhutias female population (30036) of this state, according to 2001 census. Again out of the total Bhutias workers, 76.51 per cent are the main workers and 23.49 per cent are the marginal workers. Further among the total Bhutias male workers, overwhelming majority (83.02%) are the main and only 16.98 per cent are marginal workers. But among the female Bhutias workers, 65.39 per cent are the main and 34.61 per cent are the marginal workers.

In Table 5.13 we have cited the Census figures of 2001 on the workers of the Scheduled Tribe population of Sikkim and also of the Bhutias population of Sikkim. The table shows that out of the total Scheduled Tribe population 48.59 per cent are the workers. Again 54.58 per cent of the total male and 42.33 per cent of the total female Scheduled Tribe population are also workers. We further notice that 77.64 per cent of the total Scheduled Tribe workers are the main workers while the remaining 22.36 per cent are marginal workers. Similarly 85.15 per cent male and 67.52 per cent female Scheduled Tribe workers are the main workers while the remaining 14.85 per cent male and 32.48 per cent female Scheduled Tribe workers are the marginal workers.

Among the Bhutias population of Sikkim the 2001 Census gives us the similar trend. Here among these people 47.90 per cent of the total population are the workers, 54.98 per cent total Bhutias male population and 40.69 per cent of the total female Bhutias population are workers. Again out of the total Bhutias workers, 79.00 per cent are the main and 21.00 per cent are the marginal workers. Among the Bhutias male workers 86.19 per cent are the main and the remaining 13.81 per cent are the marginal workers. The Bhutias female workers of Sikkim according to

Table 5.12: Distribution of Total Workers, Main Workers and Marginal Workers among the Scheduled Tribes and the Bhutias of West Bengal, Census 2001

Tribe		*Total Workers*			*Total Main Workers*			*Total Marginal Workers*		
		Person	*Male*	*Female*	*Person*	*Male*	*Female*	*Person*	*Male*	*Female*
All Scheduled Tribes	No.	2149255	1195480	953775	1412133	936302	475831	737122	259178	477944
	%	100.00	100.00	100.00	65.70	78.32	49.89	34.30	21.68	50.11
Bhutias	No.	21831	13763	8068	16702	11426	5276	5129	2337	2792
	%	100.00	100.00	100.00	76.51	83.02	65.39	23.49	16.98	34.61

Source: Census of India, West Bengal 2001.

2001 Census, returned 68.96 per cent as the main and the rest 31.04 per cent as the marginal workers (Table 5.13).

Workers, Main Workers, Marginal Workers and Non-Workers of the Bhutias of West Bengal and Sikkim

Before we proceed further to catch the Sherpas of our studied villages in Sikkim order to know their number of workers, non-workers and also the main workers involved in different economic activities, we shall examine the number of workers, non-workers and the main workers in different economic activities of the Bhutias of West Bengal and Sikkim according to 2001 census as in both States the Sherpas have been included in the broad category, Bhutias, along with some other communities. So, the readers may get some rough idea about the workers, non-workers and different economic activities of the Sherpas of the two states, through the Bhutias.

From Table 5.14 reveals that in West Bengal majority of the Bhutias (person 63.67%, male 54.21% and female 73.14%) are non-workers. That means that these huge numbers of non-workers depend on the earning of workers (person 36.33%, male 45.79% and female 26.86%) who are minority in the Bhutias society of West Bengal. Again out of the total workers 76.51 per cent are the main workers and the rest 23.49 per cent, marginal workers.

In case of the Bhutias males of West Bengal out of the total Bhutias workers, 83.02 per cent are the main workers and the remaining 26.98 per cent are marginal workers. Among the Bhutias females of this state 65.39 per cent of the total females are main workers and the rest 34.61 per cent are marginal workers.

But the picture available from Table 5.14 about the Bhutias of Sikkim is slightly different from that of their congeners living in West Bengal. Among these people of Sikkim as seen from the figures of 2001, we get that the number of the workers among the total Bhutias population and the total female Bhutias population is less than half of the total Bhutia population and total female population (47.90% and 40.69% respectively). But the strength of the Bhutias male workers is a little over half (54.87%) of the total Bhutias male population of Sikkim. It means that here in this state majority, though slender, of the total Bhutias and total female Bhutias are the non-workers (52.10% and 59.31% respectively). Only male Bhutias non-workers are less than 50 per cent of the total Bhutias male

Table 5.13: Distribution of Total Workers, Main Workers and Marginal Workers among the Scheduled Tribes and the Bhutias of Sikkim, Census 2001

Tribe		*Total Workers*			*Total Main Workers*			*Total Marginal Workers*		
		Person	*Male*	*Female*	*Person*	*Male*	*Female*	*Person*	*Male*	*Female*
All Scheduled Tribes	*No.*	54132	31077	23055	42030	26463	15567	12102	4614	7488
	%	100.00	100.00	100.00	77.64	85.15	67.52	22.36	14.85	32.48
Bhutias	No.	33680	19628	14052	26607	16917	9690	7073	2711	4362
	%	100.00	100.00	100.00	79.00	86.19	68.96	21.00	13.81	31.04

Source: Census of India, 2001, Sikkim.

Table 5.14: Total, Main and Marginal Workers of the Bhutias of West Bengal and Sikkim, 2001 Census

Area	*Population*	*Workers*		*Main Workers*		*Marginal Workers*		*Non Workers*	
		Total	*%*	*Total*	*%*	*Total*	*%*	*Total*	*%*
West Bengal	P	21831	36.33	16702	76.51	5129	23.49	38260	63.67
	M	13763	45.79	11426	83.02	2337	16.98	16292	54.21
	F	8068	26.86	5276	65.39	2792	34.61	21968	73.14
Sikkim	P	33680	47.90	26607	79.00	7073	21.00	36628	52.10
	M	19628	54.87	16917	86.19	2711	13.81	16142	45.13
	F	14052	40.69	9690	68.96	4362	31.04	20486	59.31

Source: Census of India, 2001, West Bengal and Sikkim.

population. So, a large number of the Bhutias non-workers of both West Bengal and Sikkim depend on the Bhutias workers.

Like the Bhutias of West Bengal, the Bhutias of Sikkim also have significant number of the marginal workers, though their strength is slightly lower than that of their congeners living in West Bengal.

So, we see that according to 2001 Census the number of the total Bhutias workers, male workers and female workers are more than those of the Bhutias of West Bengal. Therefore, we see that the Bhutias non-workers are more in number in West Bengal than in Sikkim.

Now, let us examine the economic pursuits of the Bhutias main workers of the two states, West Bengal and Sikkim (Table 5.15).

In West Bengal out of a total of 16,702 Bhutias workers, majority are in 'Other Trades' (65.97%). Similarly in case of both male and female main workers, majority are in 'Other Trades' (66.82% and 64.18% respectively).

The next higher number of the main workers are in cultivation (24.98%, 24.80% and 25.36% for person, male and female Bhutias main workers respectively). The strength of the main workers as agricultural labouers and in household industry are much less than 10.00 per cent in person, male and female Bhutias categories.

As we came down to the Bhutias of Sikkim, we get that a large number of the total and female Bhutias main workers and more than half of the male main workers are in 'Other Trades', but no doubt quite a significant number of the Bhutias main workers of Sikkim are cultivators (45.77%,

42.30% and 51.84% for the total male and female main workers respectively). The strength of the main workers working as agricultural labourers and working in household industries is significantly low (less than 5.00% each).

It is thus seen from Table 5.15 that more Bhutias of Sikkim have preferred to work as cultivators than those of West Bengal. In case of the 'Other Trades' more West Bengal Bhutias workers have accepted this category than the Bhutias main workers of Sikkim.

Table 5.15: Distribution of the Main Workers in Different Economic Pursuits among the Bhutias of West Bengal and Sikkim, 2001 Census

Area	Population	Main workers		Main Workers							
				Cultivators		Agri. Labourers		Household Industries		Other Trades	
		Total	%	Total	%	Total	%	Total	%	Total	%
West Bengal	P	16,702	—	4,172	24.98	1,008	6.04	501	3.00	11,021	65.97
	M	11,426	—	2,834	24.80	662	5.79	295	2.58	7,635	66.82
	F	5,276	—	1,338	25.36	346	6.56	206	3.90	3,386	64.18
Sikkim	P	26,607	—	12,179	45.77	964	3.62	372	1.40	13,092	49.21
	M	16,917	—	7,156	42.30	551	3.26	206	1.22	9,004	53.22
	F	9,690	—	5,023	51.84	413	4.26	166	1.71	4,088	42.18

Source: Census of India, 2001, West Bengal and Sikkim.

The Workers and Non-Workers among the Sherpas of Darjeeling District

From two locations of Kalimpong Sub-Division of Darjeeling District, Raha has got 57.57 per cent workers and 42.43 per cent non-workers among the Sherpas. Among the male Sherpas the same is 56.79 per cent and 43.21 per cent and among the female Sherpas 58.33 per cent and 41.67 per cent respectively (2011:78). Raha has further shown that in the some locations of Kalimpong the average Sherpa workers per family is 2.84. The average Sherpa male workers per family is 1.38 and average female workers is 1.46. That means the average Sherpa female workers per family is slightly higher than that of the male workers per family. The average Sherpa non-workers per family is 2.10, male non-workers 1.05 and female non-workers 1.04 (Table 5.16).

Table 5.16: Distribution of the Combined Sherpa Workers and Non-Workers of Two Locations of Kalimpong, Darjeeling

Population	*No. %*	*Workers*	*Non-Workers*	*Total*
Person	No.	327	241	568
	%	57.57	42.43	100.00
Male	No.	159	121	280
	%	56.79	43.21	100.00
Female	No.	168	120	288
	%	58.33	41.67	100.00

Source: Raha 2011: 78.

Expected and Actual Workers: The Sherpas of the Studied Villages

For the purpose of our study we have calculated the expected workers as those who belong to the age-group, 15-59. We have considered people belonging to this age-group, as the expected work force of a society or of a group of people. But the actual work force includes those who actually work. They may belong to this age-group or may have come from the age-group other than the above age-group. This means that if a person having age 60 or above and also a boy or a girl 14 or below years of age who works and earns, is also considered as an actual worker but they are not considered as the expected workers. Again if a person who belongs to the age-group, 15 to 59, does not work and earn but depends on other's income, is not considered as actual worker because he or she does not actually work. So, the number of actual workers may be the same with the number of expected workers, may be more or may even be less than that of the expected workers.

In the light of this if we examine the Sherpas of our four studied villages, two from Kalimpong sub-division of Darjeeling district and two from South District of Sikkim, we shall find that at the village Sherpaguri of Darjeeling the strength of the expected workers and also expected male and female workers (who belong to the age-group 15-59) are over 62.00 per cent. But at Sherpapur village both total and female expected workers are less than 60.00 per cent but the expected male workers are a little over 60.00 per cent. At Sherpagaon village of Sikkim while expected male workers are a little more than 60.00 per cent, the female expected workers are a little less than 60.00 per cent. At Sherpahat village of Sikkim the total and also both male and female expected workers are only a fractionally over 52.00 per cent (Table 5.17).

Now, we shall examine the actual number of the Sherpa workers in these four villages. At Sherpaguri and Sherpapur villages the actual number of workers are little over half of the Sherpa population of these two villages of Darjeeling District. That means the rest of the Sherpa population that is, a little less than half, depend on the income of little over half of the Sherpa population of these two villages. Again in these two villages a little less than 60.00 per cent of the Sherpa males are the actual workers, but unfortunately a little over 45.00 per cent of the females of these two villages (46.79% and 45.25%) are the actual workers.

The Sherpas of two villages of Sikkim that is, Sherpagaon and Sherpahat, show slightly different trend. In these two villages less than half (47.06% and 41.48% respectively) of the Sherpa population are the actual workers. This means that more than half of the total Sherpa population of these two villages depend on these Sherpa population. Again among the male Sherpas of these two villages 52.60 per cent and 46.20 per cent respectively are the actual workers. But among the female Sherpas of these two villages even much less number of them are the actual workers (46.62% and 37.02% respectively).

Table 5.17: Distribution of Expected and Actual Workers among the Sherpas of Studied Villages of Darjeeling and Sikkim

Workers	Popu-lation	*Villages of Darjeeling*				*Villages of Sikkim*			
		Sherpaguri		*Sherpapur*		*Sherpagaon*		*Sherpahat*	
		No.	*%*	*No.*	*%*	*No.*	*%*	*No.*	*%*
Expected	P	136	62.67	205	58.40	206	60.59	185	52.56
	M	67	62.04	105	61.05	119	61.98	90	52.63
	F	69	63.30	100	55.87	87	58.78	95	52.49
Actual	P	115	53.00	182	51.85	160	47.06	106	41.48
	M	64	59.26	101	58.72	101	52.60	79	46.20
	F	51	46.79	81	45.25	69	46.62	67	37.02
Difference	P	61	9.67	23	6.55	46	13.53	39	11.08
	M	23	2.78	4	2.33	18	9.38	11	6.43
	F	18	16.51	19	10.62	18	12.16	28	15.47

Source: Field study by the authors.

Now, when we compare between the expected and the actual workers we see that the gap or difference between the expected and actual number of workers. While the difference between these two is less than 10.00 per cent (9.67% and 6.55% respectively) among the Sherpas of the two Sherpa villages of Darjeeling, the same is a little over 10.00 per cent (13.53% and 11.08% respectively) among the Sherpas the two Sherpa villages of Sikkim. While the said different is less than 3.00 per cent among the male Sherpa workers of the two villages of Darjeeling, the same difference is 9.38 per cent and 6.43 per cent respectively among the male Sherpa workers of the two villages of Sikkim. But in case of the female Sherpa workers of all the four villages studied, the different between expected and actual female workers is significantly high. The same is between 10.62 per cent to 16.51 per cent.

It is thus seen that there is difference between expected (here it is all the members belonging to the age-group, 15 to 59) and the actual workers among the Sherpas of all the four studied villages of both Darjeeling, West Bengal and South District, Sikkim. In some case while the gap is quite small as low as 2.33 per cent, in some other case the same is as high as 16.51 per cent.

Among the Sherpas of two locations of Kalimpong Sub-Division, Darjeeling District, Raha has got 60.04 per cent of the total Sherpa population of the two villages as expected Sherpa workers whereas the actual workers being 57.57 per cent (Table 5.18). In the same way the expected and actual Sherpa male workers are 61.43 per cent and 56.79 per cent respectively. In case of the Sherpa females the expected and actual Sherpa workers are 58.68 per cent and 58.33 per cent respectively. So, it is clear that in case of the Sherpa persons and the Sherpa males the difference between expected and actual Sherpa workers is quite significant. But same is not so in case of the female Sherpa expected and actual workers (Raha 2011: 80).

Table 5.18: Combined Expected and actual Workers among Sherpas in Two Settlements of Kalimpong, Darjeeling

Population	*Expected Workers*		*Actual Workers*		*Difference*		*Total population*
	No.	*%*	*No.*	*%*	*No.*	*%*	
Person	341	60.04	327	57.57	14	2.46	568
Male	172	61.43	159	56.79	13	4.63	280
Female	169	58.68	168	58.33	01	0.35	288

Source: Raha 2011: 80.

Workers and Non-Workers or Dependants: The Sherpas of the Studied Villages

The Sherpas of Darjeeling District, West Bengal and South District, Sikkim live in undulating and unkempt terrain in the mountainous areas having harsh climate. They do not have a smooth life and have to toil hard to earn their bread. As their landholding is small and that too in small plots on the stony hilly slopes, wherefrom they do not get much crops, and as their other sources of income are also very limited, so all the adults do not get job to earn their living. Therefore among them, in most of the villages, the number of workers is much less than that of non-workers or dependants. A large number of non-workers depend on the earning of the workers for their survival.

In our studied villages both in Darjeeling and also in Sikkim the same condition prevails. At Sherpaguri of Darjeeling out of a total Sherpa population of 217, only 34.56 per cent are workers. Therefore, the non-workers among them number nearly double (65.44%). The condition of Sherpapur village of Darjeeling is almost the same. Here 40.45 per cent of the population are workers. Therefore, the number of dependants here is much more than the workers (Table 5.19).

But at Sherpagaon and Sherpahat villages of South District of Sikkim the number of the Sherpa workers is much less (35.29% and 30.11% respectively) than that of the non-workers or dependants. Therefore, it may rightly be assumed that among the Sherpas of these two areas (Darjeeling and South District) a large number of family members depend economically on much less number of workers of the respective family.

Table 5.19: Strength of Workers and Non-workers or Dependants on the Total Sherpas Population of Four Studied Village, of Darjeeling and Sikkim

Villages	*Total Population*		*Workers*		*Non-Workers*	
	No.	*%*	*No.*	*%*	*No.*	*%*
Sherpaguri	217	100.00	75	34.56	142	65.44
Sherpapur	351	100.00	142	40.45	209	59.55
Sherpagaon	340	100.00	120	35.29	220	64.71
Sherpahat	352	100.00	106	30.11	246	69.89

Source: Field study by the authors.

Table 5.20: Average Number of Workers and Non-Workers per Family Among the Sherpas of Four Studied Villages

Villages	*Total Families*	*Workers*		*Non- Workers*	
		Total	*Average*	*Total*	*Average*
Sherpaguri	43	75	1.74	142	3.30
Sherpapur	72	142	1.97	209	2.90
Sherpagaon	64	120	1.88	220	3.44
Sherpahat	60	106	1.77	246	4.10
Total	239	443	1.85	817	3.42

Source: Field study by the authors.

Now, let us examine the average number of workers and non-workers or dependants in these four villages. In the total number of families of these four villages (239) the average number of workers per family is 1.85 and that of non-workers is 3.42. At Sherpaguri it is 1.74 and 3.30, and at Sherpapur 1.97 and 2.90 respectively. In Sikkim at Sherpagaon village the number of average workers is 1.88 and average non-workers 3.44 per family and at Sherpahat village the same are 1.77 and 4.10 respectively. So, it clearly seen that in all the villages the number of dependants per family is much more than that of workers (Table 5.20).

After finding out average number of members per family, we shall now take up sex-wise distribution of the Sherpa workers and non-workers or dependants of the four studied villages two from Darjeeling and two from Sikkim. It is seen that out of a total of 443 workers more than half (57.56%) are male workers and less than half (42.44%) are female workers. At Sherpaguri more than half are male workers and a little over 40 per cent are female workers. But at Sherpapur village of Darjeeling the condition is almost same as that of Sherpaguri village. In Sikkim on the other hand, the male workers range between 56.56 per cent (Sherpahat) and 59.17 per cent in the other village. The female workers remain between 40.83 per cent and 42.44 per cent in Sherpagaon and Sherpahat villages respectively (Table 5.21).

Sex-wise Distribution of Workers and Non-workers

Among the Sherpas of both Darjeeling and Sikkim, both males and females are very hard workers. One will find many of them doing some work in order to earn livelihood. Here below (Table 5.22) we have analyzed sex-

Table 5.21: Sex-wise Distribution of Male and Female Workers in Total Workers in different Studied Sherpa Villages of Darjeeling and Sikkim

Villages	*Total Workers*		*Total Male Workers*		*Total Female Workers*	
	No.	*%*	*No.*	*%*	*No.*	*%*
Sherpaguri	75	100.00	44	58.67	31	41.33
Sherpapur	142	100.00	81	57.04	61	42.96
Sherpagaon	120	100.00	71	59.17	49	40.83
Sherpahat	106	100.00	59	55.56	47	44.34
Total	443	100.00	255	57.56	188	42.44

Source: Field study by the authors.

wise distribution of workers in different studied villages of Darjeeling, West Bengal and South District, Sikkim.

From Table 5.22 it is seen that out of a total of 643 Sherpa males of the four villages, only 39.66 per cent are actual workers but the majority (60.34%) are non-workers. Similarly, among the total Sherpa females (617) only a minority (30.47%) are actual workers but the vast majority (69.53%) are non-workers. Now, we come down to the village level.

In Sherpaguri village out of a total of 108 males much less than half are workers (40.74%) and the remaining males, who are mostly children and old, are non-workers. But in this village most of the females except (28.44%) are non-workers, this is not true for the other village, Sherpapur, of Darjeeling. Here as usual the male workers (47.09%) have been overshadowed the male non-workers (52.91%) but unlike their female congeners of Sherpaguri, the female workers here have the strength much less than half (28.44%) of the total females. That means that the female workers here are much less in number than the female non-workers.

At Sherpagaon village of Sikkim, out of a total of 192 males, 36.98 per cent are workers, the non-workers are naturally less than half in number. The femalc workers as usual, are very small in number (33.11%) and so the females non-workers have the overwhelming majority (66.89%). Almost same is the picture among the Sherpas of Sherpahat village (Table 5.22). Here in this village 34.50 per cent of the total males and only 25.97 per cent of the total females are workers. So the number of both male and female workers are quite low. We also see that while the

Table 5.22: Sex-wise Distribution of Sherpa Workers and Non-workers in Total Sherpa Male and Female Population in Four Studied Villages

Village	*Total Population*				*Total Workers*				*Total Non-Workers*			
	Total Males		*Total Female*		*Male Workers*		*Female Workers*		*Male Non-workers*		*Female non-workers*	
	No.	*%*	*No.*	*%*	*No.*	*%*	*No.*	*%*	*No.*	*%*	*No.*	*%*
Sherpaguri	108	100.00	109	100.00	44	40.74	31	28.44	64	59.26	78	71.56
Sherpapur	172	100.00	179	100.00	81	47.09	61	34.08	91	52.91	118	65.92
Sherpagaon	192	100.00	148	100.00	71	36.98	49	33.11	121	63.02	99	66.89
Sherpahat	171	100.00	181	100.00	59	34.50	47	25.97	112	65.50	134	74.03
Total	643	100.00	617	100.00	255	39.66	188	30.47	388	60.34	429	69.53

Source: Field study by the authors.

non-earner males have some strength, a large number of females. Sherpa females of this village are non-workers.

It may therefore be said that among the Sherpas of these four villages while more than half of the total males (55.83%) are workers, only 21.72 per cent of the combined total females of these four villages are non-workers.

Among the Sherpas of both Darjeeling and Sikkim different types of labourers are present. There are labourers who are exclusively meant for agricultural purposes whereas there are some other type of labourers who do some non-agicultural jobs. The agricultural labourers have the skill in different agricultural operations. They are generally engaged by those Landlords (both the Sherpas and non-Sherpas) who have largers areas of cultivable land and less manpower. The agricultural labourers are employed to do all the agricultural jobs from the preparation of land and making it suitable for cultivation to the harvest and bringing crops at home.

Sometimes, these labourers are employed for the whole operation, but sometimes for some particular operation or operations. Both adult males and females are employed. But there is no restriction for employing teen-agers belonging to the age-group, 13 to 17. Though there are official rates for the payment of wages to the labourers for the jobs done by them, still in most of the cases the rate per day is fixed through negotiation between the landlord and the labourers. Whatever may be the case, no doubt rates are not same for all ages and also for both sexes. The rate varies in case of male and female labourers. The female labouers in both Darjeeling and Sikkim get less wage than their male counterparts even for doing same type and amount of work. Similarly non-adult labourers get lower rate of wages even for the same type and same load of work. Possibly this tradition is continuing in every part of India. It seems it is a pan-Indian picture, but surely it is true for the Sherpas. Now, the labourers, besides their wages, usually get a cup of tea in the morning and also the mid-day meal. In the evening they again get a cup of tea before they leave for their own home after the end of their day's work. Occasionally, in stead of tea a pot of *Chhang* (home brwn liquor) is also served to the adult male labourers.

Sometimes, some big landowners keep permanent labourers by providing them accommodation close to their house. These permanent labourers are meant for all purposes. They do both household as well as agricultural works. Instead of daily wage, they get wages on monthly basis. They take breakfast, meals both in the daytime and also at night and also tea or sometimes *Chhung* in the afternoon, free of cost, in the house of the landowners. The permanent labourers are mainly males, mostly adults. Their monthly wages vary according to the age. Normally younger and older permanent labourers get a little less than the able bodied adults. The monthly salary of the permanent labourers is fixed through negotiation.

The work exchange system is also present among the Sherpas. Under this system members of one Sherpa family, provide free labour for a particular job to another family, related or unrelated and living in the same village or in the neighbouring villages, for a fixed number of days. For this labour provided, they do not charge any remuneration or wage. Instead when they have any such works the members of the other family come forward and provide necessary labour to this family which rendered free labour to them. That means one family provides free labour to another, and in exchange, get back free labour when needed. The work exchange system is employed in the agricultural field, construction of house, construction of ridges around agricultural plots, repairing the irrigational channels, clearing the field from pebbles and boulders and some such works. Normally those families which do not have sufficient man power for different types of jobs (agricultural or non-agricultural), generally go for the work exchange system. They seek such labour either from their relatives or neighbours in the same village or in the neighbouring villages. In case of work exchange system, a family provides same number of days of labour and also by same number of persons to the other family from whom this family got the help. No payment is made in the work exchange system, but usually tea, lunch etc. are given to the persons providing labour.

In general for all types of labour, the working hours is from 8.00 AM in the morning to 4.00 PM in the afternoon. In between they get break of one hour usually from 12.00 noon to 1.00 for lunch. Normally the persons hired as labourers do different types of jobs like ploughing, weeding, sowing of seeds, harvesting, pruning etc. when hired for agricultural works or do other jobs if provided for non-agricultural purposes. The non-agricultural labourers usually do different types of works such as bringing fodders for the animals, fuel wood for the family, construction of building, repair of the irrigational channel, and different such jobs. Normally, the wages given to the female labourers is a little less than that of the male labourers. The same is the case with the teen-ager-labourers. They get even leser wages than that paid to the female labourers. Again in case of the agricultural works, wages paid to the labourers vary for the land situated in different altitudes. Labourers in the higher altitudes get higher wages. Again on the steepness of the land situated on the hill slopes, depends the rate of wages. No doubt among the Sherpas all the family members, from teen-ages to the old, from males to the females, work in their land, upto their capacity. The very young or very old and also the sick persons and handicapped are given exemption. Otherwise, all other persons if not employed elsewhere do work, though harder works, like ploughing, are done by the adult males. In case of household works, similarly, all such members remain engaged, still no doubt, adult women do more works, in comparison to the adult males. Cooking, cleaning, washing, bringing drinking water etc. are mostly done by the females, besides agriculture.

Economic Activities

The traditional economic activities of the Sherpas of Darjeeling, Sikkim and Nepal are agriculture and animal husbandry. They were also remained engaged in trade with Tibet and other areas. But with the Chinese occupation of Tibet the said trade of the Sherpas ceased to function. This of course, brought a set-back in their economy. For the same reason their animal husbandry has also suffered. A good number of the Sherpas got involved in trekking and mountain expeditions as porters and guides since long as they have proved as excellent mountaineers and trekkers. Some other Sherpas have accepted different other jobs like manufacturing and household industries, service, daily labour, business etc.

In Darjeeling district, the Sherpas are basically the cultivators. Agriculture is their main source of livelihood. Their "prolonged association with other agricultural communities" have helped them to lean towards agriculture, and for this they have learnt the know-how of farming. At present a large number of them have become totally agriculturists. Bagchi also holds the same view (1991: 174). Many of them are also engaged as agricultural and daily labourers. Some of them also work as porters. But "livestock plays a vital part in the economic life of the Sherpas" (Bagchi: *ibid*). Most of the Sherpa houses keep domestic animals like cattle, sheep, poultry birds, etc. Again a good number of the Sherpas are found to remain engaged in trade, manufacturing and household industry. According to Bagchi "In Kalimpong Sub-Division about 35 trading and manufacturing establishments belong to the Sherpas including 19 in the town of Kalimpong ...." (*ibid*). In Darjeeling and Kurseong they also have similar such manufacturing establishments. The number of such establishments were 49 in Darjeeling and 23 in Kurseong (*ibid*). Horticulture is another economic activity of these people. In their kitchen gardens they produce potato, different vegetables like cabbage, cauliflower, tomato, squash, fruits etc. Some of them have business while some others work as porters. A few of them are found to work as labourers in tea estates. Mitra has found that "The corps of special porters used in all the Mount Everest expeditions and other rock climbing expeditions are recruited almost entirely from the Sherpa community, and they have proved their worth on a every Himalayan expedition" (2008: 1185). The educated Sherpas have shown their interest towards white colour jobs in Government and private sectors, and now many of them are seen to work in these sectors.

Among the Sherpas of Darjeeling District like all other hilly areas, the cultivable lands are distributed in different altitude. So, the "physiography in the area has made agricultural condition extremely diverse. Agriculture is greatly impacted by altitude and slope aspects" (Desai: 2013). During winter it is difficult to grow crops beyond 2895.6 meters. Moreover, the lands are full of rocks and pebbles the depth of the surface soil is quite low, and many slopes are exceedingly steep. All these restrict the agricultural operations to a great extent. Moreover, the soil is not that fertile, and therefore yield is comparatively low. Over and above for the hilly condition of the agricultural land, more input of human labour is essential (Desai: *ibid*). So, the cost of agricultural operation is higher.

According to Kapoor and Gupta the traditional occupation of the Sherpas of Darjeeling was cultivating potato in the hilly terraces. At present many of them draw their income from carrying luggage of the tourists and in mountain expeditions. Some of them are also found to work in offices or undertake business and practices horticulture (2008: 132).

According to 1991 census majority of the inhabitants of Sikkim depended on agriculture and related activities. But unfortunately only 15.00 per cent of the total geographical areas of this state were available for cultivation. In this state the net cultivated area according to 1991 Census, was 79,723.00 hectares of which net area under cultivation was 74,365.00 hectares and area under current fallows was 5,358.00 hectares. Besides, there was cultivated waste land of 3,366.00 hectares. The smallness of the cultivable land was mainly because a very large areas of this state is either barren or uncultivable while another large areas are under forest and pastures. "With the increase in population, the pressure on land has also increased substantially" (1993: 21).

In 2004-2005 only 13.67 per cent of the total geographical areas of 709,600 hectares, are meant for cultivation in Sikkim. During this period the net area sown was 63,250 hectares, current fallow 3,910 hectares, other cultivable land excluding fallow land was 10,830 hectares and cultivable waste land was 9,810 hectares. In 2004-2005, the areas under irrigation were 11,310 hectares. Total un-irrigated areas was 49,310 hectares and the areas under large cardamom cultivation were 21,220 hectares (Subba 2008: 79-80). So, we see that the land is the main source of their livelihood, and over land individual ownership is there. Therefore, land is managed and controlled individually.

Gangopadhyay has also found in Sikkim that the land is their main source of livelihood, and the same is controlled individually (1993: 159). As their lands are situated on the terraces, so, they depend on terrace cultivation. Bisht and Bankati too have seen land as the main source of livelihood, and they are terrace cultivators (2004: 1492).

In Sikkim the main agricultural crops are maize, rice, wheat, large cardamom, finger millet, *urd*, *rai* mustard, barley, soyabeans, potato etc. Besides, different varieties of fruits are also produced. Subba has reported that paddy, maize, wheat, pulses, oil seeds etc. are cultivated. Apart from these fruits, vegetables, potato, large cardamom, ginger etc. are also produced (2008: 83). "They are specialized on production of seed potato, off-season vegetables such as cabbage, peas, radish etc. as they inhabit above 2,700m from the sea level" (*ibid*: 283-284).

In case of the surplus agricultural production, the Sherpas of both Darjeeling and Sikkim directly sell the same in the local market. The middle men are not much encouraged to come in between them and the market. In fact middlemen have little role to play. Particularly, after the harvest of when the Sherpas get crops like potato, ginger, large cardamom etc., they normally go to the local market and sell their surplus crops directly to the purchasers (wholesellers and retailers) at the existing market rate. In one our studied villages in Kalimpong of Darjeeling, some Sherpa families in order to sell their surplus milk, have selected one person belonging Chhetri caste (Nepali) who collect milk from the families willing to sell the milk every morning and sell the milk thus collected in the market or shops at Kalimpong town. He makes payment on monthly basis to each and every Sherpa family of this village who gives milk to him, the cost of whole month's milk thus collected by him from the villagers. The ratge of milk he charges from the villagers is one rupee less than the market rate of the milk per litre. This one rupee per litre of milk is his charge for collecting milk from the households of the village and carrying the milk to the market at Kalimpong town and sell there. The Sherpas of this village have accepted the rate per litre of milk charged by this man as they consider it to be the minimum charge offered by this man for his labour. Further, the Sherpas also consider it is not profitable to take by themselves the small quantity of milk they have, to the market at Kalimpong town every morning and sell the milk there for small profit hampering the day today agricultural and household works.

For selling potato, ginger, large cardamom, they do not go to the market every day, but only twice or thrice a week after the harvest depending on the load of works they have in their hand, for their kitchen garden production, that is, vegetables like *rai* (mustard plant), cabbages, cauliflower, squash etc. they sell only what is left after their consumption.

Occupation: The People of Darjeeling District

Table 5.23 below clearly shows the trend of change of the occupational pattern of the people of Darjeeling District from 1901 to 1931, 1931 to

Table 5.23: No. of Workers in Different Years (Their Percentages to Total Workers) in Darjeeling District

Category of Workers	*1901*	*1931*	*1961*	*1991*
Total workers	154489 (100.00)	122904 (100.00)	266105 (100.00)	444832 (100.00)
Cultivators	56811 (36.77)	23346 (18.99)	99703 (37.47)	110051 (24.74)
Agricultural Labourers	691 (0.45)	9069 (7.38)	7807 (2.94)	52579 (11.82)
Mining, Quarrying, Livestock, Forestry, Fishing, Hunting, Plantations, Orchards etc.	71555 (46.32)	67568 (54.98)	82236 (30.90)	93504 (21.02)
Manufacturing including Household Industry	4925 (3.19)	3838 (3.12)	9306 (3.51)	32072 (7.21)
Construction	3729 (2.41)	550 (0.45)	3160 (1.19)	10676 (2.40)
Trade and Commerce	7033 (4.55)	6781 (5.52)	15592 (5.86)	50533 (11.36)
Transport, Storage and Communication	2627 (1.70)	2423 (1.97)	7756 (2.92)	20640 (4.64)
Other Services	7118 (4.61)	9329 (7.59)	40545 (15.21)	74776 (16.81)

Source: Das & Bhuimali 2011:122.

1961 and from 1961 to 1991. From this table we get that the number of cultivators which was 36.77 per cent in 1901, came down to 24.74 per cent in 1991. But proportionately the number of agricultural labourers has significantly increased from 0.45 per cent in 1901 to 11.82 per cent in 1991. The strength of workers has been in increased from 1901 to 1991.

Manufacturing including household industries, trade and commerce, transport, storage and communication and 'Other Services'. On the other hand, the number of workers dropped down during the same period in mining, quarrying, livestock, forestry, fishing, hunting, plantations, orchards etc. During 90 years time from 1901 to 1991 no significant change is noticed. Rather the strength of workers remains almost constant in construction.

The other significant thing that one can notice from the above table is that the number of cultivators dropped significantly from 1901 to 1931 (18.99%) but gained significant momentum in 1961 (34.47%). The strength of this category again dropped in 1991. In case of the agricultural labourers the strength rose to 7.38 per cent in 1931 but dropped to only 2.94 per cent in 1961. The number of workers engaged in mining, quarrying, livestock etc. increased to 54.32 per cent in 1931 from 1901 (46.32%), but dropped to 30.90 per cent in 1961. Both construction and transport, storage and communication got very low priority among the workers of this hilly district of West Bengal. But the trend shows that the workers here have started selecting 'other services' more and more.

From two locations of Kalimpong, Darjeeling, Raha has been able to give an idea about the occupational pattern of the Sherpa workers. From table 5.24 as given by Raha (2011:80) we get:

Table 5.24: Occupational Pattern of the Combined Sherpa workers of Two Locations of Kalimpong and Darjeeling

Workers	*No. %*	*Agriculture*	*Labour*	*Skilled Labour*	*Business*	*Service*	*Religious Specialist*	*Household Work*	*Total*
Person	No.	178	10	21	4	31	8	75	327
	%	54.43	3.06	6.42	1.22	9.48	2.45	22.94	100.00
Male	No.	93	7	21	1	29	8	—	159
	%	58.49	4.40	13.21	0.63	18.24	5.03	—	100.00
Female	No.	85	3	—	3	2	—	75	168
	%	50.60	1.79	—	1.79	1.19	—	44.64	100.01

Source: Raha 2011: 80.

From the above table we get that a little over half of the workers have involved in agricultural activities (Person 54.43%, Male 58.49% and Female 50.60%). As skilled labourers a good number of the Sherpa males (13.21%) remain engaged in different activities. In the same way a good number of the Sherpa males (18.24%) are also in service. While all religious specialists (5.03%) are males, all household workers (44.64%) are the female Sherpas.

Table 5.25: Land-use Statistics of Darjeeling District

Year	*Percentage of arable land to geographical Area*	*Area under forest*	*Percentage of forests to geographical area*	*Other lands and water bodies*	*Per capita agricultural area in hectares*	*Per capita forest area in hectares*
1901	19.76	1554	51.54	865	0.24	0.62
1911	23.45	1554	55.55	754	0.25	0.59
1921	21.39	1481	49.14	889	0.21	0.52
1931	20.38	1427	45.46	1072	0.20	0.44
1941	24.50	1414	45.81	917	0.16	0.37
1951	36.67	1430	46.01	538	0.19	0.32
1961	31.92	1432	46.07	684	0.16	0.23
1971	44.51	1372	40.73	—	0.19	0.18
1981	53.61	1204	38.23	—	0.16	0.12
1991	56.41	1155	34.12	—	0.15	0.08

Source: Das & Bhuimali 2011: 148.

Table 5.25 above shows clearly that with the growth of population in Darjeeling District, the demand for the arable land has also increased. And with the increase of the area of the arable land keeping in cope with the demand for the arable land by the increasing population, the area under forest started reducing. In the same way, with the increase of the per capita agricultural land, the per capita forest area has also started decreasing. In 1901 while the percentage of arable land to the geographical area was 19.76 per cent, in 1991 it went up to 56.41 per cent. Reversely while the percentage of the forest area to the total geographical area was 51.54 per cent in 1901, it came down to 34.12 per cent in 1991.

When we look at the per capita agricultural land in different periods, we shall see from the same table that while the per capita agricultural area was 0.24 hectare in 1901 in Darjeeling District, it came down 0.15 hectare in 1991 because of the rapid growth of population. For the same

Table 5.26: Temporal Changes in Occupational Structure by Sex (1971 to 2001) in Sikkim

Sector	1971			1981			1991			2001*		
	Male	*Female*	*Total*	*Male*	*Female*	*Total*	*Male*	*Female*	*Total*	*Male*	*Female*	*Total*
Cultivators	74.53	92.28	81.00	50.16	79.52	60.10	50.96	71.74	57.84	42.3	49.9	66.8
Agriculture Labourers	4.12	3.16	3.77	3.45	3.06	3.31	8.04	7.37	7.81	5.3	4.3	6.5
Livestock, forestry, hunting, fishing, plantation and allied	0.60	0.48	0.55	1.93	0.92	1.59	2.99	1.58	2.53	—	—	—
Mining & quarrying	0.09	0.00	0.05	0.17	0.00	0.11	0.30	0.05	0.22	—	—	—
Manufacturing, processing, servicing and repairing												
(a) Household industry	0.50	0.04	0.34	1.25	0.74	1.08	0.99	0.33	0.77	1.7	1.6	1.1
(b) Other than household industries	1.31	0.26	0.93	3.14	1.29	2.51	3.94	1.88	3.26	—	—	—
Construction	4.85	0.87	3.40	10.47	4.98	8.62	8.84	3.54	7.09	—	—	—
Trade & Commerce	3.09	0.48	2.14	5.08	1.00	3.70	6.79	2.08	5.23	—	—	—
Transport, storage and communication	2.27	0.42	1.59	1.55	0.07	1.05	2.62	0.24	1.82	—	—	—
Other services	8.64	2.01	6.23	22.80	8.42	17.93	14.53	11.19	13.43	53.4	46.7	31.0
Total workers % of main	100.00	100.00	100.00	100.00	100.00	100.00	100.00	100.00	100.00			
workers to total population	62.97	41.82	53.17	56.55	34.69	46.60	50.82	28.63	40.45			

Source: Census of India 1971, 1981, 1991, 2001*(Provisional); Subba 2008:95

reason the per capita forest area which was 0.62 hectare in 1901, was reduced to 0.08 hectare in 1991.

No doubt cultivation as a source livelihood, is the first choice of the people of Sikkim though the strength of the workers has decreased in different census years from 1971 to 2001. While 81.00 per cent of the workers were involved in cultivation in 1971, their number came down to 60.40 per cent in 1981, 57.84 per cent in 1991 and finally increased in 66.8 per cent in 2001 (Table 5.26). The number of agricultural labourers who were 4.12 per cent in 1971, were increased to 7.39 per cent in 1991 though in the midway they suffered a decrease to 3.31 per cent in 1981. In 2001 they were again decreased to 6.5 per cent. In trade and commerce and construction slight increase in the number of workers in Sikkim from 1971 to 1991 is noticed. But significant increase in the number of workers in 'Other Services' from 1971 (8.64%) to 2001 (31.0%) is clearly visible. That means the Sikkimese workers (belonging to all communities) have started preferring 'Other Services'.

The Sherpas of Sikkim are found to have other subsidiary occupations such as labour, service, acting as helpers or as guides on mountain expeditions. More and more Sherpas are looking for service and also join as daily labourers (Gangopadhyay 1993: 159). Subba also found different subsidiary occupations like livestock rearing (stall fed cattle rearing), labour, service, helpers and guides of Himalayan expeditions etc. (2008:284). Bisht and Bankoti have also seen the above as the subsidiary occupations of the Sherpas of Sikkim. But Coomar and Raha have found the Sherpas of Sikkim as agriculturists as well as horticulturists. Generally, the landless and marginal land-owners work as agricultural labourers. But those Sherpas who live in the urban centers, like to have other jobs such as service, business, teachings or act as professionals etc. (1999:193; 2013: 37).

Now, we shall look at the economic activities of the Sherpas of Nepal. According to Shrestha, Singh and Pradhan the Sherpas of Nepal have three main occupations, and these are agriculture, trade, and yak farming and sheep rearing. In the cultivable area they grow rice, wheat, maize and potatoes. Some of them are engaged in trade with Tibet and India. Some others prepare *ghee* (clarified butter), *Durukho* (a kind of cheese) and also Nepali paper (1975:13). Some of them also prepare wooden utensils, baskets etc., while some others weave blankets and carpets. Many of them also work as porters for the mountain expeditions (*ibid)*.

According to Bista "The Sherpa economy is directly related to their mountain environment, and falls into four distinct categories: field agriculture, animal husbandry, trade and a recent innovation–mountaineering" (1976:161). Bista also found that a large number of the Sherpas are preferring the profession of guides to the trekkers. While a good number of the Sherpas of Khumbu are found to be engaged in pastoral activities, their congeners at Solu remain satisfied with agriculture. They produce maize, wheat and potatoes. The farming in Khumbu being limited, the Khumbu Sherpas concentrate their efforts on their livestock particularly on the cattle and yak. They also practice crossbreeding of cow and yak and get valuable male *dzopkyo* and female *dzum*. Both yak and *dzopkyo* are used as pack and also as draught animals. The *dzopkyo* is also used for ploughing the cultivable land. On the other hand, cow and *dzum* are meant for milk products (*ibid*: 161-162).

In connection with the economic activities of the Sherpas of Nepal. Bisht and Bankoti have stated that a good number of the Sherpas are involved in business and trade. They also weave carpets, rear yak, *dzo* and *dzuma*. Currently, they are very much engaged in trekking and mountaineering business. Many Sherpa women are found to run shop of catering food and other luxury items (2004:1488).

Being situated in high altitude of Nepal, the soil of Khumbu remains frozen for six months a year during winter season, as noticed by Fürer-Haimendorf. So, the Sherpas of Khumbu are unable to cultivate any crop during this period. On the other hand, the Sherpas of Solu and Pharak are able to cultivate both winter and summer crops. During winter they produce wheat and barley while during summer they cultivate buckwheat, maize and potato. The Sherpas of Khumbu get only a short span of time, from middle April to early Octobar for cultivation. In most of the villages the Sherpas grow bitter buckwheat, potatoes, turnips and coarse greens (1964:7).

Among the Sherpas of Khumbu "Potatoes form mainstay of Sherpa diet and economy" (*ibid*:8). According to Fürer-Haimendorf the potatoes entered Eastern Nepal from the gardens of European settlers in Darjeeling and the gardens of the British residency in Kathmandu (*ibid*: 8-9). In the light sandy soil of Khumbu the yield of potatoes is undoubtedly good.

> "Thus, the potato has revolutionized Sherpa economy. At a time when the old-established trade with Tibet is threatened by a new orientation in that country's economy and relations with its neighbours, the existence of this crop will at least prevent the Khumbu Sherpas from starving while they adjust themselves to the new condition, and may cushion the blow which any reduction

> or rerouting of the Tibetan trade with Nepal inevitably due to their economy" (*ibid:*11).

But again when Fürer-Haimendorf visited Khumbu in 1983 he found dramatic change of the economy of the Sherpas of Khumbu. The development of tourism has brought most of the changes in the economy of the Khumbu. From 1974 a large number of tourists started visiting this area. This helped the Sherpas to earn good amount of money. "Even women and adolescents worked for tourists within their home area and thereby saved themselves from trouble of going to Kathmandu and searching there for employment" (Fürer-Haimendorf 1984:117).

Ortner has also studied the Sherpas of Solu in Nepal. The Solu valley situated south of Khumbu, is in lower altitude with more moderate climate. The soil here is relatively fertile and spread over in gentle slopes. The Sherpas here devote most of their economic energy to agriculture (1979:13).

The Sherpas of Solu valley are terrace cultivators and also practice animal husbandry. So "The Sherpa economy may be characterized as one of mixed agriculture and animal husbandry, supplemented by cash from labour and trading venture" (Ortner *ibid*:14). Though the economy of the Sherpas of Solu is predominantly agricultural still both pastoralism and trade play important roles in the economy.

In another article Ortner has mentioned that a mixture agriculture and dairying supplemented by some petty trading and cash labour form the economic base of the Sherpas (1978:265-266).

The Sherpas here as seen by Ortner, grow in their garden beans, peas, radishes, squash, greens, garlic and chili. They also produce barley, wheat and of course potatoes. But according to Ortner potato was introduced here only 100 years ago, and the seeds were brought from the garden of the British Ambassador in Sikkim. Corn is also grown. Squash is also introduced in recent years.

> The Sherpas, having contact with so many exotic nationalities, are rather adventurous about growing new foods, although in the manner of preparing them they all tend to boil down (as it were) to the same thing (1979:15).

Most of the cultivable land in the Sherpa region of Nepal is rocky. So, one of the most important job for preparing a cultivable land ready for cultivation, is to clear the rocks from the bed of the land.

The Sherpas inhabiting different areas of Nepal also have different occupations. Agriculture, animal husbandry and trade were their traditional occupations. In Khumbu region the Sherpas are depending on livestock rearing since time immemorial as they are considering it as one of the most profitable occupations. They move from place to place for grazing their animals. So, they lead a transhumance mode of life. "They graze their cattle though transhumance system in which seasonal migration of domesticated livestock and their herders for the purpose of grazing at different pasturers at different time of the year between highlands or summer land (*yar sa*) and low land or winter grazing land (*lun sa*) has been practiced (source: *internet*). The animals they keep are yak, *nak*, *zhum* and *zopkyo*. Out of these they use yak and *zopkyo* for carrying goods from one place to another, and other two animals (*nak* and *zhum*) for milk. They also had trade with Tibet. But now the young Sherpas prefer trekking, mountaineering and trade. But the educated youths love to get a service.

Sacherer while studying the Sherpa of Rolwaling of Nepal has found the traditional base of the Sherpa economy, "was potato agriculture and yak rearing, supplemented with man-carried trade in other regions of Nepal and Tibet" (1981:158). Because of the extreme climate, the Sherpas of Rolwaling had no option but to device a unique system of rotation of crops and herds based on changes of altitude. To operate this sytem they have built three large villages and three yak camps in three separate altitudes so that the Sherpa population of Rolwaling can be accommodated there to carrying on their economic activities (*ibid*: 158). Touring was also another important economic activity of the Sherpas of Rolwaling. Here in this area the Sherpas did not have opportunity to come in contact with tourist activities. Till 1972 Rolwaling was closed to "all mountaineering and tourist groups", and so, the Sherpas here became economically backward in comparison to Sherpas of other regions (*ibid:* 160).

> The fall of 1974 saw the first large scale visitations by foreign tourists who even at that time, outnumbered the local residents at the height of the season. Since then, ever increasing numbers of them have come as Rolwaling has gained an international reputation as one of the most traditional and beautiful Nepalese tourist sports (*ibid*).

As already said earlier that besides agriculture, the Sherpas of Nepal were and still are involved in animal husbandry and trade. According to Fürer-Haimendorf the Sherpas of Nepal, particularly of Khumbu region,

> regard the breeding of yak and other cattle for nobler occupation. No other form of property has quite the same prestige value as a herd of yak, and rich men, who would never put their hand to a hoe or sickle, unhesitatingly undergo the hardships of grazing their herds for weeks and months on high pastures (1964:11).

Still they cannot be considered as the pastoral people. To them yak breeding is one of their many economic choices. Apart from using these animals for their own purposes like using diary products or use them as pack and draught animals, they also sell these animals, particularly their calves. These calves are mostly from Tibetan bull (*Chang*) and female yak (*nak*). "The female cross-breeds (*zhum)* give more milk than yak-cows (*nak*) and the male cross-breeds (*zopkyo*) are more manageable pack and draught-animals than pure yak" (*ibid*:12).

Ortner has also found animal husbandry as an important economic resource among the Sherpas of Nepal. According to Ortner the Sherpas of Solu keep cow, yak, *zom*, *zopkyo*. They also sell the diary products like butter, cards, yoghurt, some kind of dry cheese etc. and earn a good amount of money. They also use yak as pack and draught animal (1979: 16-17).

Trade with Tibet was and is an important economic pursuit of the Sherpas of Khumbu. Because of this trade the Sherpas of Khumbu achieved a standard of living far superior to many other communities of Nepal like the Rais, Tamang, Gurung and the Magan living in the middle ranges of Eastern Nepal (Fürer-Haimendorf 1964:13).

> It was the trade with Tibet which gave the Sherpas the chance of acquiring valuable jewellery, clothing, household goods and ritual objects of Tibetan and Chinese origin, while the many journeys connected with this trade, kept them in touch with the aesthetic and intellectual interests of their Tibetan neighbours (*ibid*).

The Sherpas of Khumbu did not have many goods for the markets of Tibet but they acted as middlemen. Moreover, at that time the Nepalese government by an order prohibited the Sherpas of Solu for going to Tibet market for trade after crossing the Nangpa La Pass at an altitude of 18,000 ft., the route that the Sherpas of Khumbu followed. This gave the Sherpas of Khumbu a monopoly of trade to along the Nangpa La route (*ibid*). During trade the Sherpas used to import salt and wool from Tibet market and used to export grain, butter, cattle, paper, hides, sugar and different other Indian commodities.

When the Chinese occupied Tibet the border between Nepal and Tibet was closed, and naturally the trade of the Sherpas with the Tibet was stopped. After some years the Sherpas were allowed "to dispose their wares at the Chinese trade depot in Dingri where prices were unpredictable with no possibility to bargain" (1984: 23). This was definitely a big set back for the Sherpas. However, development of tourism and the Himalayan mountaineering helped them to compensate their loss in trade.

In another article Fürer-Haimendorf has mentioned the Sherpas of Namche Bazar and also the Bhotias of Walongchung and Mugu, the Takhalis of Tukche and the Taralis of Tichurong "developed trade as their central economic interest while the people of Humla pursued it as an occupation intimately intertwined with their pastoral activities" (1978: 339).

The village Khumbu where Brower also studied the Sherpas, is situated in the high altitude of the Himalayas in the eastern part of Nepal. The village is situated in a very difficult terrain with a harse climatic condition. "The area occupied by the people represent a tiny fraction of the fundamentally forbidden mountain landscape of Sagarmatha National Park, yet the area has maintained a sizeable population for hundreds of years (Brower 2003: 51).

The land of the Sherpas of Khumbu for cultivation and settlement, are scatteredly distributed in different altitudes and environment.

> "... but such a dispersal of activity requires control of a number of widely scattered tracts of land of different types. This accounts for the widespread ownership of houses in subsidiary settlements. It is also a reason behind variety of Sherpa land tenure arrangements. In addition to private ownership of houses, and walled fields, there are community controlled lands as well. These include the forest and grazing lands that lie outside the perimeter of the village proper, but within village boundaries, as well as grazing and hay-gathering areas up the main valleys and beyond the highest temporary settlements" (Brower 2003: 51).

To survive in such a hostile environment, the Sherpas of Khumbu have no option but to depend on their cultivable land and also on the forest. While cultivable land give them main food items like barley, buckwheat, potato and other vegetables, spices etc., forests give them varieties of products such as house-building materials like beams and poles, floorboards, framing timber, roofing materials, wood for making tools and kitchen implements, and also pack-saddles etc., grass for broom, fruits, mushrooms, condiments, tea, medicinal plants, aromatic leaves etc. Forests are also main grazing field for their animals throughout the year (Brower 2003:52).

The traditional occupations of the Sherpas of Khumbu, Nepal, according to Brower were agriculture, trade and animal husbandry. For transportation, particularly in the high altitude areas and also for trade, yak is essential for them. Brower states—

> "Yak-keeping was a part of that tradition, and is probably the oldest occupation. Along with agriculture and trade, animal husbandary enabled the Sherpa to live in a forbidding environment, mostly rock and ice" (2003:1-3).

The present-day Sherpas of Khumbu have multifarious occupations besides their traditional occupations like agriculture, trade and animal husbandary. Apart from their traditional occupations, the Sherpas here remain engaged as "expedition climber, hotel keeper, tourist guide, government worker, globe-trottering, traders, politician etc. These new jobs reflect the major changes that have come to the area over last few decades" (*ibid*:3). Brower also thinks that the present day economy of the Sherpas has become somewhat complicated because of the tourism (*ibid*: 54).

Because the Sherpas of Eastern Nepal, particularly in the Solu-Khumbu region, live in the undulating hilly terrain of the high Himalayas, they get very small geographical areas for cultivation and other purposes. Brower has also marked this.

According to Brower,

> "Although high altitude and steep gradients impose constrain on Sherpas' use of environment, these same factors make for opportunities as well. A series of micro-environment is created by variation in altitude, aspect and landscape history. Different locations undergo the sequence of seasonal changes in different times and at varying intensifies" (*ibid*: 51).

In fact the Sherpas of Khumbu also intelligently and wisely take advantage of these sequential changes and undertake different agricultural activities like ploughing, planting, harvesting etc. during the time they get in their high altitude habitat and also other sustainable activities "through an extended seasonal period in a number of different locations, and thus both increase the productivity of a relatively small labour pool, and reduce the risk of total crop failure or other environmental disaster" (*ibid*).

In the cultivable land they possess, the Sherpas of Khumbu utilize these for the cultivation of different crops like potatos, buckwheat, barley, hardy vegetables like cabbages, white tunip, leafy vegetables, garlic, spices, chilli, etc. At present the Sherpas of Khumbu have given stress on the cultivation of potato, and potato (*rigi*) has somewhat disrupted the production of barley and buckwheat which were grown in abundance in the past. Brower thinks that potato is not very old among the Sherpas of Khumbu. They probably got potato from the west (*ibid*: 54). But according to Hooker potato entered Khumbu area from Darjeeling (1854: 167). Introduction of potato has revolutionized the Sherpa agriculture and social system, as the same grows in abundance, and has almost become staple food in Khumbu. Normally, three varieties of potato (*rigi*) are grown in Khumbu area, and these three varieties are *maru* (red), *ceru* (yellow) and *bikas* (an improved variety in Nepal). No doubt to the Sherpas the red variety (*maru*) is the tastiest and more nutritious, still the present day the Sherpas prefer *rigi ceru* (Yellow) and *rigi bikas* varieties (Brower 2003: 54-59). In addition to potato, barley is also an important food for the Sherpas of Khumbu.

Trade as also an important economic pursuit of the Sherpas of Khumbu, is also found by Brower. According to her

> The Sherpa of Khumbu have traditionally dominated the local trade across their stretch of mountains, both acting profitably as middlemen in low-land-Tibet exchange, and also trading their own locally produced items, such as dried potatoes, which are taken to Tibet or Sherpa-made textiles, which are traded south (2003: 58).

They are a part of brotherhood of trans-Himalayan traders who had their settlements along the crest of the Himalayas. Brower also marked that the Sherpas change the character of their trade along with the change of the demand for different types of commodities "as permeability of political boundaries tightens and loosens, and as the other economic options available to Sherpa vary accordingly" (*ibid*: 59).

Domestic animals are also very important in the life of the Sherpas of Khumbu. Though only a few families depend mainly on the livestock, still cattle are absolutely essential to every economic activity of the Sherpas here, like agriculture, trade etc. and "every other facit of both traditional and transitional Sherpa life" (2003: 93).

No. 1: Collection data with a backdrop of flower plantation

No. 2: A local Buddhist monastery

No. 3: Road side decoration ahead of a Buddhist festival

No. 4: A Buddhist 'stupa'

No. 5: An elderly Sherpa couple in front of their house with the lady wearing local dress named 'Baku'

No. 6: A young Sherpa nuclear family

No. 7: Village Primary School under the Darjeeling District School Board

No. 8: Author (right) with a Sherpa informant

No. 9: Sherpa women working in a kitchen garden

No. 10: Flower plantation with a nursery in the back drop

No. 11: A nursery inside flower plantation field; sheds are used to avoid direct sunlight

No. 12: Road carved through bushes and shrubs leading to a house

No. 13: A new built office building waiting for inauguration

No. 14: A double storied house with slope tin roof

No. 15: A residential house of a economically well off Sherpa

No. 16: School going children

No. 17: A village grocery shop

No. 18: Local 'hut' with pig shed outside covered with wood

6
THE DIVISIONS IN THEIR SOCIETY

Among the Sherpas of both Darjeeling and Sikkim we have not seen any social division like sub-tribe, moity, phratry etc. This tribal society of both areas is directly divided into a number of exogamous clans, known as *ru*. But Gangopadhyay in connection with the Sherpas of Sikkim, has stated that this tribal group is divided into two endogamous divisions known as the Sherpas and the Yukpas. Among these two divisions the former, that is, the Sherpas enjoy a higher social status than the later. Again these two divisions are again sub-divided into a number of exogamous clans known as *ru* (1993: 155). But we did not find such type groups among the Sherpas either in Darjeeling or in Sikkim. Our Sherpa informants in both areas clearly stated that their tribe was divided into a number of *ru*. No other division was present. Mitra also has not found any group among the Sherpas of Darjeeling except only clan (*ru*) (2008: 1183). Bisht and Bankoti have on the other hand, mentioned the same two endogamous divisions: (i) the Sherpas and (ii) the Yukpas as mentioned by Gangopadhyay. Among these two groups, the former is superior to the later. These two groups are gain sub-divided into a number of exogamous clans (*ru*) (2004:1489). But they have not mentioned any such divisions or groups among the Sherpas of Nepal. According to them in Nepal "The Sherpas are divided into many *thars* or septs ...." (*ibid:* 1483).

In connection with the Sherpas of Nepal Fürer-Haimendorf also has not mentioned any social divisions of the Sherpas except clans or *ru* (1964: 18-38).

In his second book on the Sherpas of Nepal published in 1984, he has stated that the Sherpa society in Nepal in un-stratified. According to him the Sherpas have several exogamous clans (1984: 27-33).

Bista is of the view that the Sherpa society of Nepal is divided into a number of exogamous clans. But

> These many clans fit into two endogamous groups, *khadev* and *khemdu*, the former being of higher status. All members of one or the other of these divisions are equal. They can share a common cup among themselves and can intermarry freely so long as they do not violate the restriction of marrying within their own clan. If, for example a *khadev* man or woman marries or lives for a long period of time with a *khamendu*, he or she will lose the higher status and be forced to live as a *khamendu* (1976:163).

In connection with the social equality of all residents in a Sherpa village in Nepal, Fürer-Haimendorf opines that there are two classes of people present there. One class of people considered inferior by both the Sherpas and the Khambas. These people are the immigrants from Tibet. This inferior class of people are known as the Khamendeu meaning mouth-bad. The opposite to Khamendeu is Khadeu or mouth-good. The Khadeu class of people will never "drink from a vessel touched by the mouth of any person of Khamendeu status", though the Khadeu people "freely eat the food cooked and served by members of Khamendeu class and the only restriction on commensality is the rule that those may not drink from a cup which passes in usual Sherpa fashion from mouth to mouth" (1964:35). Fürer-Haimendrof has also mentioned that there is a ban on intermarriage between these two classes of people "…any one of superior status who entertains permanent sexual relations with a person of Khamendeu class, loses his or her Khadeu status, and henceforth treated as Khamendeu" (*ibid*). The Yemba is another group of lower class people. Both the Khamendeu Khambas and the Yembas are debarred from becoming Lamas (*ibid*).

Ortner has also not mentioned any social division among the Sherpas other than the exogamous patrilineal clans. According to Ortner the Sherpa society of Nepal is directly divided into a number of clans without having any other social groupings (1979:18). But T.B. Subba has stated that the Sherpa society of Darjeeling is broadly divided into groups, Khadev and Khemedu. Both are again divided into a number of clans. "If any marriage takes place between these two groups the member of the former group will lcse his or her status and fall in the second group" (1989:46). But J.R. Subba has not found any such social groupings like the Khadev and the Khemendu among the Sherpas of Sikkim. According to him clan (*ru*) is the basic element of their social structure (2008:283).

Ru (Clan) Organization

Among the Sherpas of our studied villages of both Darjeeling in West Bengal and South District in Sikkim, the clan is called as *ru*. The Sherpa society of these four villages have a number of clans. While some of the clans are numerically quite large, the others have lesser population. In a village the number of clans increased with the coming of the different clan members from other villages. The members come to the village either through marital ties or through immigration or for business or other purposes and finally settled in this village. Among the Sherpas the clans (*ru*) are exogamous in nature. The members of a particular clan are not permitted to marry in their own clan. Marriage in the same clan is considered as the heinous sin and incestuous. No Sherpa will ever think of marrying or having sex with any member of his or her own clan. So, marriage regulation is one of the important functions of the Sherpa clans or *ru* as these clans are exogamous in character. The Sherpas of these two areas do not consider their clans having higher or lower status. To them these are of the same status whether or not they are numerically strong or weak. Fürer-Haimendorf in connection with the clans of the Sherpas of Nepal, writes,

> None of these clans lay any claim to seniority or higher status on the ground of prior arrival in Solu and Khumbu, nor is numerical predominance of the one or other clan in any specific area considered a significant indication that its members were the first settlers (1964:18-19).

Among the Sherpas of both Darjeeling and South Districts, the Sherpa term for the clan is *ru*, that is, 'bone' because, according to them, every Sherpa inherits his or her father's bone. Fürer-Haimendorf has also endorsed this view. According to him, "The idea is that children inherit their father's bones, and that all descendants of one ancestor in the male line are hence of 'one bone' "(*ibid*:20). So, the Sherpas belonging to 'one bone' are considered as blood related. And for this reason those Sherpa who belong to the same *ru* or clan, cannot marry one another nor can they indulge in sex relation between them. This rule of clan exogamy is present among the Sherpas of both Darjeeling and South Districts as well as among the Sherpas of Nepal. Every Sherpa will avoid this sort of incestuous relation. During our study in four villages – two from Darjeeling and two from South District, we failed to unearth a single case of intra-clan sex-relation or marriage. Fürer Haimendorf also "failed to discover a single case of even a fleeting amorous attachment between members of the same clan ..." (*ibid*:20). However, theoretically if at all such incidence happens then the couples as well as their respective family are supposed to face dire consequences. Excommunication, fine etc. are usually imposed on them as with such a marriage the couple and their respective families are supposed to have committed incest and sin, and also defamed their own society..

Among the Sherpas of our studied areas there is no uni-clan village. The Sherpas belonging to different clans live in the village. That means, the villages are all multi-clan villages. The Sherpas having a particular clan but living in different villages, consider themselves as blood related, i.e. agnatic kins. So, they cannot marry one another. That means if the Paldorje clan members are found to live in three different villages, X, Y and Z, and even if the villages are far away from one another, the members of this clan of X village cannot marry the same clan members living in Y or Z village and *vice versa.* This is because they treat themselves as agnatic kins. Fürer-Haimendorf has also found such prohibition among the Sherpas of a particular clan living in different villages of Nepal. According to him

> All Sherpas of the same *ru*, irrespective of the distance which may separate their villages and the impossibility of tracing genealogical links, consider themselves as agnetic kins and debarred from marriage. Sexual relations between clan members are regarded as incest and are virtually unheard of (1964:20).

Among the Sherpas of Darjeeling and Sikkim, the clan (*ru*) descent is routed through the male line. This means the children always get their father's clan. The mother's clan has no much role to play so far as the clan descent is concerned, while the sons bear the father's clan throughout their life, the daughters hold the same so long they remain unmarried. After marriage they of course, accept their husbands' clan.

Among the Sherpas of Nepal as Ortner further stated that the "true Sherpa clans now number fifteen, derived by fission from an original set of four "proto-clans" two of which have remained conceptually intact under single clan names, thirteen of which are divisions from the two other original clans" (1979:18). Ortner on referring to Oppitz, further states that

> These thirteen now function as full-fledged clans with distinct names, exogamy rules, but they form two sets (of eight and five clans, respectively), each set retaining a tradition of its common descent from, a proto-clan and thus not intermarrying among themselves (*ibid*).

As the Sherpas of Darjeeling originally migrated from Sikkim and some from Nepal. Those who came from Sikkim, were originally the settlers of Nepal, even then among them there is no such concept like core clan as mentioned by Fürer-Haimendorf (1964:18-19) and Ortner (1979:18-19). Both of them have reported the presence of core clans which are considered as "the full-fledged Sherpa clan in every respect". Originally, these core clans migrated from southwest Tibet about 150 years ago. But in Nepal also there are clans which came into existence because of the marriage of the Sherpas with other ethnic groups in Nepal. In both Darjeeling and Sikkim also we get the same picture. Here, like Nepal, some Sherpas have married some non-sherpas like the Bhutias, Lepcha and some other caste groups of the Nepali like the Pradhan, Limbu, Subba, Rai, Thapa, Gurung etc. These non-Sherpa people are now staying with the Sherpas and consider themselves as the members of the Sherpa families. But these non-Sherpa clans do not have the same social status as those of the original Sherpa clans. Here also like those of Nepal they "Nevertheless style themselves as Sherpa, formed themselves into exogamous clan units, and established continuous marriage relationship with other Sherpa clans" (Ortner 1979:19).

No doubt the *Lama* clan is considered a bit higher in status, but all the original Sherpa clans of all the three regions, Nepal, Sikkim and Darjeeling, have the same social status.

In connection with the clans of the Sherpas Oppitz is of opinion that in Nepal "the first colonization is identical with the separate movements of the first clans to arrive" (1977:234). He further states that the general pattern of settling is as follows:

- Each of the different clans selects a clearly defined locality for settlement and demarcates the boundaries of its clan property;
- The number of clan's members increases and the small settlements develop into first discernable clan-villages, the centers of clan activities;
- From the first clan-villages new satellite settlements are founded within the confines of a clan's area;

- The new settlements grow and become independent clan-villages;
- The dislocation from the old villages produces naturally an increasing disintegration of the original homogenous proto-clans; and
- The final result of disintegration is the split of the proto-clans into several sub-clans which by adopting new clan names, become independent social units (*ibid*).

Oppitz again mentions that two–proto-clans the Minnagpa and Thimmi, out of the four, first of all occupied and established their settlements in the eastern and western parts of Khumbu while the other two proto-clans Serwa and Charpa moved towards Solu without lapse of time.

> In the course of their geographical dispersion only the first two proto-clans mentioned, split up into a number of independent sub-clans which however, preserve to the present day common ancestry. This can be seen from the fact that members of sub-clans belonging to a common proto-clan do not intermarry, just as if they still were one single clan, which by definition strictly follows the rules of clan exogamy. The descendants of the four proto-clans, including their different split branches—lineages or sub-clans—now form the core of Sherpa society, in rank, in age and in number (*ibid*).

Among the Sherpas the membership of a clan

> does not involve any definite obligation other than the observance of the rule of exogamy and the worship of the clan deities three times a year, it is of supreme importance as being the indispensible symbol of a person's status within the core Sherpa society (Fürer-Haimendorf 1964:23).

That some non-Sherpas penetrated into the Sherpa society by virtue of marriage with the Sherpas, has also been noticed by Fürer-Haimendorf. He has also seen "the presence of so strong 'Gurung' element in Sherpa society" (*ibid*:25). Even in Nepal though the number of core clan remaining the same as no new agnatic clan was added, still "fresh blood is continuously being introduced into it by marriages between men of the old Sherpa clans and women of immigrant families" (*ibid*: 26). This means that in all the three regions, Darjeeling, Sikkim and Nepal, the Sherpas do practice inter-community marriages. Here, in Darjeeling and Sikkim though they mostly marry in their own group, but cases are there when the Sherpas married non-Sherpas like the Bhutias Lepcha and different caste groups of the Nepalese like the Gurung, Limbu, Pradhan, Thapa, Rai and others.

In our studied villages of both Darjeeling and Sikkim we get a number of clans present among the Sherpas while undertaking household census and drawing genealogy in the Sherpa families. In the village Sherpaguri in Kalimpong, Darjeeling, we have got 22 clans while at Sherpapur village, also of Kalimpong Sub-Division of Darjeeling, we also get 22 clans. But in our studied villages of South District, Sikkim, i.e. Sherpagaon and Sherpahat we find the Sherpas having 25 clans in each village. Some of these clans are common to all the four villages while some other clans are found only in a particular village and not in other villages. Again some of the clans are found in two or three villages but not in the remaining villages. Those clans which are common to all the four of our studied villages, are Ghola, Goparma, *Lama* Sherpa, Pankarma, Odomba, Rickpho, Shalaka, and Temang. All these clans are found among the Sherpas of all the four villages we have studied. This means that these clans are found among the Sherpas of both Darjeeling and Sikkim. Again the clans like Chukule, Noumi, Lepcha and Bhutias are found among the Sherpas of Sherpapur village of Darjeeling and Sherpagaon and Sherpahat villages of Sikkim. Similarly, clans like Thapa, Pradhan and Khambochan are present among the Sherpa of Sherpaguri village of Darjeeling and also in the two villages, Sherpagaon and Sherpahat of Sikkim. There is only one clan, Pianasha, common to the Sherpas of the two villages, Sherpaguri and Sherpapur of Darjeeling; but in case of the Sherpas of the two villages, Sherpagaon and Sherpahat of Sikkim, a number of clans are common. These clans are Cherithakpo, Gangthakpo, Haluri, Jelibork, Kongsherpa, Kulunge, Kulungsherpa, Luma Rimbuche, Lhasa, Nonghola, Rakha, Sikkimese, Subba and Thakpo. These clans are common to the two villages of Sikkim we studied. Chuyeni is the only clan which is common to the Sherpas of Sherpapur village of Darjeeling and Sherpahat village of Sikkim. Apart from these common clans, the Sherpas of the individual village have their specific clans which are not found among the Sherpas of the other three villages. For example the Sherpas of Sherpaguri village have such clans like Affangme, Chaba, Gurung, Payame, Shari *Lama* and Yakumdghola. These Sherpa clans are not found in other three villages. Similarly, clans like Durbigha, *Lama* Gorma, Nyunpa, and Sunar are found only in Sherpapur village. In Sikkim the clan Pradhey is traceable only among the Sherpas of Sherpagaon village and the clan *Lama* Limbu only at Sherpahat village. It is thus seen that while some of the Sherpa clans are found among the Sherpas of more than one village, some other clans are found among the Sherpas of one village only. The latter clans are not found among the Sherpas of other villages (Table 6.1).

Table 6.1: List of the Sherpa clans of our studied villages in Darjeeling district and Sikkim

Darjeeling		*Sikkim*	
Sherpaguri	*Sherpapur*	*Sherpagaon*	*Sherpahat*
Affangme	Basmat	*Bhutia	*Bhutia
*Bhutia	*Bhutia	Cherithakpo	Cherithakpo
Chaba	Chukte	Chukale	Chukale
Chuyemi	Chukule	Chuyemi	Gangthakpo
Dhakal	Chuyemi	Gangthakpo	Ghola
Ghola	Durbigha	Ghola	Goparna
Gholey	Garje	Goparna	Haluri
Goparna	Ghole/Ghola	Haluri	Jalibork
*Gurung	Goparna	Jalibork	Khambachan
Khambochan	Lama Sherpa	Khambachan	Kong Sherpa
Lama Sherpa	*Lepcha	Kong Sherpa	Kulunge
*Lepcha	Noumi	Kulung Sherpa	Kulung Sherpa
Monger	Nyunpa	Kulunge	Lama Gorma
Odomba	Odamba	Lama Rimbuche	*Lama Limbu
Pankarma	Ongba	Lama Sherpa	Lama Rimbuche
Payame	Pan Karma	Lhasa	Lama Sherpa
Phinasha	Paya	*Lepcha	Lhasa
*Pradhan	Pianasha	Nonghola	*Lepcha
*Rai	*Rai	Noumi	Nonghola
Rickpho	Rickpho	Odamba	Noumi
Shalaka	Shalaka	Pankarma	Odomba
*Sharma	Shorey	*Pradhan	Pan Karma
Shari Lama	Sunar	Pradhey	*Pradhan
Temang	Temang	*Rai	*Rai
*Thapa		Rakha	Rakha
Yakumdghola		Rickpho	Ricktho
		Shalaka	Shalaka
		* Sikkimese	*Sikkimese
		Temang	* Subba
		Thakto	Temang
		* Thapa	Thakto
			*Thapa

*Note:** These are not Sherpa clans. These are of different neighbouring communities like the Bhutias, Lepcha and the Nepali who were married to the Sherpas.

Source: Field study by the authors.

Apart from our data we also come to know about the presence of clans in the Sherpa society of Darjeeling, Sikkim and Nepal from the writings of different scholars. T.B. Subba has mentioned about the presence of a number of clans among the Sherpa of Darjeeling (1984:46). Mitra has also found about clans like Chiula, Ganza, Gola, Goarna, Khambaza, Lama, Pinasa, Salakha, Thaktu, Sang-gu, Lukpa, Mormin-Cho, Chu-Sherwa, Lak-Shinda etc. among the Sherpa of Darjeeling District (Table 6.1).

In Sikkim, as mentioned by Gangopadhyay the Sherpa society is divided into a number of exogamous clans (*ru)* such as Shalakha, Rinasha, *Lama* Sherpa, Choyaba, Goperna etc. (1993: 155).

Bisht and Bankoti have also found different clans or septs (*thars*) among the Sherpas of Sikkim. Bisht and Bankoti have recorded clans like Lama, Chhusherwa, Chiyawa, Garja, Golae Goparra, Hirgoma, Lakshindu, Mendae, Mope, Dawa, Paldorje, Pankarma, Penasa, Salaka, Sagup, Serwa, and Yakut among the Sherpa of Nepal (2004:1483). J.R. Subba has also noted the some clans such as Shulakha, Phinasha, *Lama* Sherpa, Chayaba, Goperma etc. among the Sherpas of Sikkim (2008: 283).

Among the Sherpas of Nepal, Fürer-Haimendorf has traced out twenty one of such clans or *ru*. These twenty one clans are: Chiawa, Chusherwa, Gardza, Gole, Goparna, Jongdomba, Khambedze, Lakshindu, Lama, Lukpa, Mende, Munming, Nawa, Paldorje, Pankarma, Pinasa, Salaka, Shangup, Sherwa, Shire and Thaktu. But according to the notion of the Sherpas, as heard by Fürer-Haimendorf, the Sherpas of Nepal had eighteen such clans or *ru* in Khambu, Pharak and Solu regions. But he actually got the above twenty one clans (*ibid*: 19). Fürer-Haimendorf has also mentioned that some of the clans known by different names in different regions, are in fact identical. Thus, according to his informants the clans Paldorje and Shalaka are one and the same clan but this clan is known as Paldorje in Khumbu and Shalaka in Solu (*ibid*).

In both Darjeeling and South District some of the Sherpa clans have clan deities. They worship these deities once or twice a year. Only the numerically large clans organize these worships. Those clans which have very few members in the village, do not venture for such worship. Even in case of the clan deity worship by the large clans, all the clan members of the village may not always take part in such worships because of the financial or some other reasons. The worship is conducted by a Lama. These sorts of worship lasts for a day only. Only the members of a particular clan who organize such worship, take part in it. Usually, the members of the other clans or non-Sherpa do not participate in these worships. These worships are arranged in a small scale basis.

The clans of the Sherpas of Nepal also, besides obeying the rule of exogamy, worship certain deities thrice a year and this gives each Sherpa a definite status in the core Sherpa society (*ibid:23*). Fürer-Haimendorf has further stated that the clans play an important role in the religious activities. "...they do appear as distinct units in a limited number of ritual matters" (*ibid*). Among these people of Nepal the members of every clan

> "Recognize certain mountain gods as their specific protective deities and on some occasions clan members resident in the same village, may combine for the worship of such clan deities" (*ibid*).

These deities who are treated as the "Lords of the Soil" (*Zidag*), have inferior status, and they occupy in the lower rank in the hierarchy of the Buddhist deities. They are worshipped in the months of May, August and October. Among the Sherpas of Nepal the clans do not have any official to organize the co-operation of the clan members on a permanent basis nor any priest to perform *lhachetu* (*lha*=god; *chetu*=ceremony) on a regular basis. The celebration of the ancestral deities of the clan by several members belonging to a particular clan, is only a matter of convenience and also "a way to invest the rite with additional solemnity" (*ibid*:23). But such celebration is not prescribed by the tradition, and therefore, it is optional to the members of the clan. All the families belonging to a particular clan may not organize such celebration jointly or take part in it.

Fürer-Haimendorf in connection with the clan (*ru*) of the Sherpas of Nepal in his second book, '*The Sherpa Transformed*', has also mentions that among the Sherpas of different villages, the same clan is known in different names. He has cited the example of Paldorje clan of Khumbu village. This clan of Khumbu village is known as Salaka at Solu. So, the members of these two clans observe the taboos of clan endogamy because "they are regarded as consanguineous kin folk" (1984:28).

Ortner through her study on the Sherpas of Solu valley of Nepal, has informed that the "whole Sherpa society today is divided into named, exogamous, patrilineal clans. Every person inherits a clan affiliation of his or her father and must marry someone from of different clan affiliation" (1979:18). According to Ortner 90 per cent of the present day Sherpa population of her area of study belong to some clans which were descended from the original immigrant families. Ortner has further stated that among the Sherpas of Solu, Nepal, there are core clans which originally descended from the original immigrants who came from South-west Tibet about 150 years ago. They never married in their own clan nor did they marry members of the non-Sherpa groups. There are some other clans among the Sherpas which were created by the intermarriage with other ethnic-groups of Nepal. They consider themselves also as the Sherpas. These clans have retained their exogamous characters and go on marrying with other Sherpa clans (*ibid:* 19). Ortner has further noted the informal hierarchical order among the Sherpa clans. Among these clans found by Ortner, *Lama* clan is considered as the highest specially by its own members. The clan, Gordza is treated as lower one as they were formerly a blacksmith caste-like group. But this form of hierarchy was quite informal except "for the undisputed economic and political dominance of the *Lama* clan. Otherwise all the core clans have almost equal status" (*ibid*). Among the Sherpas marriage between the members of the core clans and those of first ring creates no problem. Again "marriage between members of the full Sherpa clans and members of clans deriving from mixture with other ethnic groups, is frowned upon but not forbidden" (*ibid*). Normally, the members of the mixed clans marry the members of other mixed clan. In some cases marriage of the members of the mixed clans with those of first ring clans are also found. But marriage of the members of the mixed clan with those of the core clans is very rare. Ortner has also found that the primary function of the clan is to regulate marriage. While a Sherpa adheres to the rule of clan exogamy, he or she also avoid marrying in his or her mother's and grand mother's clan, though it is not strictly adhered to. Among the Sherpas of Nepal, as Ortner has found the clans divided into lineages.

Goldstein in connection with the Sherpas of Nepal, mentions that these people have a number of patri-clans. They are exogamous in nature and they are not "corporately organized and seem to function exclusively with respect to marriage exogamy" (1975: 58). Goldstein has found three clans the members of these are prohibited to eat beef or pork or chicken; but a few of them sometimes eat chicken. But they are allowed to eat mutton. The clans here follow the patrilineal rule of descent (*ibid*).

Bista is of the view that the Sherpa society of Nepal is divided into a number of clans. These clans are exogamous in nature, and so the members are compelled to get married outside their own clan (1976: 163). In Darjeeling and Sikkim also the Sherpas never marry in his or her own clan (that is his or her father's clan). He or she will also not marry in his or her mother's and grand mother's clan.

Clan Population

As already said the Sherpas of Kalimpong, Darjeeling has a number of clans. Each clan includes a number of the Sherpas as members. But the number of members is variable from clan to clan. That mean all the clans do not have equal number of the Sherpa population.

At Sherpapur village of Darjeeling there are a good number of clans. These clans have a total population of 351. Out of these Sherpa population the clan Rickpho has the highest population (21.37%). Next to Rickpho, comes Paya which has covered a total of 16.52 per cent. The third and fourth positions in this regard, have been secured by Durbigha and Gorja clans which have taken in their fold 13.96 per cent and 11.68 per cent respectively of the Sherpa population of this village. There are three more clans among the Sherpas of this village such as Pankarma (8.83%), Odomba (7.41%) and Chukte (6.27%) which have population between 5.00 per cent and 10.00 per cent. The rest of the clans have less than 5.00 per cent population (Table 6.2).

Now, we come down to the male Sherpa population of this village, Sherpapur.

Here we see that the clan, Rickpho has the highest Sherpa population (25.58%). Paya clan has the next higher population (22.67%). Three clans, Gorje, Odomba and Chukte have population between 5.00 per cent and 10.00 per cent. The rest of the clans among the Sherpas of Sherpapur have less than 5.00 per cent male population (Table 6.2).

Among the Sherpa females of this village, the clan, Rickpho has the highest population (17.32%). Next come clans like Pankarma and Gorje, each with 13.41 per cent Sherpa female population. The third position in this regard, has been secured by Durbigha clan (12.85%). The clan, Paya also has significant strength (10.61%). There are two clans, namely, Odomba and Chukte which have population ranging from 5.00 per cent to 10.00 per cent. The rest of the clans have population 5.00 per cent.

From the above table (Table 6.2) it is clearly seen that only four clans namely, Rickpho, Gorje, Durbigha and Paya covers 63.53 per cent clan population where as the remaining 20 clans have secured only 36.47 per cent of the Sherpa population of the village, Sherpapur.

At Sherpaguri village of Kalimpong, Darjeeling, the Sherpas also have a good number of clans. The Ghola clan among them has the highest population. Out of a total of 217 clans population, 16.59 per cent belong to this clan. The clan, *Lama* Sherpa has the next higher population (14.75%). Another clan, e.g. Pankarma has covered 13.82 per cent of the

Table 6.2: Sex-wise Distribution of Population belonging to different Sherpa clans

Name of the Clans	*Villages of Darjeeling*											
	Sherpapur						*Sherpaguri*					
	Person		*Male*		*Female*		*Person*		*Male*		*Female*	
	No.	*%*	*No.*	*%*	*No.*	*%*	*No.*	*%*	*No.*	*%*	*No.*	*%*
1. Ghola	5	1.42	4	2.33	1	0.56	36	16.59	26	24.07	10	9.17
2. Rickpho	75	21.37	44	25.58	31	17.32	3	1.38	—	—	3	2.75
3. Lama Sherpa	1	0.28	—	—	1	0.56	32	14.75	18	16.67	14	12.84
4. Pankarma	31	8.83	7	4.07	24	13.41	30	13.82	19	17.59	11	10.09
5. Shalaka	13	3.70	5	2.91	8	4.47	13	5.99	7	6.48	6	5.50
6. Gorje	41	11.68	17	9.88	24	13.41	—	—	—	—	—	—
7. Goparna	2	0.57	—	—	2	1.12	8	3.69	6	5.56	2	1.83
8. Rai	2	0.57	—	—	2	1.12	4	1.84	—	—	4	3.67
9. Shari Lama	—	—	—	—	—	—	18	8.29	7	6.48	11	10.09
10. Odomba	26	7.41	13	7.56	13	7.26	—	—	—	—	—	—
11. Khambochan	—	—	—	—	—	—	13	5.99	7	6.48	6	5.50
12. Pradhan	—	—	—	—	—	—	7	3.23	3	2.78	4	3.67
13. Chukte	22	6.27	11	6.40	11	6.15	—	—	—	—	—	—
14. Temang	2	0.57	—	—	2	1.12	4	1.84	—	—	4	3.67
15. Durbigha	49	13.96	26	15.12	23	12.85	—	—	—	—	—	—
16. Ghole	—	—	—	—	—	—	8	3.69	5	4.63	3	2.75
17. Paya	58	16.52	39	22.67	19	10.61	17	9.83	7	6.48	10	9.17
18. Others	24	6.84	6	3.49	18	10.06	24	11.06	3	2.78	21	19.27
Total	351	99.99	172	100.01	179	100.02	217	99.99	108	100.00	109	99.97

Source: Field study by the authors.

Sherpa population of this village. Out of the remaining clans of this village, clans like Shalaka (5.99%), Shari *Lama* (8.29%), Khambachan (5.99%) and Paya (7.83%) have the Sherpa population between 5.00 per cent and 10.00 per cent. The rest of the clans do have the Sherpa population but below 5.00 per cent.

Among the male Sherpas of this village the clan, Ghola has the highest population (24.07%). The clan, Pankarma comes next after covering 17.59 per cent of the total population of the Sherpa males of this village. *Lama* Sherpa clan has secured the third position in this regard with 16.67 per cent male population. Five clans, namely Shalaka, Goparna, Shari Lama, Khambachan, and Paya have male Sherpa population between 5.00 per cent and 10.00 per cent. The rest of the clans have male population below 5.00 per cent.

So far as the female Sherpa population of this village is concerned, the *Lama* Sherpa clan has the highest population (12.84%). The clans, Pankarma and Shari *Lama* have the next higher female Sherpa population,the numerical strength with each clan having 10.00 per cent of the total Sherpa female population. The third position in this regard has been secured by both Ghola and Paya clans each with 9.17 per cent female Sherpa population. Two clans, Shalaka and Khambachan have each 5.50 per cent. The rest of the clans have female Sherpa population below 5.00 per cent.

Table 6.2 shows that at Sherpaguri, only three Sherpa clans each of whom has more than 10.00 per cent population, have taken in their fold 45.16 per cent of the total population whereas the rest of the clans, total 23, have held 54.84 per cent of the total population of this village. Another interesting feature of the Sherpa population in these villages of Darjeeling, is that while some of the clans which are found in Sherpapur village such as Gorje, Odomba, Durbigha and Chukte, are not found in the village Sherpaguri. Again clans like Shari Lama, Khambachan, Pradhan and Ghole are found only at Sherpaguri and not at Sherpapur, whereas other clans are common in both villages.

Further it is also seen in case of some of the clans of Sherpapur that these have no male population, but these have the female population. For example, the clans *Lama* Sherpa, Goperna, Rai and Tawang do have female population but not the male population. Again at Sherpaguri village clans like Rickpho, Rai and Temang do not have male population, but have female population. These clans have come to these two villages from other villages on marriage. There is no clan in these two villages which has male population, but not the female population. All the others clans which have male population, also have female population.

In the South District of Sikkim one of the two studied villages of ours, is Sherpagaon. In this village the total Sherpa population of 340 are unevenly distributed among different clans of the Sherpas of this village. Out of these clans, *Lama* Sherpa has secured the highest population (25.59%) followed by two other clans, Khambachan and Goparna, each with 11.18 per cent Sherpa population. Numerically, the next position has been secured by the clan, Ghole. Two clans, namely Rickpho and Chukale have population between 5.00 per cent and 10.00 per cent. The rest of the clans, have less than 5.00 per cent population each (Table 6.3).

Among the Sherpa male population of this village the clan, *Lama* Sherpa has the highest male population strength (22.92%). Next comes the clan, Ghole which has a male population of 12.50 per cent. Khambachan comes next with 11.46 per cent of the total male population. The clan, Goparna has secured 10.29 per cent of the male population. There are two clans which have male population between 5.00 per cent and 10.00 per cent. The rest of the clans have less than 5.00 per cent population each.

In case of the Sherpa female population of this village (Table 6.3), the highest population is held also by the *Lama* Sherpa clan (29.05%). Next in order comes the clan, Goparna (12.16%) followed by the clan, Khambachan (11.49%). There are only two clans, Ghole and Rickpho which have population strength between 5.00 per cent and 10.00 per cent. The each of the remaining clans has population lying below 5.00 per cent.

It is clear from Table 6.3 that in the village Sherpagaon only four clans, namely, *Lama* Sherpa, Khambachan, Goparna and Ghola have jointly secured majority of the population (58.53%). The remaining 41.47 per cent are shared by all the other 28 clans.

Now, we come to the second studied village of Sikkim, Sherpahat. When we examine the clan population of the Sherpas of this village, we see that here also the clan, *Lama* Sherpa has the highest population (25.28%). The next higher population strength is held by the clan, Khambochan (12.22%) followed by Goparna (11.08%) and Ghola (10.28%). Only two clans, viz., Rickpho and Chukale have population between 5.00 per cent and 10 per cent. The each of the remaining clans has population below 5.00 per cent. Next we come to the Sherpa male population strength of the clans. In this village the clan, *Lama* Sherpa has the highest Sherpa male population (22.81%). The next higher male population is held by Ghola clan (13.45%) followed by the clan, Khambachan (11.11%).

There are four clans here at Sherpahat each of which has the population strength ranging from 5.00 per cent to 10.00 per cent. Each of the remaining clans has population below 5.00 per cent of the total. In case of the female Sherpa population we find that the *Lama* Sherpa clan has the highest female Sherpa population (27.62%). Next comes the clan, Khambachan with 13.26 per cent female population followed by the clan, Goparna (12.71%). There are two clans which have female Sherpa population ranging from 5.00 per cent to 10.00 per cent. All the remaining clans have quite low population strength each below 5.00 per cent of the total female Sherpa population of this village.

From this table (Table 6.3) it is clear that in this village (Sherpahat) there are only four clans which jointly hold 58.86 per cent of the total female Sherpa population of this village. That means majority of the female Sherpa population is held by these four clans only, while the remaining population (41.14%) are held by the remaining 28 clans.

It is thus seen that among all the clans of the Sherpas of both Darjeeling and Sikkim villages, only a few clans, may be three or four, hold the majority population whereas some other clans have significantly low population. In these two villages all the clans are not same. Some of the clans are different for different villages.

In South district, Sikkim the two studied villages, Sherpagaon and Sherpahat, have the same clans except two, Pradhaey at Sherpagaon and *Lama* Limbu at Sherpahat. The rest of the clans of these two villages are same.

In connection with the clan population we have included the non-Sherpa clan or ethnic groups like the Bhutias, Lepcha, Pradhan etc. as they are living in the Sherpa family after their marriage with the Sherpa members of the family.

Inter-Clan Marriage

As already said the clans (*ru*) of the Sherpas of both Darjeeling and Sikkim are exogamous. No one is allowed to marry in one's own clan. One must marry in the clan other than his or her clan. In Table 6.4 we have listed the inter-clan marriages among the Sherpa of the four studied villages, two from Darjeeling, West Bengal, while the other two from South District, Sikkim.

Table 6.3: Sex-wise Distribution of Population belonging to different Sherpa clans

Name of the Clans	Villages of Sikkim											
	Sherpagaon						Sherpahat					
	Person		Male		Female		Person		Male		Female	
	No.	%	No.	%	No.	%	No.	%	No.	%	No.	%
1. Lama Sherpa	87	25.59	44	22.92	43	29.05	89	25.28	39	22.81	50	27.62
2. Khambochan	39	11.47	22	11.46	17	11.49	43	12.22	19	11.11	24	13.26
3. Goparma	38	11.18	20	10.42	18	12.16	39	11.08	16	9.36	23	12.71
4. Ghola	35	10.29	24	12.50	11	7.43	36	10.28	23	13.45	13	7.18
5. Rickpho	24	7.06	12	6.25	12	8.11	25	7.10	10	5.85	15	8.29
6. Pankarma	13	3.82	8	4.17	5	3.38	13	3.69	5	2.92	8	4.42
7. Shalaka	7	2.06	3	1.56	4	2.70	7	1.99	3	1.74	4	2.21
8. Rakha	5	1.47	3	1.56	2	1.35	6	1.70	3	1.75	3	1.66
9. Thakto	5	1.47	3	1.56	2	1.35	6	1.70	4	2.34	2	1.10
10. Lama Rimbuchi	10	2.94	7	3.65	3	2.03	7	1.99	4	2.34	3	1.66
11. Chukale	17	5.00	11	5.73	6	4.05	19	5.40	11	6.93	8	4.42
12. Haluri	7	2.06	3	1.56	4	2.70	7	1.99	3	1.75	4	2.21
13. Lahsa	4	1.18	4	2.08	—	—	6	1.70	4	2.34	2	1.10
14. Gangthakpa	7	2.06	4	2.08	3	2.03	7	1.99	4	2.34	3	1.66
15. Kong Sherpa	13	3.82	9	4.69	4	2.70	13	3.69	9	5.26	4	2.21
16. Others	29	8.53	15	7.81	14	9.46	29	8.24	14	8.19	15	8.29
Total	340	10.00	192	100.00	148	99.99	352	100.04	171	99.99	181	100.00

Source: Field study by the authors.

In the village Sherpaguri of Darjeeling, out of 33 Sherpa couples (both husbands and wives are the Sherpas), the largest number of husbands (8) have Pankarma as their clan, and these eight husbands have taken eight wives, one each, from seven different clans (Ghola, Khambachan, Ricktho, Odamba, Chuyeri, Chaba and Paya), two of these wives have the same Ghola clan. The next higher number of husbands (7) comes from *Lama* Sherpa clan. They have married seven Sherpa women, one each, who come from five different clans. These five clans are Shalaka, Goparna, Paya, Ghola and Khambachan. Out of these seven husbands, two have wives from Shalaka clan and two other husbands have taken Ghola wives. Five husbands belong to Ghola clan and four of them have taken wives, one each, from the clans like *Lama* Sherpa, Shalaka, Ricktho and Payame. The remaining husbands were unable to name the clan of his wife. In a similar way, husbands having some other clans, also have married in other clans different from their own clans.

In case of the Sherpas of the other village of Darjeeling, that is, Sherpapur, the largest number of husbands (16) have Ricktho as their clan. Out of these 16 Ricktho husbands, three have married three women with Ungkha clan, four have taken four women as wife having Pankarma clan, three husbands have wedded three women with Chukale clan, four husbands have married four women with, one each, with Basmat, Gorja, Odamba and Goparna clans respectively. In case two wives the clan name could not be traced. In this village again, 12 Sherpa husbands with Paya as their clan, have married 12 Sherpa women, one each. Two of these 12 wives have Pinasha as their clan other two have Pankarma, another two Gorja, two more have Ricktho, one with Shalaka and the other with Durbigha clan. Two wives of two husbands, forgot their clan name. There are 10 Ungkha husbands in this village, and they have married one each, 4 Gorja women, 2 Ricktho, one each of Sarey, Pankarma, Shalaka and Cheyeni women. Out of the remaining husbands, 4 belong to Durbigha clan, 4 to Gorja, 3 to Shalaka, and the last 5 husbands, one each, belong to Odamba, Nymba, Pinasha, Ghola and Pankarma. They have married in different other clans (Table 6.4).

When we shift to the two Sherpa villages of South District, Sikkim, we get almost similar picture. At Sherpagaon village there are 71 husbands who have married in clans other than their own. Among these 71 husbands 22 have Kulung as their clan. These 22 Kulung husbands have married 22 wives, one each. Out of these 22 wives, 8 belong to Khambachan clan, 3 belong to Halung, 2 to *Lama* Sherpa, 2 to Rakhali, 2 to Thakto, and one each to Ricktho, Lamaborga, and Zumba. Two husbands have failed to

Table 6.4: Inter-Clan Marriages among the Sherpas of Two Villages of Darjeeling District, West Bengal

Sherpaguri				*Sherpapur*			
Sl. No.	*No. of husbands*	*Clan of husband*	*Married to (clan of the wife)*	*Sl. No.*	*No. of husbands*	*Clan of husband*	*Married to (clan of the wife)*
1.	1	Paya	Lama Sherpa	1.	16	Ricktho	Basmat Ungkha-3 Pankarma-4 Chukale-3 Unknown-2 Gorja, Odamba, Gopama
2.	3	Payame	Paya, Ricktho, Ghola	2.	4	Durbigha	Ricktho-2, Pankarma, Chukale,
3.	2	Gopama	Unknown, Chaba	3.	4	Gorja	Ricktho, Chukale, Nyumi, Odamba
4.	3	Shalaka	Yakum Ghola, Unknown, Pinasha	4.	7	Chukale	Pankarma-3, Gorja, Ricktho, Gopama, Odamba,
5.	1	Haluri	Ghola	5.	1	Odamba	Gorja
6.	5	Ghola	Lama Sherpa, Shalaka, Ricktho, Unknown, Payame	6.	10	Ungkha	Sarey, Pankarma, Ricktho-2, Shalaka, Gorja-4, Chuyemi
7.	7	Lama Sherpa	Shalaka-2 Gopanma, Paya, Ghola-2 Khambachan	7.	3	Shalaka	Gorja, Unknown, Gorja
8.	8	Pankarma	Ghola-2, Khambachan, Ricktho, Odamba, Chuyemi, Chaba, Paya	8.	1	Nyumba	Chukale
9.	1	Assangme	Ghola	9.	1	Pinasha	Shalaka
10.	2	Khambachan	Ghola, Chaba	10.	1	Pankarma	Odamba
				11.	12	Paya	Pinasha-2 Unknown-2 Pankarma-2 Gorja-2, Ricktho-2 Shalaka, Durbigha
				12.	1	Ghola	Ricktho

Source: Field study by the authors.

remember the clan name of their wives. In this village there are 9 husbands who have *Lama* Sherpa as their clans. Their 9 wives, one each, have different clans. Three of the wives have Khambachan as their clan, and each of the remaining 6 wives have clans like Cheyeni, Tamang, Lamagomte, Thapasherpa, Goparna and Shalaka. Again another 8 husbands are of Lamagorba clan. Out of their 8 wives, one each, 2 belong to Kulung clan, 4 other wives belong four different clans like Khambachan, Noumi, Yayatha and Rakhali. The husband of two wives have failed to tell the clan of their wives. Eight husbands have Khambachan as their clan, and the wives of 7 of them have come from 7 different clans like Halung, Lamasherpa, Kulung, Ungkha, Sherpatamang, Ricktho and Pankarma. The remaining husband was unable to tell the clan name of his wife. Another 8 husbands having Pankarma as their clan, have married, one each, 3 Kulung women and one each of *Lama* Sherpa, Noumi, Khambachan, and Goparna women. One husband did not remember the clan name of his wife during investigation. The remaining husbands belong to different other clans like Rakhali (3 husbands), Halung (3 husbands), Goparna (3 husbands), Paya (2 husbands), Haluri (2 husbands) and also Ricktho, Shalaka, and Gorja (one husband each). They have taken wives, one each from different other clans. In case of Halung, Goparna and Haluri husbands, one each, failed to tell the clan name/of their wives (Table 6.5).

Table 6.5: Inter-Clan Marriages among the Sherpas of Two Villages of South District, Sikkim

Sherpagaon				*Sherpahat*			
Sl. No.	*No. of husbands*	*Clan of the husband*	*Married to (clan of the wife)*	*Sl. No.*	*No. of husbands*	*Clan of the husband*	*Married to (clan of the wife)*
1.	8	Lamagorba	Unknown, Khambachan, unknown, Kuling, Noumi, Yayatha, Rakhali, Kuling	1.	19	Lamasherpa	Unknown, Goparna, Khambachan, Haluri, Cheri Thakto, Unknown, Khambachan, Khambachan, Unknown, Goparna, Goparna, Pankarma, Kulung, Lamagompa, Gangthakpa, Unknown, Chukale, Goparna.

(*Contd.*)

Table 6.5 (*Contd.*)

Sherpagaon				*Sherpahat*			
Sl. No.	*No. of husbands*	*Clan of the husband*	*Married to (clan of the wife)*	*Sl. No.*	*No. of husbands*	*Clan of the husband*	*Married to (clan of the wife)*
2.	2	Paya	Momba, Noumi	2.	1	Jalbork	Ghola
3.	22	Kulung	Ricjthu, Lama Sherpa, Khambachan, Rakhali, Lamagorba, Unknown, Khambachan, Thakto, Khambachan, Halung, Khambachan, Halung, Khambachan, Halung, unknown, Lama sherpa, Rakhali, Thakto, Khambachan, Zumba, Khambachan, Khambachan	3.	5	Chukale	Lama Sherpa, Goparna, Lamasherpa, Ricktho, Shalaka
4.	9	Lama Sherpa	Chuyeni, Khambachan, Tamang, Lamagomte, Thapa Sherpa, Goparna, Khambachan, Shalaka, Khambachan	4.	2	Pankarma	Unknown, Lamasherpa,
5.	8	Khambachan	Unknown, Halung, Lamasherpa, Kuling, Ungkha, Sherpatamang, Ricktho, Pankarma	5.	8	Goparna	Khambachan, Lamasherpa, Khambachan, Unknown, Lamasherpa, Lama Sherpa, Khambachan, Lamasherpa.
6.	8	Pankarma	Lamasherpa, Unknown, Kulung, Noumi, Kulung, Khambachan, Goparna, Kulung	6.	3	Gangthakpa	Unknown, Haluri, Unknown

(*Contd.*)

(*Contd.*)

Sherpagaon				Sherpahat			
Sl. No.	No. of husbands	Clan of the husband	Married to (clan of the wife)	Sl. No.	No. of husbands	Clan of the husband	Married to (clan of the wife)
7.	3	Rakhali	Lamasherpa, Odamba, Halung	7.	1	Kulung	Khambachan
8.	3	Halung	Bhotia, Ricktho, Unknown	8.	2	Shalaka	Goparna, Unknown
9.	3	Goparna	Khambachan, Thakto, Unknown	9.	9	Ghola	Ricktho, Haluri, Unknown, Lamasherpa, Pankarma, Pankarma, Kulunge, Pankarma, Ricktho.
10.	1	Ricktho	Kulung	10.	2	Lamarimbuchi	Goparna, Shalaka
11.	2	Haluri	Goparna, Unknown	11.	1	Lhasa	Ghola
12.	1	Shalaka	Halung	12.	9	Khambachan	Pankarma, Lamasherpa, Goparna, Goparna, Shalaka, Lamasherpa, Odamba, Unknown, Lama Sherpa
13.	1	Gorja	Kulung	13.	3	Kongsherpa	Lamasherpa, Pankarma, Lamashrpa
				14.	2	Ricktho	Noumi, Unknown
				15.	1	Rakla	Ricktho
				16.	2	Nonghola	Khambochan, Pankarma
				17.	1	Thakto	Khambachan

Source: Field study by the authors.

We now came to the second studied village from Sikkim that means, Sherpahat. In this village there are 71 husbands who have taken Sherpa wife. Out of these 71 husbands, 19 husbands have taken 19 wives, one each. Now out of these 19 wives, 4 are Goparna, 4 Khambachan, one each of Haluri, Cherithakto, Pankarma, Kulung, Lamagompa, Gangthakpa and Chukale. In case of 4 husbands, the clan of their wives could not be traced. There are 9 husbands having Khambachan clan. They have 9 wives, one each, and of these 9 wives 3 have come from Lamasherpa clan, 2 from Goparna, and one each from Pankarma, Shalaka and Odamba. The ninth husband failed to reveal the clan name of his wife. Another clan Ghola also have 9 husbands who have married to 9 women, one each. Three of the 9 husbands have taken 3 Pankarma wives, one each, 2 husbands have taken 2 Ricktho wives, one each, 3 husbands have taken 3 wives having Lamasherpa, Haluri and Kulunge clans respectively. Only one of these 9 husbands could not tell his wife's clan name. There are 8 Goparna husbands in this village. Four of these 8 husbands have taken 4 Lamasherpa wives, one each. Another 3 husbands have married to 3 Khambachan wives one each. One husband could not remember his wife's clan name. Five Sherpa husbands of this village belong to Chukale clan. Two of them have taken wife from Lamasherpa clan, and the remaining three husbands have taken wife one each, from Goparna, Ricktho and Shalaka clans respectively. The rest of the husbands who have come from different other clans, have also taken wife from different clans. Of course, in a few cases some Sherpa husbands were unable to tell the clan name of their respective wife. For example, out of three Gangthakpa husbands, two failed to tell the clan of their respective wife. The third husband of course, married a Haluri wife.

It is thus seen in most of the marriages among the Sherpa have taken place between different clans (*rii*). Not a single case we could locate where marriage took place in the same clan which they consider, is incestuous and therefore tabooed. So, the Sherpa of both Darjeeling and Sikkim have followed clan exogamy strictly.

7

IN THE FAMILY THEY LIVE

Like marriage, family is also a very important universal institution and is found in all human societies, 'backward' or 'advanced'. It is the smallest social unit present in the human society. According to Murdock "the family is a social group characterized by common residence, economic co-operation and reproduction" (1949:1). Rivers has also defined family as "a small social grouping consisting of parents and children". He has also mentioned family 'as the basis' of the society (1932:12). The *Dictionary of Anthropology* has stated that family is the "key institution in society, consisting of one or more women along with one or more men and their children" (Tylor 1999:199). This Dictionary has also referred to that the family is characterized by the socially approved sex relationship, and various rights and obligation (*ibid*:199:200). Murdock has further mentioned that the family "includes adults of both sexes, at least two of whom maintain a socially approved sexual relationship, and one or more children, own or adopted, of the sexually cohabiting adults" (1949:1). The family is not only made up of individuals but it is also a part of bigger social network (Goode 1964:2) and so in it the individual members who have important role to play. The family expands with the birth, adoption or marriage. On the other hand, it breaks up with the death of a member. Divorce is also a factor that changes the type and size of the family.

Family is a very important social institution. "It is *through the family* that society is able to elicit from the *individual* his necessary contribution" (Goode 1965:3). "The family is the only social institution other than religion which is *formally* developed in all societies" (*ibid*:4). In a family the members are to perform specific duties, and there is division of labour among the members of a family.

> Family duties are the *direct* role responsibility of everyone in the society with rare exception ....Many people, on the other

> hand, may escape the religious duties which others take for granted or the political burdens of the society. Almost no family role responsibilities can be delegated to others, as more specialized obligations can be in a work situation (Goody: *ibid*).

"The family is the fundamental instrumental foundation of the larger social structure, in that all other institutions depend on its contributions" (*ibid*).

The family has many functions. From food supply and general security to sex-relation, child-birth and rearing of children to maintain the continuity of the progeny and family identity and restrict the family property within the family. So sex, descent and inheritance are very important aspects of the family.

In the Sherpa society of both Darjeeling and Sikkim, the family is considered as the very important institution which acts as the link for the family members to the broader society. The Sherpa society of both Darjeeling and Sikkim here has different forms, types and sizes of family. The readers will have a glimpse of these in the forthcoming pages. Among these people of Darjeeling and Sikkim though monogamous family is the norm only a very few polygynous families are also met with. But no polyandrous form is present. The families among these people are mostly nuclear though extended and some other types are also present. Sometimes some distant relatives are found to stay in the nuclear or extended family as adhesions. Different sizes of family are also present among the Sherpas of both Darjeeling and Sikkim, but medium size families are numerically dominant. In the Sherpa family the members have a strong bond among them, and every one of them has a significant but allotted duties to perform. These duties are of different types, economic, social or religious. A Sherpa is always proud of his/her family. While an addition in a family is always welcome, separation or death of a family member is also treated as a very sad incident. The Sherpa family also helps its members to establish link with members of the wider network and also of the society at large. They also keep contact as much as possible with the relations from father, mother and wife's sides, and also with both near and distant relatives. A family also gives its members a definite and distinct identity, and they get recognition in the society through this identity. The Sherpa families are patrilinear in nature, with patripatestal authority and patrilocal residence.

We shall now examine the Sherpa families of Darjeeling as reported by Mitra. According to him the Sherpas of Darjeeling prefer nuclear families at present. Still a 'mixed extended' families are found to be present. The father in each family acts as the head of the family. Among them "The eldest son succeeds his father as the head of the family with all social and ritual rights" (2008:1184).

Among the Sherpas of Darjeeling as reported by Bagchi, "most of their families are of the nuclear type, but joint families are not uncommon" (1991:174). He has also mentioned that two third of the Sherpa families in a village near Kalimpong were of nuclear type while the remaining one third were intermediate or joint. Out of 34 Sherpa families of Kalimpong town, "as many as 24 are nuclear. Almost all the Sherpa families are patrilocal in residence" (*ibid:* 174-175).

In connection with the family of the Sherpas of Sikkim, Gangopadhyay is of the view that among these people nuclear families are common and the nuclear families are on the rise. Among them also the eldest son succeeds after the death of his father (1993:156). Bisht and Bankoti have also noticed the dominance of nuclear families among the Sherpas of Sikkim (2004: 1430).

In connection with the Sherpa families of Sikkim Subba, J.R. writes:

> The Sherpa family is patrilocal and descend is reckoned through the male. The father is economically head of the family. The types of families among the Sherpas are Nuclear, Stem, Nascent and Broken family. The nuclear family is common. The Sherpa society is basically patricentric monogamous, residence is normally patrilocal and inheritance is normally patrilineal (2008:282).

Now, let us see the pattern of family among the Sherpas of Nepal. Fürer-Haimendorf has mentioned that the Sherpas in Nepal as having husband, wife and unmarried children in most of the Sherpa families. That means they also have nuclear families in most of the cases. But where there is polyandrous marriage, the family is polyandrous one which consists of two husbands with a common wife. In the polygynous family one husband and two wives live with their respective children. In connection with the peculiarity of the families of the Sherpas of Nepal, Fürer-Haimendorf states,

> ...the Sherpa families is not permanently embedded in a wave of close kinfolk. From the moment of its establishment as a separate unit, a moment which coincides usually not with the inception of the husband-wife relationship but with the husband's separation from the parental household, a married couple stands by itself, responsible to no one and relying on one's support (1964:39).

As Fürer-Haimendorf has already said that the Sherpas of Nepal have mostly nuclear families. He has further mentioned another interesting point that they do not have any extended or joint family. Among them "every married couple should set up an independent household, even if at first this aim can only be achieved by partitioning the house of the husband's parents' (*ibid*). Among these people of Nepal each Sherpa family has its own household. But establishment of such household is sometimes postponed till the birth of one or two children.

Ortner, in connection with the Sherpas of Nepal, has remarked that "The private-property-owning, highly independent" nuclear family is the 'atom' of the Sherpa social structure" (1979:39). Each family among the Sherpas has a network of kin group, and this kin group is activated as and when required, particularly on different occasions. According to Ortner the Sherpa families depend on "mutual-aid relationship for various forms of vital material assistance nonetheless a whole range of cultural and structural factors emphasize the ideal autonomy and self sufficiency of the nuclear family unit" (*ibid:* 39). Among these people the family members as a team, work in order to earn from their livelihood. Ortner has further mentioned some important features as mentioned below:

1. Far-reaching economic independence of the unit, and economic interdependence of the members,
2. Strong emotional ties between parents and children,
3. Real internal intimacy of domestic life,
4. Symbolic beliefs and practices that input a sort of vital essence that must be hoarded and stored up.
5. Actual historical and contemporary examples of families that isolate themselves from village social life (*ibid*:41).

We have thus tried to give our readers some general features of the families of the Sherpas of Darjeeling, Sikkim and Nepal. We shall now move to the analysis and interpretation of quantitative data collected by us on the families of the Sherpas of our studied villages of Darjeeling (West Bengal) and South District (Sikkim).

Family of the Sherpas

The family is the basic social unit and universal in nature. All human societies of the world have this social unit. There is not a single community in the world which does not have family. Like all other societies of the world, the Sherpas of Darjeeling, Sikkim and Nepal also have family. This is their basic but smallest social unit. Among the Sherpas each family consists of some members who are affinally and/or consanguinally related. Among them the number of members in a family is not fixed; it is variable. In our studied villages in Darjeeling and Sikkim the number of members in the Sherpa families also varies from family to family. In our two studied villages of Darjeeling district, there are a total 115 Sherpa families. Out of these 115 families 43 or 37.39 per cent are found at Sherpaguri village and the remaining 72 or 62.61 per cent at Sherpapur village. Again in these 115 families a total of 568 Sherpas live. Out of these 568 Sherpas 217 or 38.20 per cent live at Sherpaguri and 351 or 61.80 per cent reside at Sherpapur village. The average size of these 115 families of these two villages is 4.94; that means, on an average 4.94 members live in a family. The average size of the families at Sherpaguri village is 5.05 and that of Sherpapur village is 4.88. Now if we come down to our two studied Sherpa villages of South District Sikkim, we see that in these two villages reside 124 Sherpa families. Out of these 124 Sherpa families, 64 or 51.61 per cent are found at Sherpagaon village and the remaining 60 (48.39%) are located at Sherpahat village. Again these 124 Sherpa families consist of 692 members of which 340 (49.13%) live at Sherpagaon village but more than half (352 or 50.87%) reside in 60 families of Sherpahat village. The average size of all the 124 Sherpa families of the two villages of South District, Sikkim is 5.58. In the individual villages the average size of the Sherpa families at Sherpagaon village is 5.31 and that of Sherpahat village is 5.87 (Table 7.1).

When we compare the strength of the Sherpas and their families of the studied villages of Darjeeling with that of the Sherpas and their families in the studied villages of Sikkim, we see that total Sherpa families of the later areas are more in number than those of the former areas though the number of the Sherpa families of the Sherpapur village, Darjeeling is more than those of any of the two villages of Sikkim. But the number of members of the Sherpa families in the villages of Sikkim is more than that of the members of Sherpa families of the villages of Darjeeling, both total and individual village. Similarly, the average members per family are more in Sikkim villages than those of Darjeeling villages.

Table 7.1: Distribution of Family and Average Family Members in Different Villages of Darjeeling and Sikkim

Family/ Population	*Percentage/ Average*	*Darjeeling District, West Bengal*			*South District, Sikkim*		
		Sherpaguri	*Sherpapur*	*Total*	*Sherpagaon*	*Sherpahat*	*Total*
Family	No.	43	72	115	64	60	124
	%	37.39	62.61	100.00	51.61	48.39	100.00
Family Members	No.	217	351	568	340	352	692
	%	38.20	61.80	100.00	49.13	50.87	100.00
Average Size		5.05	4.88	4.94	5.31	5.87	5.58

Source: Field study by the authors.

Family Types

Among the Sherpas different types of families are found to be prevalent. The formation of these different types of families depends on the difference of the relation between members of these families. So, the presence of different types of relations in a family helps in the formation of different types of families. But with the departure or death of any one or more members of a family or any addition in the families through marriage, birth or adoption, may change the types of the family. What is a nuclear family or an extended family today may not remain as nuclear or extended forever. With the addition or departure or death of a member in the family, a nuclear family will not remain as a nuclear one or an extended family may not remain as an extended one. Similarly, partition also changes the size and type of the family. With the marriage of a son and then birth of a child, a nuclear family may be changed into an extended one. Again death of one of the parents in a nuclear family, it becomes a broken one. In a vertically extended family of the parents, unmarried children and married son, if the parents die or if the son and his wife leave the family, then it comes nuclear family. However, we shall now discuss about the types of families among the Sherpas of the two studied villages of Darjeeling District, West Bengal and also two studied villages of South District, Sikkim.

Out of a total of 115 families of the two villages of Darjeeling District more than half (54.78%) of the total families are nuclear type. The next

Table 7.2: Distribution of Family Types of the Sherpas in Different Villages of Darjeeling and Sikkim

Family Type	*Total of Two village of Darjeeling*		*Sherpaguri*		*Sherpapur*		*Total of Two villages of Sikkim*		*Sherpagaon*		*Sherpahat*	
	No.	*%*	*No.*	*%*	*No.*	*%*	*No.*	*%*	*No.*	*%*	*No.*	*%*
Nuclear	63	54.78	24	55.81	39	54.17	71	57.26	39	60.94	32	53.33
Nuclear with adhesion	6	5.22	3	6.98	3	4.17		27.42				
Extended	27	23.48	9	20.93	18	25.00	34	0.81	16	25.00	18	30.00
Extended with adhesion	1	0.87	1	2.33			1	0.81	1	1.56		
Nascent	4	3.48			4	5.56						
Broken	13	11.30	6	13.95	7	9.72	15	12.10	6	9.37	9	15.00
Broken with adhesion	1	0.87			1	1.39	3	2.42	2	3.13	1	
Total	115	100.00	43	100.00	72	100.01	124	100.01	64	100.00	60	1.67

Source: Field study by the authors.

come the extended families with a strength of 23.48 per cent. The broken families are also insufficient in number (11.30%). In case of the village, Sherpaguri also the nuclear families have occupied highest position (55.81%) followed by extended families (18.60%). The broken families are also in good number (13.95%). The same is the picture at Sherpapur village of Darjeeling District. Here also the nuclear and the extended families have first (54.17%) and second (25.00%) position respectively (Table 7.2).

Among the Sherpas of the two villages of South District, Sikkim, the strength of different types of families is almost the same. In these two villages out of a total of 124 families, the nuclear families have secured numerically the highest position (57.26%). The extended families have the next higher position in this regard (27.42%). The broken families are also in a good number. At Sherpagaon and Sherpahat villages of South District the picture is almost the same. Here in these two villages the nuclear families have the highest strength (60.94% and 53.33% respectively). The next position is held by the extended families (25.00% and 30.00% respectively).

It is thus seen that in both Darjeeling District of West Bengal and South District of Sikkim, the family types of the Sherpas are also same only that all types of family are not found in all the villages, while some types of family are common to all the villages, the others are not present in all the villages. Further while nuclear families, among the Sherpas have secured highest number more than half of the total families in all the villages, the extended families come next everywhere.

Family Size and the Distribution of Members in Different Sizes of Family

The Sherpas, everywhere, have different sizes of family, and the family among them, is their smallest social unit. These families have given shelter to the varied number of members. In our studied villages also we get different sizes of families among the Sherpas, and these consist of variable number of members. In the two villages of Kalimpong sub-division of Darjeeling district we get different sizes of families. In these two villages the medium sized families (4 to 6 members per family) of the Sherpas have more than half (53.04%) of the total families (115). The small families have the next higher number of families (25.22%). These are closely followed by the large families (7 to 9 members per family). The very large families have the lowest number of families (less than 4.00%).

Now, in these two villages of Darjeeling district there are a total of 115 Sherpa families which have 568 members. Out of these 568 members of 115 Sherpa families, more than half of the total members (53.17%) reside in the medium sized families. So far as male members are concerned this size of families has taken more than half of the total male members (51.07%) under the control of these. More than half of the total female members (55.21%) also live in this size of families. The large families with 7 to 9 members per family, have accommodated the next higher number of family members (total as well as male and female members). The very large families (10 or more members per family) have given shelter to the lowest number of members. The same is the case with both male and female members of these very large families (Table 7.3).

When we come down to the individual villages, we see that in the village, Sherpaguri, the same picture is reflected. In this village also the medium sized Sherpa families have retained the largest number of families (48.84%).

Table 7.3: Family Size and the Distribution of Members in Different Sizes of Family among the Sherpas of Two Villages of Darjeeling District

Size of the Family	*Total Families*		*Total Members*		*Total Male Members*		*Total Female Members*	
	No.	*%*	*No.*	*%*	*No.*	*%*	*No.*	*%*
1-3	29	25.22	69	12.15	38	13.57	31	10.76
4-6	61	53.04	302	53.17	143	51.07	159	55.21
7-9	23	20.00	175	30.81	88	31.43	87	30.21
10+	2	1.74	22	3.87	11	3.93	11	3.82
Total	115	100.00	568	100.00	280	100.00	288	100.00

Source: Field study by the authors.

The next higher number of families is in the fold of large sized families (27.91%). The small sized families also have a significant number of families (20.93%). The very large families of the Sherpas have kept lowest number of the families. So, far as the number of members in these families is concerned, the medium sized families have the largest share of total members as well as male and female members (45.62%, 42.59% and 48.62% respectively). The large families have retained the next higher number of members (total as well as male and female members). (Table 7.4)

But there is very little difference in strength of the male members in medium sized families (42.59%) from that of large sized families (41.67%). Here in this village the strength of the male members per family is lowest in the very large families. In case of the female members in this village the lowest concentration is seen in very large families (Table 7.4).

Table 7.4: Family Size and the Distribution of Members in Different Sizes of Family among the Sherpas of Sherpaguri Village of Darjeeling District

Size of the Family	*Total Families*		*Total Members*		*Total Male Members*		*Total Female Members*	
	No.	*%*	*No.*	*%*	*No.*	*%*	*No.*	*%*
1-3	9	20.93	20	9.22	11	10.19	9	8.26
4-6	21	48.84	99	45.62	46	42.59	53	48.62
7-9	12	27.91	88	40.55	45	41.67	43	39.45
10+	1	2.33	10	4.61	6	5.56	4	3.67
Total	43	100.01	217	100.00	108	100.01	109	100.00

Source: Field study by the authors.

As we step in the other village of Darjeeling district, West Bengal, that is, Sherpapur, (Table 7.5) we see that the medium sized families (4 to 6 members per family) of the Sherpas have the largest number of families. The next higher number of families have been retained by the small size families (27.78%). The very large families are insignificant in number. Again medium sized families have also occupied more than half

Table 7.5: Family Size and the Distribution of Members in Different Sizes of Family among the Sherpas of Sherpapur Village of Darjeeling District

Size of the Family	*Total Families*		*Total Members*		*Total Male Members*		*Total Female Members*	
	No.	*%*	*No.*	*%*	*No.*	*%*	*No.*	*%*
1-3	20	27.78	49	13.96	27	15.70	22	12.29
4-6	40	55.56	203	57.83	97	56.40	106	59.22
7-9	11	15.28	87	24.79	43	25.00	44	24.58
10+	1	1.39	12	3.42	5	2.91	7	3.91
Total	72	100.01	351	100.00	172	100.01	179	100.00

Source: Field study by the authors.

of the total members (57.83%). The next higher strength of members goes to the large families (24.79%). The very large families as usual have somehow kept the lowest number of members (3.42%). The same is the case with the strength of the male members of different sizes of families. The medium sized families have been able to capture more than half the total number of male members (56.40%). The next higher concentration of members is seen in the large sized families. The very large sized families of the Sherpas have the lowest concentration of male members. The same is the case with the female members. The medium sized families have retained almost 60 per cent of the total female members. The next higher concentration of the female members is seen in the large sized families (24.58%). The very large families have as usual the lowest number of female members per family (Table 7.5).

Thus, we see that among the Sherpas of Darjeeling district the medium sized families have the highest number, and these have retained the highest number of members (total as also sex-wise). Both small and large families also have significant number and have also retained significant number of members.

In South District of Sikkim the two villages, Sherpagaon and Sherpahat, have a total of 124 Sherpa families. Out of these 124 Sherpa families the largest number of families (48.39%) are medium sized (4 to 6 members per family). The next higher number of families (23.39%) are small sized one (1 to 3 members per family). The large sized families (7 to 9 members per family) come next. The very large families (10 or more members per family) have the lowest strength.

Now, in these 124 Sherpa families of the two villages of Sikkim 692 members reside. Out of these 692 members the largest number of members (41.91%) live in the medium sized families. Next in order come large families where 25.00 per cent of the total members live. The very large families also have a substantial number of members (22.98%). The small families have retained the lowest number of members.

The male members of these families have also followed the path of the total members. The medium sized families have kept highest number of male members (42.78%). The next higher number of male members live in the large families (26.72%) followed by the very large families. The small families have the lowest number of male members.

There are a total of 329 female members live in these 124 Sherpa families of the two villages of South District, Sikkim. Out of these 329 female members, the largest number of them live in the medium sized families (40.73%). The very large families have the next higher number of female members (25.53%). The large sized families (23.00%) closely follow the very large families. The small families retain the lowest number of female members (Table 7.6).

Table 7.6: Family Size and the Distribution of Members in Different Sizes of Family among the Sherpas of Two Villages of South District, Sikkim

Size of the Family	Total Families		Total Members		Total Male Members		Total Female Members	
	No.	%	No.	%	No.	%	No.	%
1-3	29	23.39	70	10.12	35	9.64	35	10.64
4-6	60	48.39	290	41.91	156	42.78	134	40.73
7-9	22	17.74	173	25.00	97	26.72	76	23.10
10+	13	10.48	159	22.98	75	20.66	84	25.53
Total	124	100.00	692	100.01	363	100.00	329	100.00

Source: Field study by the authors.

The village, Sherpagaon has reflected the same picture as the combined families and members of the two villages have. In this village as usual, the medium sized families have the highest strength (48.44%). Next in order come small families which have retained one fourth of the total Sherpa families of this village. The large families are also significant in number. In this village, in a similar way, the medium sized families have retained the largest number cf members (43.24%), the male members (43.75%) and also the female members (42.57%). The next higher number

Table 7.7: Family Size and the Distribution of Members in Different Sizes of Family among the Sherpas of Sherpagaon Village of South District, Sikkim

Size of the Family	Total Families		Total Members		Total Male Members		Total Female Members	
	No.	%	No.	%	No.	%	No.	%
1-3	16	25.00	41	12.06	23	11.98	18	12.16
4-6	31	48.44	147	43.24	84	43.75	63	42.57
7-9	13	20.31	101	29.70	59	30.73	42	28.38
10+	4	6.25	51	15.00	26	13.54	25	16.89
Total	64	100.00	340	100.00	192	100.00	148	100.00

Source: Field study by the authors.

of total members, total male members and female members are found to live in the large sized families. The lowest number of total members, total male members and also female members reside, in the small sized families (Table 7.7).

As we come to Sherpahat village of South district, Sikkim, we find that the medium sized families among the Sherpas are the numerically the most dominant ones (48.33%). Then come small families (21.67%). The large and very large families have equal strength (15.00% each). The distribution of members in different sizes of family, follows a little different pattern. In this village, in a similar way, the medium sized families are the highest retainers of the total members, total male members as well as female members (Table 7.8).

Table 7.8: Family Size and the Distribution of Members in Different Sizes of Family among the Sherpas of Sherpahat Village of South District, Sikkim

Size of the Family	Total Families		Total Members		Total Male Members		Total Female Members	
	No.	%	No.	%	No.	%	No.	%
1-3	13	21.67	29	8.24	12	7.02	17	9.39
4-6	29	48.33	143	40.63	72	42.11	71	39.23
7-9	9	15.00	72	20.45	38	22.22	34	18.78
10+	9	15.00	108	30.68	49	28.65	59	32.60
Total	60	100.00	352	100.00	171	100.00	181	100.00

Source: Field study by the authors.

But in this village the very large families have taken the second position in so far as the strength of the total members and also total male and female members in different sizes of the families are concerned, keeping the large sized families in the third position in this regard. The small sized families have as usual, kept the lowest number of total members, also lowest number of male and female members.

Thus, it is seen that among the Sherpas of all the four villages studied by us, two from Darjeeling, West Bengal and two from South District, Sikkim, the medium sized families among the Sherpas are numerically the most dominant ones retaining either little over half or almost half of the total families the Sherpas of these villages have. The next higher number goes either to the large families or the small families. Then in case of the distribution of the members of the families, we see that the medium sized families of the Sherpas both in Darjeeling and also in Sikkim

Table 7.9: Average number of Members of Different Sizes of Family of the Sherpas of Four Studied Villages of Darjeeling and Sikkim

Size of the Families	Sherpaguri				Sherpapur				Total				Sherpagaon				Sherpahat				Total			
	Family		Members		Family		Members		Family		Members		Family		Members		Family		Members		Family		Members	
	No.	%	No.	%	No.	%	No.	%	No.	%	No.	%	No.	%	No.	%	No.	%	No.	%	No.	%	No.	%
1-3	9	31.03	20	2.22	20	68.97	49	2.45	29	100.00	69	2.38	16	55.17	41	2.56	13	44.83	29	2.30	29	100.00	70	2.41
4-6	21	34.43	99	4.71	40	65.57	203	5.08	61	100.00	302	4.95	31	51.67	147	4.74	29	48.33	143	4.93	60	100.00	290	4.83
7-9	12	52.17	88	7.33	11	47.83	87	7.91	23	100.00	175	7.61	13	59.09	101	7.77	9	40.91	72	8.00	22	100.00	173	7.86
10+	1	50.00	10	10.00	1	50.00	12	12.00	2	100.00	22	11.00	4	30.77	51	12.75	9	69.23	108	12.00	13	100.00	159	12.23
Total	43	37.39	217	5.05	72	62.61	351	4.88	115	100.00	568	4.94	64	51.61	340	5.31	60	48.39	352	5.87	124	100.00	692	5.58

Source: Field study by the authors.

have retained the largest number of total members and also largest number of male and female members. But in the Sherpa villages of Darjeeling district while the very large families have the lowest number of total members as well as male and female members, in Sikkim villages the lowest position has been retained by the small families and not by the very large families, so much, so, that at Sherpahat village the very large families have secured the second place, after medium sized families so far as the total number of members, total number of male members and female members in the families are concerned.

Average Number of Members per Family

Among the Sherpas of the Himalayas the families are constituted of more than one member who are somehow related either affinally and/or consanguinally or through adoption. At the same time, the number of members residing in a family also vary from family to family. Among the Sherpas also the number of members in the family is not constant but variable. Through Table 7.9 we have examined the number of members (total and average) living in different sizes of the Sherpa families of the two studied villages of Darjeeling, West Bengal and also two studied villages of South District, Sikkim. Among the Sherpas of the two studied villages of Darjeeling district, that is, Sherpaguri and Sherpahat, there is a total of 115 families where live 564 members. Therefore, the average number of members in each of these 115 families is 4.94. Out of these 115 families 43 (37.39%) Sherpa families are found to live at Sherpaguri village with 217 members giving rise to an average of 5.05 members per family here. At Sherpapur village of this district, the Sherpas have 72 families forming 62.61 per cent of the total families of the two villages. Now, in these 72 families a total of 351 members reside. Therefore, the average number of members per family of the Sherpas of this village is 4.88.

Now, we come down to the average number of members per family in different sizes of families of the Sherpa of these two Sherpa villages of Darjeeling district.

Out of the total families of these two Sherpa villages, 29 families have 1 to 3 members per family. The average number of members per family in this size of the Sherpa families of the two villages is only 2.38. At Sherpaguri village there are a total of 9 families with 1 to 3 members per family. There are 20 members in these 9 families with an average of 2.22 members per family. At Sherpapur village all the 20 Sherpa families with 1 to 3 members per family, the average number of members per family is 2.45 members.

The average number of members of the total Sherpa families of these two villages with 4 to 6 members per family is 4.95. The average members of the Sherpa families with 4 to 6 member per family of Sherpaguri village is 4.71 and that of Sherpapur villages is 5.08. As we come to the Sherpa families of the two villages of Darjeeling district with 7 to 9 members per family, the average number of members per family is 7.61. The same for Sherpaguri village is 7.33 members per family and that of Sherpapur village is 7.91. In case of the Sherpa families of these two villages with 10 and more members per family, the average number of members per family is 11.00 per family. The same for the Sherpa families of Sherpaguri village of Darjeeling District is 10.00, but that of Sherpapur village is as high as 12.00 members per family. Therefore, it is seen that the average number of members per family of the Sherpas of Sherpapur village is much higher than that of Sherpaguri village.

In South District of Sikkim we have studied the Sherpas of two villages, Sherpagaon and Sherpahat. The total Sherpa families of these two villages combined together is 124 where 692 members live. The average number of members per family in these two villages jointly is 5.58. At Sherpagaon the total Sherpa families is 64, and these families form 51.61 per cent of the combined families of the two villages (Table 7.9). The average number of members per family here is 5.31. Sherpahat village has given shelter to 60 Sherpa families which have accommodated 352 members. The average number of members per family here is 5.87. When we come down to the average number of members per family in different sizes of the Sherpa family of this village, we see that there is a total of 29 families with the family size of 1 to 3 members. In these families the average number of members per family is only 2.41. At Sherpagaon village the same size of the Sherpa families have an average of 2.56 members live in each Sherpa family. At Sherpahat village a total of 13 Sherpa families give rise to 2.30 members on an average per family in the families of 1 to 3 members. In the families with 4 to 6 members the two villages of Darjeeling district have a total of 61 families with a size of 4 to 6 members per family. The average members per family is 4.95. At Sherpaguri village the Sherpa families with this size (4 to 6 members) of families have an average of 4.71 members per family and at Sherpapur village this average is 5.58 members per family.

In South District, Sikkim on the other hand, there is total of 60 Sherpa families in two studied villages with 4 to 6 members per family. The average number of members per family here is 4.83. At Sherpagaon village in this South District, the average number of members per family is 4.74 in the families with 4 to 6 members and at Sherpahat village here the same is 4.93 (Table 7.9).

In Darjeeling district of West Bengal the two studied Sherpa villages have a total of 23 families with a size of 7 to 9 members per family. Here the average number of members per family is 7.61. At Sherpaguri village of this district this size of families have an average of 7.33 members per family and the same at Sherpapur village is 7.91.

When we come to the studied villages of South District, Sikkim we see that there are a total of 22 Sherpa families with a size of 7 to 9 members per family. In these families the average number of members per family is 7.86 members. At Sherpagaon village this average is 7.77 and at Sherpahat villages this is 8.00.

Among the Sherpas of the two villages of Darjeeling district there is a total of 22 families with a size of 10 or more members per family. Now, these families have 11.00 as the average number of members per family. At Sherpaguri village the family of this size (only one family) has 10 or more members. At Sherpapur village also there is only one family of this size and in this family live 12 members.

As we come to the studied Sherpa villages of South District, Sikkim we get 13 families with the size of 10 or more members per family. These families has an average of 12.23 members per family. At Sherpagaon village this average is 12.75 members per family and at Sherpahat village is 12.00 (Table 7.9).

From the above tables and also from the discussion, it is apparent that the average number of members per family in different sizes of family is higher at Sherpapur village of Darjeeling District than that of Sherpaguri though the average number of members per family of the total families of Sherpaguri village is higher than that of Sherpapur village. But the picture is somewhat different in case of the two villages of South District. Here the average number of members per family of the family sizes, 1 to 3 and 10 or more members per family is higher at Sherpagaon than that of Sherpahat village. Reversely the average number of members per family of the family sizes 4 to 6 and 7 to 9 members per family is higher at Sherpahat than that of Sherpagaon village (Table 7.9).

But when we compare the Sherpas of two sets of villages of two different areas, Darjeeling and South District we find that the total Sherpa families of two villages reveal that the average number of members of all sizes of families of South District except the size 4 to 6 members per family, is higher than that of the Sherpas of two villages of Darjeeling District. The size, 4 to 6 members per family of the Sherpa families of Darjeeling District, is higher than that of South District. Again the total families of four different villages indicate that Sherpahat village has the highest average members per family (5.87 members) followed by Sherpagaon village. Sherpapur village has the lowest average number of members per family. Again the average number of members per family of the Sherpas of South District villages is higher than that of the Sherpa of Darjeeling district villages.

Size of the Family and Distribution of Members

In Darjeeling district of West Bengal the Sherpas have, as we get from our study, different sizes of families. These families have the maximum of 12 members in our two studied villages. When we examine the size of all the Sherpa families of the two villages studied, we see that the families with five members have the highest strength (22.61%). Next come families with four members (16.52%) followed by the families with six (13.61%) and three (12.17%) members. Families with ten and twelve members have the lowest strength (0.87% each). Following this trend we see that the families with five members have retained highest number of the total members (22.89%), highest number of the total male and also female members (22.86% and 22.92% respectively). Next come families with six members which have 16.90 per cent of the total members, 16.79 per cent of total male members and 17.01 per cent of the total female members followed by families with eight members (14.08% of the total members, 14.64% of the total male members and of the total 13.54% female members). These two Sherpa inhabited villages do not have any family with eleven members (Table 7.10).

At Sherpaguri village of Kalimpong sub-division of Darjeeling district, there are 43 Sherpa families having the highest of ten members. Among these families, the some with four members have the highest frequency (10 or 23.26%). Next in order come families with eight members (18.60%) followed by the families with five members (16.28%). If population-wise distribution of families is counted then the families with seven members retain the highest number of the total members (25.81%). In this regard the second position is held by families with five members (16.13%). The highest number of male and female members is also present in the families with seven members (25.93% and 25.69% of the total respectively). Next come families with four members. These families have

Table 7.10: Family Size and Sex-wise Distribution of Members in the Sherpa Families of Two Villages of Darjeeling, West Bengal

Sl. No.	Family size	No. of Family		Population		Male		Female	
		No.	%	No.	%	No.	%	No.	%
1.	1	3	2.61	3	0.53	2	0.71	1	0.35
2.	2	12	10.43	24	4.23	12	4.29	12	4.17
3.	3	14	12.17	42	7.39	24	8.57	18	6.25
4.	4	19	16.52	76	13.38	32	11.43	44	15.28
5.	5	26	22.61	130	22.89	64	22.86	66	22.92
6.	6	16	13.91	96	16.90	47	16.79	49	17.01
7.	7	11	9.57	77	13.56	39	13.93	38	13.19
8.	8	10	8.70	80	14.08	41	14.64	39	13.54
9.	9	2	1.74	18	3.17	8	2.86	10	3.47
10.	10	1	0.87	10	1.76	6	2.14	4	1.39
11.	12	1	0.87	12	2.11	5	1.79	7	2.43
	Total	115	100.00	568	100.00	280	100.01	288	100.00

Source: Field study by the authors.

retained 18.43 per cent of the total members, 16.67 per cent of the total male members and 20.18 per cent of the total female members. This village does not have any Sherpa family with nine members (Table 7.11).

Table 7.11: Family Size and Sex-wise Distribution of Members in the Sherpa Families of Sherpaguri Village of Darjeeling, West Bengal

Sl. No.	Family Size	No. of Family		Population		Male		Female	
		No.	%	No.	%	No.	%	No.	%
1.	1	2	4.65	2	0.92	1	0.93	1	0.92
2.	2	3	6.98	6	2.76	2	1.85	4	3.67
3.	3	4	9.30	12	5.53	8	7.41	4	3.67
4.	4	10	23.26	40	18.43	18	16.67	22	20.18
5.	5	7	16.28	35	16.13	17	15.74	18	16.51
6.	6	4	9.30	24	11.06	11	10.19	13	11.93
7.	7	8	18.60	56	25.81	28	25.93	28	25.69
8.	8	4	9.30	32	14.75	17	15.74	15	13.76
9.	10	1	2.33	10	4.61	6	5.56	4	3.67

Source: Field study by the authors.

The other Sherpa village of Kalimpong, Darjeeling, Sherpapur, has the highest of twelve members in a family. In this village families with five members have the highest strength (26.37%) followed by the families with six members (16.67%) and three members (13.86%). Families with one member (if we at all call it a family) and twelve members have the lowest strength (1.39% each). Again in this village families with five members have the highest number of the total members (27.07%), highest number of the total male (27.33%) and also highest number of total female members (26.82%). Next come families with six members as these families retain 20.51 per cent of the total members, 20.93 per cent of the total male and 20.11 per cent of the total female members followed by families with eight members. These families with eight members each, have kept 13.68 per cent of the total members, 13.95 per cent of the total male and 13.41 per cent of the total female members (Table 7.12).

Table 7.12: Family Size and Sex-wise Distribution of Members in the Sherpa Families of Sherpapur Village of Darjeeling

Sl. No.	Family Size	No. of Family		Population		Male		Female	
		No.	%	No.	%	No.	%	No.	%
1.	1	1	1.39	1	0.28	1	0.58		
2.	2	9	12.50	18	5.13	10	5.81	8	4.47
3.	3	10	13.89	30	8.55	16	9.30	14	7.82
4.	4	9	12.50	36	10.26	14	8.14	22	12.29
5.	5	19	26.39	95	27.07	47	27.33	48	26.82
6.	6	12	16.67	72	20.51	36	20.93	36	20.11
7.	7	3	4.17	21	5.98	11	6.40	10	5.59
8.	8	6	8.33	48	13.68	24	13.95	24	13.41
9.	9	2	2.78	18	5.13	8	4.65	10	5.59
10.	12	1	1.39	12	3.42	5	2.91	7	3.91
	Total	72	100.01	351	100.01	172	100.00	179	100.01

Source: Field study by the authors.

In Sikkim the Sherpa families of the two villages of South District have a maximum of 14 members. There are a total of 124 Sherpa families in these two villages, and in these families the four member families have the highest strength (20.16%). The next higher strength goes to the families with five members (16.13%) followed by the families with three (12.90%) and six (12.10%) members. Here, the only family with 14 members has the lowest strength (0.81%). So far as the number of members is concerned, the families with both four and five members have retained the highest but equal number of members (14.45%each). Next higher number of members retained are families with six members (13.01%) followed by the families with seven members (10.12%). The one membered families have housed the lowest number of members (0.58%). Just above one membered families, lies the family with 14 members (2.02%) (Table 7.13).

In these two villages the highest number of male members is found in the Sherpa families with five members. In these families live 14.88 per cent of the total male members (363) of these two villages. Families with four members are very close to the families with five members. These have retained 14.60 per cent of the total male members. Families with six members are also not far behind with 13.50 per cent of the total male members. Families with one member have the lowest number of male members. So far as the female members of these families are concerned, we find that families with four members have retained the highest number of female members (14.29% of the total female members of all the families). Next come families with five 13.98%, twelve (12.77%) and six (12.46%) members. These families are closely behind families with four members in this regard. Families with one member have the lowest number of female members (0.61%) followed by families with 14 members (1.82%) (Table 7.13).

Table 7.13: Family Size and Sex-wise Distribution of Members in the Sherpa Families of Two Villages of South District, Sikkim

Sl. No.	Family Size	No. of Family		Population		Male		Female	
		No.	%	No.	%	No.	%	No.	%
1.	1	4	3.23	4	0.58	2	0.55	2	0.61
2.	2	9	7.26	18	2.60	8	2.20	10	3.04
3.	3	16	12.90	48	6.94	25	6.89	23	6.99
4.	4	25	20.16	100	14.45	53	14.60	47	14.29
5.	5	20	16.13	100	14.45	54	14.88	46	13.98
6.	6	15	12.10	90	13.01	49	13.50	41	12.46
7.	7	10	8.06	70	10.12	38	10.47	32	9.73
8.	8	7	5.65	56	8.09	33	9.09	23	6.99
9.	9	3	2.42	27	3.90	15	4.13	12	3.65
10.	10	2	1.61	20	2.89	11	3.03	9	2.74
11.	11	2	1.61	22	3.18	10	2.75	12	3.65
12.	12	7	5.65	84	12.14	42	11.57	42	12.77
13.	13	3	2.42	39	5.64	15	4.13	24	7.29
14.	14	1	0.81	14	2.02	8	2.20	6	1.82
	Total	124	100.01	692	100.01	363	99.99	329	100.01

Source: Field study by the authors.

At Sherpagaon village of South District, Sikkim, the Sherpas have a total of 64 families. The highest number of members in a family is 14 but there is no family with 10 or 11 members. In this village the Sherpa families with four members have the highest strength (21.88%). Families with three and five members have the next higher strength (17.19 each). Families with 13 and 14 members have the lowest strength (1.56% each). So far as the distribution of members in these families is concerned, we find that families with four members have retained the highest number of the total members (16.47%). Families with five members are following closely by retaining 16.18 per cent of the total members followed by the families with seven members (12.35%). In this village the Sherpa families with four members have kept highest number of male members (17.19%). Next come families with five members (15.10%) and then families with seven members (13.02%). Families with one member have retained the lowest number of male members (1.04%) followed closely by the families with two members (1.56%). In case of the female members, families with five members have kept the highest (17.57%) of the total female members of the Sherpa families of this village. The next higher number of female members is retained by families with four members (15.54%) followed by families with seven members (11.49%) and three members (10.14%). Families with two members have the lowest number of female members (2.03%) (Table 7.14).

Table 7.14: Family Size and Sex-wise Distribution of Members in the Sherpa Families of Sherpagaon Village of South District, Sikkim

Sl. No.	*Family Size*	*No. of Family*		*Population*		*Male*		*Female*	
		No.	*%*	*No.*	*%*	*No.*	*%*	*No.*	*%*
1.	1	2	3.13	2	0.59	2	1.04	—	—
2.	2	3	4.69	6	1.76	3	1.56	3	2.03
3.	3	11	17.19	33	9.71	18	9.38	15	10.14
4.	4	14	21.88	56	16.47	33	17.19	23	15.54
5.	5	11	17.19	55	16.18	29	15.10	26	17.57
6.	6	6	9.38	36	10.59	22	11.46	14	9.46
7.	7	6	9.38	42	12.35	25	13.02	17	11.49
8.	8	4	6.25	32	9.41	19	9.90	13	8.78
9.	9	3	4.69	27	7.94	15	7.81	12	8.11
10.	12	2	3.13	24	7.06	12	6.25	12	8.11
11.	13	1	1.56	13	3.82	6	3.13	7	4.73
12.	14	1	1.56	14	4.12	8	4.17	6	4.05
	Total	64	100.03	340	100.00	192	100.01	148	100.01

Source: Field study by the authors.

The next studied Sherpa village of South District, Sikkim that is Sherpahat, has 60 Sherpa families. Out of these sixty families, families with four members have the highest strength (18.33%). The next higher strength goes to families with five and also six members, each with 15.00 per cent strength. The families with one, ten, eleven, twelve and thirteen members have the lowest strength, each carried 3.33 per cent strength. As the Sherpa families retain varied number of members, our analysis shows that among the Sherpas of this village families with eleven members have retained the highest number of members (17.05%) and also the highest number of both male and female members (17.54% and 16.57% respectively). The next higher number of members is retained by families with six members (15.54%) which also retains the highest number of male (15.79%) and female (14.92%) members. Here families with one member have the lowest number of members (0.57%) and also lowest female members (1.10%), no male member lives in one membered family. Families with two members have the lowest male members (2.92%). (Table 7.15).

Table 7.15: Family Size and Sex-wise Distribution of Members in the Sherpa Families of Sherpahat Village of South District, Sikkim

Sl. No.	Family Size	No. of Family		Population		Male		Female	
		No.	%	No.	%	No.	%	No.	%
1.	1	2	3.33	2	0.57			2	1.10
2.	2	6	10.00	12	3.41	5	2.92	7	3.87
3.	3	5	8.33	15	4.26	7	4.09	8	4.42
4.	4	11	18.33	44	12.50	20	11.70	24	13.26
5.	5	9	15.00	45	12.78	25	14.62	20	11.05
6.	6	9	15.00	54	15.34	27	15.79	27	14.92
7.	7	4	6.67	28	7.95	13	7.60	15	8.29
8.	8	3	5.00	24	6.82	14	8.19	10	5.52
9.	10	2	3.33	20	5.68	11	6.43	9	4.97
10.	11	2	3.33	22	6.25	10	5.85	12	6.63
11.	12	5	8.33	60	17.05	30	17.54	30	16.57
12.	13	2	3.33	26	7.39	9	5.26	17	9.39
Total		60	99.98	352	100.00	171	99.99	181	99.99

Source: Field study by the authors.

Distribution of the Sherpa Families with Members of Different Age-Groups

The Sherpa families of both Darjeeling and Sikkim like the families of many other groups of people in different parts of the world, have members belonging to different age-groups. Members of all age-groups are not always found in all the families. While some families have members belonging to some age-groups, in case of some other families, members are found to belong to all the age groups. So on the basis of different categories of age-groups if the members living in the Sherpa families are classified, then we shall find that in Darjeeling district the two studied villages taken together, have families with the members belonging to the age-groups 'Upto 14' and 15-59 have the highest strength (63.48%). The next higher numbers of families (13.91%) have kept members of all age-groups. The lowest number of families (1.74%) have members belonging to the age-groups 60+ (Table 7.16).

At Sherpaguri village of Darjeeling District, the families with members of the age-groups 'Upto 14' and 15-59, have the highest strength (56.16%). Families with the members belonging to all age-groups, come next with 20.93 per cent strength. At Sherpapur village of this district, as usual the families with members belonging to the age-groups 'Upto 14' and '15 to 59' come first with the strength of 66.67 per cent strength. In this village also families with members of all age-groups, retain the next position.

Now, we shall see how the families of the Sherpas of Sikkim villages are distributed age-group-wise. The age-group-wise distribution of the combined families of the two studied villages of the Sherpas show that

Table 7.16: Distribution of Sherpa Families with Members of Different Age-groups in Studied Village of Darjeeling and Sikkim

Age-Groups	*Sherpaguri*		*Sherpapur*		*Total*		*Sherpagaon*		*Sherpahat*		*Total*	
	Families		*Families*		*Families*		*Families*		*Families*		*Families*	
	No.	*%*	*No.*	*%*	*No.*	*%*	*No.*	*%*	*No.*	*%*	*No.*	*%*
15-59	5	11.63	9	12.50	14	12.17	13	20.31	5	8.33	18	14.52
60+	2	4.65			2	1.74			2	3.33	2	1.61
Upto 14 & 15-59	25	58.16	48	66.67	73	63.48	34	53.13	35	58.33	69	55.65
Upto 14 & 60+												
15-59 & 60+	2	4.65	8	11.11	10	8.70	10	15.62	3	5.00	13	10.48
All Age-groups	9	20.93	7	9.72	16	13.91	7	10.94	15	25.00	22	17.74
Total	43	100.00	72	100.00	115	100.00	64	100.00	60	99.99	124	100.00

Source: Field study by the authors.

here also families with the members belonging to the age-groups 'Upto 14' and '15 to 59' have kept the highest position covering 55.65 per cent families, and like the Sherpa families of Darjeeling District, the Sherpa villages of Sikkim have also kept the Sherpa families with members of all age-groups in the second position with 17.74 per cent strength.

At Sherpagaon village of South District, Sikkim as usual, families with members belonging to the age-groups 'Upto 14' and '15 to 59' have the highest strength (53.13%).

But the next position has been retained by the families with the members belonging only to the age-group 15 to 59. Families with the members belonging to all age-groups have the lowest strength. But the Sherpa families of the Sherpahat village of South District, have followed the path of their counterparts in Darjeeling district. Like the Sherpa families of the Darjeeling villages, here also the families with members belonging to the age-groups 'Upto 14' and '15 to 59' have the highest strength (58.33%) and families with the members of all age-groups have retained the second position (25.00%) (Table 7.16).

Type and Size of the Sherpa Families and Distribution of Family Members

Among the Sherpas of both Darjeeling and Sikkim, different types and sizes of the families are found to exist, and in these families varied number of members live. When we analyse the data on the Sherpa families of these two areas, we see that among the Sherpas of the two studied villages of Darjeeling the total number of families is 115. Out of these families the highest number of families (54.78%) are nuclear type. The next higher number of families are extended type. In the small (1 to 3 members) and medium sizes (4 to 6 members) of families the nuclear type secures the highest number (56.62% and 67.21% respectively). But in case of large (7 to 9 members) and very large families (10+ members) the extended type has the highest stake (65.22% and 100.00% respectively). Again when the distribution of the average number of male and female members is counted, it is seen that the highest average number of male members is in the extended type but the highest average number of female members is in the extended with adhesion type of families. In the small sized families, the nuclear type has the highest male and also female members. But in the medium sized families the broken type with adhesion has the highest average male members, and the extended type has the highest average female members. In case of the large families the nuclear type has the highest average male and the extended type has the highest average female members. The extended type of the very large families has the highest average male as well as female members (Table 7.17).

At Sherpaguri village of Darjeeling District, as usual, the nuclear type has the highest number of families (55.81%). The extended type has the next higher strength (18.60%). The highest average number of both male and female members is found to stay in the extended type with adhesion. In this village the nuclear type is found in the highest number in both small (77.78%) and medium size families (57.14%). But the highest number of extended families is found in the large families. The very large family is only one in number and extended type with adhesion while the small sized nuclear family has the highest average male as well as female members. In the medium sized families, the extended type has the highest average male and also female members. The large sized families have nuclear families with highest average male members and extended type with adhesion has the highest average female members. In case of very large families the extended type with adhesion has the highest average number of both male and female members (Table 7.18).

We shall now move to Sherpapur village of Darjeeling District to see the family types, sizes and the distribution of average members in different types and sizes of families. In this village also the nuclear type of families has the highest strength (54.17%). The extended type has the next higher number (25.00%). The nuclear type with adhesion has the highest average male members and extended type, the highest average female members. As we see the distribution of different types of families in different sizes of families and also the distribution of average members in these families, we find that in this village, the nuclear type has retained half of the total number of small sized families, and also these small sized nuclear families have also retained the highest average number of both male and female members. The same is the condition with the medium sized families which have covered overwhelming majority of nuclear families (72.50%). But in this case the highest average male members are found in the nuclear type with adhesion, and the extended type has the highest average female members. Again among the Sherpas of this village, both large and very large size extended families are enjoying the highest position covering 81.81 per cent and 100.00 per cent of the total families. The average number of both male and female members is also the highest in these families (Table 7.19).

Now, if we look at the type and size of the Sherpa families from a different angle, we will see that in the two villages of Darjeeling district

Table 7.17: Distribution of Average Male and Female Members in Different Types and Sizes of Family among the Sherpas in Two Villages of Darjeeling, West Bengal

Family type	Family Size																			
	1-3				4-6				7-9				10+				Total			
	Total Family		Avg male	Avg female	Total family		Avg male	Avg female	Total family		Avg male	Avg female	Total family		Avg male	Avg female	Total family		Avg male	Avg female
	No.	%			No.	%			No.	%			No.	%			No.	%		
Nuclear	17	58.62	1.53	1.18	41	67.21	2.41	2.51	5	21.74	4.40	3.00					63	54.78	2.33	2.19
Nuclear with Adhesion					4	6.56	2.50	2.75	2	8.70	3.50	3.50					6	5.22	2.83	3.00
Extended					10	16.39	2.20	3.20	15	65.22	3.73	4.07	2	100.00	5.50	5.50	27	23.48	3.33	3.81
Extended type with adhesion									1	4.35	3.00	4.00					1	0.87	3.00	4.00
Nascent	3	10.34	0.67	0.33	1	1.64	2.00	2.00									4	3.48	1.00	0.75
Broken	9	31.03	1.11	1.11	4	6.56	1.75	2.25									13	11.30	1.31	1.46
Broken with adhesion					1	1.64	3.00	2.00									1	0.87	3.00	2.00
Total	29	99.99	1.31	1.07	61	100.00	2.34	2.61	23	100.01	3.83	3.78	2	100.00	5.50	5.50	115	100.00	2.43	2.50

Source: Field study by the authors.

Table 7.18: Distribution of Average Male and Female Members in Different Types and Sizes of Sherpa Family in Sherpaguri Village of Darjeeling, West Bengal

Family type	Family Size																			
	1-3				4-6				7-9				10+				Total			
	Total Family		Avg male	Avg female	Total family		Avg male	Avg female	Total family		Avg male	Avg female	Total family		Avg male	Avg female	Family		Avg male	Avg female
	No.	%			No.	%			No.	%			No.	%			No.	%		
Nuclear	7	77.78	1.43	1.14	12	57.14	2.33	2.50	5	41.67	4.40	3.00					24	55.81	2.50	2.21
Nuclear with Adhesion					3	14.29	2.00	2.67									3	6.98	2.00	2.67
Extended					2	9.52	2.50	3.00	6	50.00	3.33	4.00					8	18.60	3.13	3.75
Extended type with adhesion									1	8.33	3.00	4.00	1	100.00	6.00	4.00	2	4.65	4.50	4.00
Nascent																				
Broken					4	19.05	1.75	2.25									6	13.95	1.33	1.67
Broken with adhesion	2	22.22	0.50	0.50																
Total	9	100.00	1.22	1.00	21	100.00	2.19	2.52	12	100.00	3.75	3.58	1	100.00	6.00	4.00	43	99.99	2.51	2.53

Source: Field study by the authors.

Table 7.19: Distribution of Average Male and Female Members in Different Types and Sizes of Sherpa Family in Sherpapur Village of Darjeeling, West Bengal

Family Size	1-3				4-6				7-9				10+				Total			
Family type	Total Family		Avg male	Avg female	Total family		Avg male	Avg female	Total family		Avg male	Avg female	Total family		Avg male	Avg female	Total family		Avg male	Avg female
	No.	%			No.	%			No.	%			No.	%			No.	%		
Nuclear	10	50.00	1.60	1.20	29	72.50	2.45	2.52									39	54.17	2.23	2.18
Nuclear with Adhesion					1	2.50	4.00	3.00	2	18.18	3.50	3.50					3	4.17	3.67	3.33
Extended					8	20.00	2.13	3.25	9	81.81	4.00	4.11	1	100.00	5.00	7.00	18	25.00	3.22	3.89
Extended type with adhesion																				
Nascent	3	15.00	0.67	0.33	1	2.50	2.00	2.00									4	5.56	1.00	0.75
Broken	7	35.00	1.29	1.29													7	9.72	1.29	1.29
Broken with adhesion					1	2.50	3.00	2.00									1	1.39	3.00	2.00
Total	20	100.00	1.35	1.10	40	100.00	2.43	2.65	11	99.99	3.91	4.00	1	100.00	5.00	7.00	72	100.01	2.39	2.49

Source: Field study by the authors.

Table 7.20: Distribution of Male and Female Members in Different Types and Sizes of Sherpa Family in Two Villages of Darjeeling, West Bengal

Family Type		Family Size																			
		1–3				4–6				7–9				10+				Total			
		Family	Person	Male	Female	Family	Person	Male	Female	Family	Person	Male	Female	Family	Person	Male	Female	Family	Person	Male	Female
Nuclear Type	No	17	46	26	20	41	202	99	103	5	37	22	15					63	285	147	138
	%	26.98	16.14	17.69	14.49	65.08	70.88	67.35	74.64	7.94	12.98	14.97	10.87					100.00	100.00	100.01	100.00
Nuclear with adhesion	No					4	21	10	11	2	14	7	7					6	35	17	18
	%					66.67	60.00	58.82	61.11	33.33	40.00	41.18	38.89					100.00	100.00	100.00	100.00
Extended Type	No					10	54	22	32	15	117	56	61	2	22	11	11	27	193	89	104
	%					37.04	27.98	24.72	30.77	55.56	60.62	62.92	58.65	7.41	11.40	12.36	10.58	100.01	100.00	100.00	100.00
Extended with adhesion type	No									1	7	3	4					1	7	3	4
	%									100.00	100.00	100.00	100.00					100.00	100.00	100.00	100.00
Nascent Type	No	3	3	2	1	1	4	2	2									4	7	4	3
	%	75.00	42.86	50.00	33.33	25.00	57.14	50.00	66.67									100.00	100.00	100.00	100.00
Broken type	No	9	20	10	10	4	16	7	9									13	36	17	19
	%	69.23	55.56	58.82	52.63	30.77	44.44	41.18	47.37									100.00	100.00	100.00	100.00
Broken with adhision total	No					1	5	3	2									1	5	3	2
	%					100.00	100.00	100.00	100.00									100.00	100.00	100.00	100.00
Total	No	29	69	38	31	61	302	143	159	23	175	88	87	2	22	11	11	115	568	280	288
	%	25.22	12.15	13.57	10.76	53.04	53.17	51.07	55.21	20.00	30.81	31.43	30.21	1.74	3.87	3.93	3.82	100.00	100.00	100.00	100.00

Source: Field study by the authors.

Table 7.21: Distribution of Male and Female Members in Different Types and Sizes of Sherpa Family at Sherpaguri Village, Darjeeling, West Bengal

Family Type		Family Size																			
		1—3				4—6				7—9				10+				Total			
		Family	Person	Male	Female	Family	Person	Male	Female	Family	Person	Male	Female	Family	Person	Male	Female	Family	Person	Male	Female
Nuclear Type	No.	7	18	10	8	12	58	28	30	5	37	22	15					24	113	60	53
	%	29.17	15.93	16.67	15.03	50.00	51.33	46.67	56.60	20.83	32.74	36.67	28.30					100.00	100.00	100.01	99.99
Nuclear with adhesion	No.					3	14	6	8									3	14	6	8
	%					100.00	100.00	100.00	100.00									100.00	100.00	100.00	100.00
Extended Type	No.					2	11	5	6	6	44	20	24					8	55	25	30
	%					25.00	20.00	20.00	20.00	75.00	80.00	80.00	80.00					100.00	100.00	100.00	100.00
Extended with adhesion type	No.									1	7	3	4	1	10	6	4	2	17	9	8
	%									50.00	41.18	33.33	50.00	50.00	58.82	66.67	50.00	100.00	100.00	100.00	100.00
Nascent Type	No.																				
	%																				
Broken type	No.	2	2	1	1	4	16	7	9									6	18	8	10
	%	33.33	11.11	12.50	10.00	66.67	88.89	87.50	90.00									100.00	100.00	100.00	100.00
Broken with adhesion total	No.																				
	%																				

Source: Field study by the authors.

Table 7.22: Distribution of Male and Female Members in Different Types and Sizes of Sherpa Family at Sherpapur Village, Darjeeling, West Bengal

Family Type		Family Size																			
		1—3				4—6				7—9				10+				Total			
		Family	Person	Male	Female	Family	Person	Male	Female	Family	Person	Male	Female	Family	Person	Male	Female	Family	Person	Male	Female
Nuclear Type	No	10	28	16	12	29	144	71	73									39	172	87	85
	%	25.64	16.28	18.39	14.12	74.36	83.72	81.61	85.88									100.00	100.00	100.00	100.00
Nuclear with adhesion	No					1	7	4	3	2	14	7	7					3	21	11	10
	%					33.33	33.33	57.14	30.00	66.67	66.67	63.64	70.00					100.00	100.00	100.00	100.00
Extended Type	No					8	43	17	26	9	73	36	37	1	12	5	7	18	128	58	70
	%					44.44	33.59	29.31	37.14	50.00	57.03	62.07	52.86	5.56	9.38	8.62	70.00	100.00	100	100	100
Extended with adhesion type	No																	0	0	0	0
	%																	0	0	0	0
Nascent Type	No	3	3	2	1	1	4	2	2									4	7	4	3
	%	75.00	42.86	50.00	33.33	25.00	57.14	50.00	66.67									100.00	100.00	100.00	100.00
Broken type	No	7	18	9	9													7	18	9	9
	%	100.00	100.00	100.00	100.00													100.00	100.00	100.00	100.00
Broken with adhesion total	No					1	5	3	2									1	5	3	2
	%					100.00	100.00	100.00	100.00									100.00	100.00	100.00	100.00
Total	No	20	49	27	22	40	203	97	106	11	87	43	44	1	12	5	7	72	351	172	179
	%	27.78	13.96	15.70	12.29	55.56	57.83	56.40	59.22	15.28	24.79	25.00	24.58	1.39	3.42	2.91	3.91	100.01	100.00	100.01	100.00

Source: Field study by the authors.

the nuclear type of families has retained the highest number of the medium sized families (65.08%). These families have also retained the highest number of members (70.88%), male (65.35%) and also female (74.64%) members. Same is the case with the nuclear type with adhesion.

On the other hand, the extended type large families have secured the highest position in all respects (55.56% of the total families, 60.62% members, 62.92% male members and 58.65% female members)(Table 7.20).

At Sherpaguri village of Darjeeling District, out of 24 nuclear type families the medium sized families have in the fold, half of the total nuclear families. These families have also retained the highest number of total members, and also the highest number male and female members. The large sized families have, on the other hand, retained the highest number of extended families, the highest number of members, highest number of male members and also female members (Table 7.21).

In the second studied village of Darjeeling District, Sherpapur, the medium sized families have kept the highest number of the nuclear families (74.36%) and also highest share of the total members, male and female members. But in case of the extended families the large sized families have the highest number of families as well as members (Table 7.22).

Now, we shall come down to the studied villages of South District, Sikkim to see the type and size of the Sherpa families and distribution of members of the Sherpa families. Out of the total of 124 Sherpa families of the two villages, the nuclear type has retained the highest position capturing 57.26 per cent of the total families. Next come the extended families (27.42%). The extended families have also kept highest number of both male and female members. From here if we shift to different sizes of the families, we shall see that in the small and medium sized families the nuclear type has kept the highest number of families (65.52% and 68.33% respectively). But in case of the large and very large sized families, the extended type has captured the highest number of families. In case of the large sized families the nuclear type has also a good number of families (Table 7.23).

At Sherpagaon village of South District, Sikkim, out of a total of 64 families, the nuclear type has the highest strength (60.94%). The extended type has a strength of only one fourth of the total.

Now, when we examine the size and type of the Sherpa families of this village we see that the small and medium sized nuclear type families have the highest strength (68.75% and 67.74% respectively). In case of the large sized families both nuclear and extended types have equal and

Table 7.23: Distribution of Average Male and Female Members in Different Types and Sizes of Sherpa Family in Two Villages of South District, Sikkim

Family type	Family Size																			
	1-3				4-6				7-9				10+				Total			
	Family No	Family %	Avg male	Avg female	Family No	Family %	Avg male	Avg female	Family No.	Family %	Avg male	Avg female	Family No.	Family %	Avg male	Avg female	Family No	Family %	Avg male	Avg female
Nuclear Type	19	65.52	1.05	1.16	41	68.33	2.44	2.29	9	40.91	3.78	3.56	2	15.38	5.50	6.50	71	57.26	2.32	2.36
Nuclear with Adhesion Type																				
Extended Type	2	6.90	2.00	1.00	10	16.67	2.90	2.70	12	54.55	4.75	3.50	10	76.92	5.90	6.50	34	27.42	4.38	4.00
Extended type with adhesion					1	1.67	4.00										1	0.81	4.00	
Nascent type																				
Broken type	7	24.14	1.29	1.43	7	11.67	3.00	1.57					1	7.69	5.00	6.00	15	12.10	2.33	1.80
Broken with adhesion	1	3.45	2.00	1.00	1	1.67	2.00	2.00	1	4.55	6.00	2.00					3	2.42	3.33	1.67
Total	29	100.01	1.21	1.21	60	100.01	2.60	2.33	22	100.01	4.41	3.45	13	99.99	5.77	6.46	124	100.01	2.93	2.65

Source: Field study by the authors.

the highest strength (46.15%each). The very large families have provided the extended type the highest strength (75.00%) (Table 7.24).

At the second studied village of South District, Sikkim, i.e. Sherpahat, out of a total of 60 Sherpa families a little over half (53.33%) are nuclear type. 30.00 per cent families here are extended type. In the family size level the nuclear type of both small and medium sized families has the highest strength (61.54% and 68.97% respectively). On the other hand, extended type in case of the large and very large families, has retained the highest position (66.67% and 77.77% respectively) (Table 7.25).

We shall now move to the other aspect of type and size in the Sherpa family organization. Out of the total of 71 nuclear families of the two studied villages of South District, Sikkim the medium sized families have the highest strength (57.75%). The small sized families have the next higher strength. In case of the extended type of families, large sized families have the highest strength (35.29%). Both medium and very large families have the next higher strength (29.41% each). The medium sized nuclear families have retained the highest number of family members (Table 7.26).

At Sherpagaon village of South District, Sikkim, out of a total of 39 nuclear families the medium sized families have the highest position (53.85%). These families have also retained the highest number of members (53.33% and the highest number of both male (53.61%) and female (53.01%) members. In case of the extended families the large families have the highest position (37.50%). These families have also retained the highest number of members and also the highest number of both male and female members (Table 7.27).

Now, as we move to Sherpahat village of this district, we see that there are 39 nuclear types of Sherpa families in this village which have very large number (62.50%) of medium sized families. The next higher number goes to the small sized families. The medium sized nuclear families have also taken in the fold, more than half of the total members, total male and also female members (67.42%, 61.54% and 64.10% respectively). As we examine the extended families of the Sherpa of this village, we find that the very large sized extended families have retained the highest number of the total extended families (38.89%). Next come the large sized extended families (33.33%). The very large sized extended families have also kept the highest number of total members and also the highest number of male and female members.

It is thus seen that among the Sherpa of both Darjeeling, West Bengal and South District, Sikkim the nuclear type has retained the highest number

Table 7.24: Distribution of Average Male and Female Members in Different Types and Sizes of Sherpa Family in Sherpagaon Village of South District, Sikkim

Family type	Family Size																			
	1-3				4-6				7-9				10+				Total			
	Family		Avg male	Avg female	Family		Avg male	Avg female	Family		Avg male	Avg female	Family		Avg male	Avg female	Family		Avg male	Avg female
	No	%			No.	%			No.	%			No.	%			No.	%		
Nuclear Type	11	68.75	1.27	1.09	21	67.74	2.48	2.09	6	46.15	4.17	3.33	1	25.00	6.00	7.00	39	60.94	2.49	2.13
Nuclear with Adhesion Type																				
Extended Type	2	12.50	2.00	1.00	5	16.13	3.00	2.80	6	46.15	4.67	3.33	3	75.00	6.67	6.00	16	25.00	4.19	3.13
Extended with adhesion type					1	3.23	4.00										1	1.56	4.00	
Nascent type																				
Broken type	2	12.50	1.50	1.50	4	12.90	3.25	1.25									6	9.34	2.67	1.33
Broken with adhesion	1	6.25	2.00	1.00					1	7.69	6.00	2.00					2	3.13	4.00	1.50
Total	16	100.00	1.44	1.13	31	100.00	2.71	2.03	13	99.99	4.54	3.23	4	100.00	6.50	6.25	64	99.97	3.00	2,31

Source: Field study by the authors.

Table 7.25: Distribution of Average Male and Female Members in Different Types and Sizes of Sherpa Family in Sherpahat Village of South District, Sikkim

Family Size	1-3				4-6				7-9				10+				Total			
Family type	Total Family		Avg male	Avg female	Total Family		Avg male	Avg female	Total Family		Avg male	Avg female	Total Family		Avg male	Avg female	Family		Avg male	Avg female
	No.	%			No.	%			No.	%			No.	%			No.	%		
Nuclear Type	8	61.54	0.75	1.25	20	68.97	2.40	2.50	3	33.33	3.00	4.00	1	11.11	5.00	6.00	32	53.33	2.13	2.44
Nuclear with Adhesion Type																				
Extended Type					5	7.24	2.80	2.60	6	66.67	4.83	3.67	7	77.77	5.57	6.71	18	30.00	4.56	4.56
Extended with adhesion type																				
Nascent type																				
Broken type	5	38.46	1.20	1.40	3	10.34	2.67	2.00					1	11.11	5.00	6.00	9	15.00	2.11	2.11
Broken with adhesion					1	3.45	2.00	2.00									1	1.67	2.00	2.00
Total	13	100.00	0.92	1.40	29	100.00	2.48	2.45	9	100.00	4.22	3.78	9	99.99	5.44	6.56	60	100.00	2.85	3.02

Source: Field study by the authors.

Table 7.26: Distribution of Male and Female Members in Different Types and Sizes of Sherpa Family at Two Villages of South District, Sikkim

Family Type		*Family Size*																			
		1—3				*4—6*				*7—9*				*10+*				*Total*			
		Family	*Person*	*Male*	*Female*	*Family*	*Person*	*Male*	*Female*	*Family*	*Person*	*Male*	*Female*	*Family*	*Person*	*Male*	*Female*	*Family*	*Person*	*Male*	*Female*
Nuclear Type	No.	19	42	20	22	41	194	100	94	9	66	34	32	2	24	11	13	71	326	165	161
	%	26.76	12.88	12.12	13.66	57.75	59.51	60.61	58.39	12.68	20.25	20.61	19.88	2.82	7.36	6.67	8.67	100.01	100.00	100.01	100.00
Nuclear with adhesion	No.																				
	%																				
Extended Type	No.	2	6	4	2	10	56	29	27	12	99	57	42	10	124	59	65	34	285	149	136
	%	5.88	2.11	2.68	1.47	29.41	19.65	19.46	19.85	35.29	34.74	38.26	30.88	29.41	43.51	39.60	47.79	99.99	100.01	100.00	99.99
Extended with adhesion type	No.					1	4	4										1	4	4	
	%					100.00	100.00	100.00										100.00	100.00	100.00	
Nascent Type	No.																				
	%																				
Broken type	No.	7	19	9	10	7	32	21	11					1	11	5	6	15	62	35	27
	%	46.67	30.65	25.71	37.04	46.67	51.61	60.00	40.74					6.67	17.74	14.29	22.22	100.01	100.00	100.00	100.00
Broken with adhesion	No.	1	3	2	1	1	4	2	2	1	8	6	2					3	15	10	5
total	%	33.33	20.00	20.00	20.00	33.33	26.67	20.00	40.00	33.33	53.33	60.00	40.00					99.99	100.00	100.00	100.00
Total	No.	29	70	35	35	60	290	156	134	22	173	97	76	13	159	75	84	124	692	363	329
	%	23.39	10.12	9.64	10.64	48.39	41.91	42.98	40.73	17.74	25.00	26.72	23.10	10.48	22.98	20.66	25.53	100.00	100.01	100.00	100.00

Source: Field study by the authors.

Table 7.27: Distribution of Male and Female Members in Different Types and Sizes of Sherpa Family at Sherpagaon Villages of South District, Sikkim

Family Type		Family Size																			
		1—3				4—6				7—9				10+				Total			
		Family	Person	Male	Female	Family	Person	Male	Female	Family	Person	Male	Female	Family	Person	Male	Female	Family	Person	Male	Female
Nuclear Type	No.	11	26	14	12	21	96	52	44	6	45	25	20	1	13	6	7	39	180	97	83
	%	28.21	14.44	14.43	14.46	53.85	53.33	53.61	53.01	15.38	25.00	25.77	24.10	2.56	7.22	6.19	8.43	100.00	99.99	100.00	100.00
Nuclear with adhesion	No.																				
	%																				
Extended Type	No.	2	6	4	2	5	29	15	14	6	48	28	20	3	38	20	18	16	121	67	54
	%	12.50	4.96	5.97	3.70	31.25	23.97	22.39	25.92	37.50	39.67	41.79	37.04	18.75	31.40	29.85	33.33	100.00	100.00	100.00	99.99
Extended with adhesion type	No.					1	4	4										1	4	4	
	%					100.00	100.00	100.00										100.00	100.00	100.00	
Nascent Type	No.																				
	%																				
Broken type	No.	2	6	3	3	4	18	13	5									6	24	16	8
	%	33.33	25.00	18.75	37.50	66.67	75.00	81.25	62.50									100.00	100.00	100.00	100.00
Broken with adhesion total	No.	1	3	2	1					1	8	6	2					2	11	8	3
	%	50.00	27.27	25.00	33.33					50.00	72.73	25.00	66.67					100.00	100.00	100.00	100.00
Total	No.	16	41	23	18	31	147	84	63	13	101	59	42	4	51	26	25	64	340	192	148
	%	25.00	12.06	11.98	12.16	48.44	43.24	43.75	42.57	20.31	29.71	30.73	28.38	6.25	15.00	13.54	16.89	100.00	100.01	100.00	100.00

Source: Field study by the authors.

Table 7.28: Distribution of Male and Female Members in Different Types and Sizes of Sherpa Family at Sherpahat Villages of South District, Sikkim

Family Type		Family Size															
		1—3				4—6				7—9				10+				Total			
		Family	Person	Male	Female	Family	Person	Male	Female	Family	Person	Male	Female	Family	Person	Male	Female	Family	Person	Male	Female
Nuclear Type	No.	8	16	6	10	20	98	48	50	3	21	9	12	1	11	5	6	32	146	68	78
	%	25.00	10.96	8.82	12.82	62.50	67.42	61.54	64.10	9.38	14.39	13.24	15.38	3.13	7.53	7.35	7.69	100.01	100.00	99.99	99.99
Nuclear with adhesion	No.																				
	%																				
Extended Type	No.					5	27	14	13	6	51	29	22	7	86	39	47	18	164	82	82
	%					27.78	16.46	17.07	15.85	33.33	31.10	35.37	26.83	38.89	52.44	47.56	57.32	100.00	100.00	100.00	100.00
Extended with adhesion type	No.																				
	%																				
Nascent Type	No.																				
	%																				
Broken type	No.	5	13	6	7	3	14	8	6					1	11	5	6	9	38	19	19
	%	55.56	34.21	21.58	36.84	33.33	36.84	42.11	31.58					11.11	28.95	26.32	31.58	100.00	100.00	100.01	100.00
Broken with adhesion total	No.					1	4	2	2									1	4	2	2
	%					100.00	100.00	100.00	100.00									100.00	100.00	100.00	100.00
Total	No.	13	29	12	17	29	143	72	71	9	72	38	34	9	108	49	59	60	352	171	181
	%	21.67	8.24	7.02	9.39	48.33	40.63	42.11	39.23	15.00	20.45	22.22	18.78	15.00	30.68	28.65	32.60	100.00	100.00	100.00	100.00

Source: Field study by the authors.

of families, and either small or medium sized families have the highest number of nuclear families. These families have also retained the highest number of members of both sexes. In case of the extended families, large or medium size families have kept in their fold, the highest number of extended families and the highest number of members.

Generation-wise Gradation of the Sherpa Families

In the families of the Sherpas of both Darjeeling and Sikkim, like the families of different other communities of the world, the family members belong to different generations. Members of both ascending generations as well as descending generation from ego do live in some of the Sherpa families with members of the generation of self. Of course, it is not that members belonging to different ascending generations, ego's generations and also different descending generations, live in the same family. While the members of one family belong to both ascending and descending generation, the other family may have members of one generation only. However, we shall now examine the generation-wise distribution of the members in the Sherpa families. For the purpose of our study we have been able to divide the Sherpa families on the basis of the members belonging to different generations, into following five grades:

- Grade-I Families composed of members from ego's generation, ego's first ascending generation and ego's first descending generation.
- Grade-II Families composed of members from generation of ego only.
- Grade-III Families composed of members from generation of ego and ego's second descending generation.
- Grade-IV Families composed of the members from generation of ego, first descending and second descending generations of ego.
- Grade-V Families composed of members belonging to the generation of ego, and ego's first descending generation.

We shall now examine our data which we collected from the Sherpas of two villages, Sherpaguri and Sherpapur of Kalimpong Sub-Division of Darjeeling District and another two villages, Sherpagaon and Sherpahat, from South District, Sikkim.

Generation-wise Gradation

In the two villages, that we studied in Kalimpong Sub-division, Darjeeling District, there are a total of 115 Sherpa families having 568 members. Out of these 115 sherpa families, Sherpaguri village has the lowest number (43 or 37.39%) of the Sherpa families. But highest number of the Sherpa families (72 or 62.61%) are located at Sherpapur village. Similarly Sherpapur village also have higher number of Grade-IV and Grade-V families in comparison to those of other village. While there is only one Grade-I family and that is located at Sherpaguri village, Grade-III family (only one) is situated only at Sherpapur village and not at Sherpaguri. But Grade-II families are present in equal number in these two villages (Table 7.29).

Now, as we come to the distribution of family members in different grades of these two villages, we found that out of the total families (115) of these two villages, Sherpapur village has the higher number of family members (351 or 61.80%). The rest of the members (217 or 38.20%) are in the village Sherpaguri. The grade-wise distribution of the family members shows that Grade-II, Grade-IV and Grade-V have the large number of family members at Sherpapur village, higher than those of Sherpaguri village. While all the members of Grade-I family (only one) live at Sherpaguri village, all the members of Grade-III family (only one) reside at Sherpapur village.

Now, we come down to the two villages we studied in South District, Sikkim. Out of a total of 124 families of all grades of these two villages of Sikkim, a little over half (64 or 51.61%) are located at Sherpagaon village and the remaining families (60 or 48.39%) are at Sherpahat village. When we look at grade-wise distribution of the Sherpa families of these two villages we find that Grade-I has a total of only three families of which two are in the village, Sherpahat and the remaining one at Sherpagaon village. Out of 7 Grade-II families, majority (71.43%) are in Sherpahat village. The two families of Grade-III are both at Sherpahat village and none at Sherpagaon village. In case of Grade-IV families also the majority (65.22%) out of 23 families, are in Sherpahat village. But the majority of Grade-V families (59.55%) are in Sherpagaon village. The rest of the families are in the other village of Sikkim. Following grades of these two villages, the members of the families of all the grades except Grade-V are in majority in the Sherpahat village. The family members of only Grade-V are in majority at Sherpagaon village though no doubt Sherpagaon village has more number of families (64) than that of Sherpahat village (60).

Table 7.29: Generation-wise Gradation of the Sherpa Families of the Studied Villages of Darjeeling and Sikkim

Generation-wise Gradation	Sherpaguri				Sherpapur				Total				Sherpagaon				Sherpahat				Total			
	Family		Members		Family		Members		Family		Members		Family		Members		Family		Members		Family		Members	
	No.	%	No.	%	No.	%	No.	%	No.	%	No.	%	No.	%	No.	%	No.	%	No.	%	No.	%	No.	%
I	1	100.00	5	100.00	—	—	—	—	1	100.00	5	100.00	1	33.33	6	42.86	2	66.67	8	57.14	3	100.00	14	100.00
II	4	50.00	6	40.00	4	50.00	9	60.00	8	100.00	15	100.00	2	28.57	2	20.00	5	71.43	8	80.00	7	100.00	10	100.00
III					1	100.00	12	100.00	1	100.00	12	100.00					2	100.00	8	100.00	2	100.00	8	100.00
IV	10	47.62	69	47.92	11	52.38	75	52.08	21	100.00	144	100.00	8	34.78	63	31.50	15	65.22	137	68.50	23	100.00	200	100.00
V	28	33.33	137	34.95	56	67.67	255	65.05	84	100.00	392	100.00	53	59.55	269	58.48	36	40.45	191	41.52	89	100.00	460	100.00
Total	43	37.39	217	38.20	72	62.61	351	61.80	115	100.00	568	100.00	64	51.61	340	49.13	60	48.39	352	50.87	124	100.00	692	100.00

Source: Field study by the authors.

As we come down to Table 7.29 we find that out of a total of 115 families of the two villages of Darjeeling District, the largest number of the families are Grade-V families (73.04%). The next larger number (18.26%) of families is in Grade-IV, followed by Grade-II (6.96%).

As we move to the individual village, we see that at Sherpaguri village also Grade-V has the largest number of families (65.12%). In this village also Grade-IV has the next higher number of families (23.25%) followed by Grade-II. But this village does not have Grade-III family.

The other village, Sherpapur also follows the same trend. Here in this village Grade-V also holds the largest number of families (77.78%). Next in order comes Grade-IV which has 15.28% of the total families of this village. This village does not have Grade-I family.

Now, we shall come to the distribution of family members of these two villages in different generational grades. In these two villages a total of 568 members live in 115 families. Following the trend of the distribution of families in different grades, Grade-V holds the largest number of family members (69.01%). Grade-IV has the next higher number of family members (25.35%). The two villages, individually, have followed the same line of distribution of family members in different grades. Grade-V holds the largest number of family members (63.13% and 72.65% respectively) and in a similar way Grade-IV has the next higher number of family members (31.80% and 15.37% respectively).

Now, we like to come to the studied villages of South District, Sikkim, to see the gradewise distribution of the Sherpa families and family members.

The combined number of the Sherpa families of the two villages, Sherpagaon and Sherpahat is 124. In these two villages the trend of distribution of families is also similar to that of Darjeeling villages. Here in these Sikkimese villages, Grade-V in a similar way, holds the highest number of families (71.77%). Grade-IV here has the next higher number of the Sherpa families (18.55%). In this area the individual villages also follow the same trend. Both Sherpagaon and Sherpahat villages also have Grade-V holding the largest number of families (82.81% and 60.00% respectively). In these two villages also Grade-IV has the next higher number of families (12.50% and 18.53% respectively (Table 7.30).

Now, if we look at the distribution of family members in different grades, we find that in these villages of Sikkim this distribution has followed the same path as that followed by the Sherpa families. There is a combined total of 692 members living in 124 Sherpa families of these villages. Now, out of these 692 family members, Grade-V as usual, has

Table 7.30: Generation-wise Gradation of the Sherpa Families of the Studied Villages of Darjeeling and Sikkim

Generation-wise Gradation	Sherpaguri				Sherpapur				Total				Sherpagaon				Sherpahat				Total			
	Family		Members		Family		Members		Family		Members		Family		Members		Family		Members		Family		Members	
	No.	%	No.	%	No.	%	No.	%	No.	%	No.	%	No.	%	No.	%	No.	%	No.	%	No.	%	No.	%
I	1	2.33	5	2.33	—	—	—	—	1	0.87	5	0.88	1	1.56	6	1.76	2	3.33	8	2.27	3	2.42	14	2.02
II	4	9.30	6	2.77	4	5.56	9	2.56	8	6.96	15	2.64	2	3.13	2	0.59	5	8.33	8	2.27	7	5.65	10	1.45
III					1	1.39	12	3.42	1	0.87	12	2.11					2	3.33	8	2.27	2	1.61	8	1.16
IV	10	23.25	69	31.80	11	15.28	75	21.37	21	18.26	144	25.35	8	12.50	63	18.53	15	25.00	137	38.92	23	18.55	200	28.90
V	28	65.12	137	63.13	56	77.78	255	72.65	84	73.04	392	69.01	53	82.81	269	79.12	36	60.00	191	54.26	89	71.77	460	66.47
Total	43	100.00	217	100.00	72	100.01	351	100.00	115	100.00	568	99.99	64	100.00	340	100.00	60	99.99	352	99.99	124	100.00	692	100.00

Source: Field study by the authors.

the highest number of family members (66.47%) followed by Grade-IV (28.90%). The distribution of the Sherpa families in the two villages if shown separately, also follows the same trend. At Sherpagaon as well as at Sherpahat village the majority of the family members live in Grade-V families. But at Sherpagaon village while overwhelming majority of family members (79.12%) live in Grade-V, at Sherpahat village also Grade-V families hold only slender majority of family members (54.26%). In both the villages Grade-IV families retain the next higher number of family members. But here on the other hand, Sherpahat village has kept in its fold more family members in Grade-IV families (38.92%), the other village, Sherpagaon, holds much less number of family members in Grade-IV families, only 18.53 per cent. In both villages Grades-I, II and III do not have significant number of families and family members. Sherpagaon village, of course, does not have any Grade-III families and, therefore, family members.

Thus, from the above discussion, it is revealed that among the Sherpas of both Darjeeling and Sikkim Grade-V families are numerically the most dominant grade as this grade holds the largest number of families as also the family members. Grade-IV holds the next higher number of families as well as family members. The other three grades do not enjoy much numerical significance.

Hereafter, we shall examine our data on different sizes of the Sherpa families having members belonging to different generations. In the two studied villages at Darjeeling District there are a combined total of 115 families of which majority (73.04%) belong to Grade-V (Table 7.31).

The next higher number of families (18.26%) belongs to the Grade-IV. The lowest number of families belongs to the Grade-I and Grade-III, each with one family only (0.87% each). The members living in the Grade-V families also have the highest number of members, the highest number of male members and also the highest number of female members.

Now, as we come to the village, Sherpaguri of Darjeeling District, we get the same picture. In this village also the Grade-V retains the highest number of the Sherpa families (65.12%). The Grade-IV has the next higher number of families (23.26%). The Grade-V families here also retain the highest number of members, and also the highest number of male as well as female members (Table 7.32).

The Sherpa families of the village, Sherpapur of Darjeeling District also show the same trend. Here also the highest number of families are found to belong to the Grade-V (77.78%) and these families have also retained the highest number of members, male members and as well as

Table 7.31: Generation-wise Gradation of Members in the Sherpa Family of Two Villages of Darjeeling, West Bengal

Family Size		Generation-wise Gradation of Family																					
		I				II				III				IV				V				Total			
		Family	Person	Male	Female	Family	Person	Male	Female	Family	Person	Male	Female	Family	Person	Male	Female	Family	Person	Male	Female	Family	Person	Male	Female
1-3	No.					7	11	6	5									22	58	32	26	29	69	38	31
	%					24.14	15.94	15.79	16.13									75.86	84.06	84.21	83.87	100.00	100.00	100.00	100.00
4-6	No.	1	5	2	3	1	4	2	2					8	43	18	25	51	250	121	129	61	302	143	159
	%	1.64	1.66	1.40	1.89	1.64	1.32	1.40	1.26					13.11	14.24	12.59	15.72	83.61	82.78	84.62	81.13	100.00	100.00	100.01	100.00
7-9	No.													12	91	44	47	11	84	44	40	23	175	88	87
	%													52.17	52.00	50.00	54.02	47.83	48.00	50.00	45.98	100.00	100.00	100.00	100.00
10+	No.									1	12	5	7	1	10	6	4					2	22	11	11
	%									50.00	54.55	45.45	63.64	50.00	45.45	54.55	36.36					100.00	100.00	100.00	100.00
Total	No.	1	5	2	3	8	15	8	7	1	12	5	7	21	144	68	76	84	392	197	195	115	568	280	288
	%	0.87	0.88	0.71	1.04	6.96	2.64	2.86	2.43	0.87	2.11	1.79	2.43	18.26	25.35	24.29	26.39	73.04	69.01	70.36	67.71	100.00	100.00	100.01	100.00

Source: Field study by the authors.

Table 7.32: Generation-wise Gradation of Members in the Sherpa Family of Sherpaguri Village of Darjeeling, West Bengal

Family Size		I				II				III				IV				V				Total			
		Family	Person	Male	Female	Family	Person	Male	Female	Family	Person	Male	Female	Family	Person	Male	Female	Family	Person	Male	Female	Family	Person	Male	Female
1-3	No.					4	6	3	3									5	14	8	6	9	20	11	9
	%					44.44	30.00	27.27	33.33									55.55	70.00	72.73	66.67	99.99	100.00	100.00	100.00
4-6	No.	1	5	2	3									3	15	7	8	17	79	37	42	21	99	46	53
	%	4.76	5.05	4.35	5.66									14.29	15.15	15.22	15.09	80.95	79.80	80.43	79.25	100.00	100.00	100.00	100.00
7-9	No.													6	44	21	23	6	44	24	20	12	88	45	43
	%													50.00	50.00	46.67	53.49	50.00	50.00	53.33	46.51	100.00	100.00	100.00	100.00
10+	No.													1	10	6	4					1	10	6	4
	%													100.00	100.00	100.00	100.00					100.00	100.00	100.00	100.00
Total	No.	1	5	2	3	4	6	3	3					10	69	34	35	28	137	69	68	43	217	108	109
	%	2.33	2.30	1.85	2.75	9.30	2.76	2.78	2.75					23.26	31.80	31.48	32.11	65.12	63.13	63.89	62.39	100.01	100.00	100.00	100.00

Source: Field study by the authors.

Table 7.33: Generation-wise Gradation of Members in the Sherpa Family of Sherpapur Village of Darjeeling, West Bengal

Family Size		Generation wise Gradation of Family																							
		I				II				III				IV				V				Total			
		Family	Person	Male	Female	Family	Person	Male	Female	Family	Person	Male	Female	Family	Person	Male	Female	Family	Person	Male	Female	Family	Person	Male	Female
1-3	No.					3	5	3	2									17	44	24	20	20	49	27	22
	%					15.00	10.20	11.11	9.09									85.00	89.80	88.88	90.90	100.00	100.00	99.99	99.99
4-6	No.					1	4	2	2					5	28	11	17	34	171	84	87	40	203	97	106
	%					2.50	1.97	2.06	1.89					12.50	13.79	11.34	16.04	85.00	84.24	86.60	82.08	100.00	100.00	100.00	100.01
7-9	No.													6	47	23	24	5	40	20	20	11	87	43	44
	%													54.55				45.45				100.00			
10+	No.									1	12	5	7									1	12	5	7
	%									100.00	100.00	100.00	100.00									100.00	100.00	100.00	100.00
Total	No.					4	9	5	4	1	12	5	7	11	75	34	41	56	255	128	127	72	351	172	179
	%					5.56	2.56	2.91	2.23	1.39	3.42	2.91	3.91	15.28	21.37	19.77	22.91	77.78	72.65	74.42	70.95	100.01	100.00	100.01	100.00

Source: Field study by the authors.

female members. Grade-IV has the next higher number of families (Table 7.33).

Now, let us examine the Sikkim scenario. In the two Sherpa villages together, the total number of the Sherpa families is 124. Out of these families, the largest number of families belong to the Grade-V, and this grade also retains the highest number of families (71.77%), and the highest male as well as female members. The Grade-IV has the next higher number of families, the next higher number of members, male members and also female members. Now, as we reach Sherpagaon village and also Sherpahat village of this district, we see the same trend in the generation-gradation of the Sherpa families. In these two villages also the Grade-V has secured the highest position in concentrating highest number of families, the highest number of members, and also the highest number of male as well as female members. And similar to the trend in the villages of Darjeeling, the second position in the village of Sherpagaon has been secured by the Grade-IV. The only difference is that at Sherpahat Grade-IV has quite significant strength of the families and the members (Tables 7.34, 7.35 and 7.36).

Now, let us see the position of different generation grades in different sizes of the Sherpa families. In the two villages of Darjeeling District taken together, out of a total of 84 families of Grade-V, the highest number of families (60.71%) are medium sized families. The next higher strength of the Grade-V families goes to small families. There is no very large size families in Grade-V. The next higher number of families (21) belong to the Grade-IV. In the Grade-IV large sized families have the highest strength (57.14%). Next in order come the medium sized families (38.10%). In Grade-III there is only one family, and that is a large family. Grade-II has eight families, of which seven (87.50%) belong to small families. Grade-I also has one family which is a medium sized one (Table 7.37).

As we come down to the individual village we see that at Sherpaguri village there are a total of 28 families in Grade-V of which the highest number of families (17 or 60.21%) are medium sized. But in the Grade-IV families of this village majority of the families (60.00%) are large families. There is no small family in this Grade. At this village there is no Grade-III family. The Grade-II has only 4 families and all are small families. Grade-I has only one family, a medium sized one (Table 7.38).

Now, let us see the position of the other Sherpa village of Darjeeling District, that is, Sherpapur. In this village families belong to Grade-V are 56 in number. Out of these 56 families 34 (60.71%) are medium sized

Table 7.34: Generation-wise Gradation of Members in the Sherpa Family of Two Villages of South District, Sikkim

Family Size		Generation-wise Gradation of Family																							
		I				II				III				IV				V				Total			
		Family	Person	Male	Female	Family	Person	Male	Female	Family	Person	Male	Female	Family	Person	Male	Female	Family	Person	Male	Female	Family	Person	Male	Female
1-3	No.					7	10	5	5	1	2		2					21	58	30	28	29	70	35	35
	%					24.14	14.29	14.29	14.29	3.45	2.86		5.71					72.41	82.86	85.71	80.00	100.00	100.01	100.00	100.00
4-6	No.	3	14	7	7					1	6	3	3	6	31	14	17	50	239	132	107	60	290	156	134
	%	5.00	4.83	4.49	5.22					1.67	2.07	1.92	2.24	10.00	10.69	8.97	12.69	83.33	32.41	84.62	79.85	100.00	100.00	100.00	100.00
7-9	No.													10	83	50	33	12	90	47	43	22	173	97	76
	%													45.45	47.98	51.55	43.42	54.55	52.02	48.45	56.58	100.00	100.00	100.00	100.00
10+	No.													7	86	59	47	6	73	36	37	13	159	75	84
	%													53.85	54.09	52.00	55.95	46.15	45.91	48.00	44.05	100.00	100.00	100.00	100.00
Total	No.	3	14	7	7	7	10	5	5	2	8	3	5	23	200	103	97	89	460	245	215	124	692	363	329
	%	2.42	2.02	1.93	2.13	5.65	1.45	1.38	1.52	1.61	1.16	0.83	1.52	18.55	28.90	28.37	29.48	71.77	66.47	67.49	65.35	100.00	100.00	100.00	100.00

Source: Field study by the authors.

Table 7.35: Generation-wise Gradation of Members in the Sherpa Family of Sherpagaon Village, South District, Sikkim

Family Size		Generation-wise Gradation of Family																							
		I				II				III				IV				V				Total			
		Family	Person	Male	Female	Family	Person	Male	Female	Family	Person	Male	Female	Family	Person	Male	Female	Family	Person	Male	Female	Family	Person	Male	Female
1-3	No.					2	2	2										14	39	21	18	16	41	23	18
	%					12.50	4.88	8.70										87.50	95.12	91.30	100.00	100.00	100.00	100.00	100.00
4-6	No.	1	6	4	2									2	10	3	7	28	131	77	54	31	147	84	63
	%	3.23	4.08	4.76	3.17									6.45	6.80	3.57	11.11	90.38	89.12	91.67	85.71	100.00	100.00	100.00	99.99
7-9	No.													5	41	23	18	8	60	36	24	13	101	59	42
	%													38.46	40.59	38.98	42.86	61.54	59.41	61.02	57.14	100.00	100.00	100.00	100.00
10+	No.													1	12	5	7	3	39	21	18	4	51	26	25
	%													25.00	23.53	19.23	28.00	75.00	76.47	80.77	72.00	100.00	100.00	100.00	100.00
Total	No.	1	6	4	2	2	2	2						8	63	31	32	53	269	155	114	64	340	192	148

Source: Field study by the authors.

Table 7.36: Generation-wise Gradation of Members in the Sherpa Families of Sherpahat Village, South District, Sikkim

Family Size		Generation-wise Gradation of Family																							
		I				*II*				*III*				*IV*				*V*				*Total*			
		Family	Person	Male	Female	Family	Person	Male	Female	Family	Person	Male	Female	Family	Person	Male	Female	Family	Person	Male	Female	Family	Person	Male	Female
1-3	*No.*					5	8	3	5	1	2		2					7	19	9	10	13	29	12	17
	%					38.46	27.59	25.00		7.69	6.90		2					53.85	65.52	75.00		100.00	100.01	100.00	
4-6	*No.*	2	8	3	5					1	6	3	3	4	21	11	10	22	108	55	53	29	143	72	71
	%	6.90	5.59	4.17	7.04					3.45	4.20	4.17	4.23	13.79	14.69	15.28	14.08	75.86	75.52	76.39	74.65	100.00	100.00	100.01	100.00
7-9	*No.*													5	42	27	15	4	30	11	19	9	72	38	34
	%													55.56	58.33	71.05	44.12	44.44	41.67	28.95	55.89	100.00	100.00	100.00	100.01
10+	*No.*													6	74	34	40	3	34	15	19	9	108	49	59
	%													66.67	68.52	69.39	67.80	33.33	31.48	30.61	32.20	100.00	100.00	100.00	100.00
Total	*No.*	2	8	3	5	5	8	3	5	2	8	3	5	15	137	72	65	36	191	90	101	60	352	171	181
	%	3.33	2.27	1.75	2.76	8.33	2.27	1.75	2.76	3.33	2.27	1.75	2.76	25.00	38.92	42.11	35.91	60.00	54.26	52.63	55.80	99.99	99.99	99.99	99.99

Source: Field study by the authors.

Table 7.37: Generation-wise Gradation of Members in the Sherpa Family of Two Villages of Darjeeling, West Bengal

Family size	Generation-wise Gradation of Family																							
	I				II				III				IV				V				Total			
	Family		Person		Family		Person		Family		Person		Family		Person		Family		Person		Family		Person	
	No.	%	No.	%	No.	%	No.	%	No.	%	No.	%	No.	%	No.	%	No.	%	No.	%	No.	%	No.	%
1-3					7	87.50	11	73.33									22	26.19	58	14.80	29	25.22	69	12.15
4-6	1	100.00	5	100.00	1	12.50	4	26.67					8	38.10	43	29.86	51	60.71	250	63.78	61	53.04	302	53.17
7-9													12	57.14	91	63.19	11	13.10	84	21.43	23	20.00	175	30.81
10+									1	100.00	12	100.00	1	4.76	10	6.94					2	1.74	22	3.87
Total	1	100.00	5	100.00	8	100.00	15	100.00	1	100.00	12	100.00	21	100.00	144	99.99	84	100.00	392	100.01	115	100.00	568	100.00

Source: Field study by the authors.

Table 7.38: Generation-wise Gradation of Members in the Sherpa Family of Sherpaguri Village of Darjeeling, West Bengal

Family size	Generation-wise Gradation of Family																							
	I				II				III				IV				V				Total			
	Family		Person		Family		Person		Family		Person		Family		Person		Family		Person		Family		Person	
	No.	%	No.	%	No.	%	No.	%	No.	%	No.	%	No.	%	No.	%	No.	%	No.	%	No.	%	No.	%
1-3					4	100.00	6	100.00									5	17.86	14	10.21	9	20.93	20	9.22
4-6	1	100.00	5	100.00									3	30.00	15	21.74	17	60.21	79	57.66	21	48.84	99	45.62
7-9													6	60.00	44	63.77	6	21.42	44	32.12	12	27.91	88	40.55
10+													1	10.00	10	14.49					1	2.33	10	4.61
Total	1	100.00	5	100.00	4	100.00	6	100.00					10	100.00	69	100.00	28	99.99	137	99.99	43	100.01	217	100.00

Source: Field study by the authors.

Table 7.39: Generation-wise Gradation of Members in the Sherpa Family of Sherpapur Village of Darjeeling, West Bengal

Family size	Generation-wise Gradation of Family																							
	I				II				III				IV				V				Total			
	Family		Person		Family		Person		Family		Person		Family		Person		Family		Person		Family		Person	
	No.	%	No.	%	No.	%	No.	%	No.	%	No.	%	No.	%	No.	%	No.	%	No.	%	No.	%	No.	%
1-3					3	75.00	5	55.56									17	30.36	44	17.24	20	27.78	49	13.96
4-6					1	25.00	4	44.44					5	45.45	28	37.33	34	60.71	171	67.06	40	55.56	203	57.83
7-9													6	54.55	47	62.67	5	8.93	40	15.69	11	15.28	87	24.79
10+									1	100.00	12	100.00									1	1.39	12	3.42
Total					4	100.00	9	100.00	1	100.00	12	100.00	11	100.00	75	100.00	56	100.00	255	99.99	72	100.01	351	100.00

Source: Field study by the authors.

Table 7.40: Generation-wise Gradation of Members in the Sherpa Family of Two Villages of South District, Sikkim

Family size	Generation-wise Gradation of Family																							
	I				II				III				IV				V				Total			
	Family		Person		Family		Person		Family		Person		Family		Person		Family		Person		Family		Person	
	No.	%	No.	%	No.	%	No.	%	No.	%	No.	%	No.	%	No.	%	No.	%	No.	%	No.	%	No.	%
1-3					7	100.00	10	100.00	1	50.00	2	25.00					21	23.60	58	12.55	29	23.39	70	8.73
4-6	3	100.00	14	100.00					1	50.00	6	75.00	6	26.09	31	15.50	50	56.18	241	52.16	60	48.59	290	36.16
7-9													10	43.48	83	41.50	12	13.48	90	19.48	22	17.74	273	34.04
10+													7	30.43	86	43.00	6	6.74	73	15.80	13	10.48	169	21.07
Total	3	100.00	14	100.00	7	100.00	10	100.00	2	100.00	8	100.00	23	100.00	200	100.00	89	100.00	462	99.99	124	100.00	802	100.00

Source: Field study by the authors.

ones. Majority of the Grade-IV families (54.55%) here are large families while the remaining 45.55 per cent families are medium sized. Again at Sherpapur village there is only one family in Grade-III and that one is a very large family. Three fourth of the Grade-II families (75.00%) are small families. This village does not have any Grade-I family (Table 7.39).

After analyzing the generation-wise gradation of the Sherpa families of the two Sherpa villages of Darjeeling district, we shall now move to our two studied villages of the South District, Sikkim to analyse and discuss about the same point, i.e. generation-wise gradation of the Sherpa families.

When we take up the combined strength of the families in these two villages, we see that there are a total of 89 families in Grade-V of which more than half (56.18%) are medium sized families. Another significant number of families (23.60%) are small families. In case of the Grade-IV families 43.48 per cent are large families, 30.43 per cent are very large families and the rest are medium families. In Grade-III there are only two families of which one is small and the other one, medium family. Grade-II has 7 families, and all the seven families are small families. Similarly, all the 3 families of Grade-I are small families (Table 7.40).

As we come down to the village level we see that at Sherpagaon village of South District, Sikkim, there are a total of 53 families of which more than half (52.83%) are medium sized families. Another significant number of families (26.42%) is small families. The majority of the Grade-IV families (62.50%) are large families whereas one fourth of total families of this Grade are medium families. There is no small family in this Grade. In this village there is no Grade-III family. In Grade-II all the two families are small families. Grade-I has the lone family, and that is a medium one (Table 7.41).

At Sherpahat village of South district, Sikkim, Grade-V has 36 families of which much over half (61.11%) are medium sized families. In Grade-IV the highest number of families (40.00%) are very large families while medium (26.67%) and large families (33.33%) also have significant strength. The number of families of Grade-III are only two of which one is small and the other is medium family. All the five families of Grade-II are small families while all the families of Grade-I are medium families (Table 7.42).

Thus, we see that among the Sherpas of both Darjeeling, West Bengal, and South District, Sikkim have varied sizes of families in different Grades where members of different generations stay together.

Table 7.41: Generation-wise Gradation of Members in the Sherpa Family of Sherpagaon Village of South District, Sikkim

Family size	Generation-wise Gradation of Family																							
	I				II				III				IV				V				Total			
	Family		Person		Family		Person		Family		Person		Family		Person		Family		Person		Family		Person	
	No.	%	No.	%	No.	%	No.	%	No.	%	No.	%	No.	%	No.	%	No.	%	No.	%	No.	%	No.	%
1-3					2	100.00	2	100.00									14	26.42	39	14.50	16	25.00	41	12.06
4-6	1	100.00	6	100.00									2	25.00	10	15.87	28	52.83	131	48.70	31	48.44	147	43.24
7-9													5	62.50	41	65.07	8	15.09	60	22.30	13	20.31	101	29.71
10+													1	12.50	12	19.04	3	5.66	39	14.50	4	6.25	51	15.00
Total	1	100.00	6	100.00	2	100.00	2	100.00					8	100.00	63	99.99	53	100.00	269	100.00	64	100.00	340	100.01

Source: Field study by the authors.

Table 7.42: Generation-wise Gradation of Members in the Sherpa Family of Sherpahat Village of South District, Sikkim

Family size	Generation-wise Gradation of Family																							
	I				II				III				IV				V				Total			
	Family		Person		Family		Person		Family		Person		Family		Person		Family		Person		Family		Person	
	No.	%	No.	%	No.	%	No.	%	No.	%	No.	%	No.	%	No.	%	No.	%	No.	%	No.	%	No.	%
1-3					5	100.00	8	100.00	1	50.00	2	25.00					7	19.44	19	9.95	13	21.67	29	8.01
4-6	2	100.00	8	100.00					1	500.00	6	75.00	4	26.67	21	15.33	22	61.11	108	56.54	29	48.33	143	39.50
7-9													5	33.33	42	30.65	4	11.11	30	15.71	9	15.00	72	19.89
10+													6	40.00	74	54.01	3	8.33	34	17.80	9	15.00	118	32.60
Total	2	100.00	8	100.00	5	100.00	8	100.00	2	100.00	8	100.00	15	100.00	137	99.99	36	99.99	191	100.00	60	100.00	362	100.00

Source: Field study by the authors.

8

THE WAY THEY MARRY

Marriage is the social norm of the Sherpa society of Darjeeling and Sikkim as it is the case with all other human societies of this world. It is the general expectation among the Sherpas that all young men and women must marry except those who want to become monk or nun. The Sherpa parents do not like that their young children remain unmarried throughout their life. Similarly, when a Sherpa boy or a girl reaches marriageable age, he or she develops a desire to get married. To remain unmarried in this society is considered below dignity, and an unmarried one is looked down in this society. The people normally suspects some wrong with him or her. They often think that an unmarried person has some wrong, and so, the person could not marry or failed to marry. At the same time the Sherpas do not like to give marriage to their child with some one who suffers from some contagious or incurable and serious disease, or if that some one is physically handicapped or mentally disabled. People will also not like to marry such person.

The Sherpas are in general an endogamous tribe. In Darjeeling as well as in Sikkim they in general practice endogamy. In these two areas they prefer to marry in their own community. Particularly, in case of negotiation marriage the parents/guardians always like to have a spouse for their child from the Sherpa community. But there are cases in the Sherpa society of both areas when this rule of endogamy has been violated. In these cases the Sherpa boys and girls have married or have been given marriage with non-Sherpas who belong to different neighbouring communities like the Nepali, Bhutias and the Lepcha. But most of these cases happened due to love affair between the Sherpa boy/girl with the non-Sherpa girl/boy. Love does not care for caste, creed, religion etc. But even in case of the love marriage boys and girls always take care of their clan. A boy or a girl will never love a girl or boy belonging to the same clan as he or she considers his or her clan members as his or her close relative with whom marriage is prohibited.

Again the Nepali, Bhutias or the Lepcha boys are sometimes seen to fall in love with the Sherpa girls, and in some cases their love ripens into marriage. So, at present we see some cases of marriage between the Sherpa boys and non-Sherpa girls or the same between the Sherpa girls and the non-Sherpa boys. The persons (the Sherpa or non-Sherpa) do not face any difficulty in living with the other members of the Sherpa society. These Sherpa-non-Sherpa marriages are at present, well accepted by the Sherpa society without having any inhibition in their mind, and the partners of such inter-community marriages are not in any way, discriminated. They enjoy equal status as are enjoyed by the Sherpa-Sherpa couples because these children are also considered as members of the Sherpa society. Even the children of such inter-community marriages are not differentiated against the children of Sherpa-Sherpa couples. These children whose either of the parents is the non-Sherpa, are brought up in the Sherpa society of Darjeeling and Sikkim in the same way as the pure Sherpa children are brought up. Even when they enter the marriageable age, they can easily marry the pure Sherpas or Sherpas whose one of the parents is the non-Sherpa or they even can marry non-Sherpa. The Sherpa parents keep no inhibition against such marriage and do not restrain their children from marrying such person whose one of the parents is the non-Sherpa.

As we have said that the Sherpa woman and non-Sherpa man couples and their children enjoy equal status in the Sherpa society of Darjeeling and Sikkim. The only difference is that unlike the pure Sherpa children or children of the Sherpa father and non-Sherpa mother, the children of the Sherpa mothers and non-Sherpa fathers cannot carry any Sherpa clan name. They keep either the community name of their fathers or clan name, if any of their fathers or simply add the word 'Sherpa' after their name.

Among the Shrpas of Nepal Fürer-Haimendorf also found the entry of the non-Sherpa element with marital ties. According to him

> The absence of any sentiment comparable with the caste consciousness of Hindu society and even the present-day Buddhist society of the Nepal valley, has facilitated the absorption of various alient ethnic elements into the body of Sherpa society. We have seen that men of such non-Bhotia groups as Newars and Chetris experience no difficulty in entering temporary or permanent unions with Sherpa women. Their presence in a Sherpa village produces no problem, for Sherpas will admit members of other societies to commensality and normal social intercourse (1964:37).

Even Fürer-Haimendorf found no prejudice against the children born of such inter-community marriages. In the Sherpa society of Nepal such children enjoy equal status with the children of the Sherpa-Sherpa couples. The only difference is that when non-Sherpa male marries a Sherpa female, the children do not have any Sherpa clan. In the Sherpa society of Nepal, as seen by Fürer-Haimendorf "the descendants of Newars, Chetris, Gurung and Tamangs are accepted as the social equals of pure Sherpa" (*ibid*).

Fürer-Haimendorf has also traced some cases of temporary union between the Sherpa women and non-Sherpa men. Usually, such cases take place when some non-Sherpa traders, businessmen, labourers and some such people come to the Sherpa villages and stay there temporarily for a period of time. During their stay they come in close contact with the Sherpa women and get intimated. Their union sometimes leads to child-birth. "Such children are accepted and cared for by the mother's family, whether the father is a Sherpa or an outsider ...." (*ibid*).

In the villages of Nepal studied by Fürer-Haimendorf

> there are several descendants of non-Sherpa men and all of them are fully privileged members of the village community and socially indistinguishable from pure Sherpas, except for the fact that they have no Sherpa clan name. Several of these men, known as Newar Sherpa, are the sons and grandsons of a Newar trader ....(*ibid*).

This trader stayed in that village for about a decade with two Sherpa wives, both having Pankarma clan. Another man was born of the Chetri man and a Sherpa woman married a Sherpa. Their children are known as the Chetri-Sherpa. Fürer-Haimendorf noticed the Sherpa societies at Khumbu Pharak and Solu of Nepal are basically open societies which show marked contrast from the closed caste societies of different parts of Nepal.

In his later publication on the Sherpa (*The Sherpas Transformed*), Fürer-Haimendorf is of openion that the entry of the Newar and the Chetri blood into the Sherpa society is mainly due to their matrimonial relation and also because of the casual intercourse between the Newar or Chetri men and the Sherpa women. The children and grand-children of this intercourse are called the Newar Sherpas or the Chetri-Sherpas as the case may be. Fürer-Haimendorf has also seen a number of cases of marriage between the Sherpa men and the western women

(1984:32). He has further reported the cases of marriage of the Sherpas with the American, German, Swiss, French and also people from other European countries and also of Japan. In most of the cases the Sherpa men married foreign women. But there are a few cases as reported by Fürer- Haimendorf, where the Sherpa women married the foreign men (*ibid*: 76:77). But in our studied villages of Darjeeling and Sikkim we have not met a single case of marriage between the Sherpas and the foreigners.

Shrestha and others have also marked that 'when a boy grows young, he is free to choose his own lady-love and marry her' (1975:16).

In connection with the Sherpas of Darjeeling Mitra writes that they 'practise endogamy at the community level, i.e. they marry within the society' (2008:1184).

Ortner in connection with the rule of endogamy among the Sherpas of Nepal states that these people usually marry in their own community. 'Marriage between Sherpas and Khambas is supposedly a serious offence.... Involving loss of one's status and rights in the community, Marriage with Yembas is more or less unthinkable (1979:19).

The Sherpas of both Darjeeling and Sikkim follow the rule of exogamy in the clan level. They strictly follow the rule of clan exagomy. Among them no one is allowed to marry in his or her clan. The parents invariably check up the clan of the parents of the boy or the girl with whom they negotiate for their daughter or son's marriage. Similarly, no boy or girl will make love with any girl or boy having the same clan with him or her. To marry, to make amorous relation or any sex relation with any Sherpa with same clan is a heinous and despicable act, like incest, and no Sherpa will dare to do this. Any breach of the rule of clan exogamy is dealt with severity. If some Sherpa is found to break this rule, he or she is usually fined and excommunicated. Even a child knows this rule. In the villages of Darjeeling and Sikkim where we undertook our study among the Sherpas, we did not come across any such case of violation of clan exogamy (Raha 2014). Under this rule a Sherpa with Poldorje clan cannot marriages a Poldorje, a Garza- a Garza, a Salakha –a Salakha, a Chukte- a Chukte and so on. According to Mitra the Sherpas of Darjeeling 'maintain exogamy at the level of *ru*. A man cannot marry a girl of his own *ru* (2008:1184). Again Gangopadhyay has also reported that among the Sherpas of Sikkim 'Marriage is prohibited within the sub-division (*pin*) of the same *ru* (1993:155). He has further stated that the rules of exogamy is observed at the level of clan (*ru)* (*ibid*: 156).

Among the Sherpas of Sikkim Bisht and Bankoli have mentioned that clan exogamy is strictly followed by the Sherpas of this Himalayan state. No Sherpa can marry within his or her own clan. Similarly, marriage within the sub-clan (*pin*) is also prohibited. Any breach of these rules is severely dealt with.

Subba, J. R. has found the clans (*ru*) of the Sherpas of Sikkim and their sub-clans (*pin*) as exogamous. Marriage is totally prohibited in the same clan or sub-clan among them (2008: 283, 286).

In Nepal the Sherpas also observe clan (*ru*) exogamy. According to Fürer-Haimendorf

> The essential feature of the Sherpa clan is its role as the basic exogamous unit. All Sherpa of the same *ru*, irrespective of the distance which may separate their villages and the impossibility of tracing genealogical link, consider themselves as agnetic kin and debarred from marriage. Sexual relation between clan members are regarded as incest, and are virtually unheard of. Though there is a great tolerance of casual sex relation, I have failed to discover a single case of even a fleeting amorous attachment between members of the same clan ... dire punishments would be meted out to anyone offending against the rules of clan exogamy (1964:20).

Out of 567 Sherpa mariages recorded from different villages of Nepal, Fürer-Haimendorf failed to trace a single case of union between members of the same clans or brother-clans. Marriage of members between brother-clans is also prohibited (*ibid*: 21).

Ortner has also stated that regulation of marriage is the main function of the clans of the Sherpas. Among them "Every person inherits a clan affiliation from his or her father and must marry someone of a different clan affiliation". Ortner has further informed that no Sherpa can marry a member of his or her mother's or grandmother's clan and lineage. But the "marriage between members of full Sherpa clans and members of clans deriving from mixture with other ethnic groups is frowned upon but not forbidden. I would guess the mixed clans primarily marry with other mixed clans, and secondarily with first ring rather than core Sherpa clans" (1979: 19).

Bista has also noticed the rule of clan exogamy among the Sherpas of Nepal. Among them no one will marry in his or her own clan (1976:163).

Forms and Types of Marriage

Monogamy is the general norm of the Sherpa society. In fact during our field work both in Darjeeling and Sikkim, we have not come across any form of marriage other than monogamy. We met with not a single case of polygyny or polyandry or polygynandry. But our older informants were of the openion that polygyny and polyandry were accepted by the Sherpas in the past, and even at present these are not prohibited though no one is inclined to go for a plural marriage. At present the Sherpas in general, prefer monogamy and avoid the other two forms of plural marriage. They have now acceptged "one man-one wife" policy. Even the women do not like to have more than one husband or co-wife. And for the men, their economy also does not permit to bring one more wife except when the first wife is barren or mentally unstable or suffering from incurable disease. Even Subba, J.R. has also seen monogamy as the usual norm of the Sherpa society of Sikkim (2008: 286). Bisht and Bankoti have also got monogamy being the usual norm of the Sherpas of Sikkim (2004:1490). The same is the view of Gangopadhyay for the Sikkimese Sherpas (1993:156). In case of the Sherpa of Darjeeling also Mitra found the Sherpas practicing only monogamy (2008:1184).

So, it is clear that the Sherpas of both Darjeeling and Sikkim at present do not like to go for any form of plural marriage like polygyny or polyandry. They remain satisfied with "one husband – one wife policy" and so, they go for monogamous marriage.

But this is not so in case of the Sherpas of Nepal. They practice both monogamy and plural marriages, and of the plural marriages, both polygyny and polyandry are present in their society. According to Fürer-Haimendorf both polyandry and polygyny are present in the Sherpa society or Nepal. But the cases of polyandry are much more than that of polygyny. Out of 236 Sherpa marriages of in Khumjung, Kunde, and Phortse areas, Fürer-Haimendorf could trace 19 polyandrous and only 5 polygynous marriages.

> This is in accordance with the Sherpa belief that polyandrous marriages are a time-honoured and highly respectable device to prevent the fragmentation of property and foster the solidarity of brothers, whereas a man's marriage with more than one wife at a time is more in nature of an emergency measure resorted to, if the first wife has remained childless, but neither of the spouses desires a divorce (1964:68).

Among the Sherpas of Nepal as seen by Fürer-Haimendorf, because of the parental arrangements the number of polyandrous union is more when the parents arrange for the marriage of their eldest son, they select a wife for both elder and younger sons. The younger brother at that time may be too young to count his choice. Usually, the elder brother take major role in the arrangement of this polyandrous marriage. It is he who goes to marry the girl and as per marriage rule he is the first husband to initiate sexual relation with the newly betrothed wife (*ibid*). Normally, at the time of *sodene* the girl and her family members are informed that she would be the joint wife of two brothers. The marital negotiation is finalized if the girl and her family members agree to this proposal. After betrothal brothers are allowed to become night visitors to the girl. But normally the eldest brother only visit her at night. Though younger brother's inclusion in the marriage is done in the *dem-chang* ceremony, but only in the wedding ceremony "both brothers appear in the role of bridegroom" (*ibid*:69). Among the Sherpas as reported by Fürer-Haimendorf, if there are three brothers, normally, the middle brother goes to monastery as a trainee *Lama* and the other two brothers marry jointly. The Sherpa girls usually like to marry two brothers.

But in 1984 Fürer-Haimendorf saw a marked change in the forms of marriage. At this time the Napalese Sherpas became almost monogamous and the number of polyandrous and polygynous marriages has much been reduced. While Fürer-Haimendorf found 19 cases of polyandrous marriages, in 1983 he found only one polyandrous marriage in Ku:.de, none in Khumjung and only three in Phortse. In 1983 this form of marriage was not as prestigious and popular as the same in 1950s (1984:44).

Ortner has also reported about the presence of polyandry among the Sherpas of Nepal, though the number of cases of polyandrous marriage is quite low. But no details of polyandry are received from Ortner (1979:21).

Bisht and Bankoti have also noticed the practice of polyandry among the Sherpas of Nepal. They have found that among this people "a single woman may be the wife two or three husbands or she may have a couple of husbands who are unrelated" (2004: 1487). This means the Sherpas of Nepal have both fraternal and non-fraternal types of polyandry according to them. But now-a-days the system of having more than two husbands has been replaced by one woman –two husbands system. All children born of the common wife are considered as the children of the eldest brother, though some of other brothers may be biologically responsible for the birth of some or even all children (*ibid*).

The Sherpas of Nepal as found by Bishta, practice fraternal polyandry. Usually, the two brothers marry a common wife. He has also reported the presence of polygyandry among these people of Nepal when he reports that "sometimes two brothers marry two common wives". Bishta has further stated that "since only two brothers, and not more than two, can marry one wife, parents of three sons usually make a celibate monk of the middle child. The elder and the younger can then take a common wife". Bishta has got only one family with four brothers. Of these four brothers the first and second married one wife and third and fourth another common wife (1976: 163-164).

Robert Paul (1989:66) and Barbara Brower (2003:11, 52) both have found the Sherpas practicing fraternal polyandry. Paul found them to continue with two brothers marrying a common wife (*ibid*:66) while Brower opines that "the Sherpa occassionally engage in plural marriage. The more common traditional arrangement involved in single woman marrying two brothers..." (*ibid*:52).

Besides polyandry the Sherpas of Nepal are also found to practice other form of plural marriage that is, polygyny. But this form of plural marriage is not widespread or popular. Only a few cases of polygyny can be met with a Sherpa village of Nepal. But Brower has noticed a recent trend among this people ".... in recent years the number of marriages involving a single man with more than one wife, one often maintained in Kathmandu while the other stays at Khumbu, has become more common" (2003:52). Fürer-Haimendorf has also found the same trend among the Sherpas of Nepal. According to him those Sherpas who are engaged in tourism, polygyny is more common. Many of them are found to keep one wife in Kathmandu while the other one lives at the village, i.e. Khumbu (1984:44).

The Sherpas of Darjeeling and Sikkim are not found to practice any type of cousin marriage, cross-cousin or parallel-cousin. Here levirate is also not present, but in rare cases sororate is practiced only when the first wife is dead. In our studied villages we have not met with any case of both levirate and sororate.

In Nepal among the Sherpas both levirate and sororate are not allowed. According to Fürer-Haimendorf "to marry one's mother's brother's or father's sister's daughter used to be a strictly forbidden one except a few stray cases. The marriages between a Sherpa and his real or classificatory elder brother's widow (levirate) or wife's younger sister (sororate) are allowed but not very common (1964:47, 1984:38). Ortner has also spoken about the prohibition of cross and parallel cousin marriage.

According to Ortner "Although this is not strictly adhered to, it is part of the rationale that rules out matrilateral cross-cousin marriage, that is, marriage with one's mother's brother's daughter.... Patrilateral cross-cousin marriage, that is marriage with one's father's sister's daughter (who also does not belong to one's own clan) also consider repugnant" (1979: 119). That is cross-cousin marriages, both MBD and FSD types, are forbiddened in the Sherpa society of Nepal, has also been observed by Bista (1976:163).

Normally, the Sherpas of both Darjeeling, West Bengal and South District, Sikkim practice negotiation and love marriage. So in their cases, the marriage partner is either selected by the parents or guardians or the young men and women themselves select their live partner. Their friendship often matures into love, and ultimately their love in most of the cases results in marriage. At present, the incidents of love marriage are speedily increasing. In and around their villages the young boys and girls get enough opportunity to meet one another, and so they have enough scope to make love. In some cases pre-marital sex-relation also takes place. Forests, cultivable land and some such isolated places are suitable for the boys and girls to make love. Their love affairs and even their pre-marital sex-relation do not raise eye-brows of their parents and other elderly person. A few may get annoyed but normally they do not advance much as if it is taken for granted that it is a common affair that the young boys and girls will make love. The parents do not normally impose their decisions on them.

In Darjeeling negotiation is the norm of marriage among the Sherpas (Mitra 2008:1184). Subba has mentioned about the presence of both negotiation (*Lung jang*) and elopement (*Kabtindop*) marriges practiced by by the Sherpas of Sikkim though arranged marriage is the norm (2008:286). Gangopadhyay also thinks that among the Sherpas of Sikkim arranged marriage is the norm, but marriage by elopement is also in vogue (1993: 156).

Fürer-Haimendorf has also found the Sherpa boys and girls have freedom "to form attachments and become lovers naturally results in many marriages which entirely of the making of the two partners" (1964:41). Fürer-Haimendorf has also found that the unmarried Sherpa boys and girls are free to have sex-relations "with any unmarried person not excluded from range of potential mates by rules of clan exogamy or prohibition of sexual intercourse between persons of *khaden* and *khamendeu* status". In their society also no one makes any adverse comments (*ibid*: 40, 1984: 36-37). Ortner has also found negotiation and love marriages among the Sherpas of Nepal (1979: 19-21).

We shall now present the analysis of the quantitative data on marriage system which we collected from the Sherpas of four villages, two from Darjeeling and another two from Sikkim.

INTRA AND INTER-COMMUNITY MARRIAGES

The Sherpas of both Darjeeling district, West Bengal, and South District of Sikkim practice endogamy. But this rule guiding the Sherpas to marry in their own community, has not always been strictly followed. There are cases where some Sherpa males after breaking this rule, married in other communities. Similarly, some non-Sherpa males after marrying Sherpa women, have started living in the Sherpa society. Table 8.01 will throw some light about the nature and extend of intra and inter-community marriages among the Sherpas of the studied villages of Darjeeling and South district, Sikkim.

At Sherpaguri village of Darjeeling district, out of 53 Sherpa couples studied, 96.23 per cent cases the Sherpa men have married the Sherpa or non-Sherpa women and only in 2 (3.77%) cases the non-Sherpa males have married the Sherpa females. Among the non-Sherpa men who have married the Sherpa women, one is a Pradhan and the other one is a Sharma. Again out of 51 cases where the Sherpa males have married the Sherpa or non-Sherpa females, in 33 (64.74%) cases the Sherpa men have taken the Sherpa wife and in the rest 18 (35.29%) cases the Sherpa men have union with the non-Sherpa women. Out of these 18 Sherpa men have married to the non-Sherpa men, the Sherpa have married the Gurung women in 4 (7.84%) cases, the Sherpa men have married the Tamang women in also 4 (7.84%) cases, the Sherpa men have married the Rai women in 3 (5.88%) cases. In 2 (3.92%) cases the Sherpa men have taken a Lepcha wife. In five other cases five Sherpa men have taken five wives, one each, from the Pradhan, Dhakal Chetri, Thapa, Magar, and the Bhotia communities respectively.

In the other studied village, i.e. Sherpapur of Darjeeling District, all the 66 Sherpa husbands have taken either the Sherpa wife or wife from other communities. But no non-Sherpa has taken any Sherpa wife in this village. In these 66 cases, all but five have taken the non-Sherpa wife. Those five cases two Sherpas have taken wife from the Tamang community and one from the Rai, the other one from the Bhotia and the last Sherpa from the Lepcha community (Table 8.1).

Table 8.1: Intra and Inter-Community Marriages among the Sherpas of the Studied Villages of Darjeeling and Sikkim

Community of the Husband	*Community of the wife*	*Sherpaguri*		*Sherpapur*		*Sherpagaon*		*Sherpahat*	
		No.	*%*	*No.*	*%*	*No.*	*%*	*No.*	*%*
Sherpa	Sherpa	33	64.71	61	92.42	71	94.67	71	87.65
Sherpa	Gurung	4	7.84			1	1.33		
Sherpa	Pradhan	1	1.96					1	1.23
Sherpa	Dhakal Chetri	1	1.96						
Sherpa	Tamang	4	7.84	2	3.03			2	2.47
Sherpa	Rai	3	5.88	1	1.52	1	1.33		
Sherpa	Thapa	1	1.96					1	1.23
Sherpa	Magar	1	1.96						
Sherpa	Sikkimese							1	1.23
Sherpa	Bhotia	1	1.96	1	1.52	2	2.67	2	2.47
Sherpa	Lepcha	2	3.92	1	1.52			3	3.70
Total		51	99.99 (96.23)	66	100.01 (100.00)	75	100.00 (98.88)	81	99.98 (96.43)
Subba	Sherpa					1	100.00	1	33.33
Pradhan	Sherpa	1	50.00					1	33.33
Bhotia	Sherpa							1	33.33
Sharma	Sherpa	1	50.00						
Total		2	100.00 (3.77)			1	100.00 (1.12)	3	99.99 (3.57)

Source: Field study by the authors.

The Sherpagaon village of South District, Sikkim has 76 couples living in the Sherpa community. Out of these 76 couples, 75 (98.88%) Sherpa husbands have taken wife from the Sherpa or non-Sherpa communities. In only one case a non-Sherpa (Subba) after marrying a Sherpa woman, is living with the Sherpas of this village. Again out of 75 cases in 71 (94.67%) cases the Sherpa husbands have taken Sherpa wives and in 4 cases non-Sherpa wives. Out of the Sherpa- non-sherpa marriages, in one case a Sherpa man has taken a Gurung wife, in 2 cases the Sherpa husbands have taken the Bhotia wives and in the fourth cases another Sherpa man has taken one Rai woman as his wife.

We shall now examine the intra and inter-community marriages among the Sherpas of the second village, i.e. Sherpahat of Sikkim. There are 84 couples in this village among whom either the husband or the wife or both are the Sherpas. Out of these 84 couples in case of 81 (96.43%) couples the Sherpa husbands have either the Sherpa or the non-Sherpa wife. Only in three cases, the husbands are the non-Sherpas but the wives are the Sherpas. Out of these three husbands one Subba married a Sherpa woman. The second one is a Pradhan and the third one is also a non-Sherpa (Bhotia) and both of them married a Sherpa woman each.

It is thus seen that in some cases the rule of endogamy in the Sherpa society of both Darjeeling and Sikkim is broken. Over and above, some non-Sherpa men after marrying Sherpa women, are also living in the Sherpa society. Fürer-Haimendorf has also reported the marriage of the Sherpa with the Khambas of Nepal. "... but among the Khambas of Namche Bazar there are several rich traders who have inter-married with some most respectable Sherpa families' mentions Fürer-Haimendorf" (1964: 45). In some other book on the Sherpas, Fürer-Haimendorf has also reported the marriage between the Sherpas and the foreigners in Nepal (1984:75-78). But in connection with the Sherpas of Nepal Ortner has reported, 'Marriage between Sherpas and Khambas is supportedly a serious offence (phrased in terms of polluting the Sherpa individual and his or her clan)" (1979:19). But in the later years Fürer-Haimendorf did not find such restriction among the Sherpas of Khumbu area. Among them "there is certainly no objection to intermarriage between Khambas and Sherpas, and danger of pollution occurs only in sexual unions of the Sherpas with persons of the unprivileged class of Khamendeu status" (1984:31).

Marital Status

In all human societies the members may normally pass thorugh four different marital status. At one phase of life one remains as unmarried as one has not married then. When one marries one becomes married. If one divorces ones married partner, one is diverced or remain separated from each other, then one earns the status of divorced or separated, and finally if ones married partner dies, one becomes a widowed person. In the Sherpa society of both Darjeeling and Sikkim, all these four status are found among the members. The same conditions are also prevailing among the Sherpas of our four studied villages, two from Darjeeling, West Bengal, and two from South District, Sikkim. Through our household census we collected data on the marital status of these Sherpas and tabulated and analysed the same. In the following pages we give the results of our analysis:

From Table 8.2 we get that among the total Sherpa population of the two villages combined together, the number of unmarried Sherpas is much more than those of the married Sherpas (54.40% against 39.44% married Sherpas). That means the number of married Sherpas of these villages is much less than unmarried Sherpas. While the number of the widowed persons of the total Sherpas of these two villages is quite less (5.59%), the number of the divorced persons is even lesser, less than 2.00 per cent. The same trend is noticed in case of both male and female Sherpas. In case of the combined total male and female Sherpas of the two villages, more than half of the total males (55.71%) and females (53.12%) are unmarried. The married Sherpas remain around 41.00 per cent (male-40.36% and female-38.54%). While the number of widowers is less than 4.00 per cent, the number of widows is a little more than the widowers. Again the strength of the divorced Sherpa males is less than 1.00 per cent, but the number of the divorced female Sherpas is a little more than divorced male Sherpas; but it stands less than 2.00 per cent.

Now, we will examine the marital status of the Sherpas inhabiting two villages of Darjeeling District, Sherpaguri and Sherpapur. At Sherpaguri village, as usual, over half of the Sherpa population of this village (56.22%) are unmarried while only 37.33 per cent are married. A very small number of the Sherpas (12 or 5.53%) are widowed, and two females are divorced. The same is the marital status in case of both male and female Sherpas. In case of both sexes, the number of unmarried Sherpas is much higher than that of the married ones, though the number of the married Sherpa females is more than that of married Sherpa males. Even in this village the number of widows is more than that of the widowers. While this village does not have any divorced male Sherpa, there are two divorced Sherpa women live in this village (Table 8.2).

At Sherpapur village the marital status of the Sherpas is almost the same. Here also more than half of the Sherpas are unmarried (53.28%). On the other hand, the number of the married Sherpas of this village is much less than half (40.74%). The number of both widowed and divorced Sherpas here is insignificant, but no doubt, they are more in number than those of Sherpaguri village.

At this village, Sherpapur, the marital status of both male and female Sherpas follows the same trend. Among them also the unmarried ones are more than half of the total Sherpa males and females of this village (52.33% and 54.19% respectively). That means the number of married males and females are less than the half (43.02% and 38.55% respectively)

Table 8.2: Marital Status of the Sherpas of Two Villages of Darjeeling

Marital Status	Sherpaguri						Sherpapur						Total					
	Person		Male		Female		Person		Male		Female		Person		Male		Female	
	No.	%	No.	%	No.	%	No.	%	No.	%	No.	%	No.	%	No.	%	No.	%
Unmarried	122	56.22	66	61.11	56	51.38	187	53.28	90	52.33	97	54.19	309	54.40	156	55.71	153	53.12
Married	81	37.33	39	36.11	42	38.53	143	40.74	74	43.02	69	38.55	224	39.44	113	40.36	111	38.54
Widowed	12	5.53	3	2.78	9	8.26	17	4.84	7	4.07	10	5.59	29	5.11	10	3.57	19	6.60
Divorced	2	0.92	—	—	2	1.83	4	1.14	1	0.58	3	1.67	6	1.05	1	0.36	5	1.74
Total	217	100.00	108	100.00	109	100.00	351	100.00	172	100.00	179	100.00	568	100.00	280	100.00	288	100.00

Source: Field study by the authors.

though the married Sherpa males are more in number than the married Sherpa females.

Here in case of both male and female Sherpas the numerical strength of widowers/widows vary between 4.00 per cent and 6.00 per cent (4.07% for the widowers and 5.59% for the widows). The number of divorced Sherpa males and females is, of course, negligible.

We shall now come down to the marital status of the Sherpas of the two studied villages of South District, Sikkim, that is, Sherpagaon and Sherpahat. The Sherpas of these two villages of Sikkim do not show much difference in the marital status from their congeners living in Darjeeling District of West Bengal. Among the combined total Sherpa population of these two villages of Sikkim, majority are unmarried. Only 34.83 per cent of them are married. The widowed persons are only 5.20 per cent but the divorced persons are insignificant in numbers. In case of the combined total male and female Sherpas of these two villages, the trend is also the same. In case of both sexes, the unmarried Sherpas have secured majority share (62.26% for the male and 55.93% for the female Sherpas). The strength of the married Sherpa males and females has not gone beyond 36.00 per cent (35.09% and 34.25% respectively). The widowed Sherpa males and females are only a few, though the widows are a little more in number than the widowers. The divorced male and female Sherpas are significantly low in number.

Now, as we come down to the individual villages, we find that the picture is almost the same. At Sherpagaon village as usual, the number of unmarried Sherpas is much more than the married Sherpas (59.22% and 35.00% respectively). Though widowed Sherpas have some strength, the divorced persons are insignificant in number. Again the sex-wise distribution of the marital status also reveal the same trend. In case of both male and female Sherpas of this village the number of married male and female Sherpas is over half of the total male and female Sherpas, though the unmarried male Sherpas (64.58%) have higher strength than the unmarried female Sherpas (52.03%) of this village. On the other hand, the strength of the married females Sherpas (39.86%) is much higher than that of the married male Sherpas (31.25%), though the number of the married male and female Sherpas is much less than that of the unmarried male and female Sherpas. In case of the Sherpa widows and widowers, the former is much higher in number (11 or 7.43%) than the latter (3.65%). There are only two divorced Sherpas, one male and one female.

Table 8.3: Marital Status of the Sherpas of Two Villages of Darjeeling

Marital Status	Sherpaguri						Sherpapur						Total					
	Person		Male		Female		Person		Male		Female		Person		Male		Female	
	No.	%	No.	%	No.	%	No.	%	No.	%	No.	%	No.	%	No.	%	No.	%
Unmarried	122	39.48	66	42.31	56	36.60	187	60.52	90	57.69	97	63.40	309	100.00	156	100.00	153	100.00
Married	81	36.16	39	34.51	42	37.84	143	63.84	74	65.49	69	62.16	224	100.00	113	100.00	111	100.00
Widowed	12	41.38	3	30.00	9	47.37	17	58.62	7	70.00	10	52.63	29	100.00	10	100.00	19	100.00
Divorced	2	33.33	—	—	2	40.00	4	66.67	1	100.00	3	60.00	6	100.00	1	100.00	5	100.00
Total	217	38.20	108	38.57	109	37.85	351	61.80	172	61.43	179	62.15	568	100.00	280	100.00	288	100.00

Source: Field study by the authors.

Table 8.4: Marital Status of the Sherpas of Two Villages of Sikkim

Marital Status	Sherpagaon						Sherpahat						Total					
	Person		Male		Female		Person		Male		Female		Person		Male		Female	
	No.	%	No.	%	No.	%	No.	%	No.	%	No.	%	No.	%	No.	%	No.	%
Unmarried	201	59.12	124	64.58	77	52.03	209	59.38	102	59.65	107	59.12	410	59.25	226	62.26	184	55.93
Married	119	35.00	60	31.25	59	39.86	122	34.66	60	35.09	62	34.25	241	34.83	120	33.06	121	36.78
Widowed	18	5.29	7	3.65	11	7.43	18	5.11	8	4.68	10	5.53	36	5.20	15	4.13	21	6.38
Divorced	2	0.59	1	0.52	1	0.68	3	0.85	1	0.58	2	0.10	5	0.72	2	0.55	3	0.91
Total	340	100.00	192	100.00	148	100.00	352	100.00	171	100.00	181	100.00	692	100.00	363	100.00	329	100.00

Source: Field study by the authors.

At Sherpahat village the strength of different marital statuses is almost the same as are present at Sherpagaon village. Here also the number of the unmarried Sherpas is about to touch 60.00 per cent (59.38% to be exact). The married Sherpas are only 34.66 per cent. While the widowed persons figure only 5.11 per cent, the divorced Sherpas of this village are significantly low in number.

In case of the male and female Sherpas also the trend is same. In both cases the unmarried Sherpas have nearly 60.00 per cent strength (59.65% and 59.12% respectively). In a similar way the married male and female Sherpas are 35.09 per cent and 34.25 per cent respectively. The widows and the widowers have somewhat higher strength than the divorced male and female Sherpas of this village.

The further analysis of the data on marital status of the Sherpas of our studied villages of Darjeeling and Sikkim, shows that a set of two villages bears the higher strength of all marital statuses of the Sherpas in comparison to the other set of two villages. Out of the combined total unmarried Sherpas of the two villages of Darjeeling District, Sherpapur village keeps 60.52 per cent whereas Sherpaguri village has the remaining 39.48 per cent. In case of the married Sherpas the former village has 63.84 per cent while the latter village has only 36.96 per cent of the married Sherpas.

In case of the widowed and divorced persons the same trend is noticed. Sherpapur village has higher number of widowed and divorced Sherpas than that of the village Sherpaguri. In case of the male and female Sherpas also Sherpapur has higher number of unmarried, married, widowed and divorced Sherpas (Table 8.3) than those of the other village.

As we come down to the two studied villages of Sikkim, we notice that the unmarried, married and divorced Sherpas of Sherpahat village have slightly higher strength than those of the Sherpas of Sherpagaon village. In the former village while the strength of unmarried Sherpas is 50.98 per cent, at Sherpagaon village the same is 49.02 per cent. In case of the married Sherpas while Sherpahat village has 50.62 per cent of the married Sherpas out of the combined total married Sherpas of the two villages, the village Sherpagaon has 49.38 per cent. In case of the divorced Sherpas while 60.00 per cent live in Sherpahat village, only 40.00 per cent are found in Sherpagaon village. The widowed Sherpas are equal in number in the two villages. But when we go for the sex-wise distribution of the marital status of the two villages we see the villages of Sikkim do not show the same trend as those of Darjeeling District.

At Sherpahat village the strength of the unmarried Sherpas of Sherpahat village (45.13%) is less than that of the unmarried Sherpas of Sherpagaon village (54.87%). But the strength of the married male Sherpas is equal in both the villages. Same is the case with the divorced males. Both villages share equal number. But quite opposite trend is noticed in case of the widowed Sherpas. In this regard Sherpahat village (53.33%) edges over Sherpagaon village (46.67%). In case of the female Sherpas of the village, Sherpahat the strength of the unmarried, married and divorced females is more than those of the female Sherpas of Sherpagaon village. At Sherpahat the unmarried female Sherpas hold 58.15 per cent of the total unmarried female Sherpas of the two villages. The remaining 41.85 per cent live in Sherpagaon village. Similarly, the married female Sherpas are 51.24 per cent in the former village, but 48.76 per cent in latter village. The divorced female Sherpas of Sherpahat occupy two third of the total divorced female Sherpas of the two villages while the remaining one third live in at Sherpagaon village. Thus, we get some idea about the distribution of the unmarried, married, widowed and divorced Sherpas of our studied villages of both Darjeeling, West Bengal and South District, Sikkim (Table 8.4).

In the studied villages of Darjeeling district, West Bengal, that is, Sherpaguri and Sherpapur, the combined Sherpa total population is 568. Of this population the major share is held by the unmarried people (54.40%). The next higher strength (39.44%) is held by the married persons. Both widowed and divorced persons have very negligible shares. The total number of male Sherpas of these two villages is 280. Out of these males majority (55.71%) is unmarried but 40.36 per cent are married. The number of the widowed and divorced are very meagre. Same is the case with the females. Out of 288 combined female Sherpa population of the two villages majority (53.12%) is unmarried while 38.54 per cent of them are married. The strength of widowed and divorced persons is also very meagre. The widows are 6.60 per cent only.

From Table 8.6 it is clearly seen that among the Sherpas of the two villages upto the age of 14 all the males and females (except one female) are unmarried. The marital age starts from the age of 15. But even in the age group of 15-19 the number of married persons is very low. In this age group (15-19) there is only one widow whose husband died of accident some times ago. The largest number of unmarried males and females (25.00% and 31.37% respectively) belong to the age-group 10-14. The age groups 5 to 9 and 15-19 also have high frequency for males (23.72% and 23.08% respectively) but unmarried females of age groups 'upto 4'

Table 8.5: Marital Status of the Sherpas of Two Villages of Sikkim

Marital Status	Sherpagaon						Sherpahat						Total					
	Person		Male		Female		Person		Male		Female		Person		Male		Female	
	No.	%	No.	%	No.	%	No.	%	No.	%	No.	%	No.	%	No.	%	No.	%
Unmarried	201	49.02	124	54.87	77	41.85	209	50.98	102	45.13	107	58.15	410	100.00	226	100.00	184	100.00
Married	119	49.38	60	50.00	59	48.76	122	50.62	60	50.00	62	51.24	241	100.00	120	100.00	121	100.00
Widowed	18	50.00	7	46.67	11	52.38	18	50.00	8	53.33	10	47.62	36	100.00	15	100.00	21	100.00
Divorced	2	40.00	1	50.00	1	33.33	3	60.00	1	50.00	2	67.67	5	100.00	2	100.00	3	100.00
Total	340	49.13	192	52.89	148	44.98	352	50.87	171	47.11	181	55.02	692	100.00	363	100.00	329	100.00

Source: Field study by the authors.

and 15-19 have the next higher strength, each with 18.45 per cent. Of course among the females age-group 5-9 also has significant strength (16.34%).

Among the males no one is married upto the age of 14. The Sherpas here start marrying from the age-group of 15-19. The largest number of the married males (15.93%) belongs to each of the age-groups 35-39 and 40-44. Age-groups 25-29 and 30-34 also have significant strength, each with 14.16 per cent, but among the females the age-group, 30-34, has largest number of married ones (17.17%). The next higher strength for the married females goes to the age-group 20-24 (15.34%).

Among these people of the two villages of Darjeeling majority of the widowers (80.00%) belong to the age-group 60+. Among the widowed females also the largest number belongs to the age-group 60+ (42.11%). As already said the number of divorced persons is very small.

Now, we shall come down to the individual village level. At Sherpaguri village of Darjeeling a total of 217 Sherpas live. Out of them majority are unmarried though a significant number (37.33%) of them is married. The strength of widowed and divorced Sherpas of this village is very low. Similarly, among both male and female Sherpas majority (61.11% and 51.38% respectively) are unmarried. The number of married males (36.11%) and married females (38.53%) have secured the second position. Among the male Sherpas the number of widowers is very low and there is no divorced male. Among the female Sherpas on the other hand, the widows have some strength (8.26%) and divorced ones are only a few (1.83%).

In this village all Sherpa males and females upto the age of 14 remain unmarried. Again among the unmarried males the largest number belong to the age-group of 15 to 19, (28.79%) followed by the age-group 10-14 (27.27%). But among the females the largest number of unmarried ones belong to the age-group 10-14. Next comes age-group 15-19 (25.00%). Again we do not find any unmarried male beyond the age-group of 35-39 except one in the age-group of 55-59. In case of females none usually remain unmarried beyond the age-group 30-34 except only three, one in each of the age groups, 45-49, 50-54 and 55-59, that means a total of three females are unmarried beyond the age group of 30-34.

Now, we come down to the marital status of the Sherpas of Sherpaguri. In this village out of the total Sherpas (217), 122 (56.22%) are unmarried, 81 (37.33%) married, 12 (5.53%) widowed persons, and only two of them are divorced. Again out of 108 Sherpa males, 61.11 per cent are unmarried and 36.11 per cent married and the rest are widowers. Among

Table 8.6: Marital Status of the Sherpas of Two Villages of Darjeeling

Age group	Unmarried				Married				Widowed				Divorced				Total			
	Male		Female		Male		Female		Male		Female		Male		Female		Male		Female	
	No.	%	No.	%	No.	%	No.	%	No.	%	No.	%	No.	%	No.	%	No.	%	No.	%
Upto 4	15	9.62	29	18.95													15	5.36	29	10.07
5-9	37	23.72	25	16.34													37	13.21	25	8.68
10-14	39	25.00	48	31.37			1	0.90									39	13.93	49	17.01
15-19	36	23.08	29	18.95	3	2.70	4	3.60			1	5.26					39	13.93	34	11.81
20-24	13	8.33	8	5.23	6	5.31	17	15.34									19	6.79	25	8.68
25-29	10	6.41	3	1.96	16	14.16	20	18.02							1	20.00	26	9.29	24	8.33
30-34	1	0.64	5	3.27	16	14.16	19	17.17	1	10.00							18	6.43	24	8.33
35-39	2	1.28	1	0.65	18	15.93	14	12.61			1	5.26					20	7.14	16	5.56
40-44			2	1.31	18	15.93	14	12.61			2	10.53	1	100.00	1	20.00	19	6.79	19	6.60
45-49	2	1.28	1	0.65	14	12.39	10	9.01			3	15.79					16	5.71	14	4.86
50-54			1	0.65	6	5.31	4	3.60			3	15.79					6	2.14	8	2.78
55-59	1	0.64	1	0.65	7	6.19	2	1.80	1	10.00	1	5.26			1	20.00	9	3.21	5	1.74
60+					9	7.96	6	5.31	8	80.00	8	42.11			2	40.00	17	6.07	16	5.56
Total	156	100.00	153	99.98	113	100.04	111	100.06	10	100.00	19	100.00	1	100.00	5	100.00	280	100.00	288	100.01

Source: Field study by the authors.

the female Sherpas out of a total 109, 51.38 per cent are unmarried, 38.53 per cent married, 8.26 per cent widowers and the rest are divorced. Here the Sherpa males are married from the age-group, 25-29 and the Sherpa females from the age-group 15-19. In this village the largest number of the married Sherpa males (20.51%) belong to the age-group, 45-49. The next higher number of the married Sherpa males (15.38%) are within the age-group 40-44. Now in case of the females the highest number of the Sherpa married females (19.05%) belong to the age-group 40-44 followed by those (16.67%) who belong to the age-group, 25-29. Among these people there are three widowers and all of them belong to the age-group of 60+. Among the Sherpa widows age-groups 50-54 and 60+ have 3 each (33.33% each). But one widow belongs to a very tender age of 15-19. Her husband recently died of accident. There are two divorced females live in this village. One of them belongs to the age-group, 40-44 while the other, 60+.

In Sherpapur village of Kalimpong, Darjeeling there are a total of 351 Sherpas. Out of these Sherpas 187 (53.28%) are unmarried, 143 (40.74%) married, and 17 (4.83%) are widowed. The rest 4 are divorced. Here in this village live 172 Sherpa males of whom 90 (52.32%) are unmarried, 74 (43.02%) married and 7 (4.07%) are widowers. Again out of 179 Sherpa females of this village 97 (54.19%) are unmarried, 69 (38.55%) married and 10 (5.59%) are widows. The remaining 3 female Sherpas are divorced ones. Now, we shall examine the age-groupwise distribution of the Sherpa males and females of different marital status of this village. Out of 90 unmarried males the highest number (27.78%) belongs to the age-group 5-9. They are followed by those who belong to the age-group, 10-14 (23.33%). The age-group 15-19 also has a significant strength (18.89%). Among the Sherpas married males, the higher number belong to the age-group of 35-39 (18.92%). Then comes age-groups 25-29 (17.57%) followed by age-groups 30-34 and 40-44, each of these has the strength of 16.22 of married males. Among the Sherpa widowers the overwhelming majority (71.43%) belongs to the age-group 60+. There is also one divorced male who belongs to the age-group, 40-44.

Among the females unmarried Sherpas of this village the highest number (28.87%) belongs to the age-group 10-14 followed by 'Upto 4' (22.68%) and 5-9 (20.62%). Out of 69 married Sherpa females of this village, the highest number is covered by the age-group 30-34 (21.14%). Next to this age-group come age-groups 20-24 and 25-29 each with 18.84 per cent married females. Out of 10 widows half belongs to the age-

Table 8.7: Marital Status of the Sherpas of Sherpaguri Village (Darjeeling)

Age group	Unmarried				Married				Widowed				Divorced				Total			
	Male		Female		Male		Female		Male		Female		Male		Female		Male		Female	
	No.	%	No.	%	No.	%	No.	%	No.	%	No.	%	No.	%	No.	%	No.	%	No.	%
Upto 4	3	4.55	7	12.50													3	2.78	7	6.42
5-9	12	18.18	5	8.93													12	11.11	5	4.59
10-14	18	27.27	20	35.71													18	16.67	20	18.35
15-19	19	28.79	14	25.00			1	2.38			1	11.11					19	17.59	16	14.68
20-24	6	9.09	4	7.14			4	9.52									6	5.56	8	7.34
25-29	5	7.58	1	1.79	3	7.69	7	16.67									8	7.41	8	7.34
30-34	1	1.52	2	3.57	4	10.26	4	9.52									5	4.63	6	5.50
35-39	1	1.52			4	10.26	5	11.90									5	4.63	5	4.59
40-44					6	15.38	8	19.05							1	50.00	6	5.56	9	8.26
45-49			1	1.79	8	20.51	3	7.14			2	22.22					8	7.41	6	5.50
50-54			1	1.79	4	10.26	4	9.52			3	33.33					4	3.70	8	7.34
55-59	1	1.52	1	1.79	5	12.82	2	4.76									6	5.56	3	2.75
60+					5	12.82	4	9.52	3	100.00	3	33.33			1	50.00	8	7.41	8	7.34
Total	66	100.02	56	100.01	39	100.00	42	99.98	3	100.00	9	99.99			2	100.00	108	100.02	109	100.00

Source: Field study by the authors.

Table 8.8: Marital Status of the Sherpas of Sherpapur Village (Darjeeling)

Age group	Unmarried				Married				Widowed				Divorced				Total			
	Male		Female		Male		Female		Male		Female		Male		Female		Male		Female	
	No.	%	No.	%	No.	%	No.	%	No.	%	No.	%	No.	%	No.	%	No.	%	No.	%
Upto 4	12	13.33	22	22.68													12	6.98	22	12.29
5-9	25	27.78	20	20.62													25	14.53	20	11.17
10-14	21	23.33	28	28.87			1	1.45									21	12.21	29	16.20
15-19	17	18.89	15	15.46	3	4.05	3	4.35									20	11.63	18	10.06
20-24	7	7.78	7	4.12	6	8.11	13	18.84									13	7.56	17	9.50
25-29	5	5.56	2	2.06	13	17.57	13	18.84							1	33.73	18	10.47	16	8.94
30-34			3	3.09	12	16.22	15	21.74	1	14.29							13	7.56	18	10.06
35-39	1	1.11	1	1.03	14	18.92	9	13.04			1	10.00					15	8.72	11	6.15
40-44			2	2.06	12	16.22	6	8.70			2	20.00	1	10.00			13	7.56	10	5.59
45-49	2	2.22			6	8.11	7	10.14			1	10.00					8	4.65	8	4.47
50-54					2	2.70											2	1.16		
55-59					2	2.70			1	14.29	1	10.00			1	33.33	3	1.74	2	1.12
60+					4	5.40	2	2.90	5	71.43	5	50.00			1	33.33	9	5.23	8	4.47
Total	90	100.00	97	99.99	74	100.00	69	100.00	7	100.00	10	10.00	1	100.00	3	99.99	172	100.00	179	100.03

Source: Field study by the authors.

group 60+. Next comes age-group 40-44 (20.00%). Divorced females are only a few in numbers.

We shall now take stock of the two Sherpa villages of South District, Sikkim. The combined total Sherpa population of the two villages, Sherpagaon and Sherpahat, is 692, and out of this Sherpa population 410 (59.25%) are unmarried. 241 (34.83%) married, 36 (5.20%) widowed persons and only 5 (50.72%) are divorced. Again among the total male Sherpas of these two villages (363) the highest number of males (226 or 62.26%) are unmarried and then come the married Sherpa males (120 or 33.06%), 15 (4.13%) are widowers and only two are divorced. Among the total females (329) same is the picture. The highest number of the Sherpa females here (184 or 55.93%) are unmarried and the second position is held by the married females (121 or 36.78%). But a significant number (21 or 6.38%) are widows and only three are divorced.

We shall now come down to the age-group-wise distribution of the Sherpas of different marital status of these two villages. Among the unmarried males the highest number (49 or 21.68%) belong to the age-group of 5-9. They are followed by those who belong to the age-groups of 15-19 (18.58%), and 'upto 4' (16.37%). In case of the Sherpa males who are married, the highest number (29 or 24.17%) belong to the age-group 30-34. Next comes the age-group 60+ (13.33%) followed by the age-group 35-39 (12.50%). Among the widowed males age-group 60+ has the majority (60.00%) followed by the age-group 55-59 (13.33%). There is no divorced male among the Sherpas of these two villages. Among the female Sherpas who are unmarried the highest number has been secured by the age-group 10-14 (23.91). The next comes age-group 'Upto 4' (22.28%) followed by the age-group, 5-9 (21.74%). Among the married female Sherpas the largest number belongs to the age-group 25-29 (19.01%) followed by the age-group 20-24 (15.70%) and then age-group 30-34 (14.88%). Among the Sherpa widows the largest number (47.62%) goes to the age-group 60+. Next in order come age-groups 45-49 and 55-59 each having the strength of 14.29 per cent. The majority of the divorced females (66.67%) are found to belong to the age-group 25-29.

We shall now come down to the individual villages. In the village Sherpagaon, there live a total of 340 Sherpas. Out of this Sherpa population the number of unmarried Sherpas (201 or 59.12%) has outnumbered the married Sherpas (119 or 35.00%). The number of widowed persons is 18 (5.29%), and only two are divorced. Among the male Sherpas of this village the trend is similar. Here also the number of unmarried males (124 or 64.58%) supercedes married males (60 or

31.25%). Only 7 males are widowers and there is one divorced male. Among the Sherpa females of this village also the number of unmarried males (77 or 52.03%) is higher than that of the females (59 or 39.86%). There are 11 (7.43%) widows and a single divorced female live in this village (Table 8.10).

Now, we shall discuss about the age-group-wise distribution of persons of different marital status. Among the unmarried male Sherpas of this village the largest number (26 or 20.97%) is found in the age-group 5-9 followed by 20-24 (19.35%) and 10-14 (16.31%). Among the married Sherpa males the highest concentration is in the age-group of 30-34 (25.00%) followed by the age-group 55-59 (15.00%). The overwhelming majority of widowers are found in the age-group of 60+ (71.43%).

Among the female Sherpas of this village the largest number of unmarried ones are found in the age-group of 10-14 (25.97%). Then come age-groups 'Upto 4' (22.08%), 15-19 (20.78%) and 5-9 (16.88%). Among the married females the highest number is found in the age-group of 20-24 (20.34%) followed by the age-groups of 34-39 (15.25%) and age-group of 25-29 (13.56%). Among the widowed females, the highest concentration is in the age-group of 60+ (36.36%) followed by the age-groups of 45-49 and 55-59 each with the strength of 18.18 per cent strength. The lone divorced female Sherpa belongs to the age-group of 25-29 (Table 8.10).

Now, we shall examine the marital status of the Sherpas of the other village, Sherpahat, of South District, Sikkim. Here in this village live 352 Sherpas of whom 209 (59.38%) are unmarried. The number of married Sherpas is much less (122 or 34.68%). The number of widowed persons is only 18 (5.11%) and only three are divorced persons. Among the male Sherpas here the number of unmarried males (102 or 59.65%) has overshadowed that of the married males (60 or 35.09%). There are 8 widowers (4.68%) live in this village along with one divorced male (Table 8.11).

Among the female Sherpas of this village out of 181 individuals, 107 (59.12%) are unmarried, 62 (34.25%) married and 10 (5.52%) widows. Only two women are divorced.

Now, we shall come down to the age-group-wise distribution of individual Sherpa with varied marital status. Among the unmarried Sherpa males of this village of Sherpahat out of a total of 102, the highest number (23 or 22.55%) is under age-group 5-9. Next comes age-group 10-14 (21.57%) followed by 'Upto 4' (20.59%) and 15-19 (18.63%). The rest of the age-groups have much lower frequencies. Again among the married

Table 8.9: Marital Status of the Sherpas of Two Villages in Sikkim

Age group	Unmarried				Married				Widowed				Divorced				Total			
	Male		*Female*		*Male*		*Female*		*Male*		*Female*		*Male*		*Female*		*Male*		*Female*	
	No.	*%*	*No.*	*%*	*No.*	*%*	*No.*	*%*	*No.*	*%*	*No.*	*%*	*No.*	*%*	*No.*	*%*	*No.*	*%*	*No.*	*%*
Upto 4	37	16.37	41	22.28													37	10.19	41	12.46
5-9	49	21.68	40	21.74													49	13.50	40	12.16
10-14	42	18.58	44	23.91													42	11.57	44	13.37
15-19	43	19.03	31	16.85	1	0.83	6	4.96									44	12.12	37	11.25
20-24	24	10.62	11	5.98	8	6.67	19	15.70	1	6.67	2	9.52	1	50.00			34	9.37	32	9.73
25-29	16	7.08	6	3.26	14	11.67	23	19.01			1	4.76			2	66.67	30	8.26	32	9.73
30-34	4	1.77	8	4.35	29	24.17	18	14.88									33	9.09	26	7.90
35-39	6	2.65	2	1.09	15	12.50	12	9.92	1	6.67							22	6.06	14	4.26
40-44	2	0.88	1	0.54	7	5.83	9	7.44									9	2.48	10	3.04
45-49	1	0.44			12	10.00	13	10.74	1	6.67	3	14.29			1	33.33	14	3.86	17	5.17
50-54	1	0.44			6	5.00	3	2.48	1	6.67	2	9.52	1	50.00			9	2.48	5	1.52
55-59					12	10.00	6	4.96	2	13.33	3	14.29					14	3.86	9	2.74
60+	1	0.44			16	13.33	12	9.92	9	60.00	10	47.62					26	7.16	22	6.69
Total	226	99.98	184	100.00	120	100.00	121	100.01	15	100.01	21	100.00	2	100.00	3	100.00	363	100.00	329	100.02

Source: Field study by the authors.

male Sherpas the highest number belongs to the age-group 30-34 (14 or 23.33%). The next in order come age-groups 60+ (16.67%) and age-group 35-39 (13.33%). There are only 8 widowers inhabiting in this village. Half of these widowers (50.00%) belong to the age-group 60+. The rest 4 widowers are distributed in 4 different age-groups with one belonging to each age-group. The only divorced male Sherpa belongs to the age-group 50-54 (Table 8.11).

Among the total unmarried female Sherpas (107), the highest number comes under age-group 5-9 (25.23%). The next higher strength goes to the age-groups 'Upto 4' and 10-14 (22.43%). Among the married Sherpa females the highest strength goes to the age-group 25-29 (24.19%). The age-group 30-34 has the next higher strength (17.74%). There are 10 widows live at Sherpahat. Out of them majority (60.00%) belongs to the age-group 60+. There are only two divorced females. They belong the age-groups 25-29 and 45-49.

In connection with the marital status of the Sherpas of Nepal, Oppitz is of the view that "22 per cent of lay men in the 30-34 age-group are unmarried, 29 per cent of lay women in the 30-34 age group are unmarried" (1968: 128 cf Ortner 1979:46).

Age at First Marriage

In all human societies, people get married when they attain a certain age. Normally, after becoming adult when they develop physical and mental maturity, they become eligible for marriage. So, their parents/guardian or sometimes they themselves search for a partner. But in many other societies without waiting for the adulthood, the parents/guardians go for the marriage of their little children, even at the age of 4 or 5 years of their children. But very few person get married after the age of 50. So, we see that people usually go for married when they are at the age-group of 15 to 40. This is also true for the Sherpas of both Darjeeling and Sikkim. They also prefer to marry when they are 20 to 40 years old.

In the following pages we shall discuss about the age at first marriage of the Sherpas of our studied villages of both Darjeeling in West Bengal and South District in Sikkim.

Among the Sherpas of the two villages of Kalimpong, Darjeeling studied by us, the largest number of males got married when they were between 20 and 24 years of age (39.52%). Next come those males who married when they were between 25 and 29 years of age (30.65%). On the other hand, the largest number of female Sherpas (48.87%) married

Table 8.10: Marital Status of the Sherpas of Sherpahat Village of Sikkim

Age group	Unmarried				Married				Widowed				Divorced				Total			
	Male		Female		Male		Female		Male		Female		Male		Female		Male		Female	
	No.	%	No.	%	No.	%	No.	%	No.	%	No.	%	No.	%	No.	%	No.	%	No.	%
Upto 4	21	20.59	24	22.43													21		24	
5-9	23	22.55	27	25.23													23		27	
10-14	22	21.57	24	22.43													22		24	
15-19	19	18.63	15	14.02	1	1.67	6	9.68									20		21	
20-24	7	6.86	7	6.54	7	11.67	7	11.29	1	12.50	1	10.00					15		15	
25-29	5	4.90	4	3.74	7	11.67	15	24.19							1	50.00	12		20	
30-34			5	4.67	14	23.33	11	17.74									14		16	
35-39	2	1.96	1	0.93	8	13.33	3	4.84	1	12.50							11		4	
40-44	1	0.98			2	3.33	4	6.45									3		4	
45-49					5	8.33	7	11.29	1	12.50	1	10.00			1	50.00	6		9	
50-54	1	0.98			3	5.00	1	1.61			1	10.00	1	100.00			5		2	
55-59					3	5.00	3	4.84	1	12.50	1	10.00					4		4	
60+	1	0.98			10	16.67	5	8.06	4	50.00	6	60.00					15		11	
Total	102	100.00	107	99.99	60	99.99	62	99.99	8	100.00	10	100.00	1	100.00	2	100.00	171		181	

Source: Field study by the authors.

Table 8.11: Marital Status of the Sherpas of Sherpagaon Village of Sikkim

Age group	Unmarried				Married				Widowed				Divorced				Total			
	Male		Female		Male		Female		Male		Female		Male		Female		Male		Female	
	No.	%	No.	%	No.	%	No.	%	No.	%	No.	%	No.	%	No.	%	No.	%	No.	%
Upto 4	16	12.90	17	22.08													16		17	
5-9	26	20.97	13	16.88													26		13	
10-14	20	16.13	20	25.97													20		20	
15-19	24	19.35	16	20.78													24		16	
20-24	17	13.71	4	5.19	1	1.67	12	20.34			1	9.09	1	100.00			19		17	
25-29	11	8.87	2	2.60	7	11.67	8	13.56			1	9.09			1	100.00	18		12	
30-34	4	3.23	3	3.90	15	25.00	7	11.86									19		10	
35-39	4	3.23	1	1.30	7	11.67	9	15.25									11		10	
40-44	1	0.81	1	1.30	5	8.33	5	8.47									6		6	
45-49	1	0.81			7	11.67	6	10.17			2	18.18					8		8	
50-54					3	5.00	2	3.39	1	14.29	1	9.09					4		3	
55-59					9	15.00	3	5.08	1	14.29	2	18.18					10		5	
60+					6	10.00	7	11.86	5	71.43	4	36.36					11		11	
Total	124	100.01	77	100.00	60	100.01	59	99.98	7	100.01	11	99.99	1	100.00	1	100.00	192		148	

Source: Field study by the authors.

when they were 15 to 19 years of age. Next come those (31.58%) who married when they were between 20 and 24 years of age.

Among the Sherpas of the two villages studied in Darjeeling, only five persons married when they were upto 14 years of age. Of them one is male who is now 60+ years of age while the other four are females who belong to different age groups. A total of 25 males and 65 females married when they were between 15 and 19 years of age. Out of the 25 males, the highest number belong to the age group 20-24 and 25-29 each having 20.00 per cent as its share. Next come those (16.00%) whose present age is 45-49 years of age. The rest belongs to different age-groups. Among the females (65 in number) who have married when they were 15-19 years of age, the largest number belongs to the age-group 20-24 at present. Next come those who belong to the age-group 30-34 (16.92%) followed by those who are at present belong to the age-group 45-49 (15.38%). The rest belong to different age-groups.

There are 49 male and 42 female Sherpas whose age-at first marriage was between 20 and 24. Among these 49 male Sherpas the largest member of males who married when they were in the age-group of 20-24, belong to three age-groups 25-29, 30-34 and 40-44, each with 18.37 per cent strength. Next come those who now belong to the age-group 40-44 at present (14.29%). Among the female Sherpas who have their age at first marriage being between 20 and 24, the largest number belong to the age-group 25-29 (23.81%) at present. They are followed by those who belong to the age-groups, 35-39, 40-44 and 60+ each with 14.29 per cent at its credit.

We, now come down to those Sherpas whose age of first marriage was between 25 and 29. There are 38 males and 15 females who married when they were between 25 and 29. Out of these 38 male Sherpas the largest number of males belong to the age-group 40-44 (21.05%). Next come those who belong to the age-groups 35-39 and 60+, each with 18.42 per cent. Among the female Sherpas who married when they were between 25 and 29 years of age, the largest number (26.67%) now belong to the age-group of 40-44. Next come those who belong to the age group 60+ (20.00%).

Lastly, out of those who married when they were in the age of 30 and more, there are only 12 males and 6 females. At present they belong to different ages.

We shall now discuss about the age-at first marriage of the Sherpa males and females of the two villages of Kalimpong, Darjeeling district, Sherpaguri and Sherpapur. First of all we shall come to Sherpaguri village.

In this village out of 42 Sherpas who married in different ages, the largest number (38.90%) of them was married when they were in the age-group of 25-29. Next are those male Sherpas (33.33%) who married when they were in the ages between 20 and 24. Among the female married Sherpas out of 52, the largest number (36.54%) married when they were in the age-group of 15-19, followed by those who married when they had the age at that time between 20 and 24 (34.62%) years.

Among the male Sherpas of this village there are 14 male Sherpas who married when they were 20 to 24 years old. The present age of the largest number (5 or 35.71%) is 60+. But the largest number of those who married when they were 25 to 29 years of age (25.00%) are now in the age-group of 45-49/while 9 males who married when they were 30+ years of age, belong to different age groups in varied numbers.

Among the female Sherpas only one married at the age of 13 and she is now 53 years of age. Out of 29 female Sherpas who married when they were between 15 and 29 years of age, the largest number are now belong to the age-groups 20-24 and 35-39 each with a strength of 21.05 per cent. Again among 18 females who married when they were 20 to 24 years of age, the largest number (27.78%) belong to the age-group of 25-29 at present. Only 10 females married when they were 25-29 years of age. The largest number of them (40.00%) are now belong to the age-group of 20-44.

We shall now examine the age at first marriage of the Sherpa males and females of the village Sherpapur of Kalimpong in Darjeeling District. Only one male Sherpa of this village who is now 60+ years of age, married when he was 14 years of age. Among those males who married when they were 15 to 29 years old, the largest number now belong to the age-group 20-24 (22.73%), followed by those who are now 25-29 years of age were married when they were 15 to 19 years of age, the largest number (10 or 21.74%) belongs to the those who are now in the age-groups of 20-24 and also 30-34 (29.74% each) followed by those who are now in the age-group of 45-49 (15.22%) followed by those who belong to the age group 25-29 (13.04%).

In case of those male Sherpas who married when they were 20-24 years of age, the largest number belongs to 30-34 years of age at present. Next come those who are now 25-29 and 40-44 years of age each with 20.00 per cent. Among the female Sherpas the largest number who are married when they were 20-24 years of age, are now in the age groups of 25-29 and 35-39 each with 20.83 per cent in strength. Now, we come down to those who married when they were 25-29 years of age. Among

Table 8.12: Showing the Age at First Marriage Among the Sherpas of Two Villages of Darjeeling

Present Age	Age At First Marriage																							
	Upto 14				15 - 19				20 - 24				25-29				30+				Total			
	Male		Female		Male		Female		Male		Female		Male		Female		Male		Female		Male		Female	
	No	%	No	%	No.	%	No.	%	No	%	No	%	No.	%	No.	%	No.	%	No	%	No	%	No.	%
15-19					3	12.00	3	4.62													3	2.42	3	2.26
20-24					5	20.00	14	21.54	1	2.04	3	7.14									6	4.84	17	12.78
25-29			1	25.00	5	20.00	8	12.31	9	18.37	10	23.81	2	5.26	2	13.33					16	12.90	21	15.79
30-34			1	25.00	2	8.00	11	16.92	9	18.37	4	9.52	5	13.16	2	13.33	1	8.33	1	16.67	17	13.71	19	14.29
35-39					3	12.00	8	12.31	7	14.29	6	14.29	7	18.42	1	6.67	1	8.33			18	14.52	15	11.28
40-44							7	10.77	9	18.37	6	14.29	8	21.05	4	26.67	2	16.67			19	15.32	17	12.78
45-49					4	16.00	10	15.38	3	6.12	2	4.76	5	13.16	1	6.67	2	16.67			14	11.29	13	9.77
50-54			1	25.00	1	4.00			2	4.08	3	7.14	1	2.63	1	6.67	2	16.67	2	33.33	6	4.84	7	5.26
55-59					1	4.00			3	6.12	2	4.76	3	7.89	1	6.67	2	16.67	1	16.67	8	6.45	5	3.76
60+	1	100.00	1	25.00	1	4.00	4	6.15	6	12.24	6	14.28	7	18.42	3	20.00	2	16.67	2	33.33	17	13.71	16	12.03
Total	1	100.00	4	100.00	25	100.00	65	100.01	49	99.99	42	100.00	38	100.07	15	100.01	12	100.01	6	100.00	124	100.00	133	100.01

Source: Field study by the authors.

the male Sherpas those who are now in the age group of 40-44 (27.27%) followed by those who are now in the age-group of 60+ (22.72%), the age at first marriage was 25-29. Among the female Sherpas who married when they were 25-29 years of age, the largest number of them (40.00%) are now in the age-group of 25-29. Only a few Sherpas married when they were 30+ years of age.

We shall now shift to analyse the combined data on age at first marriage of the Sherpas of two villages, Sherpagaon and Sherpahat of South District, Sikkim. The combined data on age at first marriage, show that the largest number of males (40.29%) married when they were 20-24 years of age. Next come those who married when they were 15 to 19 years of age (23.02%). Among the female Sherpas the largest number (73 or 50.69%) married when they were 15-19 years of age. Next come those who married when they were 20-24 years of age (25.69%). When we look into the age-group-wise distribution of the Sherpa married males and females as per age at first marriage, we see that among the male Sherpas who married when they were less then 15 years of age (upto 14), the largest number (4 or 50.00%) are now 55 to 59 years of age. Among the female Sherpas who married when they were upto 14 years of age-12 to 14, the largest number of them are now in the age-groups of 20-24 and 60+, each having a strength 18.75 per cent. Again among those Sherpa males who married when they were 15 to 19 years of age, the largest number (7 or 21.88%) now belong to the age-group, 30-34, followed by those who are now 60+(15.62%). Among the female Sherpas who married when they were 15 to 19 years of age, the largest number are now in the age-group of 23.29 per cent. Then come those who are now 20-24 years of age (21.92%).

We shall now come to those Sherpas who married when they were 20-24 years of age. In this age-group among the combined married Sherpa population of the two villages of Sikkim (Table 8.12) it is seen that out of 56 males who married when they were 20 to 24 years of age, the largest number (15 or 26.79%) are at present in the age-group of 30-34. They are followed by those who are now in the age-group of 60+ (17.85%) and then in the age-group of 25-29 (16.07%). Among the married female Sherpas who married in the above mentioned age of first marriage (20 to 24) the largest number (7 or 18.92%) are now in the age-group of 60+. Next to them come those (6 or 16.22%) who are now in the age-group of 25-29. 28 male Sherpas married at the age of 25 to 29. The largest number of them are now in the age-groups of 30-34 and 35-39, each with 25.00 per cent strength. They are followed by those who are now 60+ years of age (21.43%). Only 8 females married when were 25 to 29 years of age. The largest number of them are now in the age-group of 35-39 (37.50%) followed by those who are now 40-44 age-group (25.00%).

There are 15 male and 10 female Sherpas who married when they were 30+ years of age. Now, out of these 15 married males the largest number are at present 60+ years of age (21.43%) followed by those who are now 40-44 and 45-49 years of age, each with 20.00 per cent. Among those 10 married female Sherpas the largest number who married when they were 30+ years of age, are now 60+ years old (40.00%).

We shall now come down to the two individual villages of South District. At Sherpagaon there are a total of 68 males and 70 females who are married. Now out of these 68 males the largest number (25 or 36.96%) married when they were 20 to 24 years of age. Next come those (14 or 20.59%) who were married when they were 25 to 29 followed by those (13 or 19.12%) who were 15 to 19 years of age at the time of their first marriage. Among the married female Sherpas the largest number (32 or 45.71%) were married then when they were 15 to 19 years of age. They are followed by those (18 or 25.71%) who were married when they were 15 5o 19 years of age. Now, out of the male Sherpas who married when they were 20 to 24 years of age, the largest number (6 or 24.00%) of them belong to the age-groups 30-34 and 60+ followed by those whose present age is between 25 and 29. Again among these males who married when they were 25 to 29 years of age, the present age of the largest number (5 or 35.71%) is 30 to 34, followed by those (3 or 21.43%) who are now 35 to 39 years of age. Among the female Sherpas of Sherpagaon those who married at the age between 15 and 19, the present age of the largest number of the females is 20 to 24. They are followed by those (18.75%) whose present age is between 25 and 29. Next those Sherpa females whose age at first marriage were between 20 and 24 years of age, the largest number of them are now 35 to 39 and 60+ each with a strength of 22.22 per cent.

We shall now discuss about the age of first marriage among the Sherpas of Sherpahat village of South District, Sikkim. In this village there are 71 married Sherpa males and 74 married Sherpa females. Out of these 71 male Sherpa, the largest number (31 or 43.66%) married when they were 20-24 years of age. Next come those (19 or 26.76%) who married when they were 15 to 19 years of age, followed by those (14 or 19.72%) who married when they were 25 to 29 years of age. Among the female Sherpas the age at first marriage of the largest number (41 or

Table 8.13: Showing the Age at First Marriage Among the Sherpas of Sherpaguri (Darjeeling)

Present Age	Age At First Marriage																							
	Upto 14				15 - 19				20 - 24				25-29				30+				Total			
	Male		Female		Male		Female		Male		Female		Male		Female		Male		Female		Male		Female	
	No.	%	No.	%	No.	%	No.	%	No.	%	No.	%	No.	%	No.	%	No.	%	No.	%	No.	%	No.	%
15-19																								
20-24							4	21.05															4	7.69
25-29					1	33.33	2	10.53	2	14.29	5	27.78									3	7.14	7	13.46
30-34							1	5.26	1	7.14	1	5.56	2	12.50	1	10.00	1	11.11	1	25.00	4	9.52	4	7.69
35-39							4	21.05	1	7.14	1	5.56	3	18.75							4	9.52	5	9.62
40-44							3	15.79	2	14.29	2	11.11	2	12.50	4	40.00	2	22.22			6	14.29	9	17.31
45-49					1	33.33	3	15.79	1	7.14	1	5.56	4	25.00	1	10.00	2	22.22			8	19.05	5	9.62
50-54			1	100.00	1	33.33					3	16.67	1	6.25	1	10.00	2	22.22	2	50.00	4	9.52	7	13.46
55-59									2	14.29	2	11.11	2	12.50	1	10.00	1	11.11			5	11.90	3	5.77
60+							2	10.53	5	35.71	3	16.67	2	12.50	2	20.00	1	11.11	1	25.00	8	19.05	8	15.38
Total			1	100.00	3	99.99	19	100.00	14	100.00	18	100.02	16	100.00	10	100.00	9	99.99	4	100.00	42	99.99	52	100.00

Source: Field study by the authors.

55.40%) were between 15 and 19. Then come those (19 or 25.67%) whose age was at that time, between 20 and 24 years.

Now, among the male Sherpas, who married when they were 20 to 24 years of age the present age of the largest number (9 or 29.03%) is 25 to 29. They are followed by those (5 or 16.13%) who are now 25 to 29 years of age. Among those males whose age at first marriage was 15 to 19 years of age, the largest number (4 or 21.05%) are now 20 to 24 years of age. Among the those females who married when they were 15 to 19 years of age, the largest number (11 or 26.83%) are at present 25 to 29 years of age. Again those who are now 30 to 34 years of age (19.07%) married when they were 15 to 19 years of age.

It is thus seen that among the Sherpa males of the two studied villages by Kalimpong, Darjeeling, the largest number of males married when they were between 20 to 29 years of age. This means that out of 124 married males of those two villages, 70.16 per cent married when they were of those ages. Among the females Sherpas (total 133) 80.45 per cent married when they were 15 to 24 years of age. Of course a good number of males also married when they were 15 to 19 years of age.

In the two studied villages of South District, Sikkim 60.43 per cent male Sherpas married when they were in the age group of 25-30+ though a good number of them (23.02%) married when they were 15 to 19 years of age. Among the female Sherpas overwhelming majority (76.39%) married when they were in the age-group of 15 to 24. Again 11.11 per cent of them also married at a very tender age (upto 14).

Difference of Age between Husband and Wife

In all human societies the age of the husbands and wives normally vary though in some cases they may have the same age. Even when they have the same age, as they may not have born at the same time and on the same date, so there may be difference of months, days or hours indicating slight difference of age. But normally if they have born in the same year we take it for granted that they are of the same age. Among the Sherpas also the bride and the bridegroom have either of the same age or there is difference in their respective age. In the latter case the bridegroom is either senior to the bride or junior to the bride by age. Through Table 8.18 and Table 8.19 we like to show the frequencies of the difference of age of the Sherpa brides and bridegrooms of our studied villages. That means either the bridegrooms are senior to the brides or brides are senior to the bridegrooms by age or they have the same age.

Table 8.14: Showing the Age at First Marriage Among the Sherpas of Sherpapur (Darjeeling)

Present Age	Age At First Marriage																							
	Upto 14				15 - 19				20 - 24				25-29				30+				Total			
	Male		Female		Male		Female		Male		Female		Male		Female		Male		Female		Male		Female	
	No.	%	No.	%	No.	%	No.	%	No.	%	No.	%	No.	%	No.	%	No.	%	No.	%	No.	%	No.	%
15-19					3	13.64	3	6.52													3	3.66	3	3.70
20-24					5	22.73	10	21.74	1	2.86	3	12.50									6	7.32	13	16.05
25-29			1	33.33	4	18.18	6	13.04	7	20.00	5	20.83	2	9.09	2	40.00					13	15.85	14	17.28
30-34			1	33.33	2	9.09	10	21.74	8	22.86	3	12.50	3	13.64	1	20.00					13	15.85	15	18.52
35-39					3	13.64	4	8.70	6	17.14	5	20.83	4	18.18	1	20.00	1	33.33			14	17.07	10	12.35
40-44							4	8.70	7	20.00	4	16.67	6	27.27							13	15.85	8	9.88
45-49					3	13.64	7	15.22	2	5.71	1	4.17	1	4.55							6	7.32	8	9.88
50-54									2	5.71											2	2.44		
55-59					1	4.55			1	2.86			1	4.55			1	33.33	1	50.00	3	3.66	2	2.47
60+	1	100.00	1	33.33	1	4.55	2	4.34	1	2.86	3	12.05	5	22.72	1	20.00	1	33.33	1	50.00	9	10.98	8	9.87
Total	1	100.00	3	99.99	22	100.02	46	100.00	35	100.00	24	100.00	22	100.00	5	100.00	3	99.99	2	100.00	82	100.00	81	100.00

Source: Field study by the authors.

Table 8.15: Showing the Age at First Marriage Among the Sherpas of Two Villages of Sikkim

Present Age	Age at First Marriage																							
	Upto 14				15 - 19				20 - 24				25-29				30+				Total			
	Male		Female		Male		Female		Male		Female		Male		Female		Male		Female		Male		Female	
	No.	%	No.	%	No.	%	No.	%	No.	%	No.	%	No.	%	No.	%	No.	%	No.	%	No.	%	No.	%
15-19			2	12.50	1	3.13	4	5.48													1	0.72	6	4.17
20-24			3	18.75	4	12.50	16	21.92	6	10.71	2	5.41									10	7.19	21	14.58
25-29	1	12.50	2	12.50	4	12.50	17	23.29	9	16.07	6	16.22			1	12.50					14	10.07	26	18.06
30-34			1	6.25	7	21.88	10	13.70	15	26.79	5	13.51	7	25.00	1	12.50			1	10.00	29	20.86	18	12.50
35-39	1	12.50	1	6.25	3	9.38	3	4.11	3	5.36	5	13.51	7	25.00	3	37.50	2	13.33			16	11.51	12	8.33
40-44			2	12.50	1	3.13	3	4.11	1	1.79	2	5.41	2	7.14	2	25.00	3	20.00	2	20.00	7	5.04	9	6.25
45-49					3	9.38	9	12.33	5	8.93	4	10.81	2	7.14			3	20.00	2	20.00	13	9.35	17	11.81
50-54			1	6.25	2	6.25	3	4.11	3	5.36	1	2.70	2	7.14			1	6.67			8	5.78	5	3.47
55-59	4	50.00	1	6.25	2	6.25	2	2.74	4	7.14	5	13.51	2	7.14			2	13.33	1	10.00	14	10.07	9	6.25
60+	2	25.00	3	18.75	5	15.62	6	8.22	10	17.85	7	18.92	6	21.43	1	12.50	4	26.67	4	40.00	27	19.42	21	14.58
TOTAL	8	100.00	16	100.00	32	100.03	73	100.01	56	100.00	37	10.01	28	99.99	8	100.00	15	100.00	10	100.00	139	100.01	144	100.00

Source: Field study by the authors.

Table 8.16: Showing the Age at First Marriage Among the Sherpas of Sherpagaon (Sikkim)

Present Age	Age At First Marriage																							
	Upto 14				15 - 19				20 - 24				25-29				30+				Total			
	Male		Female		Male		Female		Male		Female		Male		Female		Male		Female		Male		Female	
	No.	%	No.	%	No.	%	No.	%	No.	%	No.	%	No.	%	No.	%	No.	%	No.	%	No.	%	No.	%
15-19																								
20-24			1	12.50			10	31.25	2	8.00	2	11.11									2	2.94	13	18.57
25-29					3	23.08	6	18.75	4	16.00	3	16.67			1	20.00					7	10.27	10	14.29
30-34			1	12.50	4	30.77	3	9.38	6	24.00	2	11.11	5	35.71					1	14.29	15	22.06	7	10.00
35-39	1	20.00	1	12.50	1	7.69	1	3.13			4	22.22	3	21.43	3	60.00	2	18.18			7	10.29	9	12.86
40-44			2	25.00	1	7.69	1	3.13					1	7.14			3	27.27	2	28.57	5	7.35	5	7.14
45-49							5	15.63	3	12.00	1	5.56	1	7.14	1	20.00	3	27.27	1	14.29	7	10.29	8	11.43
50-54			1	12.50	1	7.69	2	6.25	2	8.00			1	7.14							4	5.88	3	4.29
55-59	4	80.00	1	12.50	1	7.69	1	3.13	2	8.00	2	11.11	1	7.14			2	18.18	1	14.29	10	14.71	5	7.14
60+			1	12.50	2	15.38	3	9.37	6	24.00	4	22.22	2	14.29			1	9.09	2	28.57	11	16.18	10	14.29
TOTAL	5	100.00	8	100.00	13	99.99	32	100.03	25	100.00	18	100.00	14	99.99	5	100.00	11	99.99	7	100.01	68	99.97	70	100.00

Source: Field study by the authors.

Table 8.17: Showing the Age at First Marriage Among the Sherpas of Sherpahat (Sikkim)

Present Age	Age At First Marriage																							
	Upto 14				15 - 19				20 - 24				25-29				30+				Total			
	Male		Female		Male		Female		Male		Female		Male		Female		Male		Female		Male		Female	
	No.	%	No.	%	No.	%	No.	%	No.	%	No.	%	No.	%	No.	%	No.	%	No.	%	No.	%	No.	%
15-19			2	25.00	1	5.26	4	9.76													1	1.41	6	8.11
20-24			2	25.00	4	21.65	6	14.63	4	12.90											8	11.27	8	10.81
25-29	1	33.33	2	25.00	1	5.26	11	26.83	5	16.13	3	15.79									7	9.87	16	21.62
30-34					3	15.79	7	17.07	9	29.03	3	15.79	2	14.29	1	33.33					14	19.72	11	14.86
35-39					2	10.53	2	4.88	3	9.68	1	5.26	4	28.57							9	12.68	3	4.05
40-44							2	4.88	1	3.23	2	10.53	1	7.14							2	2.82	4	5.41
45-49					3	15.79	4	9.76	2	6.45	3	15.79	1	7.14	1	33.33			1	33.33	6	8.45	9	12.16
50-54					1	5.26	1	2.44	1	3.23	1	5.26	1	7.14			1	25.00			4	5.63	2	2.70
55-59					1	5.26	1	2.44	2	6.45	3	15.79	1	7.14							4	5.63	4	5.41
60+	2	66.67	2	25.00	3	15.79	3	7.32	4	12.90	3	15.79	4	28.57	1	33.33	3	75.00	2	66.67	16	22.53	11	14.86
TOTAL	3	100.00	8	100.00	19	99.99	41	100.01	31	100.01	19	100.00	14	99.99	3	99.99	4	100.00	3	100.00	71	100.01	74	99.99

Source: Field study by the authors.

During our field study among the Sherpas in two villages of Darjeeling District, West Bengal and also in two villages of South District, Sikkim, we collected data on the difference of age between the husbands and the wives. In the following pages we have stated the analysis of these data in order to show whether the husbands are senior to the wives or the wives are senior to the husbands or both have the same age.

When we get the difference of age between the husbands and wives of the combined total number of Sherpa couples, we find that those couples with husbands senior to wives by age, enjoy overwhelming majority while the strength of the other couples with brides senior to the husbands and husbands and wives having same age, is undoubtedly low (6.21% and 5.52%) respectively.

At Sherpaguri village of Darjeeling we get from Table 8.18 there are a total of 53 couples of whom overwhelming majority of the couples (86.79%) have the husbands senior to the wives. But in case of the other couples among whom wives senior to the husbands (5.66%) and husbands and wives have same age (7.55%) are of very low frequency. Same is the case with the Sherpa husbands and wives of the village, Sherpapur. Here, also the couples with husbands senior to the wives, enjoy overwhelming majority. The other couples with wives senior to the husband by age and both husbands and wives have very low strength.

Table 8.18: Difference of Age between Bride and Bridegroom in the Studied Villages of Darjeeling and Sikkim

Difference of age between the Bride and the Groom	*Villages of Darjeeling*						*Villages of Sikkim*					
	Sherpaguri		*Sherpapur*		*Total*		*Sherpagaon*		*Sherpahat*		*Total*	
	No.	*%*	*No.*	*%*	*No.*	*%*	*No.*	*%*	*No.*	*%*	*No.*	*%*
Bride Senior to the Groom	3	5.66	6	6.52	9	6.21	17	22.08	12	13.95	29	17.79
Groom Senior to the Bride	46	86.79	82	89.13	128	88.27	56	72.73	69	80.23	125	76.69
Bride and the Groom of the same age	4	7.55	4	4.35	8	5.52	4	5.19	5	5.81	9	5.52
Total	53	100.00	92	100.00	145	100.00	77	100.00	86	99.99	163	100.00

Source: Field study by the authors.

We shall now come to the Sherpa couples of the two villages, Sherpagaon and Sherpahat of South District, Sikkim. Out of the combined total 163 Sherpa couples of these two villages also, like the Sherpa couples of the two villages of Darjeeling District, overwhelming majority of the Sherpa couples (67.69%) goes to those couples whose husbands are senior to the wives by age. But unlike to the Darjeeling villages, the couples with wives senior to the husbands by age, have also significant strength

(17.79%). Of course, couples with husbands and wives having the same age, have quite low strength (only 5.52%).

When we see the difference of age of the Sherpa married couples of the two villages, we get that in both villages, the trend is the same. Both at Sherpagaon and Sherpahat villages, the couples with husbands senior to wives by age, sweep highest strength (72.73% and 80.23% respectively). But the strength of the couples of whom the wives are senior to the husbands, have significant frequency. At Sherpagaon village the same is 22.08 per cent and at Sherpahat village, 13.95 per cent. This means that in these two villages of Sikkim the couples with wives senior to the husbands, are good in number. But couples among whom the husbands and the wives having the same age, are quite low in number.

From Table 8.19 it is clearly seen that out of a total of 145 Sherpa couples in two studied villages of Darjeeling District, the majority of the Sherpa couples (63.45%) live at Sherpapur village and the remaining couples (36.55%) reside at Sherpaguri village. Out of these 145 Sherpa couples of the two villages put together there are 9 couples of whom the wives are senior in age to the husbands, and out of these 9 couples the majority (66.67%) live at Sherpapur village, and the remaining 33.33% couples are the residents of Sherpapguri village. Same is the case with the category, 'husbands senior to the wives'. The majority of such couples (64.06%) live at Sherpapur and the rest of the couples (36.94%) are found to reside at the other village that is, Sherpaguri. But the case of the couples having the same age, are equal in number in these two villages.

As we come to two studied villages of South District, Sikkim, the picture is somewhat different. Here, like Sherpaguri village out of 163 couples a little more than half of the couples (52.76%) reside at Sherpahat village and the remaining 47.24 per cent couples reside at Sherpagaon village. When we examine the difference of age of the wives and the husbands of these two villages, we get that out of 29 couples of whom the wives are senior to the husbands by age, the majority (58.62%) live at Sherpagaon while the rest stay at Sherpahat village. On the other hand, in case of the husbands senior to the wives and both are of same age, the village Sherpahat has overshadowed the other village in strength. In both cases, Sherpahat village has held little over 55.00 per cent while the village Sherpagaon has a little less than 45.00 per cent.

Again Table 8.19 indicates that there are a total of 145 couples in our two studied villages of Darjeeling district, and in case of the most of the couples (88.27%) the husbands are senior to their brides by age. In these cases where the husbands are senior to the wives by age the majority

(71.72%) had love marriage. Only in 16.55 per cent couples among whom husbands are senior to the wives, the marriages were held by negotiation. The couples among whom the wives are senior to the husbands by age or both wives and husbands having the same age, have very low frequency.

Table 8.19: Difference of Age between Sherpa Bride and Bridegroom in the Studied Villages of Darjeeling and Sikkim

Difference of age between the Bride and the Groom	*Villages of Darjeeling, West Bengal*						*Villages of South District, Sikkim*					
	Sherpaguri		*Sherpapur*		*Total*		*Sherpagaon*		*Sherpahat*		*Total*	
	No.	*%*	*No.*	*%*	*No.*	*%*	*No.*	*%*	*No.*	*%*	*No.*	*%*
Bride Senior to the Groom	3	33.33	6	66.67	9	100.00	17	58.62	12	41.38	29	100.00
Groom Senior to the Bride	46	35.94	82	64.06	128	100.00	56	44.80	69	55.20	125	100.00
Bride and the Groom of the same age	4	50.00	4	50.00	8	100.00	4	44.44	5	55.56	9	100.00
Total	53	36.55	92	63.45	145	100.00	77	47.24	86	52.76	163	100.00

Source: Field study by the authors.

When we examine the individual villages of this district, Darjeeling, we get the same result. At Sherpaguri village 86.79 per cent cases show that the bridegrooms are senior to the brides by age. The strength of other two cases, i.e. "bride senior to the groom by age" or "they are of the same age", is quite low. In Sherpapur village also overwhelming majority of the bridegrooms (89.13%) are senior or to the brides by age. The other two cases have very low shares. If we come again to the individual villages, we see that out of the 86.79 per cent cases of Sherpaguri where grooms are senior to the brides, in 47.17 per cent cases couples had love marriage while 39.62 per cent cases the marriages were held by negotiation. On the other hand, at Sherpapur out of 89.13 per cent cases where grooms are senior to the brides, almost all marriages (85.87%) had love marriages, negotiation marriages were negligible in number.

We shall now come down to the two studied villages of South District, Sikkim. The combined data of these two villages show that in 76.68 per cent cases grooms are senior to the brides, while in 17.79 per cent cases brides are senior to the grooms. Again, out of 76.68 per cent cases where grooms are senior to the brides by age in 37.42 per cent cases marriages were held by negotiation whereas in 39.26 per cent cases the marriages were love marriages.

Table 8.20: Difference of Age between Sherpa Bride and Groom having different Types of Marriage

Age Difference between Bride (B) and Groom (G)	*Type of Marriage*	*No. of couples in Darjeeling villages*						*No. of couples in Sikkim villages*					
		Sherpaguri		*Sherpapur*		*Total*		*Sherpagaon*		*Sherpahat*		*Total*	
		No.	*%*	*No.*	*%*	*No.*	*%*	*No.*	*%*	*No.*	*%*	*No.*	*%*
Bride Senior to Groom	Negotiation			1	1.09	1	0.69	9	11.69	9	10.46	18	11.04
	Love	3	5.66	5	5.43	8	5.52	8	10.39	3	3.49	11	6.75
Groom Senior to Bride	Negotiation	21	39.62	3	3.26	24	16.55	27	35.06	34	39.53	61	37.42
	Love	25	47.17	79	85.87	104	71.72	29	37.66	35	40.70	64	39.26
Bride and Groom of the same age	Negotiation	2	3.77			2	1.38	3	3.90	3	3.49	6	3.68
	Love	2	3.77	4	4.35	6	4.14	1	1.30	2	2.33	3	1.84
Total		53	99.99	92	100.00	145	100.01	77	100.00	86	100.00	163	99.99

Source: Field study by the authors.

When we come down to the individual villages of Sikkim we find that at Sherpagaon villages in 72.72 per cent cases grooms are senior to the brides whereas in 22.08 per cent cases the brides are senior to the grooms by age. Again, out of these 72.72 per cent cases where grooms are senior by age to the brides, in 35.06 per cent cases marriages were held through negotiation whereas in 37.66 per cent cases the couples had love marriages. In 22.08 per cent cases where brides were senior to the grooms, 11.69 per cent cases the marriage was through negotiation and in 10.39 per cent cases they had love marriages.

At Sherpahat village of South District, Sikkim, in 80.23 per cent cases the grooms are senior to the brides by age and in 13.95 per cent cases the brides are senior to the grooms. Again out of 80.23 per cent cases where grooms are senior to the brides, 39.53 per cent cases the marriages held through negotiation and in 40.70 per cent cases these were all love marriages. In 13.95 per cent cases where brides are senior to the grooms, in 10.46 per cent cases they had negotiation marriages and only 3.49 per cent cases love marriages.

Here, it is important to mention that in all the four studied villages, two villages from Darjeeling and two villages from South district of Sikkim, only in less than 8.00 per cent cases the brides and the grooms have the same age.

We shall now come down to Table 8.21. Through this Table we have tried to show the correlation between the seniority of the spouses and the type of marriage. The table shows that out of 145 couples in the two villages of Darjeeling the majority (63.45%) live at Sherpapur village whereas the remaining couples (36.55%) live at the other village.

In the two studied villages of Darjeeling there is only one couple who was married through negotiation. In this case bride is senior to the groom. This couple lives at Sherpapur village. Again out of couples having brides senior to the grooms and had love marriage, the majority (62.50%) live at Sherpapur while the rest reside at Sherpaguri villages. In case of those couples of whom grooms are senior to the brides there is a total of 24 couples who had negotiation marriage and where bridegrooms are senior to the brides. Of them the overwhelming majority (87.50%) live at Sherpaguri village. The others are the inhabitants of Sherpapur village. In these two villages there are only two couples having equal age and had marriage by negotiation. These two couples live at Sherpaguri village whereas out of 6 couples having equal age and love marriage, two third (66.67%) live at Sherpapur village and the remaining one third at Sherpaguri village.

In Sikkim the two studied villages have a total of 163 couples of which a little more than half live at Sherpahat village and a little less than half reside at Sherpagaon village. In these two villages there are a total of 18 couples who had negotiation marriage and among them brides are senior to the grooms. Each of these two villages shares half of the total couples. But 11 couples of these two villages who had love marriage and among whom brides are senior to the grooms by age, 72.73 per cent live at Sherpagaon and the rest reside at Sherpahat village. Again out of the 61 couples of these two villages among whom grooms are senior to the brides by age and who had negotiation marriage, the majority live at Sherpahat village and 44.26 per cent are the residents of Sherpagaon. There are 64 couples in these two villages who had love marriage and among whom the grooms are senior to the brides, again the majority (54.69%) live at Sherpahat and the remaining couples are the residents of the other village. The two villages of Sikkim have altogether 6 couples who married through negotiation and among whom the brides and the bride-grooms have same age, the two villages equally share these 6 couples. But those 3 couples who had love marriage and also of equal age, two third live at Sherpahat and the remaining one third at Sherpagaon village.

Educational Status of the Couples

In all modern human societies the educational status of the husbands and wives is not always the same. Of course in some cases they may have the

Table 8.21: Difference of Age between Bride and Groom having different Types of Marriage

Age Difference between Bride (B) and Groom (G)	Type of Marriage	No. of couples in Darjeeling						No. of couples in Sikkim					
		Sherpaguri		Sherpapur		Total		Sherpagaon		Sherpahat		Total	
		No.	%	No.	%	No.	%	No.	%	No.	%	No.	%
Bride Senior to Groom	Negotiation			1	100.00	1	100.00	9	50.00	9	50.00	18	100.00
	Love	3	37.50	5	62.50	8	100.00	8	72.73	3	27.27	11	100.00
Groom Senior to Bride	Negotiation	21	87.50	3	12.50	24	100.00	27	44.26	34	55.74	61	100.00
	Love	25	24.04	79	75.96	104	100.00	29	45.31	35	54.69	64	100.00
Bride and Groom of the same age	Negotiation	2	100.00			2	100.00	3	50.00	3	50.00	6	100.00
	Love	2	33.33	4	66.67	6	100.00	1	33.33	2	66.67	3	100.00
Total		53	36.55	92	63.45	145	100.00	77	47.24	86	52.76	163	100.00

Source: Field study by the authors.

same educational status, but in many cases the husbands and the wives may have different educational status. That means, in some cases the husbands have higher educational status than the wives while in some other cases the wives have higher educational status than the husbands. The same is also true in the Sherpa society in both Darjeeling and Sikkim. In this society while in case of some couples the husbands have higher educational status than the wives, in some other cases the wives have higher educational status than the husbands. Still in some other cases they have the same educational status. Our analyses of the data show that in Sherpaguri village of Darjeeling there are 23 couples who had married through negotiation. Out of these 23 couples in 47.83 per cent cases both husbands and wives have equal educational status and in 52.17 per cent cases the bridegrooms have higher educational status than the brides. But in this village there is not a single case where the brides have higher educational status than the bridegrooms. In case of the love and other types of marriage in this society while in 33.33 per cent cases the both brides and the bridegrooms have equal educational status, in 66.67 per cent cases the bridegrooms have higher educational status than the brides. In no case the brides have higher educational status than the bridegrooms. In the other village of Darjeeling, that is, Sherpapur, out of 4 couples having negotiation marriage 75.00 per cent couples have the same educational status and in case of the remaining couples the husband has higher educational status than the wife. But in this village 88 couples had love and other types of marriage and out of these 88 couples, in 51.14 per cent cases both husbands and the wives have equal educational status. In 43.18 per cent cases the bridegrooms have higher educational status than the brides. Only in 5.68 per cent cases the bridegrooms have lower educational status than the brides.

Now, as we come to Sikkim the village, Sherpagaon highlights different picture. Here in this village there are 39 couples who had marriage by negotiation. Out of these 39 couples in 79.49 per cent cases both husbands and the wives have the same educational status and in 17.95 per cent cases the husbands have higher educational status than the wives. Only in one case (2.56%) the bride has higher educational status than the husband. In this village there are 38 couples who had love and other types of marriages. In 65.79 per cent cases of whom the husbands and the wives have equal educational status and in 23.68 per cent cases the bridegrooms have higher educational status than the brides. Only in 10.53 per cent cases the brides have higher educational status than the bridegrooms.

Now, let us turn our attention to the Sherpas of the village Sherpahat in Sikkim. In this village there are 46 couples who had negotiation marriage. Now, out of these 46 couples in 78.26 per cent cases both husbands and the wives have equal educational status and in 19.57 per cent cases the husbands have higher educational status than the wives. Only in one case (2.17%) the wife has higher educational status than the husband. Again in this village another 40 couples have love and other types of marriage. Now, out of these couples in 57.50 per cent cases both brides and the bridegrooms have equal educational status, and in 40.00 per cent cases the bridegrooms have higher educational status than the brides. In this village also there is only one couple (2.50%) among whom the bride has achieved higher educational status than the bridegroom.

Thus, we see that among the Sherpas both Darjeeling and Sikkim either the husbands and the wives have the same educational status or the husbands have the higher educational status than the wives. Only in a very few cases the wives have higher educational status than the husbands.

Post-Marital Residence

In all human societies of the world, the residence after marriage varies as per norms of the societies. While in the matriarchal societies the post marital residence is mostly matrilineal, in patriarchal societies the same is mostly patrilineal. But in both types of society, other varients of post-marital residences, such as neolocal, duolocal, avanculocal etc. are also met with, but may be in a smaller number. The Sherpa society of Darjeeling, West Bengal and of South District, Sikkim is no exception. Here in their society, the Sherpas follow the norms regarding post-matiral residences as prescribed by their society.

Among the Sherpas of both Darjeeling, West Bengal and South district Sikkim, different types of post-marital residence are found among them. Like the Garos (Burling 1963:212) and the Rabhas (Raha 1989: 192-193) a clear difference between village and household residences is evidenced among the Sherpas also. When a man after marriage settles with his wife in his father's house it is obviously patrilocal residence both village and household-wise. But after marriage if he settles in his own separate residence but in his father's village, then it is neolocal residence in respect of the household residence but patrilocal residence in respect of village residence. Again if he starts living with his wife after marriage in a different village, different from that of his father, then both household residence and village residence are neolocal.

In case of the village residence the married couples may be divided into four categories:

(A) Local man (the word 'Local' indicates here that the person, man or woman, comes from same village and not an outsider) marries 'Local' woman and settles locally.
(B) 'Local' man married 'Foreign' woman (here the word 'Foreign' indicates that the person, man or woman comes from other village and not a local one) but settles locally.
(C) 'Foreign' man marries 'Foreign' woman and settles locally, and
(D) 'Foreign' man marries 'Local' woman and settles locally (Raha 1989:193, Coomar, Raha & Bhui 2009:188-189).

When a Sherpa of a particular village marries a Sherpa girl of different village and settled in his village after marriage

> "he is for this study treated as 'Local', but his wife is 'Foreign' in respect to the village residence. But if he is after marriage, settled in his wife's village, in that case he is 'Foreign', but his wife is 'Local'. If he is after marriage, settled with his wife in altogether different village (neither he nor his wife belongs to that village) then both are 'Foreign' in respect to the village residence. Finally, if he marries a woman from his own village and both settle in the same village, then both are 'Local' " (Raha 1989:193, Coomer, Raha & Bhui 2009:2009).

Here by 'Foreign' we mean a Sherpa on coming from some village, is finally settled after marriage in a different village of which he or she is not the original resident. By the term, 'Local' we mean a Sherpa of a particular village is settled after marriage in his or her own village.

From the tabulated post-marital residences among the Sherpas of the four studied villages, we find that out of the total post-marital residences of the two villages of Darjeeling District (160), Category-B holds the majority (64.37%). Next comes Category-A with 23.13 per cent share. The other two categories have very low strength, a little over 6.00 per cent. Almost same is the case with the total post-marital residences of the two villages of South District, Sikkim. Here the Category-B has the highest frequency (55.55%) followed by Category-B (35.95%). While Category-D has less than 8.00 per cent, Category-C has negligible strength (1.31%). But no doubt Category-B of Darjeeling villages holds much higher strength than that of Sikkim villages. But reverse is the case with Category-A. It is more in total of Sikkim villages than that of Darjeeling villages. Category-C is much lower in number in Sikkim villages than that in Darjeeling villages. If we further examine village-wise distribution of the same we find that Category-B, that is, the Sherpa man of a village marrying a local Sherpa woman of his village, secures highest frequency (50.91%) in Sherpaguri, 71.43 per cent at Sherpapur, 64.37 per cent at Sherpagaon and 54.67 per cent at Sherpapur. But among these four villages, Sherpapur has the highest strength and Sherpaguri holds the lowest share. Category-A hold the next higher strength among all these four villages. But out of these four villages Sherpagaon retains the highest strength (36%) followed by Sherpahat village (35.90%). Categories-C and D are in low key in all the four villages. Out of these four villages while Sherpaguri has a little over 10 per cent, in case of other categories of other three villages the same is less than 10 per cent. But among these four villages, Sherpapur has the lowest frequency.

Table 8.22: Distribution of Post-Marital Residence among the Sherpas of Studied Villages of Darjeeling and Sikkim

Residential Categories of Marriages	*Sherpaguri*		*Sherpapur*		*Total*		*Sherpagaon*		*Sherpahat*		*Total*	
	No.	*%*	*No.*	*%*	*No.*	*%*	*No.*	*%*	*No.*	*%*	*No.*	*%*
A	15	27.27	22	20.95	37	23.13	27	36.00	28	35.90	55	35.95
B	28	50.91	75	71.43	103	64.37	41	54.67	44	56.41	85	55.55
C	6	10.91	4	3.81	10	6.25	1	1.33	1	1.28	2	1.31
D	6	10.91	4	3.81	10	6.25	6	8.00	5	6.41	11	7.19
Total	55	100.00	105	100.00	160	100.00	75	100.00	78	100.00	153	100.00

Source: Field study by the authors.

When we analyse the result of Table 8.22 we find that out of the total the post-marital residence (160) of the two villages of Darjeeling district, the village Sherpahat holds 65.63 per cent of the total post-marital residences which are much more than that (34.37%) of Sherpaguri village. In these two villages while Categories A and B are much more in number than those of Sherpaguri village, opposite is the case with Categories –C and D. These later categories are more in number than those present at Sherpapur village.

In case of the Sherpas of the two villages of South District, Sikkim, no perceptible difference is noticed in case of the total post-marital residences out of combined total of the two villages. Out of a total of 153 cases of post-marital residence, while Sherpahat holds a little over half (50.98%) of the total post-marital residences, Sherpagaon villages has a little less than half (49.02%).

When we come down to the village-wise distribution of the post-marital residences, we see that at the village, Sherpahat, Categories- A and B are slightly higher in number than those of the other village, Sherpagaon. But in case of the other two Categories, that is, C and D, while both villages have equal share of Category-C post-marital residences, the Category-D residences are more in number (54.55%) at Sherpagaon village that those of Sherpahat village.

So, we see that in all the four villages there is an uneven distribution of post-marital residences.

Now, in order to look into the nature and extent of the village residence among the Sherpas of all the four studied villages—two from Darjeeling district, West Bengal and two from South district, Sikkim, we have analysed the data in tables prepared on this aspect. From the combined data of the two villages of Darjeeling we see that there are 160 married couples in these two villages. Out of these 160 couples, 130 (81.25%) had love or other types of marriage and the rest 30 (18.75%) married through negotiation. Out of the total couples (160) majority (64.78%) belong to the 'B' category. Only 23.13 per cent come under 'A' category. But the couples belonging to the 'C' and 'D' categories have equal but very low strength (6.25%). Again out of 30 couples who married through negotiation, majority (63.33%) belong to 'B' category, i.e. 'Local' Sherpa males married 'Foreign' Sherpa women and settled locally. In other categories (A, C and D) their strength is quite low. But in case of those couple who had love or other types of marriage, majority (84 or 64.62%) belongs also to the 'B' category. The next higher number of couples who had love or other types of marriage (32 or 24.62%) belong to 'A' category (Table 8.24).

As we come down to the village, Sherpaguri under Kalimpong, Darjeeling we see that there are 55 couples in this village of whom 36.37 per cent were married after negotiation but majority (63.64%) had love or other types of marriage. Again out of these 55 couples a little over half (50.91%) belong to the 'B' category followed by those belong to 'A' category (27.27%). The couples belong to 'C' and 'D' categories have quite a low, but equal strength (10.91% each). But when we examine distribution of couples having different marital types in different residential categories, we find that out of the 20 couples who had marriage by negotiation, half (50.00%) belong to the 'B' category. The next higher

Table 8.23: Distribution of Post-Marital Residence among the Sherpas of Villages of Darjeeling and Sikkim

Residential Categories of Marriages	Sherpaguri		Sherpapur		Total		Sherpagaon		Sherpahat		Total	
	No. of couples	%	No. of couples	%	No.of couples	%	No.of couples	%	No.of couples	%	No. of couples	%
A	15	40.54	22	59.46	37	100.00	27	49.09	28	50.91	55	100.00
B	28	27.18	75	72.82	103	100.00	41	48.24	44	51.76	85	100.00
C	6	60.00	4	40.00	10	100.00	1	50.00	1	50.00	2	100.00
D	6	60.00	4	40.00	10	100.00	6	54.55	5	45.45	11	100.00
Total	55	34.37	105	65.63	160	100.00	75	49.02	78	50.98	153	100.00

Source: Field study by the authors.

strength goes to 'A' category (25.00%) Group 'C' and 'D' categories have 10.00 per cent and 15.00 per cent respectively (Table 8.24).

But in case of the marriage by love or other types out of 35 couples, majority (51.43%) belong to Category 'B'. Next in order comes Category 'A' (28.57%). The Categories 'C' and 'D' have quite low frequency (33.43% and 8.57% respectively) (Table 8.24).

As we come down to Sherpapur village of Kalimpong, Darjeeling we find that there is a total of 105 couples in this village. Out of these 105 couples overwhelming majority (90.48%) had love or other types of marriage and the remaining only 9.52 per cent had negotiation marriage. Again out of these 10 couples having negotiation marriage 90 per cent belong to 'B' category and the remaining one person (10%) belongs to 'D' category. Similarly, majority of the couples having love or other types of marriage (69.47%) also belong to the 'B' category. The next higher number of couples (23.16%) belong to 'A' category. The couples belonging to 'C' and 'D' categories have very low strength (4.21% and 3.16% respectively) (Table 8.24).

In these two villages of Kalimpong, Darjeeling there are a total of 160 couples belonging to all categories of residence. Out of these 160 couples majority (65.62%) live in Sherpapur village while the rest (34.78%) in Sherpaguri village. Again out of 30 couples having negotiation marriage, two third live in Sherpaguri village. The remaining one third is in the other village. On the other hand, overwhelming majority of the couples having love or other types of marriage (73.08%) live in Sherpapur village and the remaining 26.92 per cent in the Sherpaguri village (Table 8.24).

Now, again when we count the frequency of the couples of the individual village belonging to different categories of residence in the total couples of the two villages, we see that under 'A' category there are 5 couples having negotiation marriage, all of whom belong to Sherpaguri village, but majority of the couples who had love or other types of marriage (68.75%), live in Sherpapur village. In case of the couples having negotiation marriage and belonging to the 'B' category of residence, a little over half (52.63%) reside at Sherpaguri and the rest live at the other village. But overwhelming majority (78.57%) who had love or other types of marriage and belong to 'B' category of residence, are all residents of Sherpapur village (Table 8.25). On the other hand, all the two 'C' category couples who have negotiation marriage, live in Sherpaguri village. But half of those couples under this category who had love or other types of marriage, are the residents of Sherpaguri while the other half live in the

Table 8.24: Distribution of Post-Marital Residence in different Types of Marriage among the Sherpa Couples of Two Villages of Darjeeling

VILLAGES	Residential Categories of Marriage																			
	A				B				C				D				Total			
	Negotiation		Love and other types		Negotiation		Love and other types		Negotiation		Love and other types		Negotiation		Love and other types		Negotiation		Love and other types	
	No.	%	No.	%	No.	%	No.	%	No.	%	No.	%	No.	%	No.	%	No.	%	No.	%
Sherpaguri	5	25.00	10	28.57	10	50.00	18	51.43	2	10.00	4	11.43	3	15.00	3	8.57	20	100.00	35	100.00
Sherpapur			22	23.16	9	90.00	66	69.47			4	4.21	1	10.00	3	3.16	10	100.00	95	100.00
Total Study Area of Darjeeling	5	16.67	32	24.62	19	63.33	84	64.62	2	6.67	8	6.15	4	13.33	6	4.62	30	100.00	130	100.01

Source: Field study by the authors.

other village. In case of the 'D' Category there are a total of 4 couples who had negotiation marriage, three fourth of them have their residence at Sherpaguri village and the remaining one fourth in Sherpapur village. But both villages have equal share of couples having love or other types of marriage (Table 8.25).

Now, let us come down to the Sherpa villages of Sikkim we have studied. The combined data from two villages, Sherpagaon and Sherpahat of South district, Sikkim reveal that a total of 153 couples live in these two villages. Out of these 153 couples 56.86 per cent have married through negotiation while 43.14 per cent preferred love marriage. Now, out of 87 couples having marriage by negotiation, the largest number (48 or 55.17%) belong to 'B' category of village residence while such couples belonging to 'A' category, come next with a strength of 40.23 per cent. The 'D' Category has a very negligible number of such couples but 'C' category does not have any. The couples who preferred love or other types of marriage, have also followed the same path. Out of 66 such couples having love or other types of marriage, the majority (56.06%) belong to the category 'B'. But a good number of them (30.30%) are also covered by 'A' Category. The other two categories have quite a low strength.

Now, let us come down to the individual village. At Sherpagaon village the total number of couples is 75. Out of these couples 56.00 per cent have married by negotiation and the rest 44.00 per cent have opted for love and other types of marriage. Again out of the 42 couples having negotiation marriage, the majority (56.76%) belong to the 'B' category. The next higher number belongs (38.10%) to the 'A' category. The other two categories have very low frequency. In case of those couple who had love or other types of marriage, also have major share (54.55%) and belong to 'B' category. In their case also the next higher strength (33.33%) goes to 'A' category. The rest is shared by other two categories (Table 8.26).

The other village of South district, Sikkim, i.e. Sherpahat has 78 couples of whom 45 or 54.69 per cent had marriage by negotiation and the remaining 33 or 42.31 tied up by love or other types of marriage. Again out of 45 couples who married by negotiation, majority (45 or 55.56%) belong to 'B' Category and the next higher number (19 or 42.22%) are from 'A' Category. The remaining only one couple belongs to 'D' Category. On the other hand, out of 33 couples who went for love or other types of marriage, majority (19 or 57.58%) belongs to 'B' Category. The next higher strength (9 or 27.27%) goes to those couples

Table 8.25: Distribution of Post-Marital Residence in different Types of Marriage among the Sherpa Couples of Two Villages of Darjeeling

Villages	Residential Categories of Marriage																			
	A				B				C				D				Total			
	Negotiation		Love and other types		Negotiation		Love and other types		Negotiation		Love and other types		Negotiation		Love and other types		Negotiation		Love and other types	
	No.	%	No.	%	No.	%	No.	%	No.	%	No.	%	No.	%	No.	%	No.	%	No.	%
Sherpaguri	5	100.00	10	31.25	10	52.63	18	21.43	2	100.00	4	50.00	3	75.00	3	50.00	20	66.67	35	26.92
Sherpapur			22	68.75	9	47.37	66	78.57			4	50.00	1	25.00	3	50.00	10	33.33	95	73.08
Total Study Area of Darjeeling	5	100.00	32	100.00	19	100.00	84	100.00	2	100.00	8	100.00	4	100.00	6	100.00	30	100.00	130	100.00

Source: Field study by the authors.

who belong to 'A' Category. The couples belonging to 'D' Category also have some strength (12.12%).

It is thus seen that while in Darjeeling villages love or other types of marriage have higher strength in Sikkim villages marriage by negotiation is preferred over love or other types of marriage. But in the villages of both areas, that is, Darjeeling district of West Bengal and South District of Sikkim, the largest number of couples preferred 'B' Category of marriage residence. Their next choice is 'A' Category. Only a few belong to the other two categories.

We have now discussed about the marital residence of the Sherpa couples who have different types of marriage. There are 19 couples who have negotiation marriage and belong to 'B' Category. Out of these 19 couples the largest number of husbands (26.32%) belong to the age-group 60+. Next come the husbands of those couples who belong to the age-group 45-49. Again out of 84 couples who had love or other types of marriage and belong to 'B' Category, the largest number of husbands of these couples (17 or 20.24%) belong to the age-group 35-39 followed by those who belong to the age-group 40-44 (16.67%) and then 60+ (15.48%). The other two categories (C and D) are not that significant.

Now, we shall come down to the post-marital village residence of the couples of Sherpaguri village. In this village there are 55 couples, the largest number of whom (28 or 50.91%) belong to 'B' Category. Next come those who belong to 'A' Category. The strength of the couples of the other two categories (C and D) is not that significant (each with 10.91%). Again, out of the total of 20 couples who had marriage by negotiation, half of them belong to 'B' Category. 'A' Category had 25.00 per cent couples. Out of 35 couples who had love or other types of marriage, the largest number (18 or 51.43%) belong to 'B' Category. Next come those who belong to 'A' Category (10 or 28.57%).

We shall now highlight age-group-wise distribution of the husbands of the couples who belong to different categories. All the 5 husbands who belong to 'A' Category had negotiation marriage, and are equally distributed in the age-groups from 40-44 to 60+.

In this category (i.e. 'A' Category) there are 10 couples who had love or other types of marriage. Out of these 10 couples age-groups 30-34 and 40-44 to 50-54 have two husbands each (20.00%) and age-groups 55-59 and 60+ have one husbands each (10.00%).

In case of 'B' Category there are 10 couples 50 per cent husbands of them belong to the age group 60+. Out of the 18 couples who had love or other types of marriage, age-groups 35-39 to 45-49 hold three husbands

Table 8.26: Distribution of Post-Marital Residence in different Types of Marriage among the Sherpa Couples of Two Villages of Sikkim

Villages	Residential Categories of Marriage																			
	A				B				C				D				Total			
	Negotiation		Love and other types		Negotiation		Love and other types		Negotiation		Love and other types		Negotiation		Love and other types		Negotiation		Love and other types	
	No.	%	No.	%	No.	%	No.	%	No.	%	No.	%	No.	%	No.	%	No.	%	No.	%
Sherpagaon	16	38.10	11	33.33	23	57.76	18	54.55			1	3.03	3	7.14	3	9.09	42	100.00	33	100.00
Sherpahat	19	42.22	9	27.27	25	55.56	19	57.58			1	3.03	1	2.22	4	12.12	45	100.00	33	100.00
Total Study Area of Sikkim	35	40.23	20	30.30	48	35.17	37	56.06			2	3.03	4	4.60	7	10.61	87	100.00	66	100.00

Source: Field study by the authors.

Table 8.27: Distribution of Post-Marital Residence in different Types of Marriage among the Sherpa Couples of Two Villages of Sikkim

Villages		Residential Categories of Marriage																			
		A				B				C				D				Total			
		Negotiation		Love and other types		Negotiation		Love and other types		Negotiation		Love and other types		Negotiation		Love and other types		Negotiation		Love and other types	
		No.	%	No.	%	No.	%	No.	%	No.	%	No.	%.	No.	%	No.	%	No.	%	No.	%
	Sherpagaon	16	45.71	11	55.00	23	47.92	18	48.65			1	50.00	3	75.00	3	42.86	42	48.28	33	50.00
	Sherpahat	19	54.29	9	45.00	25	52.08	19	51.35			1	50.00	1	25.00	4	57.14	45	51.72	33	50.00
	Total Study Area of Sikkim	35	100.00	20	100.00	48	100.00	37	100.00			2	100.00	4	100.00	7	100.00	87	100.00	66	100.00

Source: Field study by the authors.

Table 8.28: Post-Marital Residential Categories of the Sherpa Couples by Type of Marriage in Two Villages of Darjeeling

Age group of the husband	Residential Categories of Marriage																			
	A				B				C				D				TOTAL			
	Negotiation		Love and other types		Negotiation		Love and other types		Negotiation		Love and other types		Negotiation		Love and other types		Negotiation		Love and other types	
	No.	%	No.	%	No.	%	No.	%	No.	%	No.	%	No.	%	No.	%	No.	%	No.	%
<24			2	6.25			8	9.52											10	7.69
25-29			3	9.38	1	5.26	9	10.71					1	25.00			2	6.67	12	9.23
30-34			4	12.50	1	5.26	11	13.10									1	3.33	15	11.54
35-39			2	6.25	2	10.53	17	20.24							1	16.67	2	6.67	20	15.38
40-44	1	20.00	3	9.38	3	15.79	14	16.67			2	25.00					1	13.33	19	14.62
45-49	1	20.00	5	15.63	4	21.05	7	8.33			2	25.00			2	33.33	5	16.67	16	12.31
50-54	1	20.00	2	6.25	3	15.79	3	3.57	1	50.00	1	12.50	1	25.00	1	16.67	6	20.00	7	5.38
55-59	1	20.00	6	18.75			2	2.38			1	12.50			1	16.67	1	33.33	10	7.69
60+	1	20.00	5	15.62	5	26.32	13	15.48	1	50.00	2	25.00	2	50.00	1	16.67	9	30.00	21	16.15
Total	5	100.00	32	100.02	19	100.00	84	99.99	2	100.00	8	100.00	4	100.00	6	100.01	30	99.99	130	100.00

Source: Field study by the authors.

each (16.67%). Some other age-groups have either one or two husbands each.

In the village Sherpapur in Kalimpong Sub-division of Darjeeling district, there are 105 couples the overwhelming majority (95 or 90.48%) of them belong to 'B' Category. Next higher number (22 or 20.95%) come under 'A' Category. But in 'A' Category there is not a single couple who married by negotiation. The 'C' and 'D' Categories have only a few couples. It is interesting to note that all the 4 couples of 'C' Category have love or other types of marriage.

Now, out of a total of 10 couples who married by negotiation, 9 (90.00%) belong to 'B' Category. The remaining one couple belongs to 'D' Category. Again out of 95 couples with love or other types of marriages the largest number (66 or 69.47%) belong to 'B' Category and 22 (23.16%) belong to 'A' Category. The other categories have only a few couples.

As already said there are 22 couples in 'A' Category who love or other types of marriage. Out of these 22 couples the largest number of husbands of these couples (5 or 22.73%) belong to age-group 55-59. Next come age-group 60+ having 4 husbands (18.18%).

In 'B' Category there are 9 couples who married by negotiation. The largest number of the husbands (3 or 33.33%) belong to the age group 40-44. Again out of 66 couples of this category having love or other types of marriage, the largest number of husbands of the couples (14 or 21.21%) belong to age-group 35-39. The next larger number of the husbands of the couples (11 or 16.67%) come under age-groups 40-44. In the other two categories the husbands of the couples are uniformly distributed in different age-groups (Table 8.30).

We would now examine the combined data on post-marital residence of the Sherpa couples of the two villages of South district, Sikkim. There are a total of 153 couples in these two villages. Out of these couples the largest number (85 or 55.56%) belong to 'B' Category. The Category 'A' also has quite a good number of couples (55 or 35.95%). The other two categories have only a few couples. Category 'C' has only 2 couples. There are a total of 87 couples in these two villages having marriage by negotiation. Out of these 87 couples the largest number (48 or 55.17%) belong to 'B' Category followed by those (35 or 40.23%) belonging to 'A' Category.

Again in these two villages 66 couples with love or other types of marriage, live. Out of these 66 couples the largest number (37 or 56.06%) belong to 'B' Category. The next comes 'A' Category having 20 (30.30%) couples with love or other types of marriage.

Table 8.29: Post-Marital Residential Categories of the Sherpa Couples by Type of Marriage at Sherpaguri Village (Darjeeling)

Age Group of the Husbands	Residential Categories of Marriage																			
	A				B				C				D				Total			
	Negotiation		Love and other types		Negotiation		Love and other types		Negotiation		Love and other types		Negotiation		Love and other types		Negotiation		Love and other types	
	No.	%	No.	%	No.	%	No.	%	No.	%	No.	%	No.	%	No.	%	No.	%	No.	%
<24																				
25-29					1	10.00	2	11.11									1	5.00	2	5.71
30-34			2	20.00			2	11.11											4	11.43
35-39					1	10.00	3	16.67									1	5.00	3	8.57
40-44	1	20.00	2	20.00			3	16.67			1	25.00					1	5.00	6	17.14
45-49	1	20.00	2	20.00	2	20.00	3	16.67			1	25.00			1	33.33	3	15.00	7	20.00
50-54	1	20.00	2	20.00	1	10.00	1	5.56	1	5.00	1	25.00	1	33.33	1	33.33	4	20.00	5	14.29
55-59	1	20.00	1	10.00			1	5.56							1	33.33	1	5.00	3	8.57
60+	1	20.00	1	10.00	5	50.00	3	16.67	1	50.00	1	25.00	2	66.67			9	45.00	5	14.29
Total	5	100.00	10	100.00	10	100.00	18	100.02	2	100.00	4	100.00	3	100.00	3	99.99	20	100.00	35	100.00

Source: Field study by the authors.

Table 8.30: Post-Marital Residential Categories of the Sherpa Couples by Type of Marriage at Sherpapur Village (Darjeeling)

Age group of husband	Residential Categories of Marriage																			
	A				B				C				D				* Total			
	Negotiation		Love & other types		Negotiation		Love & other types		Negotiation		Love & other types		Negotiation		Love & other types		Negotiation		Love & other types	
	No.	%	No.	%	No.	%	No.	%	No.	%	No.	%	No.	%	No.	%	No.	%	No.	%
<24			2	9.09			8	12.12											10	10.53
25-29			3	13.64			7	10.61					1	10.00			1	10.00	10	10.53
30-34			2	9.09	1	11.11	9	13.64									1	10.00	11	11.58
35-39			2	9.09	1	11.11	14	21.21							1	33.33	1	10.00	17	17.89
40-44			1	4.55	3	33.33	11	16.67			1	25.00					3	30.00	13	13.68
45-49			3	13.64	2	22.22	4	6.06			1	25.00			1	33.33	2	20.00	9	9.47
50-54					2	22.22	2	3.03									2	20.00	2	2.11
55-59			5	22.73			1	1.52			1	25.00							7	7.37
60+			4	18.18			10	15.15			1	25.00			1	33.33			16	16.84
Total			22	100.02	9	99.99	66	100.02			4	100.00	1	100.00	3	99.99	10	100.00	95	100.01

Source: Field study by the authors.

If we look at the age-group-wise distribution husbands of the couples having different types of marriages and belonging to different categories, we see that in 'A' Category there are 35 couples having married by negotiation, the largest number of husbands (11 or 31.43%) of these couples belong to age-group 60+ followed by those (6 or 17.14%) who come under age-group 55-59. In this category there are 20 couples having love or other types of marriage. Now, out of these 20 couples the largest number husbands belong to the age-group 60+. Then come those husbands who belong to the age-group 24 and below (20%).

In the 'B' Category there are 48 couples who married through negotiation. Out of them the largest number of husbands (12 or 25%) belong to age-group 60+. On the other hand, out of those couples who had love or other types of marriage, the largest number (11 or 29.73%) belong to the age-group 30-34. The other two categories have only a few couples.

We shall now come down to the individual villages of Sikkim. At Sherpagaon village a total of 75 couples live. Out of these 75 couples the largest number of couples belong to 'B' Category (54.67%). Then comes 'A' Category where there are 27 couples (36%). Other categories had very low frequency. Again out of the total of 75 couples 56 per cent had negotiation marriage whereas the remaining 44 per cent couples had preferred love or other types of marriage. Out of those who had negotiation marriage, the largest number belong to 'B' Category and then come those (38.10%) who belong to 'A' Category. The same is the case with those who had love or other types of marriage. Among them also the largest number (54.54%) belong to 'B' Category followed by those who come under 'A' Category (33.33%). Again out of the 16 couples who married through negotiation, the husbands of the largest number of couples belong to the age-groups 55-59 and 60+, each with 31.25 per cent. The largest number of husbands of all the couples of 'A' Category who had love or other types of marriage, belong to the age-group 30-34 (27.27%). In 'B' Category similarly, the largest number of husbands of all the couples having married by negotiation, belongs to three different age-groups (25-29, 55-59 and 60+, each with 31.25%). The largest number of husbands of all the couples of 'A' Category who had love marriage, belong to the age-group 30-34 (27.27%). In 'B' Category similarly, the largest number of husbands of all the couples having married by negotiation, belongs to three different age-groups (25-29, 55-59 and 60+) each having 21.74 per cent. In case of the husbands of all the couples of 'B' Category who have

Table 8.31: Post-Marital Residential Categories of the Sherpa Couples by Type of Marriage in Two Villages of Sikkim

Age group of husbands	Residential Categories of Marriage																			
	A				B				C				D				Total			
	Negotiation		Love & other types		Negotiation		Love & other types		Negotiation		Love & other types		Negotiation		Love & other types		Negotiation		Love & other types	
	No.	%	No.	%	No.	%	No.	%	No.	%	No.	%	No.	%	No.	%	No.	%	No.	%
<24	1	2.86	4	20.00	4	8.33	3	8.11					1	25.00	1	14.29	6	6.90	8	12.12
25-29	1	2.86	3	15.00	7	14.58	4	10.81			1	50.00					8	9.20	8	12.12
30-34	5	14.29	3	15.00	7	14.58	11	29.73			1	50.00	1	25.00	3	42.86	13	14.94	18	29.27
35-39	3	8.57	2	10.00	4	8.33	4	10.81									7	8.05	6	9.09
40-44	2	5.71	1	5.00			4	10.81					1	25.00			3	3.44	5	7.58
45-49	4	11.43	2	10.00	7	14.58	2	5.41							1	14.29	11	12.64	5	7.58
50-54	2	5.71			1	2.08	3	8.11					1	25.00	1	14.29	4	4.60	3	4.55
55-59	6	17.14			6	12.50	2	5.41							1	14.29	12	13.79	3	4.55
60+	11	32.43	5	25.00	12	25.00	4	10.81									23	26.44	10	15.15
Total	35	100.00	20	100.00	48	99.98	37	100.01			2	100.00	4	100.00	7	100.02	87	100.00	66	100.01

Source: Field study by the authors.

Table 8.32: Post-Marital Residential Categories of the Sherpa Couples by Type of Marriage at Sherpahat Village (Sikkim)

Age group of husbands	Residential Categories of Marriage																			
	A				B				C				D				Total			
	Negotiation		Love & other types		Negotiation		Love & other types		Negotiation		Love & other types		Negotiation		Love & other types		Negotiation		Love & other types	
	No.	%	No.	%	No.	%	No.	%	No.	%	No.	%	No.	%	No.	%	No.	%	No.	%
<24	1	5.26	3	33.33	3	12.00	3	15.79							1	25.00	4	8.89	7	21.21
25-29			2	22.22	2	8.00	4	21.05									2	4.44	6	18.18
30-34	3	15.79			4	16.00	5	26.32			1	100.00	1	100.00	2	50.00	8	17.78	8	24.24
35-39	3	15.79			2	8.00	2	10.53									5	11.11	2	6.06
40-44	2	10.53					1	5.26									2	4.44	1	3.03
45-49	2	10.53			6	24.00											8	17.78		
50-54	1	5.26					2	10.53									1	2.22	2	6.06
55-59	1	5.26			1	4.00									1	25.00	2	4.44	1	3.03
60+	6	31.58	4	44.44	7	28.00	2	10.53									13	28.89	6	18.18
Total	19	100.00	9	99.99	25	100.00	19	100.01			1	100.00	1	100.00	4	100.00	45	99.99	33	99.99

Source: Field study by the authors.

Table 8.33: Post-Marital Residential Categories of the Sherpa Couples by Type of Marriage at Sherpagaon Village (Sikkim)

Age group of husbands	Residential Categories of Marriage																			
	A				B				C				D				Total			
	Negotiation		Love & other types		Negotiation		Love & other types		Negotiation		Love & other types		Negotiation		Love & other types		Negotiation		Love & other types	
	No.	%	No.	%	No.	%	No.	%	No.	%	No.	%	No.	%	No.	%	No.	%	No.	%
<24			1	9.09	1	4.35							1	33.33			2	4.76	1	3.03
25-29	1	6.25	1	9.09	5	21.74					1	100.00					6	14.29	2	6.06
30-34	2	12.50	3	27.27	3	13.04	6	33.33							1	33.33	5	11.90	10	30.30
35-39			2	18.18	2	8.70	2	11.11									2	4.76	4	12.12
40-44			1	9.09			3	16.67					1	33.33			1	2.38	4	12.12
45-49	2	12.50	2	18.18	1	4.35	2	11.11							1	33.33	3	7.14	5	15.15
50-54	1	6.25			1	4.35	1	5.56					1	33.33			3	7.14	1	3.03
55-59	5	31.25			5	21.74	2	11.11									10	23.81	2	6.06
60+	5	31.25	1	9.09	5	21.74	2	11.11							1	33.33	10	23.81	4	12.12
Total	16	100.00	11	99.99	23	100.01	18	100.00			1	100.00	3	99.99	3	99.99	42	99.99	33	99.99

Source: Field study by the authors.

love or other types of marriage, the largest number belong to the age-group, 30-34.

We shall now come to the second studied village of Sikkim, i.e. Sherpahat. In this village there are 78 couples of which 57.69 per cent married by negotiation and the remaining 42.31 per cent had love or other types of marriage. Again out of these 78 couples the largest number belong to 'B' category (44 or 56.41%) and 28 or 35.90 per cent belong to 'A' Category. 'C' and 'D' Categories have very low strength (in fact 'C' Category has only one couple). Again out of the total of 45 couples who had negotiation marriage, more than half (55.56%) belong to 'B' Category. Then come those who come under 'A' Category. Same is the case with those couples who had love marriage. The largest number of all the couples having love or other types of marriage, belong to 'B' Category, followed by those who belong to 'A' Category. Again among the 19 couples having married by negotiation and belonging to 'A' Category, the largest number of husbands (31.58%) belong to age-group 60+. In case of the couples of this category having love or other types of marriage, the largest number of husbands (44.44%) also belong to the age-group 60+. In case of the 'B' Category out of those couples who married by negotiations, the largest number of husbands belong to age-group 60+. The largest number of husbands of those couples of this category, who had love or other types of marriage, belong to the age-group 30-34 (26.32%), followed by those husbands who come under the age-group, 25-29.

Thus, we see that majority of the Sherpa couples belong to 'B' Category, i.e. local Sherpas have married the Sherpa women from other areas and settled locally, that is, in the husbands' village. The next larger number of couples come under 'A' Category, that means, the Sherpa men of a village have married Sherpa girls from their own respective villages and settled in the same village. The other two categories, i.e. 'C' and 'D' have a very few number of couples.

9
THE CRISES OF THEIR LIFE

During their life time the Sherpas observe different socio-religious ceremonies covering pregnancy of a woman and birth of the new-born, name giving ceremony connected with the new-born, marriage ceremony of the children when they reach marriageable age and death ceremony when a person dies. With all these crises of life, some sort of complex rituals (both social and religious) is connected. Below we shall describe the common features of these ceremonies of the Sherpas of our studied villages in Kalimpong Sub-Divisions, Darjeeling and also in South District, Sikkim. We shall also add brief-description of these ceremonies of the Sherpas living in Nepal as described by different scholars and academicians, so, that the readers get a total picture of the life cycle ceremonies of the Sherpas.

Pregnancy and Child Birth

Both pregnancy and child birth bring enough joy and delightfulness among the Sherpa family members. This joy increases manyfold when a newly wed wife becomes pregnant and gives birth of a healthy baby particularly the first child. During first and successive pregnancies the pregnant woman usually do not observe much taboos in connection with her movement, food and work till her pregnancy reaches near maturity. At that time normally she herself imposes some restriction on her movement and heavy work whenever possible.

Among the Sherpas as mentioned by Kunwar, a pregnant woman is usually refrained from going outside the village and/or to the forest and also from doing hard work. Sexual intercourse is also not indulged. But many couples get involved into such activity upto seven months of pregnancy or upto the period suited to both of them (1989:155).

In Darjeeling and Sikkim when the time comes for the delivery, the family members either take her to the health centre for the birth of the new born or call in a local midwife known as *Sundani.* In the later case the delivery takes place in a separate room meant for this purpose. In fact one of the rooms of the house is made ready for the delivery. The *Sundani* helps the pregnant woman to ease her acute labour pain by massaging or applying some oil mixed with some medicinal plants and rubbing the belly with it. She also helps the woman for smooth delivery. After the delivery she cuts the umbilical cord, cleans the blood and filth. She also cleans the new-born and mother. She then looks after the mother and the child for a few days in case there is no capable woman in the family. For her services the *Sundani* gets some amount of money. On the day of delivery and also on the days she stays with the mother and the new born, she also get meals, tea etc.

The members of the family where the child birth has taken place, observe pollution for a period of three days. On the fourth day a *Lama* is called in who performs prayer and worship to Lord Buddha and purify the whole house and also the members of the family. He puts small dot mark on the forehead of the new born and the mother and hoists religious flag on the right hand side of the house if the new born is the male or on the left hand side if it was a female. As the house and the members of the family become purified out of birth pollution, they lead a normal life. The assembled invitees and others are then served with a good feast.

The mother of the new-birth observes certain restrictions for seven days from the date of child birth. She usually does not do any heavy work, nor does she go to a distant place and forest. She also abstains from taking certain food items. After these days, if she keeps well, she leads a normal life. Mitra has stated that the Sherpas of Darjeeling observe post-delivery pollution for seven days in case of male child and for three days in case of a female child (2008:1184).

According to Gangopadhyay the purificatory rite and christening ceremony among the Sherpas of Sikkim is known as *Thoosur* or *Shang* which is held on the third day after the birth of the child. The *Lama* presides over the ceremony. He chants prayers and "plays particular kind of small drum by his right hand and a sacred bell (*tilu*) by his right hand". Thereafter, he sprinkles sacred water (*thoo*) all over the house. In order to purify themselves, all the members of the house sip a little of the *thoo*. During this occasion a good number of the relatives, friends and villagers assemble in this house and attend the function (1993:156-157). Bisht and Bankoti also said the same thing (2004:1490). Subba has also described the child birth in the same way as described by Gangopadhyay (1993: 156-157).

Name-giving Ceremony

The name-giving ceremony is observed on the fourth day after child-birth. On that day a *Lama* is called to perform purificatory ceremony. On the same day after the purificatory ceremony is over, a name is given to the new born. This ceremony is known as *minanjang*. The name for the new-born is selected by the *Lama*. Usually, according to the specific date of birth, the *Lama* fixes the name after consulting some religious book. On this occasion the family members invite their close relatives and friends as well as some neighbours in a feast hosted by the head of the family or the father of the new born. Often the number of invitees depends on the economic condition of the family. From this day the new-born child gets a name, and he/she is called by that name. According to Subba "Generally *ming daup* (to give name) occurs on the same day, but within eight days by the *Lama* or by the parents" (2008:286).

Marriage Ceremony

The marriage ceremony of the Sherpas as we observed in the villages we studied in Kalimpong, Darjeeling and also in South District, Sikkim, is a very elaborate one with a number of rituals which are spread over in different stages and continue for several days. Among the Sherpas of both Darjeeling and Sikkim usually, the winter months are considered suitable for marriage as during these months they do not have much of agricultural works. The boy's side first initiates the first stage. The members of the boy's family or their relatives or friends look for a suitable girl for the boy. After seeing one or more girls for this purpose, if they select a girl for their boy, and if the girl's side also likes the boy and considers him as a suitable match for their girl, then only the boy's side proceeds further. In that case they observe a small ceremony, called *ma Falgon* ceremony. This ceremony is performed by the *Lama*. After this ceremony, they send the marriage proposal to the girl's family through one or a few relatives of the boy's side. The girl's family members offer a good feast to the guests along with tea or *chhung*. A discussion is held covering different aspects of the marriage. During discussion the boy's party requests the parents of the girl to place the demands if any. Further, discussion is held after the girl's parents place their demands before the boy's side. Sometimes, the girl's parents take some time to place their demands. However, after the discussion on the demands if both parties come to an agreement then only both parties proceed further. If they fail to come to a conclusive agreement, then further negotiation is carried on. If the negotiation yields a good result then they proceed further. If the negotiation fails, then this marriage negotiation is abandoned, and the boy's party starts searching for another suitable girl again.

If after negotiation they come to an agreement on the demands, then another date is fixed when the boy along with his father and some other senior relatives, visits the girl's parents. There the boy, the prospective bridegroom, is introduced to the parents and other relatives of the girl. At the same time with the boy and his relatives the girl is also introduced. On this day the bride's party finalizes everything of marriage negotiation with the groom's party.

After everything is satisfactorily settled, both parties sit to finalise the auspicious date for the marriage. The local *Lama* is called in to help both parties to fix the day of marriage. The *Lama* after consulting religious book, selects a day suitable to both parties, for the marriage ceremony. The meeting of both parties ends with a sumptuous meal (lunch or dinner as the case may be) and *Chhung*.

On the evening of the before marriage the boy's family members called in a *Lama* who performs worship of the ancestors by reciting prayers from the religious book. The *Lama* also offers some sweet made of rice flour and seeks blessings of the ancestors of the boy for the long and happy married life of the boy. He also expels any action of the evil spirits and evil eyes that could harm the boy going for marriage. The same type of rituals are also performed by some *Lama* in the house of the would be bride. The *Lama* there also wards off the effects of the evil spirits etc. Then they get ready to receive the groom's party.

Among the Sherpas of our studied villages of both Darjeeling and Sikkim the *Lamas* presides over the marriage ceremonies, and for this act they get remuneration. On the affixed day of the marriage ceremony the boy's party consisting of the father, other senior members of the family, some elderly relatives of the groom, some senior villagers and also some friends of the groom, starts for the brides house. The bridegroom is dressed with a new marriage dress (*bakku*) and wears a hat (*samu*). The other members of the marriage party are also dressed in their best. The bride-grooms also accompanies with some musicians who play their musical instruments. The groom carries a metal pitcher (*pumba*) in his right hand and an umbrella in his left hand. In the house of the would be bride the relatives, friends and villagers of the bride have by this time, already assembled. When the members of the would be groom's party reach the girl's house, they are warmly welcomed by the members of the girl's family and also others led by the unmarried younger sister of the bride. In her absence any teen-aged unmarried female relative of the bride leads to welcome the groom's party. The members of the bride's party take the members of the groom's party along with the groom to a decorated room or a part of the courtyard where they sit. They are then served with a glass of milk to each.

When all the arrangements of the marriage are complete, the *Lama* first inspects the arrangements. He starts the marriage ceremony only when he gets satisfied with the arrangements. When everything is perfectly arranged he signals for the start of the marriage ceremony. The wedding ceremony takes place under a prefixed canopy called *Tshagang* which is well decorated. Just before the marriage ceremony starts the *Lama* requests both parties to bring the bride and the bridegroom in the place fixed for marriage. Both bride and the bridgegroom on their arrival at the wedding spot, sit side-by-side at per instruction of the *Lama*. The *Lama* sits in front of the bride and her prospective groom, facing them. All the assembled persons both male and female, young and old, throng around the marriage pandal to observe the marriage ceremony. Here, the musicians go on playing their musical instruments. Some people and children dance along with the rhythm of music.

With the start of the marriage ceremony the *Lama* smears pure ghee (clarified butter) on the forehead of both bride and the bridegroom while uttering incantation. This rituals is known as *gangu*. When *gangu* ceremony ends, *bakdada* ceremony begins. In this ceremony, some close male relative of the bride, generally, her own elder brother if she has or in absence, her elder cousin brother, performs an important function in this ceremony. After some rituals performed by the *Lama*, the *Lama* calls the elder brother of the bride who comes and stands by the side of the bride, and when the *Lama* instructs him, he declares that from that day onwards his sister belonging to a particular *ru* (*ru* of the bride), is given to another *ru* (name of the *ru* of the bridegroom) through this marriage ceremony.

This handing over the bride belonging to certain *ru* (clan) to the boy belonging to a different *ru* is undoubtedly important.

During the marriage ceremony the bridegroom as per instruction of the *Lama*, hands over a piece of one meter long ceremonial cloth known as *tarkhada* to the mother of the bride and another piece to the maternal uncle of the bride.

After the marriage ceremony is over the newly wed couple bows down before all the elderly persons and seek their blessing for a happy and prosperous married life. Then they retire to a room. All the relatives of the bride, members of the bridegroom's party and other invitees enjoy a grand feast and *Chhang*. The night is passed in merry making, drinking, singing and dancing.

Next morning the bridegroom's party along with the bridegroom and his newly wed wife, starts for the bridegroom's house. They are received by other relatives of the bridegroom, villagers, friends and other as the party reaches the village. On arriving at the house the newly wed couple seek blessing of the elderly persons. Day passes with merry making, drinking, dancing and singing. At noon all are given a sumptuous marriage feast. This ends the marriage ceremony.

According to Mitra the marriage ceremony among the Sherpas of Darjeeling takes place in the house of the bride. A *Lama* presides over ceremony. Though *sindurdan* (painting vermilion on the forehead and parting of the hair of the bride) is done among these people though they do not recognize this as a symbol of marriage. After the marriage ceremony the bride's parents arrange a marital feast for the members of the bride-groom's party, relatives and invitees. At bridegroom's house the marriage ceremony on his side takes place on the third day after marriage (2008:1184-1185).

Among the Sherpas of Sikkim according to Gangopadhyay, the first step of marriage is *Sodañi* or *Tinchang*. In this case relatives of the boy go to the house of the girl with two bottles of liquor (*arak*) and propose to the parents of the girl to marry her with the boy. They seek their consent from the parents of the girl in this regard. In case they give consent, then the relatives of the girl pay return visit when they give to the parents of the boy two bottles of liquor made of millet (*modo-do-zanr*), 20 kgs. of *kodo* and a white scarf (*khada*). The acceptance of the above items by the boys parents is known as *denchang* which takes place on the tenth day of the new moon (*aushiko dasami*). On another occasion the boy's parents give 30 kgs of *kodo* (millet) and *marcha* (yeast) to the girl's parents. On the day of marriage the boy's party which includes parents of the boy, his relatives, friends and some villagers (*zanti*), starts for the house of the girl. They take as many white scarfs (*khada*) as wanted by the parents of the girl. The bridegroom is dressed with a full sleeve *boku* (*chuwa*) and a cap *aptok*). The bride's wedding dress consists of a half-sleeve *boku* (*chewa-angi*), a cap (*tsering-king-gok*) and some ornaments. The *Lama* performs the *khalu puja* (*khalu-serkim*).

As the party of the bridegroom reaches the house of the bride, members are cordially welcomed, allowed to sit under a decorated canopy and served with *chhang*. The bridegroom and all his party members are then smeared vermileon on one another's forehead. Then before the actual marriage ceremony starts, the parents of the bridegroom offer five *khedas* to mother of the bride, two *khedas* to *Lama* of the bride's side, and one *kheda* to the father of the bride. The uncles and other relatives of the bride are also given one *kheda* to each.

Just before the marriage ceremony proper starts, the *Lama* instruct the bride's parents to bring the bride (*nama*) in the place where marriage ceremony will take place. As the bride arrives one of the members of the bridegroom's party, announces the arrival of the bride three times. This is known as *mola*. The bridegroom then hands over the marriage dress of the bridegroom to the bride for safe custody. The whole night is passed with a joyous mood with singing and dancing and also with a good feast.

Next morning the bridegroom's party (*zanti*) moves with the bride from the house of the bridegroom leaving one member of the party in the bride's house. This is known as *yang-chap* that is "holding back the good fortune of the house". This member leaves the bride's house next morning after drinking *chhung* and receiving a *kheda*.

On reaching the bridegroom's house, the members of the bridegroom's party, bride, and the *Lama* moves round the bridegroom's house three times while the *Lama* goes on chanting *mantras*. Then the bridegroom paints the forehead of the bride with vermilion as per instruction of the *Lama*. The *Lama* smears sacred butter (*gian*) on the forehead of both. The day and night are passed with singing, dancing and merry-making and of course, with a good feast.

On the third day of the marriage bride and the bridegroom go to the house of the bride. They carry with them three bottles of *karma loku* (*arak*).

This ends the marriage ceremony of the Sherpas of Sikkim as described by Gangopadhyay (1993:157-158). Bisht and Bankoti has written the same thing (2004:1490-1491) as written by Gangopadhyay in 1993 (*ibid*). Subba (2008:286-288) has also said almost same thing as mentioned by Gangopadhyay (1993:157-158).

Fürer-Haimendorf has studied in depils, the marriage ceremony of the Sherpas of Nepal in his book, *The Sherpas of Nepal: Buddhist Highlands* (1964). According to him to make any alliance the father or any senior relative of the prospective bridegroom propose (*sodene*) to the bride's father for such alliance at the time when both the boy and the girl are adolescents. The boy does not accompany his parent. In case the girl's parents accept the proposal, preliminary arrangement are made for the final wedding ceremony. The next ceremony is *dem-chang* (beer of tying). "The performance of a *dem-chang* necessitates preparations and involves the parents of the girl as well as those of the young man in considerable expenditure" (1964:49). For this ceremony a date is fixed, and on this date the bridegroom's party consisting parents, relatives and some invited villagers, visits bride's house. While awaiting for the bridegroom's party bride's mother and another woman relative perform a rite called *sur-chang*. One man sprinkles offerings (*sir kim*) and offer prayer. When the prayer is over the members of the bridegroom's party is entertained with beer.

On reaching bride's house the groom's party members present scarfes to the bride's parents and relatives of the bride. This is a very important ritual

> "So great is the significance of this presentation of ceremonial scarves that in the event of a *sodene* proposal made for a girl already pregnant, scarves may be offered to her parents together with the *sodene* beer in order to confer legitimacy on the unborn child" (*ibid*: 52).

As soon as the presentation of scarfes ends the father of the bride announces the marriage between the said boy and the girl. Then the members of the groom's party starts dancing and singing. Thereafter, the guests are entertained with a feast and drink.

After *dem-chang*, the final marriage ceremony takes place. This final marriage ceremony, according to Fürer-Haimendorf, may sometimes take place even after several years (*ibid*: 56).

The final wedding ceremony is known as *zendi* or *gyen – kutop*. This ceremony finally recognizes the man and the woman coming into union, as husband and wife.

> This rite terminates the girl's membership of her parental economic unit and it is at the time of the wedding that she is given a share of the family property in the form of dowry (*nor*). This dowry remains her personal property for the rest of her life, irrespective of the success or failure of marriage, and the wedding rite has thus subsidiary effect of establishing a woman as an independent legal person in possession of individual property (*ibid*: 58).

In fact though the Sherpa marriage is constituted of several social and religious ceremonies, but "the emphasis of the whole procedure is not on ritual but on the economic aspects of the change in relationship" (*ibid*). Among the Sherpas of Nepal the dowry which the bride gets from her parents, kinsmen and friends, is considered as "one of the distinctive marks of a union legalized by the full wedding rites" (*ibid*: 60). As the bride gets dowry from her parents, the groom in a similar way, gets a share of property from his parents.

The *gyen-kutop* ceremony consists of rituals and feasts, and this ceremony sometimes extends over two days. In this ceremony the groom's father anoints the bride's head with butter. In a similar way the bride's father anoints the bridegroom's forehead with butter. All these are done with the blowing of the conch shell, and then all start dancing, singing and playing musical instruments.

After the marriage, the groom's party along with the bride leaves for the groom's house. As the party reaches there, the members of the party are cordially received by the members of the groom's family, their relatives and villagers. Here they are served with drinks and also a little of curd, butter, *tsampa*, sugar and *thoma* (*ibid*: 61-65).

Ortner while studying the Sherpas of Dzemu village in Solu-Khumbu area in Eastern Nepal, has mentioned that the marriage ceremony takes place in stages "over a period of years, each stage, of course, having a specific name". The marriage is finalized by the negotiation between the parents of the boy and the girl.

The first stage of the marriage proper according to Ortner, is *demchang*. After this ritual "the couple is considered to be formally married such that children subsequently born are legitimate…." (1979:21). Among the Sherpas as mentioned by Ortner, there is a tradition that the bridegroom extends his service to his in-laws when he visit his wife who lives after the first stage of marriage, in her parents' house.

In the final stage of marriage the husband along with relatives and villagers, goes to the house of the bride to bring her along with the dowry she received. But this final stage may take place even after one or more years, and this delay may be due to economic reason, according to Ortner. These economic reasons are that the bride's family might not be able to collect required dowry or it may be able to spare the labour the bride renders to her family etc. (*ibid*: 22). In case the bride's family solves these two problems then she goes to her husband's house along with her dowry and leads the family life.

Bisht and Bankoti (2004: 1485-1486) have mentioned about the marriage ceremony of the Sherpas of Nepal. According to them to these people marriage is an occasion of great happiness and joy. Their marriage ceremony includes several rites such as *Dae Chyang, Daem Chyang, Pae Chyang* and *Gaen Kutawa.* Among these rites, *Dae Chyang* is the first rite in which the parents of the would-be bridegroom go to the would-be brides parents "with a *thake of jad* to ask for the hand of the girl". It is only after *thake of jad* is accepted, the other rites are performed. After this proposal is accepted, the would-be groom gains the right to visit the prospective bride at night and stay with her and the girl may become pregnant also.

The performance of the next rite *Daem Chang* actually seals the relation between the boy and the girl as permanent. "This rite makes the girl and the boy into the bride and the groom in the eyes of the Sherpa society and community" (*ibid*: 1486). On this occasion the groom's party goes to the house of the bride ceremonially, and this ceremonial meeting of two parties and offering of *Chyang* to the groom's party members by the members of the bride's party, is known as *sur Chyang*. Then the bride's parents, maternal uncles and agnates offer *khata* (white scarf) to the groom's party. The father of the bride thereafter declares the completion of marriage. Then all start singing, dancing and playing of musical instruments.

Gaen Kutawa is the last ritual of marriage ceremony of the Sherpas of Nepal as mentioned by Bisht and Bankoti. In this ritual bride takes a goblet of *Chyang* as mentioned by Bisht and Bankoti. In this ritual bride takes a goblet of *chyang* in her hand and gives a drink to all her relatives assembled there, and bids farewell to all the relatives and seeks leave from every one. This ceremony is known as *thuyanla.* Then the groom's party along with the bride return to the groom's house (*ibid*). They are cordially received by the relatives, friends and villagers as the party reaches the village of the bridegroom. In the house of the bridegroom drinking, singing and dancing go on throughout the day and night. A sumptuous feast is given to all.

Funeral Ceremony

While birth brings joy in a family, death brings enough of shock, sorrow and distress in a family. The same is the case with the Sherpas. To them death of a family member is great loss and a deep mournful affairs.

When a death occurs in a Sherpa family, everyone in a family breaks down in a sorrow, and starts wailing loudly. Getting the news of the death of relatives and the friends of the family as well as neighbours and the villagers start coming in the house of the dead person. Some of them give consolation to the bereaved family members.

Sometimes, after some relatives and family members, sometimes some neighbour or villagers also lift the dead body from the cot and place it on the floor of the room. So long the dying person is alive, even in a gasping stage, his or her body is allowed to keep on the cot and does not remove from the bed to the ground. Rather the Sherpas allowed the dying person to breathe his or her last on his or her own cot. It is considered as a disrespect to the dying person to remove him or her from the bed and place on the floor when still he is alive.

As the person dies they transfer the dead body from the cot and place it on the floor. Some relatives and others cover the dead body with a new white cloth. Some of them always stay or sit near the dead body, it is never kept alone in an empty room.

After the death of a person some persons go to call in a *Lama*. As the *Lama* arrives, the family members and other relatives sit around the dead body and with folded hand utter prayer along with the *Lama*. This is done, so, that the soul of the dead should live in other world in peace. Sometimes, if it is possible, a *Lama* is called in before the dying man breathes his or her last. In that case the *Lama* sits in front of the dying person and read some specific chapter from the *cho* (religious book). It is a belief among the Sherpas that if the dying person listens to this religious hymn read from hymnal, his or her soul will go to the other world peacefully and will not disturb the family members in any way. The relatives of the dead who live in the neighbouring villages are informed about the death so that they can come and see the dead man their last and also take part in the funeral. When most of the relatives, friends and others come, they start necessary preparations for the funeral.

Among the Sherpas cremation is the method of disposal of the dead, whether the dead man is a male or a female, young (above 10 years or so) or old. Normally, they bury the child if he or she is below ten years of age or so. Even in case of the accidental death of a person above ten years of age, he or she is buried.

When all the preparations for taking the dead to the cremation grounds, are ready, the *Lama* chants prayer so that the soul of the dead man leaves the house peacefully. He also offers *Suranga* and *chhung* to the departed soul for the last time in the house. The *Suranga* is a kind of food prepared of the mixture of the powder of wheat, maize and job in *ghee* (clarified butter). From this day the family members of the dead person, offer *suranga* for 21 days to the soul of the dead and place it outside the house and place a lighted lamp there also. Then as per direction of the *Lama* the assembled persons offer *shaba* (last respect) to the dead person.

In the meantime some of the assembled persons prepare a bier with bamboo. On the middle of the bier they attach an elliptical or square structure made of bamboo splits. They place dead body in a sitting position inside the structure and tie the dead body with the bier so that it does not fall while carrying the bier to the cremation ground (*thursa*).

When every rite concerning the death necessary to be observed in the house are observed, they take the dead body on the bier to the cremation ground. From the room to outside the room only the relatives of the dead who are Sherpas, can carry the bier. From outside the house any body who is Buddhist, can carry the bier to the cremation ground. But anybody belonging to any religion, can join the funeral procession and go to the cremation ground (*thursa*) which is situated not far from the village. Usually, all Buddhist people of the area (Sherpas or non-Sherpas) cremate their dead in the same *thursa*.

After the funeral procession leaves the house, the women of the house clean the room of the dead and also other rooms and courtyard.

As it leaves the house for the cremation ground, the funeral procession normaly do not stop anywhere in between, but goes straight to the cremation ground.

On reaching the cremation ground, they keep the bier on a place and some of them start preparing the funeral pyre (*sola*). After the pyre is ready they place the bier on it. The bier is then covered with fire wood. The *Lama* then utters prayers and offer different items such as cereals, mustard, black sesame, *chhung* etc. on the pyre in the name of the dead person and utter incantations. The assembled persons offer *kheda* (a piece of white cloth) to the dead person as the sign of their love and respect for the dead person. Some people play musical instruments also. Then after prayer the *Lama* first of all torches the pyre. Thereafter, some others also torch the pyre. As the cremation is over, all return to the house of the dead. From there after taking *thu* and then some tea or *chhang* they retire to their respective houses.

On the third day after cremation some of the family members of the dead, go to the cremation ground and collect unburnt or burnt (charcoal) portion of the skull of the dead (*ruche*) and keep it in a container. Then on their return, they keep the container carrying the *ruche* for 21 days in the room where the person died. The Sherpas believe that if they do not observe all the funeral rites and rituals in a proper way, the soul of the dead will not reach *sange*, but becomes *day* (devil) and will move around the house. It may create troubles to the householders of the dead person. For that reason before the funeral procession leaves the house with the dead man for the cremation ground, the senior most member of the family, in absence some senior relative or villagers belonging to the Sherpa community, requests the soul of the dead person not to disturb the family members or the villagers and promise that the family members would observe all obsequal rites with all sincerity.

The Sherpas have some belief about the soul of the dead. They believe that the soul after the death of a person, goes to the creator of the universe (*Sangechomdende*). They also believe that the soul of the dead person visits his or her house on the 7th, 14th, 21st, 49th day, after 90 days and after a year of the day of death of that person. So on these days the members of the family of the dead person offer items of food liked by the dead person, and also *chhung* and lit a number of lamps in the name of the dead person.

Though after cremation of the dead, the family members of the dead, are free to move and go anywhere and do their normal works, but they usually do not perform any social or religious ceremony within a year after death.

After death the members of the family observe *gayoa* or funeral ceremony on 7th, 14th and 21st day after the death. The *gayoa* ceremony which is observed on 21st day, is the main *gayoa* ceremony. At the time of *gayoa* ceremony, the family members invite a *Lama* who actually presides over the function. On this occasion the *Lama* makes prayers, offers food and *chhung* in the name of the dead person and performs *molomo*. He also reads passages from the *cho* (religious book) and lit lamps. The relatives of the dead man also lit lamps. This *gayoa* ceremony is celebrated in the same room where the dead person died. Then they erect a memorial tomb called *mane* which is made by stones of nine different kinds arranged in fourteen steps. The *Lama* inaugurates this *mane* by moving around the *mane* clock-wise for three or seven times. The economically poorer Sherpas cannot afford to erect such *mane*. Sometimes they emerse the *ruche* in the water of the nearby river.

On the *gayoa* of the 21st day after death, the family members of the dead hoist a flag called *jadha*. This flag is made of white cloth on which prayers are written in the Tibetan.

On the occasion of the 21 day *goyoa* ceremony, relatives, friends, other invitees and villagers particularly those who attended the funeral procession, are entertained with a feast along with *chhung*. The participants also on their part, give to the bereaved family *chhung*, money, cereals etc. This is known as the *sarai*. This ends the funeral ceremony.

Again after completing of a year after the death, the bereaved family members perform *barshokan*, i.e. annual funeral ceremony. Most of the Sherpas observe this ceremony in the monastery (*gumpha*) where the *Lama* performs the worship and *molomo* for Lord Buddha and other deities and spirits, and also for the peace of the soul of the dead person. He also lits lamps and offer food and *chhung*. The Sherpa custom allows only the sister's husband or daughter's husband of the dead person to take the responsibility of the *gayoa* function. Of course, for this responsibility the relative concern gets some money from dead person's son.

In case of the death of a minor child (generally below 10 years or so) the Sherpas do not observe *goyoa* ceremony fully. They observe this ceremony on the day they bury the dead body of the minor. A *Lama* is called in and he performs the *goyoa* ceremony fully. They observe this ceremony on the day they bury the dead body of the minor. A *Lama* is called in and he performs the *goyoa* ceremony. On this occasion he offers *molomo*, food and *chhung*, reads *cho*, worship deities and spirits and lits lamps.

Mitra has written very little of the funeral ceremony of the Sherpas of Darjeeling. According to him, the Sherpas there bury the dead and observe pollution period for thirty nine days. The *Lama* propitiates the soul of the deceased on seventh day after death. They perform purificatory ceremony on thirty ninth day (2008: 1185).

Among the Sherpas of Sikkim when a man is about to die, a *Lama* is called in as observed Gangopadhyay (1993:158-159). The family members according to him, burn *chomin* and incense sticks in the same room where the dying man is there. The *Lama* reads religious book and after the person dies, he plucks some hair from the middle of the head of the dead. He also consults religious book and finds out a suitable time to take the dead body to the cremation ground. The dead body is kept in a sitting posture on a bier. One person who leads the funeral procession, carries a *thanka* (*shiba-khola*) depicting three gods. The *Lama* who also accompanies the funeral procession, holds in his left hand a *khada* which is tied with the bier. By his right hand he holds a ritual bell (*tilu*). In the cremation ground the body is cremated on a pyre. The *Lama* lits up the pyre while uttering *mantras*. He also throws paddy and barley mixed with butter on the burning pyre several times (*zinshak hawan*). After the cremation the *Lama* prepares an image of the dead with the ashes and unburnt bone, known as *ten* putting clothes of the dead (*ibid*). The first funeral rite takes place on the third day (*nupur*) after cremation.

Many poorer Sherpas finish the funeral rites and rituals on this day itself, and so, it is known as *symbi-nupur*. The funeral ceremony comes to an end with the final purificatory rites known as *shibju-sorku* held on forty ninety day when a funeral feast is hosted by the family members of the diseased for the relatives, friends and villagers. In the evening some ceremony, known as *sindijougshi* or *sendi khingur* is performed when the *Lama* drives away the evil spirits from the house (1993: 158-159).

Subba (2008:288) has also described funeral ceremony of the Sherpas of Sikkim in brief. He has also described the same thing as described by Gangopadhyay (1993: 158-159) and Kunwar (1989: 195-197).

Among the Sherpas of Nepal, funeral ceremony requires more ministration of the *Lamas* and its features clearly show that this death ceremony is more religious one while birth and marriage among these people are more a social ceremonies. According to Fürer-Haimendorf "...death brings man face to face with those figures and forms of existence to which all religious practices and thinking is directed". It is when the death strikes a family that the surviving members set into motion a series of rites and ceremonies which, though embedded in a framework of social obligations and customs, are of an essentially religious nature" (1964: 224-225).

As soon as a death occurs in a family, the dead body is covered with a white cloth. Then the members of the bereaved family call a *Lama* and another person to prepare dead body. This is not done by the family members, but by the *Lama* and some experienced person. The *Lama* utters prayers (*pho-giau*) for sending the spirit of the dead man (*sem*) to *Devachen*, the heaven of "Boundless Light" (*Opame*). After prayers, the *Lama* finds out the manner by which the dead body would be given disposal. After the *Lama* tells about this method, the man prepares the bier which is a square structure in which the corpse is kept in a sitting position. The *Lama* then prepares an altar behind the corpse and the *tormas*, six in number, represent different deities are placed on the altar (*ibid*: 225-227).

Among the Sherpas of Khumbu, as Fürer-Haimendorf has observed, the period between death and the cremation of the death should be two to three days. The most usual form of the disposal of the dead here is cremation. The dead children are of course, buried. Sometimes very poor person who has neither property nor relatives, throw the dead body into the river.

When every thing is ready, the funeral procession consisted of a large number of mourners, relatives and villagers, proceeds toward cremation ground when the *Lama* recites from the book, *Lam-chu* (path showing). On reaching the cremation ground the bier is kept near the pyre. The *Lama* starts reciting the *Drowa-Kundrol*. Other *Lamas* play musical instruments. The dead body is then kept on the pyre in a sitting position and the *Lama* throws *tsho-torma* on the pyre as an offering to the deceased. After some other services by the *Lamas*, the pyre is set ablaze (*ibid*: 232).

After the cremation is over, all people return to the house of the dead. In the house of the dead then a number of rituals and prayers are performed by the *Lamas*. On the 8th day after death *de-dzongu* is performed to drive away the evil spirits (*shrindi*) from the house. Then the family members of the deceased make payment to the *Lamas*, *bulup* for the senior *Lama* and *te-rup* for the junior Lamas (*ibid*: 234).

Normally, the Sherpas in Nepal in general perform a post-cremation ritual (*nupur*). This ritual may be held immediately after cremation or on 3rd, 7th or 11th day after cremation. According to Fürer-Haimendorf only the wealthier section of the Sherpas perform this ritual on 11th day (*ibid*).

In this ritual the *Lama* offers food and drink and recites from the religious book. After performing some other associated rituals, the *Lama*

> despatches the departed to Devachen, "as fast as an arrow flies from a bow-string". The final adonomitions urge him to go to the West where the Buddha Sange Ngawong Tai Sakya Muni is dwelling. To his right he will see Pawa Cheresi (*Avlokitesvara*) and to his left Tudze-chenbu (*Avolokitesvara Mahakaruna*). All these are benevolent divinities who will nourish and help the deceased (*ibid*: 236)

After some other rituals and funeral feast, the funeral ceremony comes to close.

Ortner has also given brief description of the death rituals of the Sherpas of Dzemu in Solu-Khumbu areas of Nepal (1979:106-109). The first part of the ritual starts two to three days after death of a person. The dead body is bathed, purified and covered with a white sack. The body is then kept in a structure called *pungbo* (like a god's house) near the altar.

After several days of all these, the dead body is made ready for cremation and taken to the cremation ground where the body is placed on a pyre. Then the pyre is lit. according to the belief of the Sherpas "before the burning he is a god, and when they burn him he becomes an offerings". Just before the pyre is lit, the *Lama* "invites the demons to come and feast upon the corpse, and for them he is simply a hunt of meat". (*ibid*: 107). Then the *Lama* recites from the religious book so as "to guide the soul to a good rebirth." After funeral a grand *gyowa* feast is given to all the invitees, guests and relatives.

Paul has described the funeral ceremony of the Sherpas of Nepal as "the single, most common and pervasive ritual" in the life of the Sherpas. The "great amount of ritual activity which follows a death for a seven week perĩod, makes some aspect of the funerary circle a nearly ever-present reality in a Sherpa community" (1982: 102). Among the Sherpas the funeral ceremony does not include only one family but the entire community as if it is a community ritual and not a private one, according to Paul. The Sherpas according to him belief that

> The manifest purpose of Sherpa funerary rites is to ensure that the transmigrating soul of the deceased successfully leaves the body, traverses the intermediate unborn stage, and is reborn in a desirable realm, if possible in *sangye* (heaven). Since the fate of the soul in the next rebirth is supposed to be determined by the law of *karma*, it might be supposed that there is little point in trying to influence the rebirth process (*ibid*).

The funeral ceremony of the Sherpas of Khumba as dexcribed by Paul (*ibid*: 102-112) is almost same as described by Fürer-Haimendorf and some others. According to Paul the first ceremony after a person dies is *po* meaning 'to migrate' or 'change place' that means 'to instruct the departed soul in the art of changing states, from living to dead, and from containment in a body to the bodiless state. The *Lama* reads the *Book of Dead* and *Konjok Chindi* to show the path to be followed by the soul of the dead during its perilous journey. After this or a little later, *Dowa Kundul* ceremony is performed in which Pawa Chenenzi is worshipped to instruct the soul to enter the favourable one of the six realms of rebirth. Then in order to get rid the house where death has occurred, from the demonic forces responsible for inviting misfortune, some exorcism (*kurim*) is practised. At least for three days after death a number of *Lamas* are invited to read appropriate books for which they are given food, shelter and remuneration for those days.

The dead body is then taken to cremation ground for disposal. The pyre which is made for burning the dead, is treated as a *zhinsek* or "burning offering" of a benign mode. The body is placed on the pyre in a sitting posture. The *Lama* and close relatives offer different items in the burning pyre.

After cremation according to Paul, a ceremony (*nupur*) is held in which the soul which has already liberated from the dead body, is recalled into an effigy, and to this effigy the *Lama* offers food and "the soul is despatched to *sangye*". The next ceremony is known as *shetu*. The *shetu* is also performed before the cremation also. This ceremony in which passages from *konjok chindi* is read, is dedicated to Guru Rimpoche and others of his subordinate protector deities.

The final funeral ceremony is *gyowa* (virtue) which is celebrated forty-nine days after death. On this day, as the Sherpas believe, "the soul is ideally reborn, either within the cycle of existence or, less likely in *sangye*" (*ibid*: 106). For this reason the family members of the deceased arrange for a sumptuous meal for all the persons who came in their house when the person died. Even if a caste member whom the Sherpas normally do not allow to enter in the house or share food, comes when any one in a Sherpa house died, the person will be served the same food as is served to other person. The food that is prepared, includes rice, butter and sweet tea of high quality and sweetness and "peacefulness" (*ibid*).

> The point of the feast is to display complete unlimited charity on a universal scale, thereby approaching the spirit of *bodhisattva*, whose capacity for compassion is likewise without limits (*ibid*).

On the first anniversary of the death, and on subsequent anniversaries, a *tso* (gathering) ceremony may be held by the surviving family members. In this ceremony a *Lama* is called in who makes prayers to "Guru Rimpoche and his retinue; share with them and with guests an array of fine food such as rice cakes, fruits, cookies, friend dough patties and candy" (*ibid*). This ends the funeral ceremony of the Sherpas as described by Paul (1982: 102-106).

10

THEIR WORLD OF SUPERNATURALS

Buddhism in India

The Sherpas of Darjeeling, Sikkim and Nepal are Buddhists. They are Buddhists for many centuries. But before we begin Buddhism of the Sherpas we have thought of giving our learned readers some idea about Buddhism as practiced by different people of our country. This will help in understanding Buddhism of the Sherpas without any difficulty.

Buddhism was born from the soil of India. But inspite of being born in India, it is not widespread in India nor a significant number of Indian population are found embrasing this religion. Rather Buddhism is now restricted in some pockets of some States and Union Territories of India. The Buddhist people are found located in Northern India particularly in the Western Himalayas covering the States of Jammu & Kashmir, Himachal Pradesh and Uttaranchal. They are also found to reside in North-East India covering Arunachal Pradesh, Nagaland, Meghalaya, Mizoram, Assam, Sikkim and Tripura. They are also found in Maharashtra. In Jammu & Kashmir they are mostly found in Leh district (Ladakh), in Himachal Pradesh they are found to live in the districts of Lahaul and Spiti, Kinnaur and part of Simla district. In Uttaranchal they are found in some areas of Chamoli, Uttarkashi and Pithoragarh districts. They are found everywhere in Arunachal Pradesh and Sikkim and parts of Nagaland, Assam, Meghalaya, and Tripura.

In outside India they are also found in Bangladesh, Bhutan, China, Japan, Mongolia, Myanmar, Sri Lanka, and Thailand and also in some other countries.

When we look at the population strength of the Buddhist people in India we find that in our country according to 2011 Census the Buddhists have a strength of only 0.7 per cent for the total population of India. The strength of the Hindus is 79.8 per cent, Muslims 14.2 per cent, Christian 2.3 per cent and Sikh 1.7 per cent. But according to 2001 Census. 0.8 per cent of the total Indian population were Buddhists their sex-ratio being 953 females per 1000 males, according to 2001 Census. In comparison to the numerical strength of the Buddhist population in India the numerical strength of the Hindus was 80.5 per cent, Muslims 13.4 per cent, Christians 2.3 per cent and Sikhs 1.9 per cent according to 2001 Census. The strength of the 0-6 population of the Buddhist population was 14.4 per cent with sex-ratio of 942 females per 1000 males. In comparison to the Buddhists this population (0-6 age-group) among the Hindus of India was 15.6 per cent, Muslims 18.7 per cent, Christians 13.5 per cent, and Sikhs 12.8 per cent according to 2001 Census (Table 10.1).

Table 10.1: Distribution of Buddhist Population in Different States and Union Territories of India, Census 2001

States/UTs	*T/R/U*	*Persons*	*Males*	*Females*	*%*
Andhra Pradesh	Total	38,314	19,518	18,796	0.05
	Rural	24,443	12,340	12,103	0.04
	Urban	13,871	7,178	6,693	0.07
Arunachal Pradesh	Total	142,589	72,390	70,199	12.99
	Rural	131,946	66,913	65,033	15.16
	Urban	10,643	5,477	5,166	4.67
Assam	Total	51,008	26,311	24,697	0.19
	Rural	44,539	22,829	21,710	0.19
	Urban	6,469	3,482	2,987	0.19
Bihar	Total	60,606	32,709	27,897	0.07
	Rural	53,456	28,598	24,858	0.07
	Urban	7,150	4,111	3,039	0.08
Chhattisgarh	Total	65,267	32,444	32,823	0.31
	Rural	24,526	12,109	12,417	0.15
	Urban	40,741	20,335	20,406	0.97
Goa	Total	954	507	447	0.07
	Rural	440	243	197	0.06
	Urban	514	264	250	0.08
Gujarat	Total	20,640	10,763	9,877	0.04
	Rural	3,491	1,909	1,582	0.01
	Urban	17,149	8,854	8,295	0.09
Haryana	Total	14,184	7,840	6,344	0.07
	Rural	7,712	4,291	3,421	0.05
	Urban	6,472	3,549	2,923	0.11
Himachal Pradesh	Total	75,404	38,832	36,572	1.24
	Rural	63,041	32,098	30,943	1.15
	Urban	12,363	6,734	5,629	2.08

(*Contd.*)

(*Contd.*)

States/UTs	T/R/U	Persons	Males	Females	%
Jammu & Kashmir	Total	1,155	698	457	0.07
	Rural	555	353	202	0.06
	Urban	600	345	255	0.09
Jharkhand	Total	18,389	9,611	8,778	0.07
	Rural	12,327	6,343	5,984	0.06
	Urban	6,062	3,268	2,794	0.10
Karnataka	Total	400,499	210,028	190,471	0.76
	Rural	332,880	174,559	158,321	0.95
	Urban	67,619	35,469	32,150	0.38
Kerala	Total	8,790	4,401	4,389	0.03
	Rural	6,441	3,181	3,260	0.03
	Urban	2,349	1,220	1,129	0.03
Madhya Pradesh	Total	209,322	107,416	101,906	0.35
	Rural	131,356	67,031	64,325	0.30
	Urban	77,966	40,385	37,581	0.49
Maharashtra	Total	5,838,710	2,977,607	2,861,103	6.03
	Rural	3,228,573	1,639,513	1,589,060	5.79
	Urban	2,610,137	1,338,094	1,272,043	6.35
Manipur	Total	4,020	2,141	1,879	0.17
	Rural	3,776	1,993	1,783	0.21
	Urban	244	148	96	0.04
Meghalaya	Total	5,602	2,983	2,619	0.24
	Rural	3,119	1,690	1,429	0.17
	Urban	2,483	1,293	1,190	0.55
Mizoram	Total	70,411	36,499	33,912	7.92
	Rural	69,304	35,921	33.383	15.48
	Urban	1,107	578	529	0.25
Nagaland	Total	6,189	3,272	2,917	0.31
	Rural	4,727	2,509	2,218	0.29
	Urban	1,462	763	699	0.43
Orissa	Total	17,108	8,885	8,223	0.05
	Rural	13,869	7,075	6,794	0.04
	Urban	3,239	1,810	1,429	0.06
Punjab	Total	52,122	27,845	24,277	0.21
	Rural	34,207	18,172	16,035	0.21
	Urban	17,915	9,673	8,242	0.22
Rajasthan	Total	24,189	13,064	11,125	0.04
	Rural	15,452	8,204	7,248	0.04
	Urban	8,737	4,860	3,877	0.07
Sikkim	Total	151,825	78,071	73,754	28.07
	Rural	138,410	71,259	67,151	28.78
	Urban	13,415	6,812	6,603	22.41
Tamil Nadu	Total	21,787	11,368	10,419	0.03
	Rural	7,894	4,157	3,737	0.02
	Urban	13,893	7,211	6,682	0.05

(*Contd.*)

(*Contd.*)

States/UTs	*T/R/U*	*Persons*	*Males*	*Females*	*%*
Tripura	Total	98,777	50,497	48,280	3.09
	Rural	97,008	49,534	47,474	3.66
	Urban	1,769	963	806	0.32
Uttaranchal	Total	12,434	6,992	5,442	0.15
	Rural	8,241	4,753	3,488	0.13
	Urban	4,193	2,239	1,954	0.19
Uttar Pradesh	Total	356,706	188,555	168,151	0.21
	Rural	303,165	159,513	143,652	0.23
	Urban	53,541	29,042	24,499	0.16
West Bengal	Total	303,312	154,866	148,446	0.38
	Rural	209,038	105,940	103,098	0.36
	Urban	94,274	48,926	45,348	0.42
Union Territories					
Andaman & Nicobar	Total	421	310	111	0.12
	Rural	137	64	73	0.06
	Urban	284	246	38	0.24
Chandigarh	Total	1,720	937	783	0.19
	Rural	135	79	56	0.15
	Urban	1,585	858	727	0.20
Dadra & Nagar Haveli	Total	465	284	181	0.21
	Rural	88	60	28	0.05
	Urban	377	224	153	0.75
Daman & Diu	Total	130	95	35	0.08
	Rural	117	87	30	0.12
	Urban	13	8	5	0.02
Delhi	Total	25,071	13,730	11,341	0.18
	Rural	1,155	630	525	0.12
	Urban	23,916	13,100	10,816	0.19
Lakshadweep	Total	10	5	5	0.02
	Rural	8	5	3	0.02
	Urban	2	—	2	0.01
Pondicherry	Total	136	75	61	0.01
	Rural	23	11	12	0.01
	Urban	113	64	49	0.02

Source: Bhatt & Bhargava 2005: 37-85.

Now, if we come down to different States and Union Territories in search of the numerical strength of the Buddhist population, we see that they are found in varied number in different States and Union Territories. In Arunachal Pradesh their strength was 12.99 per cent of the total population of this State according to 2001 Census. In Maharashtra they were 6.03 per cent, in Mizoram 7.92 per cent, in Sikkim 28.07 per cent, in Tripura 3.09 per cent and in Himachal Pradesh 1.24 per cent of the total population of the respective State. In rest of the States and Union Territories their population was below 1.00 per cent of the total population of each of the respective States and Union Territories (Bhatt & Bhargava 2005: 37-63). The lowest strength of the total population of the respective State/UT is in Pondichery where the Buddhists were only 0.01 per cent. Then come Tamil Nadu and Kerala each with 0.03 per cent. Rajasthan and Gujarat each with 0.04 per cent, Andhra Pradesh and Orissa each with 0.05 per cent, Jharkhand, Jammu & Kashmir, Haryana and Goa each with 0.07 per cent, Daman & Diu 0.08 per cent, Uttaranchal 0.15 per cent, Andaman & Nicobar Islands 0.12 per cent, Manipur 0.17 per cent, Delhi 0.18 per cent, Assam and Chandigarh each with 0.19 per cent, Dadra & Nagar Haveli, Uttar Pradesh and Punjab each with 0.21 per cent, Meghalaya 0.24 per cent, Chhattisgarh and Nagaland each with 0.31 per cent, Madhya Pradesh 0.35 per cent, West Bengal 0.38 per cent and Kerala 0.76 per cent of the total population of each State and Union Territory according to 2001 Census (Bhatt & Bhargava 2005: 37-63).

As we have already said that 0.8 per cent of the total Indian population and 14.4 per cent of the total 0-6 year old population of this country according to 2001 Census, were Buddhists. Of this total Buddhist population 72.7 per cent were literates with 83.1 per cent male Buddhist were literates and 61.7 per cent female Buddhists were literates. These are higher than the Hindu and Muslim literates (65.1% and 59.1% respectively). Here it may be said that the Jains had the highest literacy (94.1%) followed by the Christians (80.3%).

As we come to the work participation rate among the Buddhist population of India according to 2001 Census, we find that among the people of this religious group this rate was 40.6 per cent. For the male Buddhists it was 49.2 per cent and for the female Buddhists the same was 31.7 per cent. But among the Hindus of India the same was 40.4 per cent, for males 52.4 per cent and for the females 27.5 per cent and among the Muslims the same was 31.3 per cent for the total Muslim population, 47.5 per cent for the male Muslims and 14.1 per cent for the female Muslims. Among the Christians this work participation rate was 39.7 per cent for the total Christians, 50.7 per cent for the total male Christians and 28.7 per cent for the total female Christians. So, we see that the work participation rate of the total Buddhist and total female Buddhists was more than that of the above religious groups. When we examine religious group-wise distribution of workers in different occupations, we see that in India according to 2001 Census out of the total Buddhist workers, 20.4 per cent were cultivators, 37.6 per cent were agricultural labourers,

2.9 per cent had household industry and 39.2 per cent were in other works. The Census data further show that as cultivators the number of Buddhist workers was less than those of the Hindus (33.1%), Muslims (20.7%), Christian (29.2%) and the Sikh (32.4%). But as agricultural labourers the Buddhist workers (37.6%) were much higher in number than those of any of the religious group workers (Hindus 27.6%, Muslims 22.0%, Christians 15.3%, Sikhs 16.8%). But as other works the Buddhist held the fifth position, just below the Jains (81.7%), Christians (52.8%), Muslims (49.1%) and Sikhs (47.3%). But numerically the Buddhist workers were a little above the Indian workers in general (37.6%).

Thus, we see that the Buddhist people of India though numerically they are quite weak, hold a somewhat better position in literacy, work participation and occupation.

Buddhism as already said, is mainly located in the North-Western India and also in the North-Eastern India. In fact this religion is mainly prevalent among some people of the Himalayan region. So, in the following few pages we shall discussion about Buddhism as practiced by those people in those two areas.

Buddhism in the Himalayas

The Sherpas are in general, Buddhist by religion whether they live in Darjeeling or in Sikkim. Even in Nepal they are Buddhists. The Sherpa of all the three regions practise Mahayana Buddhism and belong to the sect, Nyingmapa (Raha & Coomar 2001:81; Adam 1997: 86; Ortner 1979: 30-31; Fürer-Haimendorf 1964: 175; Fürer Haimendorf 1984: 86). Apart from the Sherpas, there are several Buddhist groups live in the Himalayan region. So, before we proceed further with the religious beliefs and practices of the Buddhist Sherpa, we like to give our readers some idea about the distribution of the Buddhist groups in the Himalayas and also history of Buddhism in the three areas, Darjeeling, Sikkim and Nepal which are the homeland of the Sherpas and also of the Buddhist population in West Bengal, Sikkim and Nepal.

In the Himalayan region a number of communities practise Buddhism. In the Western Himalayas a good number of communities have embraced Buddhism. In Leh district of Jammu and Kashmir the Ladakhi or Bodh or Botpa are Buddhists. Similarly, the Changpa, Brokpa and the Tibetan of this region are also Buddhists. According to Mann "Buddhism in Ladakh is a mixture of Bon, the old religion of Tibet, Tantrism and Mahayana. Some have also referred to Lamaism as the religion of the Ladakhi's"

(1986: 141). In Ladakh Buddhists belong to two sects—Red Hat and Yellow Hat. Mann further states that before Lamaism "two earlier religions flourished in Ladakh-Bonches and Buddhism" (1995: 12). Goldstein and Tsarong have also found Leh and Zangskar area of Ladakh as predominantly Buddhist (1987: 446). Most probably Buddhism became the dominant religion in Zangskar, a part of Ladakh as early as eighth century A.D.

> Zangskar contains rock relief and a stupa undoubtedly dating to the earliest spread of Buddhism in Northern India. The reputation of Zangskar as a holy land is further enhanced by legends suggesting that the great saints of the early Mahayana, Marpa and Naropa, both spent time in the valley meditating and preaching (Crook 1994: 449).

In Zangskar "over 95 per cent of the people are Buddhist. Every Buddhist family is affiliated to some monastery situated within or near the vicinity of the village" (Chatterjee 1992: 234).

In Kargil district of Ladakh also we find the existence two religions—Buddhism and Islam. Here a good member of people have also embraced Buddhism in which traces of *Bon* religion of Tibet (*Bon-pa*) is also seen (Rizvi 1995: 34-35).

In the district of Lahaul and Spiti of Himachal Pradesh the religion of the majority is Buddhism, and this form of Buddhism is closely akin to the Tibetan form of Tantric Buddhism (Ghosh 2002: 163). In this district of Himachal Pradesh Buddhism entered during eighth Century A.D. In fact Buddhism was brought to Lahaul and Spiti by celebrated missionary, Padmasambhava who came to Lahaul and Spiti sometimes during eighth century A.D. Sharma has also found all inhabitants of Gahr Valley of Lahaul and Spiti district as the Buddhists. In other areas of Lahaul people are found to practise Buddhism also (1987: 388). In Spiti area of Lahaul and Spiti district the Bodhs have accepted the Gelugpa sect of Buddhism (Rizvi 1987: 415; 1995: 51).

In some areas of the district of Kinnaur of Himachal Pradesh Buddhism is found to reign supreme while in some area Hinduism is predominant. In between both Buddhism and Hinduism are found to be practised by the same people. So, in this district we find curious co-existence of two religions—Mahayana Buddhism and Hinduism (Raha & Mahato 1985: 293-338; Raha 1978: 94-100). "In Kinnaur Buddhism is the most important religion next to Hinduism. It is found to be practised in Pooh and Kalpa sub-divisions" (Raha 1995: 89-90). In Kinnaur people have embraced Mahayana Buddhism (The Great Vehicle). The Mahayana Buddhists here are divided into three sects Nyingma-pa, Duk-pa and Gelug-pa. The people belonging to the first two sects are more numerous than those of the third one (Raha 2003: 132-133).

As we come down to Uttaranchal (earlier Uttar Pradesh hill areas) we find the Bhotia of Uttar Kashi, Chamoli and Pithoragarh as Buddhists. But Prasad has found "The religious life of the Bhotias has been peculiar blend of Lamaistic Buddhism, Hinduism and Animism" (1989: 100).

When we come down to the north-eastern areas of India, we find a large number of communities practicing Buddhism. The Khamtis of Arunachal Pradesh are "a Buddhist tribe with Theravada (Khamti = *to-ni*) faiths". In fact "the Tai-Khamti people were the first to bring Buddhism into the valley;...." (Tikhak 2006: 25). During Burmese invasion in Assam in the eighteenth Century the Buddhist monks came to Assam and spread *Dhamma* (Buddhism) here and there (*ibid*). In Arunachal Pradesh the Tikhas (Tangsa), Singpo, Khamti and the Chakma are the Theravada Buddhists. But the Khambas, Membas, Monpas and the Sherdukpens are the Mahayana Buddhists (*ibid*). In Arunachal Pradesh again the Nahs and the Meyors, the Tai-Phakes, Tai-Khamyang, Tai-Aitone, Tai-Turungs, Dowaniyas, besides some Shans and Mans of Assam, the Chakma and the Mags of Tripura, some Chakmas of Mizoram and Tirap and Lohit districts of Arunachal Pradesh keep faith on Theravada Buddhism (Dutta & Tripathy 2006: 15-18). In Bhutan Buddhism or Lamaism is supreme among the Bhutias and others. In Sikkim both the Bhotias and the Lepchas are Buddhists. In Nepal the Sherpas, the Tibetans and some other communities are Buddhists.

So, we find that a large number of communities living in the Western, Central and Eastern Himalayas believe in Buddhism.

Buddhism in the Western and Central Himalayas

In the Western and Central Himalayas Buddhism is mainly concentrated in the Leh district of Ladakh area of Jammu and Kashmir State, Lahaul and Spiti and Kinnaur districts of Himachal Pradesh and also in Uttarkashi, Chamoli and Pithoragarh districts of Uttaranchal. This religion is being professed there for several centuries by different groups of people. Though strong forces like Hinduism and even Christianity have invaded the strongholds of Buddhism in the Himalayan region, still somehow Buddhism is surviving, and many people particularly of the high Himalayas, have deep faith in Buddhism. However, in the following pages, we have discussed Buddhism in different parts of the Western and Central Himalayas.

Buddhism in Ladakh, Jammu & Kashmir

In the Leh district of Ladakh, Jammu and Kashmir the ethnic groups like the Ladakhi who are also known as the Boto, Bhoto, Bhautta, Bodh, Bodpa or Mangric, Gara Mon and Beda who are also known as the Dolba, practise Buddhism (Mann 1986: 16). In fact Buddhism found its way into Ladakh and the adjoining area before Emperor Ashoka ruled. According to Gannhar "...Buddhism was one of the living faiths in the valley in the time of Surendra ....Obviously Buddhism must either have been prevalent in the terriroty or was introduced into it in the time of Surendra ....Later, in Ashoka's time when Buddhism spread widely in Kashmir and other territories...." (1956: 175).

In Ladakh Buddhism is a mixture of *Bon* or *Pon* religion of ancient Tibet, Tantrism and Mahayana (Mann 1986: 141). It is also known as Lamaism.

> The chief concept of their divinity is defined under three dimensions, that is, Gautama Buddha (*Sangyas*), religious principles indicated by Buddha (*Chhos Kon chok*) and Lamas following these principles (*Gendun Konchok*). Demology and idolatry are other traits found in the religion among Ladakhis and are believed to be the outcome of *Bon* or *Pon* religion. (Mann 1992: 425; Ghosh 1986: 141)."

The Buddhism of Ladakh has two distinct sects, the Red Hat and the Yellow Hat. Here while some of the monasteries belong to Red Hat, the others come under the control of the other sect.

> Nyimapa was the earliest sect and its religious men wore red dresses. Gelukpa (the virtuous) sect was originated around the middle of fourteenth Century *Tsongkhapa*, and its religious persons wear yellow dresses. The disciples of Tsongkhapa are known as Yellow Hats. They are distinguished from the Red Hats 'of the past' (Mann 1992: 143).

While the followers of the Yellow sect do not marry and also do not drink *chang* (local liquor), the followers of the Red sect on the other hand, enjoy some laxity. They drink *chang* and are also allowed to marry.

The members of yellow sect abstain from sex, would not commit adultery and are also not supposed to indulge in killing, stealing, drinking and smoking. Inspite of having some difference among them, these two sects usually do not maintain any distance among themselves. "On some occasion, the *Lamas* from different monasteries (belonging to Red as well as Yelow sect) gather in one *Gompa* to recite the sacred text of *Kanjur* (*Shah-Hger*) and *Tanjur* (*Stan-Hgyur*).... The philosophical teachings of the two are also not different" (*ibid*: 144).

The Ladakhis living in a religion-dominated society, have a deep-rooted religious belief system. They believe in soul and rebirth. They also have a strong faith in various spirits and ghosts and also very much scared of them. This faith and fear prompted them to invent different devises of means of protection against these spirits and ghosts. Some of the spirits and ghosts of the Ladakhis are Shinde, Lhu, Lhande etc. They also have a number of gods and goddesses. Some of the important gods and goddesses are Chemresi, Chamba, Riksamganbo, Makzor Gaimo, Chham-Shing, Yul-La, Genbo and Chanlahete. But their principal god is Sangyas, Shaka Thubba or Gautam Buddha who is considered as the originator of Buddhism. Another very important god is Guru Rimpoche, Padmo Sambhava or Lobon Rimpoche. Yul-La is the village gods who is held responsible for the protection and survival of the entire village community. Along with all these gods and goddesses many other deities are also worshipped regularly. The Ladakhis also have a number of monastaries or *Gompa*, the religious institution. This sacred institution is considered as the abode of the deities. Here the Ladakhis pray and worship. Some of the monastaries also provide training to the would be Lamas.

Buddhism in Lahaul and Spiti, Himachal Pradesh

In Lahaul majority of the people practice Buddhism which has much similarity with "the Tibetan form of Tantric Buddhism" (Ghosh 2002: 163). In fact Buddhism entered Lahaul sometimes during eighth Century A.D. The District Census Handbook, Lahaul and Spiti District, Census of India, 1961, has stated that Buddhism most probably, entered this district during eighth Century A.D. The great Buddhist monk, Padma-sambhava is believed to have intoruduced Buddhism in this part of the Himalayas (Ghosh 1992: 442). "During his brief sojourn here, he was said to have founded the renowned monastery of *Guru Ghantal* which depicts the original Buddhism, differing from the shrines established after twelfth century A.D...." (Ghosh 2002: 164). Since, then Buddhism becomes the main religion of Lahual. "People are some mechanically devoted to Buddhism that prayer in this area has been reduced to a sort of reflex action and prayer wheel is a common sight" (*ibid*).

The type of Buddhism practiced by the Lahaula belongs to Red sect.

> It is said that about two hundred years back, Dewa Gyatso, a missionary sent by Nwang Namgyal, the King of Bhutan, came to Lahaul *via* Tibet and introduced the Drugpa (Red Hat) sect in this area. Namgyal was the founder of this sect and the name originates from Dug the Bhoti name for Bhutan (Gill 1972: 130; Ghosh 2002: 165).

As the *Lamas* of Lahaul belong to this sect (Red sect), they are 'not required to practice celibacy' and therefore many of them are married. Instead of staying in monastaries they stay in their houses with their families and cultivate their land. Even leading this family life they are also required to stay in the monastaries for prayer and meditation, particularly during winter. In the past the *Lamas* from this district used to go to Tibet for higher training in theology. But after 1962 with the closing of Indo-Tibetan border the *Lamas* here are unable to go to Tibet for this purpose, and many of the present day *Lamas* are not properly trained. In the present day Lahaul and Spiti society religion still holds a dominant position. The *Lamas* play important role in the socio-religious life of the people, and so they are properly respected and revered.

In the district of Lahaul and Spiti in Himachal Pradesh, almost every hamlet and village has a Buddhist monastery or *Gompa*, and these monastaries or *Gompas* are the place of worship, prayer and meditation for the *Lamas* and the *Chomos*, and the training centre for the trainee *Lamas* and the *Chomos*.

But in the recent decades, marked changes are noticed in the religious beliefs and practices in this district. The post-independence

> Developments in the area have destroyed the mythical impregnability and infallifility of the Gompa organization and have enlightened the people on secular lines. This has been fortified by newly developed ideas of sophistication and social values in preference to previous ones, grown out of the availability of secular jobs and opportunities so as to widen their outlook and contact with a wider range of people, views, ideas,

> education and cultures. These have inevitably led to the decay of the untenable position occupied by the Gompas, which, in order to maintain their supremacy had steeped the people in superstition, thus, conditioning their culture (Ghosh 2002: 166).

As a result peoples' interest in religious matters has started waning and their respect for the religious matters has also started loosening. The monastic organization is also unable to hold that command on the people and also the authoritative role they play as they had in the past. The people also are less interested to go for monastic order, and so not many people go to the *Gompas* as trainee *Lamas* and/or *Chomos*. But inspite of all these changes, the border bastion of Lahaul and Spiti of Himachal Pradesh has still the indelible imprint of Buddhism (*ibid*: 168).

Buddhism in Kinnaur, Himachal Pradesh

In Kinnaur Buddhism was brought by the Buddhist missionaries during eighth century A.D. who at that time, visited north-western part of the Himalayas including Ladakh, Lahaul and Spiti, Kinnaur and some other areas on their way back to India from Tibet. The ancient book, *Padma Bkabtang* has mentioned the name of such countries like Zahor (Tibetan for Mandi) and Garzha (Garzha was the ancient name for Lahaul) etc. where Buddhist monk, Padma-sambhava visited (Raha & Mahato 1985: 297).

In the district of Kinnaur Buddhism is found in most part of Pooh sub-division. Here Buddhism is quite dominant, may be due to its closeness to Tibet. Buddhism is also found to co-exist with local Hinduism in Kalpa sub-division. Here the same family brings *Lama* for performing some ritual and prayer in the house and again the members of this family also go to some temple for worship. The third sub-division, Nachar is exclusively ruled by local Hinduism (Raha 1974; Raha 1978; Raha 1995: 86, Raha & Mahato 1985: 297). Frazer as early as 1820 found Buddhism as followed by most of the people. Although the Kinnaurese are recognized as Hindoos by decent and general profession, they most generally follow *Lama* religion (1820: 256-257). Thornton also confirms this distribution. According to him, "The religion of Koonawar is Brahminism in the south, in the north Lamaic religion" (1854: 518). Even the District Gazetteer, Kinnaur 1971 has also reported the same type of distribution of religion (Mumgain 1971: 5). The Buddhist people normally belong to two sects, namely Nyingmapa and Dukpa. The number of the followers of Gelukpa sect is only a few. Gerard could also find Gelukpas only in a few villages (1845: 117). He further states that

> The Lamas in Koonawar are the three sects Geloopa, Dookpa and Neegma....The Geloopa or Gelookpas are reckoned the highest; since the head of their religion at Teshoo Loomboo and Lhassa are of the same sect. They wear yellow cloth garments and caps of same of various shapes. The Dookpas are dressed indifferently, but have red caps and the Neengmas wear same or go bare headed; the two former do not marry but there is no restriction on the Neengmas.... (1841: 117)

In Kinnaur also as in other Buddhist areas, the *monasties* or Gompha is the sacred temple of worship, prayer and meditation. Some of the monasteries also provide training to the trainee *Lamas* to become a full *Lama*. In all the monastaries metal idol of Lord Buddha and some of His saints like Sakya Muni, Padmasambhava, Avolokitesvara and others are found. On the roof as also on the wall paintings of all the incarnations of Lord Buddha are found. Some other deities like Nam-Chhra, Langan or Chhog-dak, Tarema or Chhering-ma, Paldan-Lamo, Ningmet-Cheebe and some others are also worshipped. Of the various saints Padma Sambhava has been given the highest place (Raha & Mahato 1985: 299-300). The Kinnaura who have embraced Buddhism, have great devotion towards these deities, saints and spirits. Many of the Kinnaura families send the middle or the youngest son to the monastery for becoming a *Lama*. Some of the daughters of the family who are not willing to lead a married life, become Zomo or chomo and join monastaries.

But gradually due to various external and/or internal forces, people have started showing some reluctance towards their religion. On the other hand, the Hinduism has spread its tentacles to the strongholds of Buddhism. A number of Hindu temples have been constructed by the side of the main road or near the villages dominated by Buddhism.

Buddhism in the Central Himalayas

In the Central Himalayas the Bhotia of Uttarkashi, Chamoli and Pithoragarh of Uttaranchal, are possibly the only group who profess Buddhism, of course not the pure form of Buddhism. The Bhotias of Uttaranchal though have some similarities with the people of Bhutan, still they most probably, do not belong to the same ethnic group. The

Bhotias of Uttaranchal are no doubt, Mongolian still there is some doubt about their Tibetan origin. The Bhotias here of course, claim their relation only with the Kshatriya people (Prasad 1989: 38). But both Wedder (1902) and Spate (1964) think of their Tibetan origin. According to Sherring (1906), "The Bhotias are of Tibetan origin, though they themselves have still current among them the belief that they were originally Hindus." But Walton (1921) has his view that the Bhotias are not identical with the Tibetans though their features are similar to the Tibetans.

Whatever may be their origin, "The religious life of the Bhotias has been a peculiar blend of Lamaistic Buddhism, Hinduism and Animism" (Prasad *ibid*: 100). During their trade with Tibet the Bhotias often came in contact with the Tibetan *Lamas* and were greatly influenced by them. Thereafter, they started to accept Tibetan *Lamas* as their priests. They also worship some Tibetan deities like Laandey, Manhfaila etc. and also offer *Sattu* (powder of grain) to the Tibetan deities like the Tibetans. It is thus seen that the present day Bhotias show traces of Buddhism, particularly the Tibetan type.

Buddhism in the Eastern Himalayas

The Eastern Himalayas which cover eight states of North-East India, Bhutan and Nepal, are the home of a large number of ethnic groups with varied cultures. In North-East India people are the believers of Shaivism, Vaishnavism, Shaktism, Jainism, Buddhism, Tantricism, and tribal religion.

> Among the religious culture of North East India, Buddhism has played a unique role, which is well reflected in nicely decorated Buddhist monasteries, stupas, other Buddhist minor structures, traditional arts and crafts, rituals, festivals and dances. In many pockets of the region, Buddhism is still a living religion (Dutta & Tripathy 2006: 16).

Normally, both Theravada and Mahayana Buddhism are found to be present among the Buddhist groups. Some of the tribes in North-East India practicing Mahayana Buddhism, are the Sherpas and Bhotias of Sikkim, Monpas, Singpos, Tikhak Tangsas of Arunachal Pradesh, the Tai-Phakes, Tai-Khamyang, Tai-Ahom, Tai-Turung, Dowaniyas, Singpos and also a few Shans and Mans of Assam, the Chakmas and Mags of Tripura. The Khamtis of Arunachal Pradesh and the Chakmas settled in Mizoram and in the district of Tirap and Lohit in Arunachal Pradesh are also the believers of Theravada Buddhism.

Buddhism entered Assam from the Gangetic valley sometimes in pre-Christian era. But this religion had its influence only in Assam. In a much later period, during early medieval period, the Buddhist missionaries brought Mahayana Buddhism in Sikkim and northern and western frontier of Arunachal Pradesh from Tibet. Thereafter, a number of Buddhist tribes migrated from Burma to the border of Assam and Arunachal Pradesh. That Buddhism was spread in different areas of North-East India, is proved by the presence of the remains of Buddhism. According to Mr. C.C. Singpho Buddhism became popular in Assam from the early historical period. Even the Tai people who migrated to Assam also "contributed to the growth of Buddhism in Assam and Arunachal Pradesh" (2006: 20-21). Mr. Singpho has also mentioned that in Arunachal Pradesh "Buddhism is a living religion". Here both Theravada and Mahayana Buddhism are embraced by different tribes. According to him the Khamtis, Singphos and the Tikhak sub-tribes of the Tangsa profess Theravada Buddhism while the Monpas, Sherdukpens, Membas, Khambas, Meyor and the Zakhring practice Mahayana Buddhism (2006: 21), "Buddhism is a living force in Arunachal Pradesh and is playing a very important role in the flourishing of Arunachal culture" (*ibid*: 21-22).

According to Tikhak though the Sherdukpens and the Monpas of Dirang and Tawang areas are practicing Buddhism for more than a thousand years, still "Buddhism in North-East India is not native to the land" (2006: 25). When Buddhism was spread in China, Thailand, Burma, Indonesia, Java, Borneo and even to Korea, it somehow missed North-East India." "The Tai-Khamti people were the first to bring Buddhism" in the Brahmuputra valley region. During the Burmese invasion in 18th Century, many Buddhist monks brought Buddhism to Assam. With them came Buddhist tribes like the Pkake, Shyam and other Buddhist people. Later on the British drove away Burmese still many Buddhist people remained in Assam. Later Buddhism entered Mizoram and Nagaland.

Buddhism in Arunachal Pradesh

In connection with Buddhism in Arunachal Pradesh Mr. C.C. Singpho opines that a good number of tribes of Arunachal Pradesh has adopted Buddhism, and among them both form of Buddhism, Theravada and Mahayana are present. Mr. Singpho has also mentioned about the Khamtis, Singphos and the Tikhak sub-tribe of the Tangsas as the Theravada

Buddhists and the Monpas, Sherdukpens, Membas, Meyor, Khambas and the Zakhrings as the Mahayana Buddhists. He further states that Buddhism is very popular among various tribes of Arunachal Pradesh and the imprint of Buddhism is clearly visible in their socio-cultural life. The monasteries, stupas, dances, festivals, arts and crafts etc. bear enough proof about how much these people have love, respect and devotion for this great religion (2006: 21). Though some changes are noticed in the practice of Buddhism among the Buddhist tribes of Arunachal Pradesh, yet Mr. Singpho still maintains thus, that "Buddhism is a living force in Arunachal Pradesh and is playing a very important role in Arunachali culture" (*ibid*: 22).

As already said in Arunachal Pradesh different communities practice Buddhism. The Khamtis of Lohit District are practicing Theravada Buddhism. In Khampti language they call their religion as *To-ni*. Their Buddhist priests *Chaw-mun*, have great influence over their society. These priests are also very much revered by the people. They train up young people who join the monastery leaving family life. Every Khampti village has a *vihara* which they call *Kyong* or *Chang*. Here on a high pedestal the images of Lord Buddha are kept. The scenes of *Jatakas*, *Vimanvathu* and *Petavathu* are painted inside the *Vihara*. The villagers have the responsibility to provide food to the *Bhikkhus* and *Samaneras*. Among these people as among other people, the Buddhist ceremonial cycle consists of a series of cycles.

> "For a pious Khamti, therefore, the first and last act of the day consist of devotions performed in front of a small shrine found in almost every Khamti household, and always on eastern side of the house above the head level which is considered auspicious (Kondinya 1987: 28)

Among the Khamti the water libation ceremony is the very important ceremony. It is the intrinsic part of all public ceremonies and public acts of meritorious giving (*ibid*: 32). Throughout the year the Buddhist Khamti perform several festivals. Some of the important festivals are Samkyen (New Year), Buddha Purnima (*Paya Puthikham*—the birthday of Lord Buddha), *Khaura* or *Vassavasa* (Buddhist Lent), *Kathina Civara* festival (Public offering of Yellow robe to the monk etc.). Pattnaik is also of the opinion that the Khamtis of Lohit district of Arunachal Pradesh profess Theravada (Teaching of Elders) Buddhism. While they came from the Borkhamti land of Upper Burma in the second half of the eighteenth Century, they brought along with them this form of Buddhism. Theravada belongs to the Hinayana (smaller vehicle) Buddhism (2006: 95). Pattnaik further mentions that the Khamtis believe in canonical literature of Buddhism (*Tripitaka)*. Every Khamti village has a *Vihara* known as *Kyong* or *Chang*, and every Khamti village has a *Bhikkhu* priest who carries out all religious functions of the village as well as of the individual. A number of Buddhist festivals are also observed according to lunar calendar. One of the important festivals is the Sankyen. Though there are changes in their culture those occurred during the present era, but they accepted the changes without sacrificing the core value of their Theravada Buddhism (Pattnaik 2006: 101-102).

The Tikhak, a sub-tribe of the Tangsas, are found to be distributed in Jairampur Nampong, Miao, Kharsang and Bordumsa circles of Changlang district of Arunachal Pradesh. They are also found to be present in different villages of Assam. During the last part of eighteenth Century the Tikhaks started embracing Theravada Buddhism. But before adopting Theravada Buddhism they used to practice their traditional religious faith, *Rang-Frahism* "which is very much identical to Hinduism and Buddhism of South-East Asian region" (Rao 2006: 37). But at present these people are following Theravada Buddhism. Due to non-availability of Buddhist monks, the Tikhak started reviving their traditional religion in nineteenth century. But again with the establishment of contact with the Buddhist monks, the Tikhak again regained their faith on Buddhism during the end of nineteenth century and beginning of twentieth century. Most probably the Tikhak are the first to bring Theravada Buddhism to India (*ibid*: 39). According to Ven. Tiringda Bhikkhu of Dibong village the Singphos became Buddhists due to their contact with the Buddhist and the Singphos in their turn converted the Tikhak into Buddhism (*ibid*: 40). The present day Buddhist Tikhak celebrate various Buddhist festivals like *Saken*, *Buddha Jayanti*, *Kando Poi*, *Changlu Poi*, *Frah-Lu-Poi*, *Wakhai Poi*, *Hikhu Chat* etc. (*ibid*: 43).

Buddhism has marked impact on the life of the Tikhak. This religion has helped the Tikhak in improving their "quality of life, health, hygiene, and sanitation. These people stopped killing of animals, and consumption of alcohol, opium and meat has been reduced" (*ibid*: 45).

The growth of Theravada Buddhism among the Tikhak has also helped some members of other Tangsa sub-tribes to adopt Buddhism. Some of the Ronrang Tangsas and also the Longri and the Mossang Tangsas became Buddhists.

The Singphos of Changlong district of Arunachal Pradesh are also Buddhists. They also profess Theravada Buddhism. They embraced Buddhism only after the visit of Rev. Pien Duin Chow Chrado of Burmah in 1882 in the Singpho areas (Showren 2006: 104). As they live surrounded by the Khamtis a marked influence of the Khamtis is seen on their socio-cultural life. In the same way the impact of the Khamti Buddhism is also seen on the Singpho religion. Rev. Chrado also introduced a number of Buddhist festivals like *Sangken*, *Maiko*, *Chumphai*, *Poi-kathing* and *Poi-Kando* among the Singpho apart from ordinating many junior monks (*Chausang*). The Singphos also maintain a number of monastaries in their area (*ibid*: 105-111).

Both the Monpas and the Sherdukpens the two major tribes of Arunachal Pradesh who reside in the West Kamang district, claim that the Guru Padmasambhava first brought the message of Buddhism in their area sometimes in eighth Century A.D. (Dondrup 2006: 185). No doubt according to "Darjee Buddhism has an overarching influence on almost all aspects of the Monpa society. This is reflected in the Monpa way of life" (2006: 195). The Monpas provide all necessary logistic and provisions to the monks of different monasteries, particularly the Tawang monastery. These selfless activities of the Monpas help the monks to perform their religious duties perfectly. On the other hand, the monastery helps the Monpas to have their much needed spiritual refuge. The socio-economic activities of the Monpas are fixed in accordance with the activities of the Tawang monastery (*ibid*: 203). Dutta and Duarah also think that Buddhist monks play significant role in almost every sphere of the socio-cultural life of the Monpas (2006: 212). They are also expert in wood-curving, mask making, scroll or *Thangka* printing, carpet making etc. In many of these the imprints of Buddhism is seen. The statue of Lord Buddha is a common item in wood-curving (*ibid*).

According to Dey "both the Monpas and Sherdukpens are the followers of Mahayana Buddhism. Besides supplying different items of arts and crafts to the monasteries, both tribes are expert in dramatic performing in the form of pantomimes associated with the Buddhist heritage. These types of performances can be seen during different festivals" (2006: 223-205).

The Membas of West Siang and Upper Siang districts of Arunachal Pradesh, profess Mahayana Buddhism. In the course of their migration from Tibet about 300 years ago, two renowned *lamas* led them to Arunachal Pradesh, while one section of them settled at Mechuka in West Siang, the other at Tuting in Upper Siang (Dutta 2006: 204). The Membas follow Vajrayana, which is the Tantrik form of Mahayana Buddhism. The Membas who also believe in supernatural beings, are taught Buddhism by the monk (*Lama*). They regularly worship Buddha for prosperity and good health. They pray to Lord Buddha before they set for journey for safety. Before starting any work they also pray to Lord Buddha. When there is no work they recite "*Om Manu Padme Hum*". They also invite monks in their house for performing rites and rituals. They have constructed *Mane* at villages, and for such construction they take advice and guidance of the *Lamas* and also hoist prayer flags on sacred places and in their houses too.

Buddhism in Mizoram

In Mizoram the only group who practice Buddhism is the Chakmas—otherwise the Mizos of Mizoram in general are Christians. The Chakmas have embraced Hinayana Buddhism though it is blended with local religious faith. They also celebrate some Buddhist festivals along with some non-Buddhist festivals also. The Buddhist festivals are the *Buddha Purnima, Kathin Chibar Dhana, Ashari Purnima, Bahu Chakma* etc. The Buddhist monks preside over the festivals (Laskar 2006: 74-76).

Buddhism in Tripura

In Tripura the Chakmas who entered here in 1840 A.D. and settled, believe in the Theravada Buddhism. But earlier before they accepted the Theravada Buddhism they used to practice Mahayana Buddhism (Poddar 2006: 65-70).

Buddhism in Bhutan

Buddhism is the state religion of Bhutan. Most of the people practice Buddhism and are followers of Mahayana Buddhism. This religion of Bhutan has its origin in Tibet, but the present day Mahayana Buddhism of Bhutan differ significantly from the Tibetan Mahayana Buddhism in its rituals, liturgy and monastic organization. There are a large number of the monasteries in this Himalayan country. There is a Central Monastic Body which has about 1000 monks (*Lama* or *Gelong*, i.e. novices). This Central Monastic Body is situated in Thimpu and also in Punakha. Besides there are a large number of monks in the district monastic bodies. Each of these bodies is headed by *Je Khenpo*. He is assisted by five *Lopons* or masters. Each of the *Lopons* is in charge of religious tradition, liturgy, lexicography or logic and university. The junior monks or monastic officials remain in charge of art, music and other areas. In late 80s were about 12,000 monks in Bhutan. There are also a large number of nuns in Bhutan. These monks and nuns belong to both Gelugpa as well as Nyingmapa sects. That means while some of them belong to the Gelugpa sect, the others come under Nyingmapa sect, the majority of the Buddhists of Bhutan are the followers of Drukpa section of Kargyupa School, one of the four major schools of Buddhism of Tibet. In order to preserve the indigenous teachings of Lord Buddha as their traditional culture, the Supreme Dharma King or His Holiness of Bhutan has formed a non-profit organization in Bhutan named *Menjong Chothun Tshogpa* in 2002. Again in 2004 another organization, *Buddha Dordenma* Foundation under the partnership of His Holiness of Bhutan with an aim to fulfil a prophecy of Guru Padmasambhava "to bestow blessings on world peace and glorious happiness". (*Source:* internet)

Bhutan has a large number of monasteries and convents where a large number of monks and nuns stay. Their daily activities include study of religious books meditations, performing rituals honouring various *Bodhisattvas*, praying for the wellbeing of the dead persons, prayers for the cure of the people suffering from illness etc. Their songs and chants are often accompanied by instrumental music. In addition to the monasteries, there are numerous symbols and structures found in different places of Bhutan. These are constructed to bring the religion close to the people. The monks also visit villages in order to propagate Buddhism among the common people and to keep their faith on this religion unshakable.

In Bhutan as mentioned by Rustomji, Guru Padmasambhava is considered as the patron saint of Bhutan. There are several monasteries (1971: 176-177). Here four *Lopons* (Abbots) are considered as important office bearers but the *Jekhenpo* is the most important one. The Dharma Raja or *Shabdrung* is the Supreme Head "whose primary responsibility was to ensure that the role and discipline of the monasteries were strictly maintained" (1971: 185:186). The more important monasteries are exclusively for the males, the females are strictly forbidden to enter and stay in these residential monasteries.

Buddhism in Nepal

Siddhartha Gautama who later on became Lord Buddha, was born in Kapilavastu, a historic town about 250 kms from Kathmandu in Nepal in sixth century B.C. So, it may be correctly said that Buddhism started from Nepal. At present about 26 per cent of the population of Nepal are

Buddhists. Three sects of Buddhism, namely Theravada, Mahayana and Vajrayana, are dominant in Nepal. In Northern Nepal the Tibetan Mahayana Buddhism is dominant and there are about 3000 monasteries of this sect. In Kathmandu valley Vajrayana is important one. The Theravada sect has lesser number of followers and is found in different pockets. In Nepal ancient stupas like Swayambhu and Bodhnath or Bouddhanatha are regarded as the most important ones.

During fourth and fifth century A.D. Indian Buddhism entered Nepal, but its influence is mostly seen in Kathmandu valley and also in the western part of Nepal. In Nepal Buddhism shows a clear marks of Hinduism. The important sites of Buddhism in Nepal are Kapilavastu, Lumbini, Svayambhunatha, Bouddhanatha etc.

In Nepal both Buddhism and Hinduism are influenced by the belief and practices of Tantrism. "Tantrism is a religion of moral percepts, meditation, yoga, mantras and a philosophy that believes in interwovenness of all things" (*Source: internet*).

In Nepal it is also believed that Buddhism were brought by the Tibetans *Lamas* and also different Buddhist groups who came to Nepal from Tibet. These *Lamas* and Buddhist groups were responsible in spreading and preaching Buddhism in Nepal and also establishing monasteries and *stupas* in different places of Nepal though in Nepal Hinduism always predominant. In connection with the historical development of Buddhism in Khumbu and Solu in Nepal Fürer-Haimendorf views that it is a problem "intimately linked with the age of Sherpa civilization in its present form". The monastic institutions here are not "older than a hundred years and the two most prominent monasteries, Tengboche and Chiwong were founded less than fifty years ago" (1964: 126-127). The Sherpas of Khumbu and the neighbouring areas associate themselves with the "Legendary figures of *Lama* Sanga Dorje, the sixth incarnation of Changna Dorje" (*Vajra Pani*).

Lama Sanga Dorje was born in Mohang a place situated in between Khumjung and Phortse, according to the local tradition. He was the son of the great *Lama*, Bundachendzen. Bundachendzen was a Sherpa by origin and belonged to the Salaka clan. It was also believed that the great country god, Khumbu-yulha used to visit *Lama* Bundachendzen regularly in the monastery at Mohang. It thus appears that though *Lama* Sanga Dorje was considered as the founder of the monastery (*Gompha*) at Khumbu, he was not the first great *Lama* of this area. There is a legend present among the Sherpas of Khumbu and the neighbouring areas is that

While his father Bundachendzen was able to converse in person with the great country god Khumbu-yulha, *Lama* Sanga Dorje had the power to fly through the air and perform other magical feats (*ibid*: 127).

The death of *Lama* Sanga Dorje was as miraculous as his life. After death his body got evaporated in the form of a rainbow. His eyes, tongue and heart were not evaporated. These were enshrined in a silver casket and preserved (*ibid*: 128).

Though Fürer-Haimendorf thinks that the monastery at Khumbu was established around the earlier part of the twentieth century, but Snellgrove believes that "Buddhism was introduced into Khumbu towards the end of seventeenth century" (1957: 213).

Again *Lama* Sanga Dorje was not reincarnated at Khumbu or its neighbouring areas. But he was reincarnated in Tibet. So after waiting for his reincarnation for three years, when it was found that *Lama* Sanga Dorje was not reincarnated, then another *Lama*, a married person, established him at Pangooche (Fürer-Haimendorf 1964: 129).

The Sherpas of Khumbu and other areas consider *Lama* Sanga Dorje as the founder and patron of their religious institutions. They believe that "the foundation of *gomba* occurred some four hundred years ago" (*ibid*). The Sherpas and other inhabitants from Khumbu and other areas visit *gombas* on different occasions in order to get the blessings of the reincarnated *Lama* or for performing some sacred rites and rituals.

During the first half of twentieth century a number of monastic institution was started in and around Khumbu and Solu and neighbouring areas, and this had given a fairly good opportunity and passage for the lays and commoners to get teachings and surmons from the incarnates, and *Lamas* on their turn, were able to disseminate their knowledge to the formers.

Buddhist in West Bengal and Darjeeling District

In West Bengal as well as in Sikkim the Sherpa practise Buddhism. In Nepal the Sherpas are also Buddhists. So, Buddhism is possibly the only religion the Sherpas of these three areas have embraced.

In West Bengal according to 2001 Census the people accepted different religions. Here in this State overwhelming majority (72.28%) embraced Hinduism. The Muslims had the next higher strength (25.14%). The rest of the religions like Christianity, Sikhism, Buddhism, Jainism and other religions had each less than 1 per cent followers. Here in West Bengal the number of the Buddhists were only 303, 212 forming 0.38 per cent of the total population (80,176,197) of this State. In the rural areas they were only 0.36 per cent of the total rural population of West Bengal (57,748,946), and in the urban centres they formed 0.42 per cent of the total urban population of West Bengal (22,427,251) (Bhatt & Bhargava 2005:47-48). Among the Buddhists of West Bengal 50.06 per cent were males and 48.94 per cent females. In the rural areas the strength of the male Buddhists was 50.68 per cent and the females 49.32 per cent, and in the urban centres of West Bengal the Buddhist males numbered 51.90 per cent and the females 48.10 per cent.

Again out of the total Buddhists (303,312) of West Bengal 209,038 (68.92%) were the inhabitants of the rural areas and 94,274 (31.08%) dwell in the urban centres. Among the Buddhist males 105,940 (68.41%) out of a total of 154,866 were living in the rural areas. The remaining 48,926 (31.59%) of the total Buddhist males were the residents of the urban sector. Similarly, out of a total of 148,446 Buddhist females of West Bengal 103,098 (69.45%) had their residence in the rural areas and the rest of 45,348 (30.55%) were urban dwellers. This clearly indicates that in West Bengal the Buddhists once had numerically a very low key position and that majority of them lived in the rural areas. Only some of them preferred urban centres as their place of residence.

In Darjeeling the Sherpas practise Buddhism. According to 2001 Census in Darjeeling district, while overwhelming majority (76.74%) in the total population, were the Hindus, only 10.96 per cent were the Buddhists. Among the other religious groups the Muslims covered only 5.29 per cent of the total population of the district, and the Christians 6.26 per cent. The other religious groups like the Sikhs, Jains and others had less than 1 per cent population each (Bhatt and Bhargava 2005: 48-49).

In the District of Darjeeling the Bhotia who include (the Tibetan, Kagete, Yolmo and the Toto) are mostly Buddhists. At the same time the Lepcha also practise Buddhism.

In this district according to 2001 Census a total of 176,413 people out of a total population of 1,609,172, had embraced Buddhism. Of these Buddhist population 88,679 (50 27%) were males and 87,734 (49.73%) were females. In the rural areas of Darjeeling district, 1,29,179 (11.86%) out of a total of 1,088,740 population of the district were the Buddhists. Again out of this rural Buddhist population 64,938 (50.27%) were males and 64,241 (49.73%) females. In the urban centres 520,432 souls live. Out of these urban population 47,234 (9.08%) had accepted Buddhism as their religion. Again out of these urban Buddhist population of 47,234, 23,741 (50.26%) were males and 23,493 (49.74%) females. Further, out of a total Buddhist population 73.23 per cent lived in the rural areas and the remaining 26.77 per cent in the urban centres. Similarly, out of a total Buddhist males 73.23 per cent resided in the rural areas and 26.77 per cent in the urban sector. Same is the case with the Buddhist females. 73.22 per cent of the Buddhist females are the residents of rural and 26.78 per cent of the urban centres of Darjeeling District (*ibid*).

Table 10.2: Religion-wise Distribution of Population in West Bengal, Census 2001

Religion	*T/R/U*	*Persons*	*Males*	*Females*	*%age*
Total population	Total	80,176,197	41,465,985	38,710,212	100.00
	Rural	57,748,946	29,616,009	28,132,937	100.00
	Urban	22,427,251	11,849,976	10,577,275	100.00
Hindu	Total	57,954,741	29,988,783	27,965,958	72.28
	Rural	39,338,079	20,197,243	19,140,836	68.12
	Urban	18,616,662	9,791,540	8,825,122	83.01
Muslim	Total	20,154,199	10,424,076	9,730,123	25.14
	Rural	16,780,035	8,594,154	8,185,881	29.06
	Urban	3,374,164	1,829,922	1,544,242	15.04
Christian	Total	577,961	290,912	287,049	0.72
	Rural	435,415	219,287	216,128	0.75
	Urban	142,546	71,625	70,921	0.64
Sikh	Total	169,671	92,753	76,918	0.21
	Rural	59,013	32,006	27,007	0.10
	Urban	110,658	60,747	49,911	0.49
Buddhist	Total	303,312	154,866	148,446	0.38
	Rural	209,038	105,940	103,098	0.36
	Urban	94,274	48,926	45,348	0.42
Jain	Total	68,388	35,559	32,829	0.09
	Rural	17,618	9,161	8,457	0.03
	Urban	50,770	26,398	24,372	0.23
Other Religions	Total	893,812	450,297	443,515	1.11
	Rural	873,434	439,510	433,924	1.51
	Urban	20,378	10,787	9,591	0.09
Religion Not Stated	Total	54,113	28,739	25,374	0.07
	Rural	36,314	18,708	17,606	0.06
	Urban	17,799	10,031	7,768	0.08

Source: Census of India, West Bengal.

In Darjeeling district as already said, 176,413, Buddhists lived according to 2001 Census. They formed 58.16 per cent of the total

Buddhist population of West Bengal. The total Buddhist male population of this district (88,679) had 57.26 per cent share in the total Buddhist male population of West Bengal. Similarly, the total Buddhist female population of Darjeeling (87,734) formed 59.10 per cent of the total Buddhist females of West Bengal. In the rural areas of West Bengal as already said, 129,179 Buddhists lived and they had a share of 61.80 per cent in the total Buddhist population living in the rural areas of West Bengal. The rural male and female Buddhists of Darjeeling covered 61.30 per cent and 62.31 per cent of the total rural Buddhist male and female population respectively of West Bengal. In the same way, the Buddhists inhabiting the urban centres of Darjeeling (47,234) had grabbed 50.10 per cent of the total urban Buddhists of West Bengal. The male and female Buddhists settled in urban areas of Darjeeling had taken 48.52 per cent and 51.81 per cent of the total male and female Buddhists of the urban areas of West Bengal.

The above discussion gives us some ideas about the numerical position of the Buddhist in West Bengal and Darjeeling district.

Buddhism in Darjeeling

O'Malley in his Gazetteer of Darjeeling has given a very brief account on the Buddhism prevalent there. This account gives us some idea about Buddhism over a century ago.

> The craving for protection against malignant gods and demons causes the people to pin their faith on charms and amulets, and to erect tall prayer flags, with strings of flag lets, which flatter from house-tops, bridges, passes and other places believed to be infested by evil spirits (1985: 49).

Here in Darjeeling the Buddhist people were often found to pray for "imploring them for freedom or release" from the cruel inflictions of the malevolent demons. They also prayed for the good things of this life". During the spare times they used to rotate their prayer-wheels and count beads uttering the mystic "*Om mani padme hum* (Om! The jewel in the Lotus, Hum)".

In connection with Buddhism in Darjeeling district, the Gazetteer of Darjeeling, 1907 writes,

> "The form of Buddhism prevalent is not a much higher type.... Prayers hang from the people's lips. The prayers are chiefly directed to the devils, imploring them for freedom or release from their inflictions or they are plain naïve request for aid towards obtaining the good things of this life, the leaves and fishes. At all spare times day and night the people ply their prayer wheels, tell their beads and mutter the mystic syllables—*Om Mani Padma Hum—Om* the jewel in the lotus, *Hum*—the sentence which gains from their great goal, the glorious heaven of eternal bliss...

In Darjeeling there are a number of Buddhist monasteries which are the sacred places for worship, prayer and meditation. All Buddhists including the Sherpas go to their respective monasteries for worship, prayer and/or meditation. A number of festivals are held in different months, and in these festivals the Buddhist people including the Sherpas attend with great devotion and joy. These monasteries are:

1. Dali Monastery

The Dali monastery or Druk Thubten Sangag Choling was founded by Kyabje Thuksey Rimpoche. The main objective of this monastery is to safeguard the Buddhist religion and Tibetan culture. His Holiness Dalai *Lama* gave religious preaching for three days during the inauguration of the new building of the monastery in 1993.

2. Bhutia Bustee Monastery

This monastery belongs to the Red sect of the Buddhist *Lamas*. This monastery was reconstructed again after it was destroyed by the earthquake in 1934.

3. Guru Shakya Monastery

It is a very old and very important monastery of the Shakya Order located at Ghoom. It was built around 1915.

4. Yiga-Choling Buddhist Monastry

This monastery is also situated at Ghoom. It is for the Yellow Sect Buddhists. It was built in 1975 by *Lama* Sherab Gyantso.

5. Makdhog Monastery

This monastery was constructed during World War-I. So, it was named as Makdhog meaning 'warding off war'. The main aim of this monastery is to safeguard the distinct social, cultural and ethnic identity of the Yolmowa community. This Yolmowa community is probably a native of north-eastern India who later settled in Darjeeling. It is built by Sangay Lama, the great religious leader of the Yolmowa sect.

Buddhists in Sikkim and South District

In Sikkim the Sherpas and all other groups under the Bhutias, practise Buddhism. Here the Lepcha are also Buddhists. But in Sikkim besides these Buddhist groups some other religions are also practised by different other groups.

In the State of Sikkim there were a total population of 540,851 according to 2001 Census. The Hindus covered 60.89 per cent of this total population while the Buddhists secured 28.07 per cent of the total population. Here in this state the Christian had a population of 6.69 per cent and the Muslim only 1.45 per cent of the total population. The other religious groups had less than 1 per cent of the total population each. In this State 28.78 per cent of the total rural population were the Buddhists and 22.41 per cent of the total urban population embraced Buddhism. Again out of the total Buddhists of this State (151,825) those inhabiting rural areas were 91.16 per cent and those residing in urban centres were 8.84 per cent. Again out of the total Buddhist males of this State 91.27 per cent lived in the rural areas and 8.73 per cent in the urban centres. Similarly, in case of the Buddhist females 91.05 per cent were the residents of the rural areas and the remaining 8.95 per cent were urban dwellers. Here, it may be mentioned that in Sikkim as also in South District the Bhutias and the Lepchas are the Buddhists.

Again the total Buddhist male population of this Himalayan State formed 27.06 per cent of the total male population and the total Buddhist female population covered 29.22 per cent of the total female population of this State. Similarly, the total male Buddhist population inhabiting rural areas and total female Buddhist population of the same areas held 27.86 per cent and 29.82 per cent of the total rural male and female population respectively of the State. In a similar way, the male and female Buddhist population of this hilly State inhabiting urban centres, secured

20.83 per cent and 24.31 per cent of the total male and female urban population of the State according to 2001 Census.

Table 10.3: Religion-wise Distribution of Population of Sikkim, Census 2001

Religion	*T/R/U*	*Persons*	*Males*	*Females*	*%age*
Total population	Total	540,851	288,484	252,367	100.00
	Rural	480,981	255,774	225,207	100.00
	Urban	59,870	32,710	27,160	100.00
Hindu	Total	329,323	177,762	151,561	60.89
	Rural	290,172	156,072	134,100	60.33
	Urban	39,151	21,690	17,461	65.39
Muslim	Total	7,860	5,450	2,410	1.45
	Rural	5,075	3,493	1,582	1.06
	Urban	2,785	1,957	828	4.65
Christian	Total	36,188	18,467	17,721	6.69
	Rural	32,268	16,527	15,741	6.71
	Urban	3,920	1,940	1,980	6.55
Sikh	Total	1,307	1,136	171	0.24
	Rural	1,198	1,074	124	0.25
	Urban	109	62	47	0.18
Buddhist	Total	151,825	78,071	73,754	28.07
	Rural	138,410	71,259	67,151	28.78
	Urban	13,415	6,812	6,603	22.41
Jain	Total	266	158	108	0.05
	Rural	116	73	43	0.02
	Urban	150	85	65	0.25
Other Religions	Total	12,913	6,511	6,402	2.39
	Rural	12,655	6,389	6,266	2.63
	Urban	258	122	136	0.43
Religion Not Stated	Total	1,169	929	240	0.22
	Rural	1,087	887	200	0.23
	Urban	82	42	40	0.14

Source: Census of India, 2001, Bhatt & Bhargava 2005: 42-43.

In the South district of Sikkim the numerical distribution of various religious groups runs unevenly. Here out of a total population of 1,31,525 the majority (63.95%) were grabbed by the Hindus. The next numerical higher position was held by the Buddhists who secured 23.59 per cent of the total population of the district. The Christians have held the third position by securing 9.74 per cent of the total population of this district and the Muslims had only 1.35 per cent. All other religious groups had less than 1 per cent of the total population of this district each (Bhatt & Bhargava 2005: 42-43).

In the South district according to 2001 Census, 31,033 persons embraced Buddhism. Of these Buddhist population 15,846 (51.06%) were males and 15,187 (48.94%) females. Again out of the total Buddhist population of this district the overwhelming majority (98.40%) lived in the rural areas and only a very negligible few (496 or 1.60%) took shelter in the urban centres. Further, among the Buddhist males almost all (98.46%) lived in the rural areas excepting a very few (244 or 1.54%) who had been left in the urban centres. The same is the case with the Buddhist females. Among them also almost all (98.34%) were the settlers of the rural areas except a few (1.66%) who were town dwellers. Again these Buddhist inhabitants of the rural areas of the South district formed 23.94 per cent of the total population of this district inhabiting rural areas. On the other hand, the urban Buddhists shared in the total urban population of the district is only 12.57 per cent.

In this connection we like to add further that the total Buddhists of South District formed 20.44 per cent of the total Buddhists of Sikkim and only 5.74 per cent of the total population of the State. Similarly, the total rural Buddhists of South District were 22.06 per cent of the total rural Buddhists of the State. The urban Buddhists of South District had a share of 3.70 per cent of the total urban Buddhists of the State of Sikkim. The total Buddhist males of South district formed 20.30 per cent of the total Buddhist males of the State. The rural male Buddhists of this South district covered only 21.89 per cent of the total male Buddhists of the rural area of the State. The urban Buddhists of South District formed only 3.58 per cent of the total urban Buddhists of the State. As we come down to the Buddhist females, we see that the female Buddhists of South District had a share of only 20.59 per cent of the total Buddhists females of the State. In the same way the female Buddhists of the rural areas of South District constituted 22.24 per cent of the total female Buddhists inhabiting rural areas of Sikkim. The urban dwelling Buddhist females of South district formed 3.82 per cent of the total Buddhist female living in the various urban centres of Sikkim. Further, we like to add that the Buddhist population of South District formed 23.59 per cent of the total population of this district. The total Buddhist male and female population held 23.22 per cent and 24.00 per cent of the total male and female population of this district respectively. Similarly, the Buddhists living in the rural areas of South district had a share of 23.94 per cent of the total rural population of the district. In the same way the Buddhist males and females living in the rural areas of this district secured 23.61 per cent and 24.29 per cent of the total male and female population of this district respectively. In South district there are only 496 Buddhists live in the urban centres. They constituted 12.57 per cent of the total urban population of this district. The Buddhist males and females living in the urban areas of this district kept in their fold 11.38 per cent and 13.99 per cent of the total male and female populations of this district respectively.

From the above discussion we get some idea about the numerical position of the people embracing Buddhism in Sikkim and South district.

Buddhism in Sikkim

In Sikkim Buddhism first entered in the eighth century A.D. Guru Rimpoche, that is, Padmasambhava actually helped in introducing and the nourishing Buddhism in this hilly State. In fact Padmasambhava "personally consecrated many of Sikkim's sacred land marks, and blessed Drakar Tashiding as the land of spiritual centre" (Subba 2008:145). The legend tells us that Guru Padmasambhava followed the "Lordly Pass" Jo-La to go to Sikkim and came back to Tibet through Je-Lep Pass. While resting en-route on the Ku-phu, he killed a fearful demon by 'tearing' up the rock. In course of time, it is believed that Guru Rimpoche along with his twenty-five disciples 'visited and blessed' this hilly land which was then known as 'Beyul Demojong' or 'the hidden fruitful valley'. The first thing that Guru Rimpoche and his disciples did was to tame all the malevolent beings, spirits and forces reigning this land. As the land became free from the hostility of the evil spirits and forces, they selected certain areas of Sikkim for monasteries and *stupas*. Thereafter, he (Guru Rimpoche) transformed all these malevolent spirits into guardian deities and brought them under Dzonga. The Supreme Guardian deity of Sikkim resided on the Kanchenjunga (*ibid*: 145). Sikkim is the place where Padmasambhava "is believed to have scripted his nine texts of "unerring prophesies". Guru Rimpoche on his return journey to Urgyen, also hid religious texts known as *Ters* at various places around Sikkim, and locked the doors to this Hidden Land" (*ibid*). Sikkim was then designated as the Hidden Land.

> These *Ters* were to be discovered later by *Tertons* during different times, each discovery reinforcing Sikkim's status as the most sacred of all hidden lands and celebrating Kanchenjunga as the most supreme of all Guardian Deities (Subba 2008: 145).

According to Kumar Lhatsun Chenpo (meaning "The Great Reverend God") a resident of Kongbo in the lower valley of the Tsangpo, is believed to have introduced Buddhism in Sikkim. His religious name was *Kun-Zong name-gye* (in Sanskrit it is Samantabhadra). He was also popular by the name *Lhatsun nam-kha-Jig-med* (in Sanskrit it is Abhijnakasadeva). It was believed that he had the power to fly. He was sometimes called by the name *Ksuho Dzog-chen chhenpo* (in Sanskrit Mahayogakshema) (*Source: Internet*).

Lhatsun Chenpo built up a number of monasteries and shrines in Sikkim in order to propagate Buddhism; Dub-de the oldest monastery of Sikkim was built by him. The monasteries such as Tashidong, Pemayangtse, Sang-nga-cho-ling etc. which were consecrated by Guru Rimpoche, ultimately became the nucleus of all the monasteries.

> "During this time the Bhutias of Sikkim had basically two faiths: the first lot, some of the early migrant Bhutias were followers of Bon religious belief system (*Bonpas*), and were not much influenced by Mahayana Buddhism as yet, while the second lot of people were the followers of Niyangmapa sect (Red Hat sect) of Mahayana Buddhism" (*ibid*: 146).

It is true that as early as eighth century A.D. Buddhism entered Sikkim. As Bhutias were minority then. So, Buddhism was established slowly. The Niyangmapa sect of Mahayana Buddhism spread in Sikkim only during Thirteenth Century. "The seventeenth Century was the turning point in the history of Sikkim" (*ibid*). During the last quarter of Thirteenth Century Shangpodar, Tsechudar, Nima Gyalpo and Guru Tashi who were grandsons of Khe-Bumsa and collectively known as *Tongduruzi* settled down in the present day Sikkim. Guru Tashi became very prominent figure and got the status of a prince.

Then during fourteenth century Rigzin Godemchen came and settled in Sikkim and opened a number of monasteries and meditation centres at Simon or Zilson near Tashiding. No doubt, that Buddhism had its entry in Sikkim as early as eighth century A.D., but in fact the Nyingmapa sect of Mahayana Buddhism could get settled here only during fourteenth century A.D. or so. But "the seventeenth century was a turning point in the history of Sikkim" (*ibid*: 146).

Phuntso Namgyul, the great grandson of Guru Tashi became the first Maharaja of Sikkim. He was enthroned in 1642 at Yoksom. "Under the patronage of the Chogyal, the monasteries, hermitages and stupas were build, and Buddhism was proclaimed as the State religion" (*ibid*:147). Later on a large number of monasteries were established to spread the religion. By 1884 a number of monasteries were constructed in Sikkim for the promotion of Nyingmapa, Sakyapa and Kagyukpa sects of Mahayana Buddhism.

> By 2006, there were 81 monasteries established and recognized by the Government of Sikkim for Nyingmapa, Sakyapa and Kagyukpa sects (Red Hat Sect) of Buddhist worship and learning centres in Sikkim. ...(*ibid*: 147).

The Buddhists of Sikkim keep faith on the different Mahayana sects like Nyingmapa, Sakyapa and Kargyupa. "However, the latter entrants from Tibet (China) to Sikkim are the believers of Gelukpa sect (Yellow Hat Sect) of Mahayana Buddhism" (*ibid*).

At the end of the seventeenth century after the death of Lhahsun Chanpo, Buddhism continued to progress steadily. A large number of monasteries was also built. So, Sikkim became a land of monasteries. At present there are 67 monasteries in Sikkim. Over and above there are 132 Manilhakhong and 22 Lhakhang and Tsamkhang (hermitage or place of meditation). Out of these monasteries, Pemayangtse and Phensang belong to the Nyingmapa sect. the monasteries of Ralang, Rumtek and Phodang are of the Kargyudpa sect (*Source*: *Internet*).

Between 1840 and 1860 a large number of *gompas* was also constructed though the first *gompa* was built at Namchi in 1836.

Foning is also of the view that Buddhism was first introduced in Sikkim by the *Lama* Lhatsun Nangkha Jigma. He contacted Thekung Mensalong, the *bonthing* who was a local shamanistic priest. He started preaching a new type of Buddhism.

> "Lama Lhatsun had taken special care and pain to prepare a treatise for the mode of worship and offering for this newly innovated special act of faith, quite permissible within the ambit of the Mahayana type of Buddhism. This accomplishment of his in no small measure helped the fusion of the native Rongfolk and the Tibetans from Kham resulting in the evolution of a new tribe called the Denjongpas, just as envisaged by the patriarchs, Thekung Tek and Khye Bumsa, long, long ago" (1987: 184).

Buddhism in Sikkim has distinct characteristics quite different from those of the Tibetan Buddhism, though in Sikkim Buddhism has retained the basic principles of Mahayana sect. But among the Lepchas of Sikkim traces of Bon religion was present during the pre-Buddhist period.

The Buddhists of Sikkim who also include the Sherpas, celebrate different festivals during different periods of the year. These festivals not only give them scope to express their faith towards their religion, but at the same time, take them away from the monotony of their day-to-day life and give them boundless joy, life element and recreation. These festivals are held on the time when they get scope to dance and sing and also display their arts and crafts (musks, dress, ornaments, musical instruments etc. specially made for this purpose). Some of important festivals of the Buddhists of Sikkim are (*Source: Internet*).

Saga Dawa

This is the Triple Blessed festival which is considered as the holiest of the holy Buddhist festivals. Lord Buddha was born, achieved Enlightenment and passed away after *Nirvana* on this day in different years of his life. This festival is celebrated on the full moon day of the fourth month of Buddhist luner calendar (May-June).

Lhabab Dhuechen

Lord Buddha descended from the heaven of the thirty three gods after visiting his mother (*Lha* = Heaven; *Bab* = descent; *Dhuechen* = festival). To mark this Lhabab Dhuechen festival is celebrated.

Losar

Losar is celebrated to mark the Tibetan New Year with great pomp and grandeur by the Sikkimese Buddhists along with the Tibetans during the month of February. The yak dance by the Tibetan youths is the most interesting feature of this festival. Among the Tibetans this festival continues for a weak.

Bumchu

This festival is celebrated in the Tashiding monastery in the month of January or February. The main feature of this festival is the opening of the sealed pot containing Holy Water (*Bum* = pot; *Chu* = water). The level of the water in the pot indicates the rate of prosperity of the coming year. A part of this Holy Water is distributed during the festivity among the devotees and the pot is again filled up with river or spring water. At the end of the festival the pot is sealed again and kept in the monastery for the *Bumchu* festival of the next year.

Guru Rimpoche's Trungkar Tshechu

The Buddhists of Sikkim including the Sherpas pay their homage to Guru Rimpoche on this day as Guru Rimpoche first blessed Sikkim as the holy land. He is responsible for providing a firm base for Buddhism in Sikkim where he introduced his own form of Tantric Buddhism. This festival marks his victory over the vanquishing demons who stood against the establishment and development of *Dharma*.

Drukpa Tsheshi

To mark the event of the first turning of wheel of *Dharma* by Lord Buddha and his first surmon (Four Noble Truths) which he gave to his five disciples at Sarnath, the Buddhists celebrate this festival. This festival is celebrated on the 4th day (*Tsheshi*) of the 6th month (*Drukpa*) of the Tibetan calendar (August).

Phang Lhabsol

This unique festival was popularized by Chakdor Namgyal, the third Chogyal of Sikkim. The main feature of this festival is the worship of the mountain Kangchendzonga. During this festival the treaty of blood-brotherhood between the Lepchas and the Bhutias by Khye Bumsa and Tetong Tek is expressed through songs. In this festival held during fifteenth day of the seventh month (August), the local deities are invoked to witness the festival. The special features of this festival are the masked *Lama* dance portraying the guardian deity and the *Pong-Toed* dance by the monks.

Losoong

This festival is celebrated during the end of the tenth month of the Tibetan calendar to mark the end of the harvest season with a pray for a better harvest of the next crop. The special feature of this festival is the *Chaam* dance in the monasteries at Palace (*Tsu-La-Khang*) Phodong and Rumtek. The archery competitions and grand festivities with songs and dances are other features.

The Religion of the Sherpa

In both Darjeeling and Sikkim the Sherpas are practicing Buddhism since time immemorial, and they belong to the Nyingma-pa sect. Among the Sherpas Buddhism is also popularly known as the Lamaism. Lamaism as defined by Waddell as "a mixture of Buddhism with a pre-pondering amount of mythology, mysticism and magic; the doctrine of incarnate *Lamas* and worship of canonized saints, now much prominent features of Lamaism, are of recent origin. It was readily accepted as it protected the people from devils" (1973:5). Buddhism or Lamaism is interwoven intimately with their life and activities. To each and every Sherpa the first and foremost thing is to observe religion with all sincerity and devotion. The major characteristic features of the religion of the Sherpas of Sikkim and Darjeeling are the performance of various rituals, religious festivals, worship etc., besides meditation and prayer. Turning of prayer wheels and circumambulation of *Gompa* and *Chorten* etc., are also part of their religious function (Raha & Coomar 2001: 81).

The Sherpas consider Lord Buddha as their *Sangchamdende*, that is the Supreme Being. They worship Lord Buddha, their supreme being, in different festivals. Apart from the supreme being they also worship different gods, goddesses and spirits. Some of their important deities are Guru Rimpoche, Hachenmaindarawa, Kanduyechoge, Cherainchi, Machihapkidama, Debjichamu, Kandu, Temanangmu, Unggura, Guru Tappu, Jha, Fhathaba, Kamrakandu, and others.

> These deities do not have the same status. The status of some of them is superior to others. Of all the deities, four are considered as most superior. These four deities are Guru Rimpoche, Hachenmaindarawa, Kanduyechoge, and Charainche. The next category of deities who have lesser status, are Unggura, Guru Tappu, Jha Fhathaba, Phanthamba, Karmakendu, Machihapkidama, Debjichamu, Kandu, Tamanangmu and others (Raha 2006: 84).

The seat of these deities on the sacred altar also indicate their respective position or status. On the centre of the sacred altar the image of Lord Buddha is placed. Guru Rimpoche, Hachenmaindarawa and Kanduyechoge have their respective place on the right side of Lord Buddha, Charainchi takes position on the left hand side of Lord Buddha (Raha & Commar 2001: 85). These deities because of their superior status, have their fixed respective place on either sides of Lord Buddha. The other deities are placed next to the superior deities. Among the Sherpas of Darjeeling as well as of Sikkim these deities are of two types. The first type is *Chulungtuksum* which includes Lord Buddha, Guru Rimpoche and God Cherainchi. All other deities such as Unggura, Guru Tappu, Jha Fhathaba, Phathamba, Karmakandu, Machihapkidama, Dobjichamu, Kandu and Tamanangmu and others come under second type. While the first type of deities have higher status, the status of the second type of deities is a little lower than the first one (*ibid*: 85).

The Sherpas of Darjeeling and Sikkim treat Lord Buddha as their Supreme Being (*Sangechamdende*). To them Lord Buddha is the greatest of all gods and goddesses. They worship him regularly in the *Gompa* as well as in the house (Raha 2006: 85). The Sherpas believe that Lord Buddha will save them from all sins, all dangers, and will not allow any malevolent spirit to harm them.

> "Lord Buddha and other deities also protect them from any kind of destruction, for example from *she* (earth), i.e. earthquake, landslide etc., from *may* (fire), from *chu* (water), i.e. flood and heavy rain, *lung* (wind), i.e. cyclone etc." (Raha & Coomar 2001: 85).

The Sherpa theology mentions about three incarnations of Lord Buddha. These are Chensi, Chaknadorje and Jamphelyang.

After Lord Buddha the next position is held by Guru Rimpoche. So far as the importance of the deities is concerned, Guru Rimpoche is second to Lord Buddha. According to Buddhism as practised by the Sherpas of Darjeeling and Sikkim, Guru Rimpoche has eight different images. These eight images are : (i) Premajungne, (ii) Khepalcandhenchosi, (iii) Shakhyasingkhe, (iv) Premasambhawaya, (v) Premagelpo, (vi) Nimayosher, (vii) Dhorjethole and (viii) Singkhedhadho.

Among the Sherpas of Darjeeling and Sikkim Cherainche or Cheransi is another main deity. They worship Cherensi with the desire that after their death their soul will have the chance to go to heaven and take refuge under the feet of lord Buddha and live in peace. The Sherpas have a strong belief that if Cherensi is pleased with them they will get salvation, and after death Cherensi will show them the path which leads them to Lord Buddha. As this faith is very strong among them and as everyone has the strongest desire to have a place at the feet of Lord Buddha after his or her death, so, "before a man dies, the *Lama* is invited to read the gospel of Cherensi, so that the dying man listens it, and thereby goes to heaven" (Raha & Coomar 1981: 86) because listening the gospel of Cherensi will sanctify the mind and heart of persons who listen it.

Charandarji is another important deity of the Sherpa pantheon. This deity is very important in the life of the Sherpas as this deity has the power to cure any disease. If this deity is pleased with the patient, he or she will definitely be cured. For this reason the Sherpas worship this deity for appeasement.

Waddel (1973: 22-26) in connection with the pantheon of the Buddhists Sherpas of Sikkim, tells that when someone enters the monasteries he or she will find images and paintings of different deities and spirits. The first three images those will be seen by the disciples and laities, are "The Three Rarest Ones" or trinity of the *Lamas*. One will find Shakya Muni in the centre, Guru Rimpoche to his right and Cherensi on the left. Shakya Muni is of yellow colour and often seen attended by two of his principal disciples, Maugdalputra and Shariputra.

Guru Rimpoche is seen to hold *dorje* (i.e. the thunderbolt of Indra, the Hindu god) in his right hand and a human skull cap with blood in his left hand. He is found attended by his two ministering wives, the Tibetan fairy, *Khando ye-she Tsho-gyal* and Indian *Lhao cham Mandarawa*.

Cherensi is considered as the patron-god of Lamaism and Tibetan Buddhism and 'incarnate in the Dalai Lama'. He has four hands and is white in colour.

In addition to the above three main deities many Sikkim monasteries are found to place some other divinities on either sides of the trinity. These deities are: (1) Dorje-phagmo (i.e. *Vajravarahi*) i.e. "The Snow-faced Lady Dorje" with three heads; (2) Dol-ma (i.e.*Tara*) is also known as "The Unloosener or the Vergin mother"; (3) Chak-dor (*Vajrapani*), i.e. "The Wielder of the Thunderbolt"; (4) Jam-yang (*Manjughosa*), i.e. "The God of Mystic Wisdom"; (5) Cheresi (*Avalokita*), i.e. "The Seer with keen eyes". He is also known as the 'God of Mercy" or The Great Pitier or "The Triard Protector"; (6) Seng-dong-ma or "The Lion-faced Goddess"; (7) Kang-Chhen-dso-nga or the 'Chief Country of Sikkim' of red colour. As he lives in the mountain 'Kangchhendsonga' so he has taken this name; and finally (8) Lha-tsiin Chembo, the pioneer *Lama* of Sikkim (Waddel 1973: 23-24).

Besides these deities in Sikkim there are a number of personal and ancestral gods and spirits. There are five such gods and spirits (Waddel 1973) and these are:

(1) *Pho-lha* or Male ancestral god.
This god sits under the armpit. He is worshipped for long life.

(2) *Mo-lha* or Mother-god or maternal uncle-god. This god is also known as *Zhang-lha* and is worshipped soon after child birth.

(3) *Srog-lha* or Life god. This god resides on the heart of the human being.

(4) *Yul-lha* or the Birth place god or country-god. This god resides on the crown of the head. He is worshipped "for dominion and fame."

(5) *Dgra-lha* or the enemy god who sits on the right shoulder. The Buddhists of Sikkim in general do not keep anything on the right shoulder as that may injure the deity (Waddle 1973: 113-114).

In addition there are Earth gods, who are worshipped in the spring, the Ancestral gods who are worshipped during summer, the three upper gods who are worshipped in autumn and the Royal Ancestor of the Sikkim King who is worshipped sometimes in winter (*ibid*: 114-115).

Besides the above gods and spirits Sikkim Buddhism (Lamaism) also presents a number of demons. Some of these demons are:

(I) House demon who is known as '*the Nang-lha* or Inside God,' and is of the nature of *Sa-dag* or 'Earth-owner demon'. As he stays in the house, he creates constant anxiety to the residents of the house.

(II) The Demons of the Earth—They are locally known as *Sab-dak-po* or Earth-owners. They are very large in number and remain under the control and authority "Old Mother *Khonma*". The earth demons live in certain trees or rocks.

(III) The Demons of the Sky—They always remain under "the control of the grand father of the three worlds-Old Father *Khen-pa* who is the owner of the sky."

(IV) Disease-producing Demons—They are known as *gshed* (or *She*) (*ibid*: 129-135).

It is thus seen that among the Sherpas, particularly of Sikkim, there are a large number of gods, goddesses, spirits and demons whom the Sherpas regularly worship.

Among the Sherpas the deities are divided into two types: firstly the peaceful or benign deities who are called *zhi-ba*, and the second types known as *khro-bo*, are those who are easily get annoyed and become wrathful. Therefore, considering the nature of the deities, the rituals performed, are also variable. There are four modes of performing rituals: peaceful (*zhi-ba*), prospering (*rgyas-pa*), powerful (*olbang-po*) and fierce (*drag-po*). These fourfold arrangement of performing rituals for different nature of deities "is a mediation of duality of peaceful and wrathful" (Paul 1989:72).

Among the Sherpas the peaceful deities are the victories Buddha, Samantabhadra, Vajrasatva, Dorje Semba and others.

The prospering deities are the two great Bodhisattvas like Pawa Cherenzi and Zhembiyang. Though Zhembiyang is more active and forceful and plays the role of a protector, still the gentle and compassionate Pawa Cherenzi is shown more rituals attention.

The best example of powerful deities are Guru Rimpoche. He is considered as the representative of the lowest of three bodies, the body of transformation.

> As such he appears in human rather then supernatural form....Guru Rimpoche is thus the prototype of the Tantric master, who through spiritual exercise, can attain supernatural power to control various forces at play in the cosmos. (*ibid*:75)

The fourth type, that is, 'Fierce' type of deities cover different violent protector gods, as well as wrathful forms of the high gods.

"Their job is to protect the religion against the enemies, demons etc. but they are also temperamental, jealous of trespasses and can easily turn against the community they are supposed to be protecting" (*ibid*). The deities come under this category, are Srungma, yi-dam or celestial divinity. These are regularly propitiated through rituals in order to appease them and also to obtain their co-operation in opposing malignant forces.

The Sherpas also have different types of gods, and each type has several number of gods. In general they are popularly called by the same term *lha*, besides the highest gods of the Tibetan Buddhism. These highest gods "are separate form and stand above all the processes of cosmic change" (Ortner 1978: 266). The Sherpas also have local gods, originally, they are pre-Buddhists (*ibid*). Their place in the pantheon is beneath the Buddhist gods. All these gods are worshipped in different religious functions

> And all are separate from the process of re-birth in which people are involved, either because like the higher gods, they transcend

it, or because, like the local gods, they are simply interdependent of the system that made it up in the first place (*ibid*).

In general the Sherpas believe that all types of gods (*lha*) live inside every human being:

> A personal god (*mi'i lha*); the white and black gods who sit on each shoulder counting merits and demerits, respectively (*lhendzikewide* and *lhendzikewilha*); the gods of lineage (*gyurpa lha*) and place of birth (*jiptak*); and gods who arrived during the persons death in a past life (Adams 1997: 90).

But according to Adams the gods of a particular Sherpa are not particular to him or her. These gods are shared by the Sherpas of ones lineage, birth place or death place....(*ibid*). He further states that

> Even though not all Sherpas are as adept at practicing Buddhism as Lamas and monks, and even though they do not always interpret the world in the same esoteric ways, Sherpa lives are in general saturated with both reminders of impermanence and opportunities for mimetic engagement with simulacra and representations, *via* Lamas and monks and *via* western visitors (*ibid*: 91).

As already said the Sherpas of Darjeeling and Sikkim belong to the Nyingmapa sect (Raha & Coomar 2001: 81, Raha 2006: 81).

> The Nyingma-pa, the wholly unreformed and unaltered section of the Lama, are considered as belonging to the 'Old School'. The people belonging to the Nyingma-pa sect wear red hats. So, they are also known as the red-hat sect (Raha 2006: 82).

The Nyingma-pa sect is considered as 'the Old School' as it is characterized by the "primitive and unreformed style of Lamaism". The Nyingma-pa sect is considered as the most traditional form of religion of the Buddhists. It is wholly unreformed section of the *Lamas* and belong to the "Old School" (Waddel 1985: 72). "It is most largely tinged with the indigenous pre-Buddhist religious practices; and celibacy and abstinence are rarely practiced" (Waddel:1973: 10). No doubt Nyingma-pa sect has a good dose of *Bon* or *Pon* or Pre-Buddhist elements which are seen in their beliefs and practices (Raha 2006: 82). Waddell has also found the presence of elements of *Bon* or *Pon* or pre-Buddhists of Tibet in high degree (1985: 72). In Sikkim Waddel has found three sub-sects of this sect. These are the *Lhatsun-pa*, *Kartok-pa* and *Nga dak-pa*. Most of the monasteries of Sikkim belong to the *Lhatsun-pa* subsect, the head of which is Pemiongchi. The *Kartok-pa* derived their name from their founder *Lama*, *Kah-tak* which means "The Understander of the Precepts". The monasteries of Kartok and Doling belong to this sub-sect. The old monastery at Darjeeling is a branch of the monastery at Doling in Sikkim. The *Nga-dak-pa* sub-sect derived its name from its founder known as "The Owner of Sway or Dominion, who was of royal lineage" (*ibid*: 10-11).

> All sections of the Nyingma-pa agree in professing the creed called *Dsog-chhen-bo* or "The Great End".... (*ibid*: 11).

Waddel has also found the Sherpas of Sikkim worshipping Lord Buddha as the Supreme Being. He rests in the heart of every Sherpa. According to Akhtar Buddhism in Sikkim also known as Lamaism or Tibetan Buddhism,

> was brought to Sikkim through Tibet in the eighth century A.D. The Guru Padmasambhava, 'the Lotus Born', also known as Guru Rimpoche, who introduced it to the people of Sikkim, was a native of Udayana (modern Swat in Pakistan) (*cf* Waddel 1973: 111)

But Waddel's view is that Guru Padmasambhava came from Udayana which is the present-day Ghajni of Afghanistan (*ibid*: 4).

The Lamaism which is and was prevalent in Sikkim may be defined as

> A mixture of Buddhism with a pre-pondering amount of mythology, mysticism and magic; the doctrine of incarnate Lamas and the worship of canonized saints, now much prominent features of Lamaism, are of recent origin. It was readily accepted as it is protected the people from devil (*ibid*:5).

Though it is a popular belief in Sikkim that Guru Rimpoche brought Lamaism in Sikkim during eighth century A.D., but in fact, according to

Waddel, the same was introduced in Sikkim sometimes in seventeenth Century A.D., when *Lhatsum Chhembo* came to Sikkim from Tibet. Lhatsun Chhembo or "the Great Reverend God" started spreading a religion known as *Kun-zang-nam-gye* meaning "The entirely victorious Essence of Goodness". He came to Sikkim along with two other lamas belonging to Nyingmapa sect. One of these two *Lamas*, Sempah Chhembo came through 'western gate' of *Singlela* whereas the other *Lama*, Rigdsin Chhembo who arrived through 'southern gate' by way of Darjeeling and Namchi. These three *Lamas* in search of a fourth one, went out towards east and finally met a person known as Phuntshog. The name of P*huntshog* appeared in the prophesy of Guru Rimpoche who was the fourth one. Phuntshog was crowned by these three *Lamas* as the Chho-gyal or Dharma-raja (religious king). Phuntshog at that time was 38 years old and became *Lama* in the year 1641 A.D. (Waddel 1973: 8-9).

As already said "Lamaism was founded by the wizard-priest Padmasambhava (Tibetan: *Pedma Jungne)* i.e. 'The Lotus Born' usually called by the Tibetans, Guru Rimpoche or "the Precious Guru or simply "Guru.... (*ibid*: 4). This type of Buddhism got momentum at the time of King Thi-Srong De-tsan, during his tenure as the ruler between 740 and 786 A.D. Padmasambhava went to Tibet during his time in order to construct building of the first monastery in Tibet. (*ibid*). He reached Samye, the place of constructing the monastery in the year 747 A.D. After defeating the demons and evil spirits with *dorje* or *Vajra*, i.e. thunderbolt and spells, he was able to construct the monastery in 479 A.D. and formed the first batch of the *Lamas*.

Among the Tibetan Buddhists there are several sects. *Kah-dam-pa* is possibly the oldest one. After three and half centuries, "it became less ascetic and more realistic" and took a new name, *Ge-luk-pa. Ge-luk-pa* was ultimately became the most important and dominant Buddhist sect in Tibet. The members of this sect started wearing yellow coloured garment and observing rigorous discipline under the guidance of Tsongkhapa.

"The Kargyupa sect was founded in the later half of the eleventh century A.D. by *Lama* Marpa...." *Lama* Marpa visited India and got special instruction from Atisha, the famous Indian Buddhist master and Naropa, Atisha's teacher. The members of this sect used to live in caves and meditate. They have their guardian deity known as "The Lord of the Black cloak", tutelary deity is Demchhok or "Chief of Happiness", and their highest teacher is mythical, Dorje-Chhang. The Kargyupa is further divided into different sub-sects known as Karmapa, Dikungpa, Talungpa, Upper Dukpa and Dukpa (*ibid*: 4-6).

The Sakya-pa is another important sect of the Tibetan Buddhism. It derived its name from the Sa-kya monastery situated in the western part of Tibet. "Its special meditative system is "*Lam-h bras*". Its guardian demons are *mgon-po-gur* or "The Guardian of the Tent" and *mgon-po-zhal*" (*ibid*: 7). The hat used by the members of Sakya-pa sect is known as *Sa-zhu*. This sect is divided into a few sub-sects like the *Ngor-pa*, *Jonang-pa* etc.

The basic characteristics of Nyingma are that they undertake special worship of Guru Rimpochhe (Rimbochhe); they consider *Kuntu zang po* (i.e. *Samanta bhadra*) as their highest god; their tutelary deity is *Dab-pa kah gye*; their special guardian deity is *Pal-gon de-nga* and their peculiar red hat is known as *Ugyen penzhu*. "With these characteristics they exhibit, as a class, a greater laxity in living than any other sect of Lamas" (*ibid*: 11).

The members of the *Nyingma-pa* sect worship "the great wizard, Guru Pema as "A second Buddha" in spite of his uncelebrated life, his semi-demoniac temper and his being altogether void of any of the admirable traits of Buddha" (*ibid*). Guru Pema is worshipped in eight forms known as *Guru Tsen-gye*, i.e. "The eight worshipful names of the Teacher". These eight forms are Guru Padma Jungne, Guru Padmasambhava, Guru Padma Gyelpo, Guru Dorje Do-Lo, Guru Nyima Od-zer, Guru Shakya Seng-ge, Guru Seng-ge-da dok, and Guru Lo-ten Chhog-se.

In the beliefs and practices of Nyingma-pa sect a good dose of *Bon* or *Pon*, i.e. the pre-Buddhist practices are found to exist. In fact both pre-Buddhist and Buddhist beliefs and practices have been amalgamated in the Nyingma-pa faith. Ortner also thinks that Nyingma-pa is the oldest and unreformed sect of the Tibetan Buddhists,

> which placed great emphasis on coercive rites, many of which were dropped or cleaned up in the later reformed sects. Specially they stress the so-called *Sang-nyak* text, which emphasize fierce rites of exorcising and destroying demons (1979: 30).

In the writings of Waddel we got the same idea about the presence of the elements of *Bon* or pre-Buddhist practices in high degree (1985:72).

When we turn over our attention to the religion of the Sherpas of Nepal we find that

> "The religious beliefs of the Sherpa are basically those of Tibetan Buddhism, and Sherpa Lamas use for the performance of private as well as public rites the liturgical text current among members of the Nyingmapa or Old Sect (Fürer-Haimendorf 1964: 175).

The Sherpas of Khumbu of Nepal among whom Fürer-Haimendorf undertook his research work, have associated themselves with *Lama* Sange Dorje, the sixth reincarnation of Changna Dorje (*Vajrapani*). According to the local tradition Mohang, a place situated between Khunjung and Phortse is the birth place of *Lama* Sange Dorje. The Sherpas and others believe that Bundachendzen, father of Sange Dorje had the power to converse with the great country god Khumbu-yulha who also visited him regularly in the monastery of Bunda Chendzen. His son, Sange Dorje had the power to fly through the air and perform other magical rites (*ibid*: 127).

Ortner while studying the Sherpas of Solu valley in Nepal, finds the Sherpas as Buddhists, follow 'the basic Buddhist principles of sin and merit and of reincarnation of various states of being, exalted or miserable depending on the amounts of sin and merit accumulated in the course of lifetime" (1979: 30).

> The religion of the Sherpa, though it has no doubt undergone much change, is still essentially that unique and exotic form of Buddhism that developed in Tibet, a school within Mahayana tradition known variously as Lamaism, Tantrayana, Vajrayana, or simply Tibetan Buddhism (*ibid*: 11).

Ortner finds the Sherpas of Nepal embracing Tibetan Buddhism. "As good Buddhists they keep strong faith on their religion. The Sherpas would certainly place first-their religion, which as far as they are concerned is the *sine qua non* of all the rest" (1979: 30). They belong to the sect, Nyingmawa (Nyingmapa), the unreformed oldest sect of the Tibetan Buddhism. They believe in a number of gods and spirits and also worship them for their wellbeing. As the Tibetan Buddhists and as belonging to the Nyingmawa sect, the Sherpas give much stress on the so-called Sangngak texts "which emphasize fierce rites of exorcising and destroying demons" (*ibid*: 30). On the Sherpa monasticism, the extraordinary leadership of the great reincarnate Lama, Tushi Rimpoche, has a marked impact. The Buddhism or Lamaism practiced by the Sherpas is the part of the Mahayana tradition, supposedly a more socially concerned "compassionate" form of the religion (*ibid*: 157).

> Sherpa Buddhism, which in many respects can hardly be called orthodox, nonetheless retains the central Buddhist tendency to isolate and atomized the individual, and devalue social bonding and social reciprocity seems a contradiction in terms. (*ibid*:157)

Very little is known about the religion rather Buddhism, practiced by the Sherpas of Tibet wherefrom they migrated to Nepal and Sikkim. Ortner has mentioned about the Buddhism of the Sherpas of Tibet.

> In Tibet, where the Sherpas originated and where their religion took the form that it retains for the most part today, the religion was supported by the theocratic state. State support of religion, in turn, allowed the monastic community to cut itself off from society more completely, because it was not directly dependent on the laity for support....(*ibid*: 159).

Fürer-Haimendorf also found that among the Sherpas the "great upsurge in religious activities had been made possible by favourable developments in the social and economic fields" (*ibid*: 127).

But these Sherpas after coming out of Tibet several centuries ago, did not give up the religion they had when they were in Tibet. They are going on continuing to retain the same religion, of course, after slight modification, even when they got settled for several centuries and established themselves properly in the places of their migration:

> When the Sherpas, several centuries out of Tibet, became prosperous enough to begin to build monasteries, they continued the Tibetan model of establishing them outside society without in fact having the political structure (centralized taxation) necessary to support them. This in turn, has involved the Sherpas in the contradictory practice of having individual families support their monk sons, a contradiction the Sherpas themselves recognized and the consequences of which remain to be seen (*ibid*: 159: 160).

This type of orthodoxy of the Buddhism practiced by the Sherpas outside Tibet because they developed a particular system which made it meaningful. "The individualistic bias of the Sherpa Buddhism orthodoxy is grounded in the structures of worldly social life" (Ortner 1979: 161). "Though it is well known that the ethics of Buddhism does not recognize all the structures of worldly social life, rather opposes these. This contradiction is because of fact that, as Ortner has explained, the Sherpas perceive the religion as antagonistic and struggle against it in their ritual". This struggle of the Sherpas against their own religion Buddhism "is partly a struggle with those aspects of their own society that in fact, make them such good Buddhists" (*ibid*).

Fürer-Haimendorf has also found the Sherpas of Khumbu of Nepal practicing Buddhism for several centuries. About 300 years ago Buddhism was established at Khumbu. "Among the Sherpas, as among the Tibetan Buddhists, the religious impulse is so strong that any margin of resources left after essential needs have been met is largely devoted to religious purpose" (1964: 11).

In connection with the religion of the Sherpas of Nepal, Paul finds them as Buddhists like the Sherpas of other area. Among these people of Nepal the triad of deities plays very important roles as they are considered as the central figures of the "Organized 'high' religion".

> The triad consists of the three gods who make up fouth of the Buddha lineage which are known to Mahayana Buddhism. Each of the five lineages consists of three tiers: the highest is that of the Dhyani-Buddha or Meditation Buddha; the second is that of the Dhyani-Budhisattva and the third is that of the human Buddha. Transcending all of these is the Adi-Buddha who represents the ultimate Buddha-ground out of which all the others emanate (Paul 1989: 57).

Among these different Buddha Dhyani Buddha who is the fourth of the five lineages, is known among the Sherpas as *Ongpame* (*Amitabha* or Boundless Light). The Dhyani-Bodhisattva is known *Pawa-Cherenzi* (*Avalokitesvara* or Glorious Eyes Looking Down). But to them the human Buddha is not Goutama, popular to all Buddhists. The Sherpa reverse him as the founder of the Tibetan Buddhism and second earthly Buddha is known as Pema Sambawa (*Padmasambhava* or Lotus self-born one or Guru Rimpoche, i.e. Precious Teacher) (*ibid*: 57). According to the Sherpas, as Paul mentions,

> This triad can be represented ichnographically in two different arrangements. In many Sherpa temples, the three gods are depicted in statues, often life-size or larger, which sit looking out from behind the altar towards the entrance. Ongpame is larger than the other two, as is placed in the center, slightly higher than and to the rear of the others. Pawa Cherenzi is seated in front of and below him, to the right; and Guru Rimpoche is seated in front of and lower than him on the left (*ibid*: 57-58).

While the sitting arrangement of statues of these Buddhist Triad in the monasteries is horizontal, the same in the religious paintings is quite different. In the religious paintings their sitting arrangement is vertical rather than horizontal. The paintings shows that Ongpame is seen to be sitting on the top, Pawa Cherenzi in the middle and Guru Rimpoche at the bottom. The size of the images of these three Buddhist deities in the paintings is also different. While the size of Guru Rimpoche is the largest and Ongpame is the smallest, Pawa Cherinzi is in between, i.e. of intermediate size. "This arrangement expresses the fact that Guru Rimpoche is an emanation of Pawa Cherenzi, who is in turn, an emanation of Ongpame" (Paul 1989: 58).

Among the Sherpas of Nepal there are a number of supernatural beings. They are of different types and grades. Ortner divided them in "two extreme types—high gods who preside over the system (and also over every ritual) and the demons who pit themselves against the system (and also against every ritual)" (1979: 137). All the deities are again divided into two types based on their modes. These two types are: (1) *shiwa* or the peaceful and benign deities and (2) *takbu* or those who are fierce and violent. "The benign form is considered more basic while the fierce form is said to be adopted for the purpose of fighting demons" (*ibid*). On the other hand, the demons are totally and extremely opposite from the gods. They are "considered to be intrinsically evil, and aggressive against humanity" (*ibid*). They not only threaten the common people, "they are also dangerous to the religion and society". "They try to tempt *Lamas* and monks into sin, to eat temple offerings, and to undermine the religion however they can". The primary objective of each and every Sherpa is to worship the gods to seek their help in combating those forces of evil and also "to get the gods to renew their primordial struggle against, and reenact their original triumph over the demons and the forces of anarchy and insolence" (*ibid*).

We have already quoted elsewhere the views of Fürer-Haimendorf about the religion of the Sherpas of Nepal. He confirms that

> The religious beliefs of the Sherpa are basically those of the Tibetan Buddhism, and Sherpa *Lamas* use for the performance of private as well as public rites the liturgical text current among members of Nyingmapa or 'Old Sect' (1964: 175)

In Nepal the Sherpas worship a large number of gods and goddesses as well as different spirits whom they worship during different occasions and festivities. Among the Sherpas of Nepal and also elsewhere like Darjeeling and Sikkim they practice religion both at home and also at the monasteries.

"There is no cleavage between the Buddhists doctrine practiced by the monasteries and the religion of the ordinary villager" (*ibid:* 126). "Similarly, there is no conflict between the village religion and more sophisticated beliefs of learned *Lamas*" (*ibid*). The Sherpas of Nepal have a number of deities which the clan members worship. It is the sacred duty of each and every member of each Sherpa clan "to recognize certain mountain gods as their specific protective deity and on the same occasions clan members resident in the same village, may combine for the worship of such clan deities". (*ibid*: 21).

These clan deities are very important to them. Some of these clan deities which Fürer-Haimendorf has mentioned, are stated below:

1. *Pari-lha-tsen-karbu.* This deity is associated with a mountain in Khambu, worshipped by the members of the Paldorje clan.
2. *Tonak-lha-tsen karbu.* This deity is the presiding deity of an area north of Gokyo and Long-gyo, associated with a dried up lake nearby of Gokyo. This deity is worshipped by the members of the Thaktu clan.
3. *Tawoche-lha-tsen.* This deity is associated with the Tawoche, a mountain close to Pangboche. This deity is worshipped by the members of the Nawa clan.
4. *Loudze-lha tsen.* This deity lives at Loudze (Lhotse) mountain which is close to Mount Everest. The members of the clan, Chusherwa, worship this deity.
5. *Arkamtse-lha-tsen karbu*. This deity is associated with the locality above Tangnak and is worshipped by the members of the Sherwa clan.
6. *Chiawitsa-kyung karbu.* This clan deity of Chiawa clan reigns in the locality above Maralung.
7. *Karte Gyelbu* ('King of Karte'). This deity is worshipped by the members of Mende clan and is the presiding deity of Karte in Tibet (Fürer-Haimendorf 1964: 21-22).

The Sherpas have kept all these clan deities in the category of *zidag* or 'Lord of the Soil' and therefore to the Sherpas their position is not that high in the Buddhist hierarchy of deities. They worship these clan deities during some ceremonies called *lhachetu (lha*=god; *chetu*=ceremony). Of these three *lhachetu* ceremonies, the *So-lha* is celebrated in the month of May, the *Yerchang* (Summer beer).

Kang-chhen-dso-nga is the chief country-god of Sikkim. The mountain Kanchenzonga or Kangchhen-dsonga which means "five repositories or ledges of the Great Snow" is another important deity. This mountain is also considered as the five 'repositories' which were the real store houses of the treasure of the mountain-god who is "on the whole a good-natured god, rather impassive, and is therefore less worshipped than more actively malignant deities" (Waddell 1973: 23-24).

In addition to Buddhism as practiced by the Sherpas in Sikkim, there are many demons and gods as believed by the Sherpas. These are found everywhere—"path, big tree, rock, spring, waterfall and lake etc." They are also found in the sky, ground, house, field, country, everywhere (*ibid*: 113). They are always invoked by the *Lamas* and also worshipped by the common people. These demons and gods are: (1) The Male Ancestral God (*Pho-lha*), (2) The Mother god or maternal uncle god (*Zhang-lha*), (3) The Life God (*Srog-lha)*, (4) The Birthplace god or country god (*Yul-lha*) and (5) The Enemy god (*Dgra-lha*). The Male Ancestral god is worshipped for long life for the protection from any sort of harm. The Mother god is worshipped for securing strength. The Life god is propitiated for wealth. The Birth place god is paid homage for securing dominion and fame, and the Enemy god is propitiated, particularly by the soldiers, for successfully defending the enemy (*ibid*: 114). Apart from all these five personal demons/gods, the *Sherpas* and other Buddhists of Sikkim also worship some other gods who are worshipped in different seasons. These are the Earth gods worshipped in the spring, the Ancestral gods worshipped in the summer, the "Three Upper gods propitiated in the autumn and the Royal Ancestor of the Sikkim king worshipped in winter" (*ibid*: 114). Besides they also have different others deities and spirits such as country gods, mountain gods, local gods etc. (*ibid*: 114-118). "The country-gods or *Yul-lha* are innumerable in number out of them the main two gods are the mountain god (*Kang-chhen-dso-nga*) who is also known as the protector of religion". The other one is *Yabbdud* or the 'Black Father Devil' who is the subordinate to the former.

Among the Sherpas and other Buddhists the *Zhi-dak* are known as red-demons or local gods. They are usually the 'spirits of the deceased novices or ill-natured *Lamas*.

It is thus seen that the Sherpas as the Lamaist Buddhists, have numerous deities, spirits and demons. They propitiate them to appease them, and to appease them only to get rid of the wrath of them.

BIBLIOGRAPHY

Adams, Vincanne, (1997), Dreams of a Final Sherpa. *American Anthropologist*, Vol. 99, No. 1.

Allen, N.J., (1976), Studies in the Myths and Oral Tradition of the Thulung Rai of East Nepal. Ph.D. Thesis, Oxford University.

Atkinson, E.T., (1973), *Religion in the Himalayas*. New Delhi, Cosmo Publications.

Bagchi, Gour, (1991), The Sherpas of Darjeeling: A Socio-Cultural Profile. In *West Bengal Tribes*: *Socio-Economic and Cultural Life*. (Eds.) A.K. Das & Others, Calcutta, Cultural Research Institute.

Bell, Charles, (1931), *The Religion of Tibet*, Oxford, Clerendon Press.

Bhasin, Veena, (1989), *Ecology, Culture and Change*: *Tribals of Sikkim Himalayas*. New Delhi, Inter-India Publication.

Bhasin, Veena, (1997), The Human Settlement and Health Status in Sikkim. In *People of the Himalayas*: *Ecology, Culture, Development, and Change*, Delhi, Kamala-Raj Enterprise.

Bhatt, S.C. and Bhargava, G.K., (2005), *Land and People of Indian States and Union Territories*: *Sikkim*, New Delhi, Kalpaz Publication.

Bisht, N.S. and Bankoti, T.S., (2004), *Encyclopaedic Ethnography of the Himalayan Tribes*. Delhi, Global Vision Publishing House.

Bista, Dor Bahadur, (1976), *People of Nepal*, Kathmandu, Ratna Pustak Bhandar.

Biswas, Samar, (2008), People of Darjeeling District in West Bengal: An Anthropological Profile. *North Bengal Anthropologist,* Vol. 1, No. 1.

Biswas, Saswati, (1993), Development Strategy in the Hill Areas of Darjeeling: A Critical Appraisal. In *Problems and Strategies of Development in the Eastern Himalayas* (Ed.) Ranju R. Dhamala. New Delhi, Gyan Publishing House.

Bose, Saradindu, (1966), The Bhot of Northern Sikkim. *Man in India*, Vol. XLVI, No. 2.

Bose, S.C., (1968), *Land and People of the Himalayas*, Calcutta, Indian Publications.

Bower, Barbara, (2003), *Sherpas of Khumbu: People Livestock and Landscape*, New Delhi, Oxford University Press.

Chakravarty, P.K., (1993), Problems and Strategies of Development in the Darjeeling Himalaya. *In Problems and Strategies of Development in the Eastern Himalayas* (Ed.) Ranju R. Dhamala. New Delhi, Gyan Publishing House.

Chatterjee, Sandhya, (1992), The Indigenous Culture of Zanskar. In *Indigenous Vision: Peoples of India Attitude to the Environment*, New Delhi, India International Centre.

Chatterjee, R. and Sekh. R Mandol, (2011), Peoples of Darjeeling Himalaya: A Profile in *Cloud Stone and The Mind: The People and Environment of Darjeeling Hill Area* (Ed.) Mamata Desai & Saptarshi Mitra. Kolkata, K.P. Bagchi & Co.

Chib, Sukdev Singh, (1977), *This Beautiful India: Sikkim*. New Delhi, Light and Life Publishers.

Coomar, P.C. and M.K. Raha, (1997), Family among the Sherpa of West Bengal. In *People of the Himalayas: Ecology, Culture, Development and Change* (Ed.) K.C. Mohanta, Delhi, Kamala-Raj Enterprise.

Coomar, P.C. and M.K. Raha, (1998), Women of the Sherpa Society in the Himalayas. In *Gender and Society in India* (Ed.) R. Indira & D.K. Behera, New Delhi.

Coomar, P.C., Raha, M.K. and S. Bhui, (2009), *Tradition and Transformation in an Immigrant Island Society: The Karen of Andaman Islands*. New Delhi, Abhijeet Publication.

Coomar, P.C. and M.K. Raha, (2013), The Sherpa of Sikkim and Their Land. In *Tribal Panorama of North East India* (Ed.) Sarthak Sengupta. New Delhi, Gyan Publishing House.

Choube, S., (1973), *Hill Politics in North-East India*. Bombay, Orient Longman.

Choudhury, N.C. and Kanchan Sarkar, (1993), Hill Villages of Darjeeling: Aspects of Economy, Ecology, and Agricultural Modernization. In *Problems and Strategies of Development in the Eastern Himalayas* (Ed.) Ranju R. Dhamala. New Delhi, Gyan Publishing House.

Choudhury, M.K. and Others, (2003), *Ethnographic Notes on the Scheduled Tribes and Scheduled Castes of West Bengal*. Kolkata, Cultural Research Institute.

Crook, John, (1994), Tradition, Development and Conservation in Ladakh. In *Himalayan Buddhist Villages* (Eds.) John Crook & Henry Osmaston, Bristol, University of Bristol.

Crook, John, H., (1994), The History of Zangskar. In *Himalayan Buddhist Villages* (Eds.) John Crook and Henry Osmaston,·Briston, University of Bristol.

Dalton, E.T., [1973 (ori. 1872)], *Descriptive Ethnology of Bengal*, Delhi, Cosmo Publication.

Dargyay, E.K., (1982), *Tibetan Village Community*, New Delhi, Vikas Publishing House (Pvt.) Ltd.

Das, Amal Kumar, (1978), *The Lepchas of West Bengal*. Calcutta, Editions Indians.

Das, A.K. and S.K. Banerjee, (1962), *The Lepchas of Darjeeling District*, Calcutta, Tribal Welfare Deptt, Government of West Bengal.

Das, A.K. and R.N. Saha, (1989), *West Bengal Scheduled Castes and Scheduled Tribes*, Calcutta, Cultural Research Institute.

Das, Amal Kumar, B.K. Roy Choudhury and M.K. Raha, (1966), *Handbook on Scheduled Castes & Scheduled Tribes of West Bengal*. Calcutta, Cultural Research Instt.

Das, A.K. and B.K. Roy Choudhury and R.N. Saha, (1978), *Scheduled Tribes and Scheduled Castes of West Bengal: Programmes, Facts and Figures*. Calcutta, Cultural Research Institute.

Das, B.S., (1983), *The Sikkim Saga*. New Delhi, Vikas Publishing House.

Das, M. and A. Bhuimali, (2011), *Darjeeling Hill Economy*, Delhi, Abhijeet Publications.

Dash, A.J., (1947), *Bengal District Gazetteers*: Darjeeling. Calcutta, Bengal Government Press.

Debnath, J.C., (2009), *Economic History and Development of Sikkim*, Delhi, Abhijeet Publications.

Desai, Mamata, (1988), *Eco-System and Ethnic Constellation of Sikkim*. Calcutta, Best Books.

Desai, Mamata, (2011), Darjeeling Hill Area Land use and Land Capability. In *Cloud Stone and The Mind: The People and Environment of Darjeeling Hill Areas*. (Eds) Mamata Desai & Saptarshi Mitra, Kolkata, K.P. Bagchi & Co.

Desai, Mamata, (2003a), Analysis and Mapping of the Land Use and Land Capability Analysis of the Darjeeling Hill Areas (unpublished Report).

Desai, Mamata, (2003b), Identification and Mapping of Hazard Prone Areas Regarding Landslides in the Darjeeling Hill Areas (unpublished Report).

Desai, Mamata, (2014), *Darjeeling: The Queen of the Hills*. Kolkata, K.P. Bagchi & Co.

Desai, Mamata and Mitra, Saptarshi (Eds.), (2011), *Cloud Stone and the Mind: The People and Environment of Darjeeling Hill Area*. Kolkata, K.P. Bagchi & Co.

Dhamala, R.R., (1991), A Socio-Economic Study of Pemayangtse Monastery in Sikkim. In *Religion and Society of the Himalayas* (Eds.) T.B. Subba & Karubaki Datta. New Delhi, Gian Publishing House.

Dey, K., (2006), Buddhist Contribution to Art forms of Arunachal: Influence of Buddhism on the Monpas and Sherdukpens. In *Buddhism in North-East India* (Eds) S. Dutta & B. Tripathy, Indus Publishing Co.

Debi, Bharati & Sikha Chatterjee, (2011), Bhutias of Darjeeling and Their Ethnic Identity: A Note. In *Cloud Stone and the Mind. The People and Environment of Darjeeling Hill Area* (Eds.) Mamata Desai & Saptarshi Mitra. Kolkata, K.P. Bagchi & Co.

Dhamala, Ranju R., (1993), *Problems and Strategies of Development in the Eastern Himalayas*. New Delhi, Gyan Publishing House.

Dhamala, Ranju, R., (1993), Panchayati Raj Institutions in Sikkim as Instruments of Development. In *Problems and Strategies' of Development in the Eastern Himalayas* (Ed.) Ranju R. Dhamala. New Delhi, Gyan Publishing House.

Directorate of Census, (1991), Census of India, 1991, Series-22. Sikkim, Part-XII A&B, District Census Handbook, North, East, South and West Districts.

Directorate of Census Operation, (1971), West Bengal District Census Handbook: Darjeeling. Part-X-C, Calcutta.

Dondrup, R., (2006), Impact of Tibetan Form of Buddhism among the Monpas and Sherdukpens. In *Buddhism in North-East India* (Eds.) S. Dutta & B. Tripathy. New Delhi, Indus Publication Co.

Dorjee, Rinchen, (2006), The Monpas: Their Social, Economic and Religious Institutions. In *Buddhism in North-East India* (Eds.) S. Dutta & B. Tripathy. New Delhi, Indus Publishing Co.

Downs, H.R., (1980), *Rhythms of a Himalayan Village*. San Francisco, Harper and Raw Publication.

Dutta, Amal, (1994), Ethnicity and Resource Management in Sikkim. In *Sikkim: Society, Polity, Economy, Environment* (Ed.) Lama, M.P. New Delhi, Indus Publishing Co.

Dutta, Archana and Subhas Dutta, (1980), Ecology, Demography and Land use change in Darjeeling Himalaya. *Bull. An S.I.*, Vol. 29.

Dutta, D.K., (2006), The Membas: Their Social, Economic and Religious Institutions. In *Buddhism in North-East India* (Eds.) S. Dutta & B. Tripathy. New Delhi, Indus Publishing Co.

Dutta, S. and Tripathy, B., (2006), *Buddhism in North-East India*, New Delhi, Indus Publishing Co.

Dutta, D.K. and Duarah, D.K., (2006), Role of Buddhist Art and Crafts in the Socio-Economic Development of the Monpas of Arunachal Pradesh. In *Buddhism in North-East India* (Eds.) S. Dutta & B. Tripathy, New Delhi, Indus Publishing Co.

Datta, S. and Tripathy, B., (2006), Introduction. In *Buddhism in North-East India* (Eds.) S. Datta & B. Tripathy, New Delhi, Indus Publishing Co.

Earl, A., (1901), *On Polyandry in Sikkim and Tibet*. Census of India, Bengal Secretariat Press, Vol.VI, Pt-I (Report).

Eliade, Mircea, (1987), *The Encyclopedia of Religion*, Vol. I and II, New York, MacMilan Publishing Co.

Fisher, James, (1986), Tourists and Sherpas. *Contribution to Nepalese Studies*, Vol. 14, No. 1.

Fisher, James, (1990), *Sherpas: Reflection on Change in Himalayan Nepal*, New Delhi, Oxford University Press.

Foning, A.R., (1987), *Lepcha: My Vanishing Tribe*. New Delhi, Sterling Publishers Pvt. Ltd.

Fraser, J.B., (1820), *Journal of a Tour through part of the Snowy Range of the Himalaya Mountains and to the Source of Jamuna and Ganges*, London.

Fürer-Haimendorf, C. Von, (1953), Pre-Buddhist Elements in Sherpa Beliefs and Rituals. In *Man*, Vol. 55, No. 61.

Fürer-Haimendorf, C. Von, (1964), *The Sherpas of Nepal: The Buddhist Highlanders*. New Delhi, Sterling Publishers Pvt. Ltd.

Fürer-Haimendorf, C. Von, (1978), Trans-Himalayan Traders in Transition. In *Himalayan Anthropology: Indo-Tibetan Interface*. The Hague, Moutan Publishers.

Fürer-Haimendorf, C. Von, (1975), *Himalayan Traders*. London, John Murray.

Fürer-Haimendorf, C. Von, (1974), Changing Fortunes of Nepal's High Altitude Dwellers. In *Contribution to the Anthropology of Nepal* (Ed.) Fürer-Haimendorf, C. Von Warminster, Aris & Phillips Ltd.

Fürer-Haimendorf, C. Von, (1984), *The Sherpas Transformed*. New Delhi, Sterling Publishers Pvt. Ltd.

Gangopadhyay, S., (1993), Sherpa. In *People of India: Sikkim*. Vol. XXXIX (Ed.) K.S. Singh. Calcutta, An S.I. & Seagull Books.

Ganhar, J.N. and P.N. Ganhar, (1956), *Buddhism in Kashmir and Ladakh*, New Delhi.

Gawloog, R.S., (2013), Traditional Religious Beliefs and Practices of the Lepcha: A study on Change and Continuity. In *Tribal Panorama of North East India* (Ed.) Sarthak Sengupta, New Delhi, Gyan Publishing House.

Gawloog, R.S., (2001), Social Organization and Change among the Lepcha of Sikkim. In *Tribes of the Eastern Himalayas* (Ed.) Sarthak Sengupta. New Delhi, Mittal Publication.

Gerard, A., (1841), *An Account of Koonauwar in the Himalayas* etc. London.

Ghosh, S.N., (1989), *Census of India 1981*, Series 23, West Bengal Part- IX (III) Special Tables for Scheduled Tribes.

Ghosh, T.K., (1992), Social Stratification in Lahaul. In *The Himalayas and the Himalayans* (Ed.) Manis Kumar Raha & Palash Chandra Coomar, Calcutta, An S.I.

Ghosh, T.K., (2002), *A Profile of the Himalayan Lahula*, Kolkata, Anthropological Survey of India

Gill, M.S., (1972), *Himalayan Wanderland*. New Delhi.

Goldslein, M.C., (1975), Preliminary Notes on Marriage and Kinship. *Contribution to Nepalese Studies*, Vol. 2.

Goldstein, M.C., (1981), High Altitude Tibetan Population in Remote Himalaya: Social Transformation and its Demographic, Economic and Ecological Consequences. *Mountain Research and Development*, Vol. I, No. 1.

Goldstein, M.C., (1987), When Brothers Share a Wife. *Natural History*, Vol. 96, No. 3.

Goldstein, M.C. and Paljor Tsarong, (1987), De-encapsulation and Change in Ladakh. In *The Himalayan Heritage* (Ed.) M.K. Raha, Delhi, Gyan Publishing House.

Goode, Willium J., (1965), *The Family*, New Delhi, Prentice-Hall of India (RI) Ltd.

Gordon, P.R.T., [2002 (Ori. 1906)], *The Khasis*. Delhi, Low Price Publication.

Gorer, Geoffrey, (1938), *Himalayan Village: An Account of Lepchas of Sikkim*, London, Machael Joseph.

Gautam, R. and A. Thapa-Magar, (1994), *Tribal Ethnography of Nepal*. Delhi.

Gupta, Ranjan, (1980), The Sherpa of Upper Khumbu and Their Migrant Counterpart in Kalimpong: A Comparative Demographic Study. In *Man and His Environment* (Eds.) I.P. Singh and S.C. Tiwari, New Delhi, Concept Publishing Co.

Gurung, Nar Bahadur, (1971), *Darjeeling*, Kalimpong.

Hermanns, M., (1954), *The Indo-Tibetans: The Indo-Tibetan and Mongoloid Problem in Southern Himalayas and North-East India*, Bombay.

Hooker, Sir J.D., (1891), *Himalayan Journals*. London, Ward, Lock Bowden & Co., Vol. XXX.

Hooker, Sir J.D., (1854), *Himalayan Journals*. 2 Vols., Calcutta.

Jest, C., (1978), Tibetan Communities in High Valleys of Nepal: Life in An Exceptional Environment and Economy. In *Himalayan Anthropology: The Indo-Tibetan Interface*. (Ed.) James F. Fisher. The Hague, Moutan Publisher.

Jina, Prem Singh, (2007), *Ladakh Buddhism: Culture and Tradition*. Delhi, Kalpaz Publications.

Kapoor, A.N., V.P. Gupta and Mohini Gupta, (2008), *Frontiers of Knowledge: A Dictionary of Scheduled Tribes in India*. New Delhi, Radha Publication.

Kohli, M.S. and B.G. Vergese, (1962), The Sherpas. In *Himalayan Endeavour* Bombay, a Times of India Publication.

Kumar, Bimalendra, N.D., A Study of Buddhism in Sikkim, *Bulletin of Tibetology* (*Source: Internet*).

Kunwar, Ramesh Raj, (1989), *Fire of Himal: An Anthropological Study of the Sherpas of Nepal Himalayan Region*. New Delhi, Nirala Publications.

Rotturen, G., (1983), *The Himalayan Gateway: History and Culture of Sikkim*. New Delhi, Sterling Publishers.

Lall, J.S., (1981), Sikkim, In *the Himalaya: Aspects of Change* (Ed.) J.S. Lall, Delhi, Oxford University Prèss.

Lama, Mahendra, P., (1994), *Sikkim: Society, Polity, Economy & Environment*, New Delhi, Indus Publishing Co.

Lama, S.T., (1971), *Sherpa a Book*, Sulukhumbu: Serlo Monastery.

Landor, A.H.S., (1975), *Tibet and Nepal: Political Cultural, Geographical & Historical*, New Delhi, Light & Life Publishers.

Lascar, N.K., (2006), Buddhism in Mizoram as practiced by the Chakmas. In *Buddhism in North-East India* (Eds.) S. Dutta & B. Tripathy New Delhi, Indus Publishing Co.

Ling, Trevor, (1991), Sikkimese Buddhism in the Nineteenth Century. In *Religion and Society of the Himalayas* (Eds.) T.B. Subba & Karubaki Datta. New Delhi, Gian Publishing House.

Liyod, W. & A. Gerard, (1946), *Narrative of the Journey from Caunpore to Boorendo Pass in the Himalaya Mountain* (2 vols). London.

O'Malley, L.S.S., [1985 (ori 1907)], *Bengal District Gazetteer: Darjeeling*. New Delhi, Logos Press.

Mamgain, M.D., (1971), Himachal Pradesh District Gazetteer, Kinnaur. Simla, Government of Himachal Pradesh.

Mann, R.S., (1986), *The Ladakhi: A Study of Ethnography and Change*. Calcutta, An S.I.

Mann, R.S., (1992), *Ladakh: Then and Now*, New Delhi, Mittal Publications.

Mann, R.S., (1995), Religious Attributes and Social Structure among the Ladakhis. In *The People of the Himalayas: Bio-Cultural and Ecological Aspects* (Ed: M.K. Raha), Calcutta, Anthropological Survey of India.

Mibang, Tamo and S.K. Chaudhuri, (2004), *Understanding Tribal Religion*. New Delhi, Mittal Publications.

Mitra, A., (1959), *District Census Handbook, Darjeeling, West Bengal*, Census 1951, Delhi, Manager of Publications.

Mitra, Amitabha, (2008), Sherpa. In *People of India*, West Bengal, Vol. XXXXIII, Part. Two. (Ed.) K.S. Singh. Calcutta, An S.I & Seagull Books.

Morris, John, (1938), *Living with the Lepchas: A book about Sikkim Himalayas*. London, Heinemann.

Murdock, G.P., (1949), *Social Structure*. New York. The Free Press.

Nakane, Chie, (1966), A Plural Society in Sikkim. In *Caste and Kin in Nepal India and Ceylon*. (Ed.) C. von Fürer-Haimendorf. Bombay, Asia Publishing House.

Namgyal, T. and Dolma, Y., (1908), *History of Sikkim.*

Oppitz, M., (1968), *Geschichte and Sozialordrung der Sherpa*, Innsbruck, Murchen.

Oppitz, M., (1977), Myths and Facts: Reconsidering some data concerning the clan history of the Sherpa. *Kailash*, Kathmandu Vol. II No. I to II, also in *Contribution to the Anthropology of Nepal* (Ed.) Fürer-Haimendorf, C. von.

Ortner, Sharry. B., (1973), Sherpa Purity. *American Anthropologist*, Vol.75.

Ortner, Sherry. B., (1978), The White Black Ones: The Sherpa View of Human Nature. In *Himalayan Anthropology: The Indo-Tibetan Interface.* (Ed.) James Fisher. The Hague, Moutan & Co.

Ortner, Sherry. B., (1979), *Sherpas through Their Rituals.* Cambridge, Cambridge University Press.

Ortner, Sherry. B., (1989), *High Religion: A Cultural and Political Profile of Sherpa Religion.*

Pattanaik, J.K., (2006), Theravada Buddhism among the Khamtis of Lohit District of Arunachal Pradesh. In *Buddhism in North-East India* (Eds.) S. Dutta & B. Tripathy. New Delhi, Indus Publishing Co.

Paul, Robert, (1982), *Tibetan Symbolic World.* Chicago, University of Chicago Press.

Paul, Robert, (1989), *The Sherpas of Nepal in the Tibetan Cultural Context.* Delhi, Motilal Banarsidass Publisher.

Poddar, Satyadeo, (2006), Buddhism in Tripura as practiced by the Chakmas. In *Buddhism in North-East India* (Eds.) S. Dutta & B. Tripathy: New Delhi, Indus Publishing Co.

Prasad, R.R., (1981), Tribal Stratification on Central Himalayas. Ranchi, *Journal of Social Research*, September.

Prasad, R.R., (1989), *Bhotia Tribals of India: Dynamics of Economic Transformation.* New Delhi, Gian Publishing House.

Raha, M.K., (1974), The Highlanders of Western and Central Himalayas, *Vanyajati*, Vol. XXII, No. 3.

Raha, M.K., (1978), Stratification and Religion in a Himalayan Society. In *Himalayan Anthropology* (Ed.) James F. Fisher. The Hague, Moutan Publishers.

Raha, M.K., (1992), Economic Strategy, Religious Dualism and Change in Diverse Cultural and Ecological Settings: A Case from Western Himalayas. In *The Himalayas and the Himalayans* (Ed.) Manis Kumar Raha & Palash Chandra Coomar. Calcutta, An S.I.

Raha, M.K., (1995), Society and Religion in Kinnaur. In *The People of the Himalayas* (Ed.) M.K. Raha, Calcutta, An S.I.

Raha, M.K , (1996), *Polyandry in the Global Context.* Calcutta, Indian Science Congress. Presidential Address in Anthropology and Archaeology Section.

Raha, M.K., (2003), Synthesis of Buddhism and Hinduism in Western Himalayas: A Study of the Kinnauras of Himachal Pradesh. In *Culture, Religion and Philosophy* (Ed.) N.K. Das, New Delhi, Rawat Publications.

Raha, M.K., (2006), Aspects of Social Organization of some Tribal Societies of Arunachal Pradesh. In *Cultural Heritage of Arunachal Pradesh* (Eds.) N. Nagaraju and B. Tripathy, New Delhi, Indus Publishing Co.

Raha, M.K., (2006), Buddhism (Lamaism) among the Sherpas of Sikkim. In *Buddhism in North-East India* (Ed.) S. Dutta & B. Tripathy. New Delhi, Indus Publishing Co.

Raha, M.K., (2007), Marriage in India with special reference to Arunachal Pradesh. In *Marriage in Tribal Societies: Cultural Dynamics and Social Realities*. (Ed.) Tamo Mibang & M.C. Behera, New Delhi, Bookwell.

Raha, M.K., (2011), Pattern of Livelihood, Ecological Involvement and Survival Strategy: The Case of the Sherpa of Darjeeling District. In *Cloud Stone and The Mind: The People and Environment of Darjeeling Hill Area* (Eds.) Mamata Desai & Saptarshi Mitra, Kolkata, K.P. Bagchi & Co.

Raha, M.K., (2015), Family and Marriage among the Sherpas of the Himalayas. In *Exploration in Anthropology* (Ed.) Sarthak Sengupta, New Delhi, Gyan Publishing House.

Raha, M.K. and P.C. Coomar, (2001), Some Aspects of the Sherpa Religion. In *Tribes of the Eastern Himalayas* (Ed.) Sarthak Sengupta, New Delhi, Mittal Publications.

Raha, M.K. and S.N. Mahato, (1985), *The Kinnaurese of the Himalayas*. Calcutta, An S.I.

Rao, N.S., (2006), Impact of Neo-Vaishnavite Movement of Tribes of East Arunachal Pradesh. In *Cultural Heritage of Arunachal Pradesh*. (Eds.) N. Nagaraju & B. Tripathy. New Delhi, Indus Publishing Co.

Rao, N.S., (2006), Tangsa Religion and Philosophy: A Note on Lord Rang-Frah. In *Cultural Heritage of Arunachal Pradesh* (Eds.) N. Nagaraju & B. Tripathy. New Delhi, Indus Publishing Co.

Risley, H.H., [1984 (Ori 1891)], *The Tribes and Castes of Bengal: Ethnographic Glossary*. Calcutta, Bengal Secretariat Press, 2 Vols.

Rivers, W.H.R., (1932), *Social Organization*. London, Kegan Paul Trench, Trubner & Co. Ltd.

Rizvi, B.R., (1995), Buddhists—Muslim Interaction in Kargil (District: Ladakh). In the *People of the Himalayas* (Ed.) M.K Raha, Calcutta, Anthropological Survey of India.

Rizvi, B.R., (1987), Class Formation and Conflict in a Polyandrous Village of Himachal Pradesh. In *The Himalayan Heritage* (Ed.) M.K. Raha, Delhi, Gian Publishing House.

Roy Burman, J.J. (2001), Ethnicity and Revivalism among the Bhutias and Lepchas of Sikkim. In *Tribes of Eastern Himalayas*. (Ed.) Sarthak Sengupta. New Delhi, Mittal Publications.

Rustomji, N.K., (1981), Sikkim, Bhutan and India's North-Eastern Borderlands: Problems of Change. In *The Himalaya: Aspects of Change* (Ed.) J.S. Lall. Delhi, Oxford University Press.

Sacherer, Janice, (1981), Recent Social and Economic Impact of Tourism on the Sherpa Community. In *Asian Highland Society: An Anthropological Perspective* (Ed.) C. von, Fürer-Haimendorf, New Delhi, Sterling Publishers Pvt. Ltd.

Sarkar, S., (2011), Colonial Social Formation and the Genesis of Separatism in Darjeeling Hills. In *Cloud Stone and the Mind: The People and Environment of Darjeeling Hill Areas* (Ed.) M. Desai & S. Mitra, Kolkata, K.P. Bagchi & Co.

Sarkar, S., (2014), Commentary: Tribal Detour in Darjeeling Hills. In *Economic and Political Weekly*, Vol. XLIX, No. 32, pp. 25-26.

Sen, Jahar, (1989), *Darjeeling: A Favoured Retreat*. New Delhi, Indus Publishing Co.

Sharma, D.D., (1987), Kinship Organization of the Polyandrous Lahuala. In *The Himalayan Heritage* (Ed.) M.K. Raha, Delhi, Gian Publishing House.

Sharma, D.D., (2000), *Peculiar Customs and Rites of the Himalayan People*. New Delhi, Mittal Publications.

Sherpa, M.N., (1982), *Sherpa Culture*. Sagarmatha National Park. Kathmandu, Gorkhapatra Sansthan Press.

Sherring, C., [1973 (ori. 1906)], *Western Tibet and British Borderland*. London.

Showren, T., (2006), Indigenous Religion and Practices of the Nyishi. In *Cultural Heritage of Arunachal Pradesh* (Eds.) N. Nagaraju & B. Tripathy. New Delhi, Indus Publishing Co.

Showren, T., (2006), Buddhism among the Singphos. In *Buddhism in North East India* (Eds.) S. Datta & B. Tripathy. New Delhi, Indus Publishing Co.

Singpho, C.C., (2006), Some observations. In *Buddhism in North-East India* (Eds.) S. Dutta & B. Tripathy. New Delhi, Indus Publishing Co.

Sinha, A.C., (1981), Resource Distribution and Multiple Ethnic Identities in Sikkim. In *Asian Highland Societies: An Anthropological Perspective* (Ed.) C. von. Fürer-Haimendorf. New Delhi, Sterling Publishers Pvt. Ltd.

Spate, O.H.K., (1954), *India and Pakistan*, London.

Spiro, M.E., (1970), *Buddhism and Society*. New York, Harpar & Row.

Snellgrove, D.L., (1957), *Buddhist Himalaya*. New York, Philosophical Library.

Snellgrove, D.L., (1981), *Himalayan Pilgrimage*. Boulder, Prajna Press.

Shrestha, D.B.C., B. Singh and B.M. Pradhan, (1975), *Ethnic Groups of Nepal and Their Ways of Living*, Kathmandu, Nepal.

Subba, J.R., (2008), *History. Culture and Customs of Sikkim*, New Delhi, Gyan Publishing House.

Subba, T.B., (1985), *The Quiet Hills: A Study of Agrarian Relations in Hill of Darjeeling*, Delhi, ISPCK.

Subba, T.B., (1989), *Dynamics of a Hill Society*. Delhi, Mittal Publications.

Subba, T.B. and K. Datta, (1999), *Religion and Society in the Himalayas*, New Delhi, Gyan Publishing House

Talukdar, S.P., (1988), *The Chakmas: Life and Struggle*. Delhi, Gian Publishing House.

Thapa, J.K., (1988), Census of India 1981, Series 19, Sikkim, Part IX, Special Tables for Scheduled Tribes.

Thornton, E., (1854), *A Gazetteer of the Territories, under the Government of East India Company and the Native States on the Continent of India*, London.

Tikhak, Yan, (2006), Buddhism in North-East India. In *Buddhism in North-East India* (Ed.), S. Dutta & B. Tripathy, New Delhi, Indus Publishing Co.

Tripathy, B., (2006), Mahayana Buddhism in Arunachal Pradesh. In *Cultural Heritage of Arunachal Pradesh*. (Eds.) N. Nagaraju & B Tripathy. New Delhi, Indus Publishing Co.

Tripathy, B., (2006), Theravada Religion in Arunachal Pradesh. In *Cultural Heritage of Arunachal Pradesh*. (Eds.) N. Nagaraju & B. Tripathy. New Delhi, Indus Publishing Co.

Tylor, E.B., (1999), *Dictionary of Anthropology*. Delhi, W.R. Goyal Publisher & Distributors.

Wadell, L.A., [1985 (ori 1894)], *The Buddhism in Tibet or Lamaism*. Jalundhar, Goutav Publishing House.

Wadell, L.A., (1973), *Lamaism in Sikkim*. Delhi, Oriental Publications.

Walton, H.G., (1911), *Almora: A Gazetteer*. Allahabad, Government Press, United Provinces.

White, J. Claude, [1971 (ori 1909)], *Sikkim and Bhutan: Twenty One years on the North-East Frontier*, 1887-1908. Delhi, Vivek Publishing House.

Xenia, Lisarevich, (1975), *Sherpa High Country*.

INDEX